'Professor Rabindra Nath Bhattacharya's research in environmental economics ranges from the micro to the macro, from investigations of common property resource institutions on land and at sea to the interrelationships among economic growth, energy consumption, and climate change. This volume assembles works written in his honour by a distinguished group of scholars from institutions in South Asia and around the world. In addition to paying tribute to Professor Bhattacharya's diverse contributions, the chapters demonstrate the ability of economics to help us understand and address some of the most challenging problems facing humanity.'

**Jeffrey R. Vincent**, *Korstian Distinguished Professor in Forest Economics and Management in the Nicholas School of the Environment and Earth Sciences, Duke University, USA*

# Environmental Economics in Developing Countries

The COVID-19 pandemic has laid bare the vulnerabilities of socio-economic systems globally and exposed the risks that natural capital degradation imposes on human health, economy, and society. This book studies the environmental challenges faced by developing economies in a post-COVID-19 world.

Exploring diverse case studies from South Asia and sub-Saharan Africa, the volume discusses the impact that economic development and, recently, COVID-19 has had on the environment, ecology, and economy of these regions. It analyzes Nature conservation policies aimed at minimizing ecological damage arising from economic development and discusses the policy objectives of sustainable development. It also highlights the significant role that environmental economics networks have played in capacity building, framing of policies using ecological economics tools, and developing a local leadership trained in addressing local sustainability issues.

An important contribution to the study of environmental economics of the Global South, this book will be of interest to students and researchers of economics, environment, development studies, development economics, environmental policies, and South Asia studies. It will also be useful for policymakers and NGOs working in this field.

**Achiransu Acharyya** is Assistant Professor in the Department of Economics at Visva-Bharati (A Central University) situated in Santiniketan, West Bengal, India. Previously he has taught at the Indian Institute of Management (IIM), Ahmedabad, and St. Xavier's University, Kolkata, India. His areas of teaching and research are mainly in natural resource and environmental economics, agricultural economics, and economics of water resources. For the past several years, he has been working on areas involving property rights and ownership of land and water, the economics of groundwater resources in agriculture, the use of energy for agriculture, and sustainable development. He has several national and international publications in journals and books to his credit. He has worked on several national and international research projects related to agriculture, the environment, and sustainable development. He visited the University of Oregon, USA, on a teaching cum research fellowship. He has also visited the University of Nijmegen in The Netherlands as a visiting scholar. He has received various awards for his research, including the third prize in the James D. Wolfensohn Essay Competition sponsored by The World Bank, Washington DC, USA and the Dr. N.A. Mujumdar Prize awarded by the Indian Society of Agricultural Economics, Mumbai, India. He is Chief Editor of the journal *Indian Groundwater*. He is also Associate Editor of the reputed Bengali social science journal *Anustup*.

# Environmental Economics in Developing Countries

## Issues and Challenges

Edited by Achiransu Acharyya

Routledge
Taylor & Francis Group
LONDON AND NEW YORK

First published 2023
by Routledge
4 Park Square, Milton Park, Abingdon, Oxon OX14 4RN

and by Routledge
605 Third Avenue, New York, NY 10158

*Routledge is an imprint of the Taylor & Francis Group, an informa business*



*British Library Cataloguing-in-Publication Data*
A catalogue record for this book is available from the British Library

*Library of Congress Cataloging-in-Publication Data*
Names: Acharyya, Achiransu, editor.
Title: Environmental economics in developing countries: issues and challenges/edited by Achiransu Acharyya.
Description: Abingdon, Oxon; New York, NY: Routledge, 2023. | Includes bibliographical references and index. |
Identifiers: LCCN 2022025954 (print) | LCCN 2022025955 (ebook) | ISBN 9781032182919 (hardback) | ISBN 9781032384504 (paperback) | ISBN 9781003253884 (ebook)
Subjects: LCSH: Economic development–Environmental aspects–Developing countries. | Sustainable development–Developing countries. | Environmental economics–Developing countries.
Classification: LCC HC59.72.E5 E5844 2023 (print) | LCC HC59.72.E5 (ebook) | DDC 333.7/091724–dc23/eng/20220601
LC record available at https://lccn.loc.gov/2022025954
LC ebook record available at https://lccn.loc.gov/2022025955

ISBN: 978-1-032-18291-9 (hbk)
ISBN: 978-1-032-38450-4 (pbk)
ISBN: 978-1-003-25388-4 (ebk)

DOI: 10.4324/9781003253884

Typeset in Sabon
by Deanta Global Publishing Services, Chennai, India

# Essays in Honour of Rabindra N. Bhattacharya

Professor Rabindra N. Bhattacharya has been a pioneer in introducing the subject of environmental economics to students and researchers in India in the late 1980s. After obtaining a PhD from Utah State University, Logan, Utah, USA, where he won the 'Outstanding Achievement Award', Professor Bhattacharya joined the University of North Bengal in West Bengal, where he taught for almost ten years before shifting to the University of Kalyani, another University of West Bengal, India, from where he retired as Professor in 2004. During his career, he has published many papers on environmental economics in topmost journals. Professor Bhattacharya has been a resource person for SANDEE (South Asian Network for Development and Environmental Economics) for more than ten years and has imparted knowledge on environmental economics to many students from South Asia.

This volume is a humble attempt to forward the legacy that he has created. All the authors in this book have contributed their chapters in his honour.

# Contents

# Figures

# Tables

# Contributors

**Bhim Adhikari** is Senior Environmental Economist at Canada's International Development Research Centre (IDRC) and works on environment, climate change, and sustainable development issues. Over the past 25 years, he has worked with several international organizations and academic institutions, including the United Nations agencies. He has worked with the Institute of Water, Environment and Health, United Nations University (UNU) in Canada, at the World Conservation Union (IUCN) in Pakistan, and at the United Nations Development Programme (UNDP) in Nepal. He was a research fellow at the School of Environment and Sustainability, University of Michigan, USA; a visiting research fellow at the Asian Development Bank Institute (ADBI) in Tokyo, Japan; and a UK Economic and Social Research Council (ESRC) postdoctoral fellow at the University of York. He taught briefly at the University of Brunel, London, and consulted for UNDP, TERI University, Portland State University, and the CIFOR.

**Gregory S. Amacher** is Julian N Cheatham Professor of Natural Resource Economics, Department of Forest Resources and Environmental Conservation, College of Natural Resources, Virginia Polytechnic Institute and State University, USA. He received a bachelor's degree from Pennsylvania State University, USA and master's degree and a PhD from the University of Michigan, USA. A member of the Virginia Tech faculty for more than 12 years, he is an international expert in forest policy analysis. His research programme centres on forest and environmental economics with a special focus on explanations of forest and natural resource user behaviour under a variety of market assumptions. His research in natural resources policy has found application in developing countries from Africa to China.

**Marina Cauchy** is a graduate student doing a master's in public policies and development at the Paris School of Economics, Paris, France.

**Ujjayant Chakravorty** is Professor of Economics at Tufts University, Massachusetts, USA and Fellow at the Toulouse School of Economics, Toulouse, France and Center for Economic Studies (CESifo), Munich, Germany. He is co-editor of the *Journal of Environmental Econom-*

*ics and Management* and associate editor of the *Journal of Economic Dynamics and Control*. He was previously Professor and Canada Research Chair at the University of Alberta, Edmonton, Alberta, Canada and has taught at Emory University Atlanta, Georgia, USA and the University of Hawaii at Manoa, Honolulu, Hawaii, USA. He has worked on the economics of fossil fuels and clean energy, the effect of environmental regulation on energy prices and the economics of water resources. He has a bachelor's degree in Civil Engineering from Indian Institute of Technology, New Delhi, India and a PhD in Resource and Environmental Economics from the University of Hawaii at Mano, East-West Center, Honolulu, USA.

**Chetana Chaudhuri** is Senior Research Associate at the Public Health Foundation of India, Gurgaon, New Delhi, India.

**Jamyang Choda** is a senior researcher at the Royal Society for the Protection of Nature, Thimphu, Bhutan.

**Kanchan Chopra** is a former director of the Institute of Economic Growth, New Delhi, India, where she had been a member of the faculty for close to three decades. She holds a PhD from the Delhi School of Economics, New Delhi, India and is a fellow of the Beijer Institute of Ecological Economics, Stockholm, Sweden and of the South Asian Network on Development and Environmental Economics (SANDEE), Kathmandu, Nepal. She was elected as a fellow of the Third World Academy of Sciences, Trieste, Italy in 2011 and is the recipient of the 2016 Boulding Award of the International Society for Ecological Economics, USA. She was a member of the assessment panel of the Millennium Ecosystem Assessment, and co-chair of its Policy Responses Group from 2001 to 2005. She is founder president of the Indian Society for Ecological Economics (INSEE) from 1998 to 2000 and was re-elected its president for 2010–2012. She has also been on the editorial and policy boards of the journals *Environmental and Development Economics* and *Ecological Economics*. Currently, she is co-editor of *Ecology, Economy and Society: the INSEE Journal*.

**Kelly M. Cobourn** is Associate Professor in the Department of Forest Resources and Environmental Conservation, College of Natural Resources, Virginia Polytechnic Institute and State University, USA. She earned a PhD in agricultural and resource economics from the University of California, Davis, USA and an MS in resource economics and policy from the University of Maine, Orono, Maine. She is a natural resource economist who specializes in identifying and understanding the linkages between natural systems and human decision-making.

**Partha Dasgupta** is the Frank Ramsey Professor Emeritus of Economics at the University of Cambridge, United Kingdom; a fellow of St. John's College, Cambridge, United Kingdom; a visiting professor at the New

College of the Humanities, London, United Kingdom; and a professorial research fellow at the Sustainable Consumption Institute, University of Manchester, United Kingdom. He taught at the London School of Economics, London, United Kingdom from 1971 to 1984 and then moved to the University of Cambridge, United Kingdom in 1985 as professor of economics, where he served as chairman of the faculty of economics from 1997 to 2001. From 1989 to 1992, he was also Professor of Economics, Professor of Philosophy, and Director of the Program in Ethics in Society at Stanford University, USA; and from 1991 to 1997 he was Chairman of the (Scientific Advisory) Board of the Beijer International Institute of Ecological Economics, Stockholm, Sweden. Since 1999 he has been Founder Member of the Management and Advisory Committee of the South Asian Network for Development and Environmental Economics (SANDEE), Kathmandu, Nepal. In 1996, he helped to establish the journal titled *Environment and Development Economics*, published by Cambridge University Press, whose purpose has been not only to publish original research on the interface of poverty and the environmental resource base but also to provide an opportunity to scholars in developing countries to publish their findings in an international journal. He was named Knight Bachelor by Her Majesty Queen Elizabeth II in her Birthday Honours List in 2002 for 'services to economics'; was co-winner (with Karl-Goran Maler of the Beijer International Institute of Ecological Economics, Stockholm) of the 2002 Volvo Environment Prize and of the 2004 Kenneth E. Boulding Memorial Award of the International Society for Ecological Economics; and was the recipient of the John Kenneth Galbraith Award in 2007 of the American Agricultural Economic Association. His report on the economics of biodiversity titled 'The Economics of Biodiversity: The Dasgupta Review' have been globally acclaimed. He was awarded the prestigious Kew International Medal in 2021 for his work to protect Nature and stop biodiversity loss.

**Susmita Dasgupta** is Lead Environmental Economist, Development Research Group, World Bank, Washington, DC, USA. Her research focuses on environmental management in developing countries. She has done extensive analysis on health hazards of pollution, poverty–environment nexus, setting priorities in pollution control, deforestation, biodiversity loss, impacts of climate change on coastal zones and climate extremes, adaptation to climate change, cost-effective regulations, and monitoring and enforcement of regulations. She has conducted research activities in Bangladesh, Brazil, Cambodia, China, Colombia, Cuba, India, Iran, Lao PDR, Madagascar, Mexico, Tunisia, Vietnam, and Yemen and has published numerous articles on issues related to development and environment. Before joining the World Bank in 1992, she taught at the American University, Washington D.C, USA and the State University of

New York at Albany, New York, USA. She holds BSc from Presidency College, India; MSc from the University of Calcutta, India; and MSc and PhD in economics from the State University of New York at Albany, New York, USA.

**Chanda Gurung Goodrich** is Senior Gender Specialist – Gender Lead at International Centre for Integrated Mountain Development (ICIMOD) Lalitpur, Nepal. Her professional specialization is in gender and participatory research and development (R&D). She has done her M. Phil and PhD in international studies from Jawaharlal Nehru University, New Delhi, India.

**Haripriya Gundimeda** is Professor in the Department of Humanities and Social Sciences at the Indian Institute of Technology, Mumbai, India. Her main areas of research are green accounting, mitigation aspects of climate change, energy demand and pricing, valuation of environmental resources, and issues relating to development in India. Gundimeda also served as president of Urban Biodiversity and Design (URBIO). She holds a master's degree in mathematics and a PhD in development policy.

**Lowine Hill** is Doctoral Researcher and Consultant at the University of Waterloo, Canada. She has more than seven years of combined experience in disaster risk reduction, climate change adaptation, and biodiversity conservation. As a consultant, she provides technical advice in the design and implementation of small- and large-scale projects, in knowledge translation, capacity-building, and community participation.

**Amelia Holmes** is Associate Program Officer at United Nations Environment Programme (UNEP), Nairobi, Kenya. Her role involves working on issues of natural capital and ecosystem services, particularly regarding mainstreaming this discourse into development and economic policy.

**Samia Islam** is an economics research consultant at United Nations Environment Programme (UNEP) in Nairobi, Kenya.

**Pushpam Kumar** is Chief Environmental Economist at United Nations Environment Programme (UNEP). In the past, he has worked as Chief of the Ecosystem Services, Economics Unit from 2010 to 2015, and as Coordinator of the Biodiversity and Ecosystem Services Branch, from 2015 to 2016, in the Ecosystems Division at the UNEP. Currently, he provides leadership to a number of initiatives. He is Report Director for Economics of Land Degradation (Africa and Asia), coordinates the Inclusive Wealth Report, and provides analytical approaches for Planetary and Human Health. He has a PhD in Environmental Economics and has been with the University of Liverpool, United Kingdom, and with the University of Delhi, India from 1991 to 2010 as Associate Professor and Professor in Environmental Economics. He also holds the position of Honorary

Research Scientist at the Earth Institute of Columbia University in New York, USA and is an Extra Ordinary Professor at the University of Pretoria, South Africa.

**Heman Das Lohano** is Professor and Program Director PhD/MS (Economics) & BS (EM) at the Institute of Business Administration, Karachi, Pakistan. He did his MS and PhD from the University of Minnesota, USA. His research interests are in applied economics.

**Muthukumara Mani** is Lead Economist in the South Asia Chief Economist's Office at The World Bank, Washington DC, USA with over 20 years of experience in leading environmental projects, policy dialogue, analytical work, and capacity-building activities. He primarily works on climate change mitigation and adaptation issues, and water and environmental issues in the region. Having a doctorate and master's in economics from the University of Maryland, College Park, USA, Mani has numerous books, journal publications, and policy papers in his name.

**Anil Markandya** is Distinguished Ikerbasque Professor and former scientific director of the Basque Centre for Climate Change in the Basque Country, Spain. He graduated from the London School of Economics, United Kingdom with a Master of Science in Econometrics in 1968 and was awarded his PhD from the same institution in the Economics of the Environment in 1975. He has held academic positions at the universities of Princeton and Harvard in the USA at University College London, and Bath University in the United Kingdom. He was a lead author for chapters of the 3rd and 4th IPCC Assessment Reports on Climate Change, which were awarded a share of the Nobel Peace in 2007. He has also been a lead author for the 5th Assessment Report published in 2014. In 2008, he was nominated by Cambridge University as one of the top 50 contributors to thinking on sustainability in the world. In 2012, he was elected the president of the European Association of Environmental and Resource Economics, and in 2013 he became a member of the Scientific Council of the European Environment Agency. Professor Markandya has also acted as a consultant to several national and international organizations and served as lead economist at the World Bank, Washington D.C, USA.

**M.N. Murty** is a former professor from the Institute of Economic Growth, New Delhi, India. He has contributed a large number of research papers in reputed national and international journals of economics. He has also taught at Delhi University, New Delhi, India; Jawaharlal Nehru University, New Delhi, India; University of Birmingham, United Kingdom and TERI University, New Delhi, India. He specializes in public economics and environmental and resource economics. He has published several books in environment and resource economics.

**Prema Sai Narasimhan** is a research consultant at the World Bank, Washington D.C, USA. He graduated with a master's in development economics from Yale University, New Haven, USA.

**Apsara Karki Nepal** currently works at International Centre for Integrated Mountain Development (ICIMOD), Lalitpur, Nepal. She has a PhD in applied economics from the University of Otago, Dunedin, New Zealand, and a masters' degree from the University of New Mexico, Albuquerque, USA. She does research in health economics and development economics.

**Mani Nepal** is the program coordinator at the South Asian Network for Development and Environmental Economics (SANDEE) and lead economist at the International Centre for Integrated Mountain Development (ICIMOD) Lalitpur, Nepal. He conducts and coordinates the South Asian Network for Development and Environmental Economics (SANDEE) research and training activities. His research interest is in non-market valuation, household energy, environmental health, programme evaluation, and development issues such as child labour, poverty/inequality, and armed conflict and its effect on social welfare.

**Jyoti K. Parikh** is Executive Director at Integrated Research and Action for Development (IRADe), India. She received her master's degree in Physics and Mathematics from the University of California, Berkeley, USA in 1964, and PhD in theoretical physics from University of Maryland, College Park, USA in 1967. She was a member of the Prime Minister's Council on Climate Change in India and is a recipient of the Nobel Peace Prize awarded to IPCC authors in 2007. She was Senior Professor at the Indira Gandhi Institute of Development Research (IGIDR), Mumbai, India. She also worked at the International Institute for Applied Systems Analysis (IIASA), Austria, and served as a senior energy consultant at the National Institution for Transforming India (NitiAayog). She was a visiting professor at the Institute of Advanced Studies (IAS) of United Nations University, Tokyo. She was Acting Director of IGIDR. She has experience for nearly 30 years in energy and environment problems in developing countries.

**Martino Pelli** is Associate Professor of Economics at the Université de Sherbrooke in Québec, Canada, a research fellow at Centre Interuniversitaire de Recherche en Économie Quantitative (CIREQ), Montreal, Canada, and a researcher at CIRANO, Montreal, Canada. His research interests are in development and resource economics, and international trade.

**Vaideeswaran Sankaran** is a consultant at the World Bank, Washington, DC, USA.

**Stella Z. Schons** is Assistant Professor in International Forest Economics and Management at Virginia Tech, Blacksburg, Virginia, USA. She did her PhD from Virginia Tech in Forestry in 2017 and MBA from Yale School of Management, USA in 2010.

**Ramprasad Sengupta** is Emeritus Professor of Economics at Jawaharlal Nehru University, New Delhi, India. He has been Mahatma Gandhi National Fellow of the Indian Council for Social Science Research (ICSSR), Government of India, till 2018. He is a former advisor to the Planning Commission, Government of India. He is also a former professor of economics at the Indian Institute of Management, Calcutta, India. He has had stints as a visiting professor/scholar at universities in India, USA, Canada Germany, the Netherlands, and Japan. He has also been Independent Director on the Board of Steel Authority of India Limited (SAIL).

**Nilesh Shinde** is a PhD scholar at the Department of Forest Resources and Environmental Conservation, College of Natural Resources, Virginia Polytechnic Institute and State University, USA.

**Priya Shyamsundar** is Lead Economist at The Nature Conservancy Arlington, VA, USA. With extensive experience on the economics of environment and development, her research covers a range of local to global urban and rural environmental problems. At The Nature Conservancy, she leads a Global Science programme on the economics of conservation that focuses on valuing green infrastructure, evaluating economic and social outcomes, identifying economic instruments, and assessing behavioural nudges that may motivate environmental actions. Previously, she was Founder Director of the South Asian Network for Development and Environmental Economics (SANDEE) based in Kathmandu, Nepal, a research network that helps examine and identify solutions to shared environment development challenges across seven countries in South Asia. She has served on advisory committees associated with the Government of India, the World Bank, and the International Geosphere-Biosphere Program. She has a PhD in environmental economics from Duke University. Her research publications cover multiple environmental areas, including forests, climate change, and watershed management.

**R. David Simpson** is Senior Professorial Lecturer and Director, Global Environmental Policy, International Development, and International Economic Relations Programs, School of International Service, American University, Washington D.C, USA. He directs the Global Environmental Policy, International Development, and International Economic Relations Programs in American University's School of International Service in Washington, DC, where he also teaches resource and international economics. He has written extensively on the economics of biodiversity, conservation, and ecosystem services.

**E. Somanathan** is Professor in the Economics and Planning Unit of the Indian Statistical Institute in New Delhi, India and Head of CECFEE (Centre for research on the Economics of Climate, Food, Energy and Environment). His research is in economics of environment and development. He received his PhD from Harvard University Cambridge, Massachusetts, USA and has taught at Emory University, Atlanta, Georgia, USA the University of Michigan, Ann Arbor, Michigan, USA and Princeton University, New Jersey, USA. He has been Executive Director of SANDEE (South Asian Network for Development and Environmental Economics), a coordinating lead author for the Fifth Assessment Report of the IPCC and is a co-editor of *Environment and Development Economics*, a Cambridge University Press journal.

**David Wheeler** is Senior Fellow Emeritus at the Center for Global Development, The World Bank, Washington D.C, USA. In his previous role as a lead economist in the World Bank's development research group, he directed a team that worked on environmental policy and research issues in collaboration with policymakers and academics in Africa, Asia, and Latin America. Before joining the World Bank, he taught at the National University of Zaire, Lengeza, Congo - Kinshasa and Boston University, Boston, Massachusetts, USA. He has a PhD from the Massachusetts Institute of Technology (MIT), USA.

# Foreword
## Understanding the Role of Nature in Economic Development

*Partha Dasgupta*

Not so long ago, the economic questions requiring urgent attention could safely be studied by excluding Nature from formal economic reasoning. At the end of the Second World War, with absolute poverty endemic in much of Africa, Asia, and Latin America, and with Europe in need of reconstruction, it made sense to focus on the accumulation of produced capital (roads, buildings, ports, machines) and human capital (health, education). Unfortunately, continued use of the resulting macroeconomic models of growth and development has encouraged us to believe that we can forever bypass Nature when we imagine our economic possibilities. That belief has been strengthened by the fact that the average person in the world today enjoys a far higher income, is less likely to be in absolute poverty, and lives significantly longer than he or she did even 70 years ago; indeed, the world economy has grown 15-fold since then. So, it would seem we are living in the best of times.

But Nature is our most precious asset. We are embedded in Nature; it is our home; and it provides us with a multitude of services we take for granted, such as regulating climate, cleansing our water, decomposing our waste, and fixing nitrogen. Even as the average person today enjoys the fruits of economic growth, the demand we have made for Nature's goods and services has for some decades exceeded her ability to supply them on a sustainable basis. One estimate is that the ratio of our current demand to Nature's ability to meet that demand has risen from one in the 1960s to 1.6 today, which is a way of saying that we need 1.6 Earths to meet our current demand on a sustainable basis.[1]

A prominent reason for the increase in the gap between demand and supply is an absence of institutions that create necessary incentives to economise on our use of Nature's services. The high seas, for example, are used for traffic and are harvested for fish, and yet we are not charged for their use. Worse, governments subsidise the use of Nature to the extent of some 4–6% of global GDP. In effect, we pay ourselves vast sums annually to eat into Nature. Because the difference between demand and sustainable supply is met by a diminution of Nature, the gap has been increasing, threatening our descendants' lives. So, it would seem we are also living in the worst of times.

And yet, academic economists, economists in governments, international organisations, and private corporations continue to use what are essentially those postwar models of growth and economic development for collecting and analyzing data, forecasting economic trajectories, evaluating options, and designing policy. Perhaps, then, it should be no surprise that those same models shape the conception we build of our economic possibilities. In turn, our acceptance of the economic possibilities the models say are open to us encourages academic economists to refine and develop them further along their tested contours. And that in turn further contributes to our beliefs about what is achievable in our economic future. The mutual influence is synergistic.

Nature entered macroeconomic models of growth and development in the 1970s, but in an inessential form (e.g., the Symposium on the Economics of Exhaustible Resources, *Review of Economic Studies*, 1974). The thought was that human ingenuity could overcome Nature's scarcity over time and ultimately (formally, in the limit) allow humanity to be free of Nature's constraints. But the practice of building economic models on the backs of those that had most recently been designed meant that the macroeconomics of growth and development continued to be built without Nature's appearance as an essential entity in our economic lives. Historians of science and technology call that feature of the process of selection 'path dependence'.[2] That may be why economic and finance ministries and international organisations today *graft* particular features of Nature, such as the global climate, onto their models as and when the need arises but otherwise continues to assume the biosphere to be *external* to the human economy.[3] It may also be why environmental and resource economics, as it was developed in the United States and then in Europe, reads the biosphere as a collection of separate resource bases (fisheries, forests, rivers, and lakes) that can be grafted into standard models of growth and development. A flavour that is added to the vast majority of models on taxation and regulation of natural resources, that income effects are negligible, puts Nature firmly in its place. We may have increasingly queried the absence of Nature from official conceptions of economic possibilities, but the worry has been left for Sundays. On weekdays our thinking has remained as usual.[4]

The synergy between academic writings and public perceptions of economic possibilities is particularly ironic in the literature on poverty and the prospects of economic development in poor countries. In no other context does the interplay of the 'macro' and 'micro' receive as much attention; and yet, whereas farmers, fishermen, woodlanders, and grazers run their eyes constantly on their natural capital assets, the one class of assets that is conspicuously missing in academic writings and government publications on poverty is the wide range of ecosystems and their services that constitute the biosphere. With but very few exceptions, mainstream economists have followed the early framing of the problem of economic development in terms of the accumulation and distribution of produced capital and human capital. Textbooks and trade books on absolute poverty make little mention that rural households in South Asia and Africa are deeply embedded in their local environmental resource base. The absence of Nature in the writings on poverty by economists raised in South Asia is a striking illustration of professional concerns eliding over even casual observation.

Rabi-da ('Professor Rabindra Nath Bhattacharya' feels inadequate here) is one exception. There is strong evidence in his writings that the bird he has wanted to catch is an economics of poverty that sees households carrying on with their lives as best as they can in the face of a deteriorating landscape. And he has wanted the economics to explain why the landscape has been deteriorating.

Original research is usually a series of reconnaissance exercises. It is revealing that Rabi-da, like the very few others who found a path in what should have been a framework in which to study deep poverty in poor countries, travelled similar intellectual paths. We have groped on the basis of hunches, built as much on taste as on experience. Such ventures are lonely because mostly there are no colleagues who can advise. Looking through Rabi-da's publications, I found that he has explored the economics of forestry, the Hill regions, and coastal zones as sites for exploring the links between Nature and economic development, the character of energy consumption in India, groundwater as a depletable resource, the health status of coal miners in India, the possible causes of differential fertility in communities, and communities and civil society as seats of collective action. The papers are tentative, some are written somewhat self-consciously, but to me, they read eerily familiar, for I too have followed a similar route. Mostly I have not known where I have been heading, and I believe Rabi-da hasn't known either.

But there is a secret pleasure in this kind of work, the pleasure of uncovering truths even when they are blurred and when few others are looking for them. Some years ago, Rabi-da and I spent a week lecturing to participants (graduate students and young teachers of economics) in the annual teaching and research workshops that are organised by the South Asian Network of Development and Environmental Economists (SANDEE). We discussed each other's lectures, and we recounted our experiences in facing the pitfalls of working in a deep and difficult field. We also discovered our shared love of teaching, which is why I am deeply grateful to Professor Acharyya for inviting me to write a Foreword to this wonderful collection of tributes to Rabi-da.

## Notes

1 For an extended discussion of economics at the environment–consumption–population interface, see *The Economics of Biodiversity: The Dasgupta Review* (London: HMTreasury, 2021).
2 A clear statement is in P. A. David, 'Clio and the Economics of QWERTY', American Economic Review, 75(2), 332-337.
3 I am using the terms biosphere and Nature interchangeably.
4 Over the years, the absence of Nature's essentiality from macroeconomic models of growth and development has been remarked upon by scholars outside the mainstream of economic thinking and practice. But while it is all too easy to criticise existing practices, it is a lot harder to develop alternative models of comparable analytical depth and empirical reach to ones that have been honed by years of patient work. That may be why the criticisms have not been taken seriously by mainstream economists.

## References

1. David, P. A. 1985."Clio and the Economics of QWERTY". *American Economic Review* 75(2): 332–337.
2. Heal, Geoffrey (ed.) 1974. *Symposium on the Economics of Exhaustible Resources*.Review of Economic Studies, Oxford University Press. Volume 41.
3. *The Economics of Biodiversity: The Dasgupta Review*. London: H.M. Treasury, 2021. https://www.gov.uk/government/publications/final-report-the-economics-of-biodiversity-the-dasgupta-review (last accessed on 3 August 2021).

# Preface

This book covers issues that are relevant to environmental economics and economics of development in today's world and that pose a challenge to the developing economies of South Asia and sub-Saharan Africa. The book attempts to address those challenges and find solutions to the problems. Issues such as the impact of COVID-19 on the environment and climate change, impact of infrastructure on climate change, regional environmental economics networks, Nature conservation, gender and environment, and current environmental policies in developing countries are covered in the 15 chapters of the book. All the contributors to the book are leading academicians in the field of environmental economics. The book is divided into four parts, covering various recent issues on environment and development. The introduction to the book extensively discusses the development of environmental economics as a subject from a historical perspective to its relevance in present times, the role of institutions and organizations in disseminating the subject across developing nations and introduces the chapters of the book in detail.

Part I is titled Environment, Ecology, and Development. The four chapters in this part attempt to cover the topics on economic growth, poverty, and environment, which are highly relevant for developing countries. The COVID-19 pandemic has put human development and human consumption patterns in serious question. Many people see the destruction of natural resources and biodiversity loss exposing humans to zoonotic diseases as the main reason for the pandemic. Several chapters in this part look at these issues and try to find solutions.

Part II is titled Economics of Nature Conservation. The economics of forestry vis-à-vis economic development is analyzed in the four chapters in this part. While forests provide carbon sequestration and ecosystem services, development literature often fails to address the full benefits of forestry. This is studied in detail. That economics can show some incentives for Nature conservation is discussed in several chapters in this part, including minimizing damage to forests while building roads in developing countries in the tropics.

Climate change is now a reality, and human beings must adjust to the changing climate. However, this will impact human lives and human development, and one must be aware and be able to adapt. Part III, Climate Change and Development, has three chapters, covering various aspects of climate change adaptation. These include a discussion on the path to sustainable development under climate change and COVID-19 pandemic, solutions to the various regional vulnerabilities that have occurred from climate change for South Asian countries, and climate smart farming, which could be one solution to the negative impact of climate change on agriculture in South Asia and sub-Saharan Africa.

Part IV of this book is titled Economics of Environmental Policy. This part has four chapters, mostly on environment policy-related issues. These include a holistic view of environmental policy in India and its impact on development and a practical policy-based approach to saving the environment. Over the years, gender has become a very important factor in Nature conservation. This is analyzed in a study of gender-based waste management in Nepal. In Bhutan, the entry of wild animals into agricultural land poses a serious problem for farmers. How the farmers and wildlife can both be saved is discussed. The concluding chapter talks about the regional environmental economic networks created in developing economies and how such networks have benefitted research activity on environmental economics in the region.

The Foreword to the book has been written by Sir Partha Dasgupta, a world-renowned expert in environmental economics. The testimonial has been written by Professor Jeffrey Vincent, another stalwart in environmental economics. The book is in honour of Professor Rabindra N. Bhattacharya, who was a pioneer in introducing the subject of environmental economics to students and researchers in India in the late 1980s. All the contributions in this book are in his honour. The book would be beneficial for undergraduate and postgraduate students who study the subjects of economics, environment, and development; research scholars in the subject; and faculty members who teach development and environmental economics, as also laymen interested in the subject.

Achiransu Acharyya
Santiniketan
May 2021

# Acknowledgements

The editor of this book would like to thank the following persons without whom this book would not have seen the light of day.

Professor Rabindra N. Bhattacharya, in whose honour this book is dedicated, for agreeing to such a book and for constant support in all difficulties.

All the authors for their contributions and, even more than that, for their perseverance. This was a long, drawn-out journey for them – from the first draft of their chapters to the final versions – outliving moments of uncertainties about the future of the book itself.

Sir Partha Dasgupta for agreeing to write the Foreword to the book and for constant moral support.

Professor Jeffrey Vincent for agreeing to write the testimonial for the back cover of the book.

Professor Ramprasad Sengupta, former professor of economics at Jawaharlal Nehru University and a contributor to this volume for all the inspiration and guidance.

Professor Kanchan Chopra, former director of the Institute of Economic Growth, for agreeing to contribute a chapter even in her most difficult times.

My students Rahul Pal and Sayak Fulmali for helping with the referencing of the chapters.

The Routledge reviewers for constructive suggestions on each of the chapters.

Mr. Narayanan Ramachandran for copyediting.

Routledge for agreeing to publish this book under its banner and bringing it out in such an elegant manner. Shoma Choudhury, the Commissioning Manager, and her colleague Anvitaa Bajaj, Editorial Assistant, who has been a great source of support and encouragement.

None of the above is, of course, responsible for any errors that may still be there in the book and for which I take complete responsibility.

**Achiransu Acharyya**

# Abbreviations

| | |
|---|---|
| ACBP | Africa Climate Business Plan |
| ADB | Asian Development Bank |
| AIDS | Acquired Immune Deficiency Syndrome |
| AQI | Air Quality Index |
| AMAF | ASEAN Ministers of Agriculture and Forestry |
| ASEAN | Association of Southeast Asian Nations |
| BAU | Business as Usual |
| BCCSAP | Bangladesh Climate Change Strategy and Action Plan |
| BCR | Benefit-Cost Ratio |
| BDBL | Bhutan Development Bank Limited |
| BECCS | Bio Energy with Carbon Capture and Storage |
| CAADP | Comprehensive Africa Agriculture Development Programme |
| CAPex | Capital Expenditure |
| CChAM | Climate Change Adaptation and Mitigation |
| CCVI | Climate Change Vulnerability Index |
| CEEPA | Centre for Environmental Economics and Policy in Africa |
| CES | Constant Elasticity of Substitution |
| CGE | Computable General Equilibrium |
| CGIAR | Consultative Group on International Agricultural Research |
| CIAT | International Centre for Tropical Agriculture |
| $CO_2$ | Carbon dioxide |
| COMESA | Common Market for Eastern and Southern Africa |
| CRED | Centre for Research on the Epidemiology of Disasters |
| CRGE | Climate Resilient Green Economy |
| CRI | Climate Risk Index |
| CSA | Climate Smart Agriculture |
| CSF | Climate Smart Farming |
| CRS | Climate Resilience Strategy |
| CRV | Climate Resilient Villages |
| CSV | Climate-Smart Villages |

| | |
|---|---|
| **DALYs** | Disability Adjusted Life Years |
| **DEMs** | Digital Elevation Data |
| **DFID** | Department for International Development |
| **DNFP** | Draft National Forest Policy |
| **DRC** | Democratic Republic of the Congo. |
| **EAC** | East African Community |
| **EAERE** | European Association of Environmental and Resource Economics |
| **ECDPM** | European Centre for Development Policy Management |
| **EE** | Environmental Economics |
| **EEA** | Experimental Ecosystem Accounting |
| **EEPSEA** | Economy and Environment Program for Southeast Asia |
| **EIA** | Environmental Impact Assessment |
| **EID** | Emerging Infectious Disease |
| **EKC** | Environmental Kuznets Curve |
| **EPW** | Economic and Political Weekly |
| **FAO** | Food and Agriculture Organization |
| **FEF** | Fabricated Electric Fencing |
| **FRA** | Forest Right Act |
| **GCM** | General Circulation Models |
| **GDP** | Gross Domestic Product |
| **GES** | Green Economy Strategy |
| **GW** | Gigawatt |
| **GHG** | Green House Gas |
| **GIS** | Geographical Information System |
| **GLOBIOM** | Global Biosphere Management Model |
| **GNH** | Gross National Happiness |
| **GOI** | Government of India |
| **GoSL** | Government of Sri Lanka |
| **GVA** | Gross Value Added |
| **HDPE** | High Density Polyethylene |
| **HIV** | Human Immunodeficiency Virus |
| **HM** | His Majesty |
| **HVI** | Heat Vulnerability Index |
| **ICIMOD** | International Center for Integrated Mountain Development |
| **IDA** | International Development Association |
| **IDRC** | International Development Research Center |
| **IEA** | International Energy Agency |
| **IECFPO** | Indonesia Estate Crop Fund for Palm Oil |
| **IGP** | Indo-Gangetic Plains |
| **IHME** | Institute for Health Metrics and Evaluation |
| **ILO** | International Labour Organization |
| **IMF** | International Monetary Fund |

| | |
|---|---|
| IPBES | Intergovernmental Science Policy Platform on Biodiversity and Ecosystem Services |
| IPCC | Intergovernmental Panel on Climate Change |
| IRENA | International Renewable Energy Agency |
| IUCN | International Union for Conservation of Nature |
| IT | Information Technology |
| IV | Instrumental Variables |
| IWI | Inclusive Wealth Index |
| JFM | Joint Forest Management |
| JRC | Joint Research Centre |
| KAN | Knowledge-Action Networks |
| kWh | kilowatt hour |
| LACEEP | Latin America and the Caribbean Environmental Economics Program |
| LDC | Less Developed Country |
| LED | Light Emitting Diode |
| LPG | Liquid Petroleum Gas |
| LPI | Living Planet Index |
| LPM | Linear Probability Model |
| LSE | London School of Economics |
| MA | Millennium Ecosystem Assessment |
| MERS | Middle East Respiratory Syndrome |
| MoAF | Ministry of Agriculture and Forests |
| MoEFCC | Ministry of Environment Forest and Climate Change |
| MoHFW | Ministry of Health and Family Welfare |
| MoSPI | Ministry of Statistics and Programme Implementation |
| MPI | Multidimensional Poverty Index |
| MSW | Managing Solid Waste |
| MT | Metric Tonnes |
| NAIPs | National Agricultural Investment Plans |
| NAP | National Action Plan |
| NAPA | National Adaptation Plan of Action |
| NbS | Nature based Solutions |
| NCF | Nature Conservation Foundation |
| NDCs | Nationally Determined Commitments |
| NEPAD | New Partnership for Africa's Development |
| NICRA | National Innovations on Climate Resilient Agriculture |
| NPIC | National Programme on Improved Chulhas |
| NPR | Nepalese Rupee |
| NPV | Net Present Value |
| NGO | Non-governmental Organization |
| NIMET | Nigeria's Meteorological Agency |
| NMSA | National Mission for Sustainable Agriculture |
| NREGA | National Rural Employment Guarantee Act |

| | |
|---|---|
| **NVCC** | National Vulnerabilities to Climate Change |
| **OBC** | Other Backward Classes |
| **OECD** | Organization for Economic Co-operation and Development |
| **OIRED** | Office of International Research, Education, and Development |
| **OLS** | Ordinary Least Squares |
| **OPex** | Operational Expenditure |
| **OSI** | Office of Science and Innovation |
| **PAMB** | Protected Area Management Board |
| **PES** | Payments for Eco-system Services |
| **PLFS** | Periodic Labour Force Survey |
| **PPP** | Purchasing Power Parity |
| **RCM** | Regional Climate Models |
| **RCP** | Representative Concentration Pathways |
| **REDD** | Reducing Emissions from Deforestation and Forest Degradation |
| **REN** | Renewable Energy |
| **RGOB** | Royal Government of Bhutan |
| **SAMREM** | Sustainable Agriculture and Natural Resource Management Collaborative Research Support Program |
| **SAARC** | South Asian Association for Regional Cooperation |
| **SADC** | Southern Africa Development Community |
| **SANDEE** | South Asian Network for Development and Environmental Economics |
| **SAR** | South Asia Region |
| **SARS** | Severe Acute Respiratory Syndrome |
| **SC** | Scheduled Castes |
| **SDG** | Sustainable Development Goals |
| **SEA** | Southeast Asia |
| **SEARCA** | Southeast Asian Regional Centre for Graduate Study and Research in Agriculture |
| **SEEA** | System of Environmental Economic Accounting |
| **SIDA** | Swedish International Development Cooperation Agency |
| **SLM** | Sustainable Land Management |
| **SRTM** | Shuttle Radar Topographic Mission |
| **SSA** | Sub-Saharan Africa |
| **ST** | Scheduled Tribes |
| **SUR** | Seemingly Unrelated Regressions |
| **TEEB** | The Economics of Ecosystems and Biodiversity |
| **TLOs** | Tole Lane Organizations |
| **TOF** | Trees outside of Forests |
| **UN DESA** | United Nations, Department of Economic and Social Affairs |

| | |
|---|---|
| **UNDP** | United Nations Development Programme |
| **UNEN** | United Nations Economist Network |
| **UNEP** | United Nations Environment Programme |
| **UNESCO** | United Nations Educational, Scientific and Cultural Organization |
| **UNFCCC** | United Nations Framework Convention on Climate Change |
| **USD** | United States of America (Dollar) |
| **UTs** | Union Territories |
| **WB** | World Bank |
| **WEF** | World Economic Forum |
| **WHO** | World Health Organization |
| **WWF** | World Wildlife Fund |

# Introduction and Overview

## Environmental Economics in Developing Countries

*Achiransu Acharyya*

### Introduction

The links between the economy and the environment are manifold: the environment provides resources to the economy and acts as a sink for emissions and waste. The environment also provides amenities in flora and fauna and other services. Natural resources are essential inputs for production in many sectors, while production and consumption also lead to pollution and other pressures on the environment. Poor environment quality, in turn, affects economic growth and well-being. This interaction between the economy and the environment is shown in Figure 0.1.

However, while the environment provides life support for the survival of human beings, the subject of economics has excluded nature, mostly taking nature to be given or granted. In his Preface to the report, *The Economics of Biodiversity: The Dasgupta Review*, Sir Partha Dasgupta writes,

> Not so long ago, when the world was very different from what it is now, the economic questions that needed urgent response could be studied most productively by excluding Nature from economic models. At the end of the Second World War, absolute poverty was endemic in much of Africa, Asia, and Latin America; and Europe needed reconstruction. It was natural to focus on the accumulation of produced capital (roads, machines, buildings, factories, and ports) and what we today call human capital (health and education). To introduce Nature, or natural capital, into economic models would have been to add unnecessary luggage to the exercise.
>
> (Dasgupta 2021)[1]

After Second World War, several developing countries attained independence from their former colonial rulers. One of the common claims made by leaders of independence movements was that colonialism had been responsible for perpetuating low living standards in the colonies. Thus, economic development after independence became an objective of policy not only

DOI: 10.4324/9781003253884-1

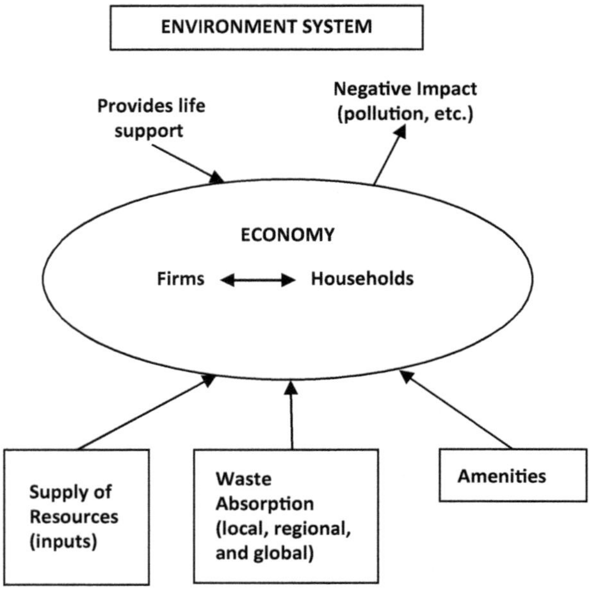


*Figure 0.1* Economy–environment linkage. *Source:* Author's illustration.

because of the humanitarian desire to raise living standards but also because political promises had been made, and failure to make progress towards development would, it was feared, be interpreted as a failure of the independence movement. Developing countries in Latin America and Asia that had been colonies accepted the analogous belief that economic domination by the industrial countries had thwarted their development, and they, too, joined the quest for rapid economic growth.

During that initial period, theorizing about development and policies to attain economic development accepted the assumption that the policies of the industrial countries were to blame for the poverty of the developing countries. Memories of the Great Depression, when developing countries' terms of trade had deteriorated markedly, producing sharp reductions in per capita incomes, haunted many policymakers. Finally, even in the developed countries, the Keynesian legacy attached significant importance to investment.

In this milieu, it was thought that a shortage of capital was the cause of underdevelopment. It followed that policy should aim at an accelerated rate of investment. Since most countries with low per capita income were also heavily agricultural (and imported most of the manufactured goods consumed domestically), it was thought that accelerated investment in industrialization and the development of manufacturing industries to supplant imports through import substitution was the path to development.

This path of economic growth and development has reaped tremendous benefits in the form of sustained economic growth, with incredibly high rates of growth starting from the second half of the twentieth century. This economic progress has allowed unprecedented improvements in human consumption, human health, education, and addressing inequality. However, many of these issues are still pertinent for developing countries of sub-Saharan Africa and Asia. It is also true that many of us have been fortunate enough to have lived without war for the past 70 years, which is widely believed to be due to the development of international institutions and a deepening of international trade that led to widespread cooperation, and with it, it brought a new era of global stability.

At the same time, the rapid increase in humankind's population, from around 2 billion in 1930 to 7.8 billion in 2020, coupled with an increase in real-world Gross Domestic Product (GDP) by a factor of roughly 40 during the same period, has led mankind to progressively push closer to the boundaries of planet Earth. To provide additional food for the surge in population, agricultural land use has increased by 30%; to provide goods and services for the rise in demand, the material footprint of our production increased by an estimated factor of 40; and to provide energy for our lifestyles, our use of non-renewable and polluting resources (coal, oil, gas) increased by a factor of 8. This increase in consumption coupled with a similar increase in input use has transformed the face of the planet Earth and has given rise to unwanted side effects and new challenges.

Some of these challenges are well known, such as local and global pollution, problems of waste, and indeed climate change. Another often neglected challenge has been consistent pressure on biodiversity due to increased land use. A mixture of burgeoning population and increasing resource use that carved deeply in nature's pristine areas has led to species conflict manifested not only in the rapid loss of other species but also in a much ignored yet increasingly visible negative feedback in the form of viral crossovers (Smith et al. 2014). The linkages between economic development, viral crossovers in the form of communicable diseases, and environmental issues have, up to now, seen little attention from environmental economists.

It is in the above light that this book is of significance. The book is in honour of Professor Rabindra N. Bhattacharyya, a pioneer in the field of environmental economics. The book addresses various environmental issues, including economic growth and environment, energy, forestry and carbon sequestration, nature conservation, sustainable development, climate change, and a history of the role of environmental economics in developing countries. The COVID-19 pandemic has significantly impacted the relationship between animals and humans. This book contains chapters on the study of the zoonotic interface of humans and their impact on the economy and ecology. The book also contains micro-level case studies on gender and waste management, road building in developing countries by minimizing ecological damage, climate-smart farming, incentives of rural households to build tree cover, the impact of electric fencing to reduce crop damages, and development under regional climate vulnerabilities. Most of these case studies are based in South Asia and Africa. The book also covers issues related to the environmental policy and regional environmental economics networks in developing countries. I discuss in detail about the book later. In this introductory chapter, initially, in the next section, I discuss the relevance of environmental economics for developing nations, an idea that is at the core of this book. Next, I briefly talk about the development of environmental economics as a subject in South Asia and India and the contribution of Professor Rabindra N. Bhattacharya. The details on the parts of the book and the chapters are discussed at the end.

## Environmental Economics in Developing Countries: Issues and Challenges

As mentioned earlier, post–Second World War, the emphasis of most of the developing countries, especially those that got freedom and had a long colonial past, was to follow a path of economic growth and prosperity following the Western model of rapid industrialization. However, being colonies of the Western world, many of these countries did not believe in the idea of competition and capitalist form of development that the Western countries preached. Instead, these countries attempted to follow industrialization through government machinery and public institutions. For them, the erstwhile Soviet Union model of development was more attractive than the Western one. The first prime minister of India, Pandit Jawaharlal Nehru, at a public meeting in Calcutta in 1949 spoke of the grand plans of industrialization. I quote:

> In two or three years we shall successfully complete the river valley projects of Damodar Valley, Mahanadi Scheme, Bhakra Dam, and others all over the country, from south to north, and that shall bring lakhs of areas under irrigation. With the completion of canals, we shall produce more food and also electricity.[2]

Science and technology were symbols of modernization and growth in these developing nations (Chakrabarty 2021).

In this light, during the 1950s, environmental economics was more concentrated on studying the optimal use of resources. It was more concerned with natural resource economics, both non-renewable (such as minerals) and renewable (such as forestry and fishery) and their optimal rates of extraction (Dasgupta 1980, Dasgupta and Heal 1982). Many of these research works were promoted by Resources for the Future (RFF), which was established in Washington, DC, USA, as an independent research organization that used both developed and applied economics to an extensive array of environmental issues. However, with the release of the book *Silent Spring* in 1962 (Carson 1962), the negative impact of economic growth and industrialization became evident. Carson's warnings about the effects of agrochemicals on the environment gained public attention and made economists think about the cost–benefit analysis of economic growth and the environment. A good amount of literature followed from this event on pollution control and negative externality issues. It was also a realization that energy derived from fossil fuels in industrial development created external diseconomies in the form of air and water pollution. Rapid industrialization in developed countries has resulted in large-scale carbon dioxide and other greenhouse gas emissions, adversely affecting the environment and creating global warming with disastrous consequences for future generations.

The environment was becoming a concern not only at the production level but also at the consumption level. The wasteful lifestyles of modern economies led many to believe that such a lifestyle will bring environmental catastrophe if followed by the large population of developing countries in Asia and Africa. Gradually, the unsustainable lifestyle issue became synonymous with the pursuit of economic growth, and the antigrowth movement was born. Many worried that their concern of Malthus about food production being unable to match the increasing consumption levels of the rising population might come true (Malthus 1798).

This idea was supported by Boulding's 1966 'spaceship Earth' essay, where he likened planet Earth to a spaceship in which there is a finite supply of energy, which can only ultimately be replaced with solar power, and a limited supply of water and materials, which can only provide a sustainable future if they are reused and recycled (Boulding 1966). This also led to the development of the subject of ecological economics, based on limits set by the Earth's carrying capacity and its environments. This is evident in the work of Herman Daly, who has long been an advocate of antigrowth as a means of keeping world economic systems within the bio-geophysical limits of the Earth (Daly 1977). Daly's work is very much in the spirit of Boulding's spaceship Earth essay and has also been heavily influenced by the work of Georgescu-Roegen's 1971 magnum opus titled 'The Entropy Law and the Economic Process', who has stressed the role of the second law of thermodynamics, increasing entropy, in making an economic system consistent with maximum recycling and maximum use of renewable energy.

In this light, the broad policy objective of sustainable development was brought to the fore with the publication of the Brundtland Report in 1987. To quote from the Brundtland Report on sustainable development, it is the 'economic development that meets the needs of the present without compromising the ability of future generations to meet their own needs'.

The concept of sustainable development led the major lending agencies to developing countries such as the World Bank and the International Monetary Fund to revise their policies, forcing the lending countries to pay more attention to the environmental costs of development projects and asking the governments to invest more in the environment, soil conservation, afforestation, watershed protection, etc. to get a loan. This forced many developing countries to give more importance to the environment in the economic development paradigm. Environmental policy also became a critical issue in this respect.

Developing countries in Asia and Africa depend in several important ways on their natural capital. Peasants, fishers, and cattle herders earn their living directly from using renewable natural resources such as farmland, water, air, forest, grazing areas, irrigation, plants, and animals. These resources are increasingly exposed to unsustainable exploitation, pollution, and conversion to other uses in many countries. To give one example, India is the largest user of groundwater in the world, and by 2030, 40% of Indians will have no access to drinking water (Acharyya 2014: Niti Aayog 2019). Along with the dwindling freshwater sources, groundwater contamination has also reached alarming levels in several parts of the country. India ranked 120 among 122 countries on a global water quality index in 2019 (Niti Aayog 2019). In eastern India and Bangladesh, many people suffer from drinking arsenic and fluoride-contaminated groundwater (Acharyya 2009). In this context, and many other such cases, the Coase theorem,[3] which states that in case of a conflict of property rights, the involved parties can bargain or negotiate terms that will accurately reflect the full costs and underlying values of the property rights at issue, resulting in the most efficient outcome (Coase 1937, 1960), will not work. Most of the people affected by property rights in developing countries are poor, be it the victim of arsenic contamination, the tribal who loses rights to the forest, the farmer who loses land to the corporate, and many more. Besides, negotiations have a transaction cost that is much high for the poor.

This is also pertinent for common property resources or open access resources such as groundwater, forestry, fishery, etc. In his paper titled 'Tragedy of the Commons' (1968), Garret Hardin hypothesized that common property resources lacking ownership would be doomed to overexploitation. Commons have suddenly emerged as a point of conflict in most developing countries, including India, as the forces of globalization have resulted in the importance of business over society. India is undoubtedly blessed with rich natural resources, but it is not free from technical and social problems of placing commons like any other country. In India, conflicts over common resources date back to the history of British colonialism (Guha 2000). Water governance crises concerning Kaveri and Yamuna Rivers; and the Bhopal gas tragedy lent credence to the vulnerability of the rich resources of the country to unabated tragedies.

However, it has also been observed that many communities historically have conserved nature on their own rules. There are good examples of commons through irrigation networks or pastures that have been managed by and for ordinary people for generations, and they are still functioning. Elinor Ostrom (1990) showed that individuals and communities could manage their collective resources. Her field research in Maine, Indonesia, Nepal, and Kenya led to the development of design principles that have supported effective mobilization for local management of common-pool resources (CPR) in various areas. Jodha (1966), while studying communities in semi-arid regions, attributed a significant role to communities in common property resource (CPR) management. He also emphasized the importance of regulatory institutions. His work on community management of natural resources in fragile mountain regions (Jodha 2002) is also widely regarded as seminal.

That cooperation within the community could be beneficial to CPRs becoming more of a global phenomenon with the problem of climate change. The industrialization that took place in the second half of the 20th century created two worlds: the dirty world of the Global South (developing countries with mass-scale poverty and dirty industries) and the Global North (developed countries with clean industries). The dirty industries were shifted to the South and dominated the North–South trade flow. This was called the phenomenon of the 'pollution haven hypothesis' (Copeland and Taylor 1994, 2004) and was supported by the Environmental Kuznets' Curve (EKC), which hypothesized the possible existence of an inverted U-shaped relationship between per capita income and pollution. This means that in the initial stages of economic growth, pollution emissions increase and environmental quality declines, but beyond some level of income per capita (which will vary for different indicators), the trend reverses so that at high-income levels, economic growth leads to environmental improvement (Stern 2004, 2018).

However, with climate change and the rapid industrialization of developing nations such as India and China, the global environment has been severely affected. Moreover, the private corporate competing in the worldwide market has also realized that they must maintain specific pollution standards even in developing economies to compete and survive (Porter and Linde 1995). Pollution checks and balances cannot wait for that time when the developing countries can come up to the standards of the developed before considering the environment. With globalization and trade integration, pollution could not have been kept only for the poor.

The prospect of global climate change has emerged as a significant scientific and public policy issue. Scientific studies indicate that accumulated carbon dioxide emitted from the burning of fossil fuels, along with contributions from other human-induced greenhouse gas emissions, are leading to warmer surface temperatures. Possible current-century consequences of this temperature increase include increased frequency of extreme temperature events (such as heat waves), heightened storm intensity, altered precipitation patterns, sea-level rise, and reversal of ocean currents. These changes, in turn, can have significant impacts on the functioning of ecosystems, the viability of wildlife, biodiversity, capital productivity, and the well-being of humans. There is considerable disagreement within and among nations as to what policies should be introduced to mitigate and prevent climate change and its various impacts. Despite the disagreements, we have witnessed the gradual emergence of a range of international and domestic climate change policies in recent years, including emissions trading programmes, emissions taxes, performance standards, and technology-promoting programmes.

Starting with Nordhaus (1982), climate change economics has focused on diagnosing the economic underpinnings of climate change and offering positive and normative analyses of policies to confront the problem. While overlapping with other areas of environmental economics, it has a unique focus because of distinctive features of the climate problem, including the long timescale, the extent and nature of uncertainties, the international scope of the issue, and the uneven distribution of policy benefits and costs across space and time.

Environment economics has become more pertinent with global negotiations on reduction in carbon emissions, starting with the Kyoto protocol adopted in Kyoto, Japan, in 1997, which started the work of the United Nations Framework Convention on Climate Change (UNFCCC) by committing industrialized countries and economies in transition to limit and reduce greenhouse gases (GHG) emissions in accordance with agreed individual targets to the Conference of Parties led Paris Agreement in 2015 where parties to the UNFCCC reached a landmark agreement to combat climate change and to accelerate and intensify the actions and investments needed for a sustainable low-carbon future. In this context, environmental economics has been instrumental in informing policy worldwide: in market creation (such as carbon), valuation, and the design of new interventions (such as payments for ecosystem services).

The other globally agreed phenomenon of development where the environment has played a vital role includes achieving the Sustainable Development Goals (SDGs), also known as the Global Goals, which the United Nations adopted in 2015 as a universal call to action to end poverty, protect the planet, and ensure that by 2030 all people enjoy peace and prosperity. The 17 SDGs are integrated into recognizing that activity in one area will affect outcomes in others and that development must balance social, economic, and environmental sustainability.

The above discussion on the environment and related issues proves that developing countries face a big challenge. On the one hand, they must improve the standard of living of their people, many of whom are poor; on the other, they must abide by the norms of carbon emission and development goals. Environmental economics can play a crucial role in achieving both.

To quote Dasgupta and Maler (1991),

> A feasible concept of sustainable development should accommodate both political and ecological concerns. In practice, this will involve the achievement of a socially necessary growth rate for developing countries while at the same time supporting environmental protection and improvement in the future.[3]

The impact of the COVID-19 pandemic has also placed many questions on our survival. COVID-19 falls into the category of emerging infectious diseases (EIDs) that are transmitted between domestic or wild animals and humans (known as 'zoonotic diseases') (WHO 2020). EIDs can significantly impact global economies and public health. More than 60% of all EID events are dominated by zoonoses; most originate in wildlife and increase considerably over time (Jones et al. 2008). The far-reaching impacts of COVID-19 on the entire planet have mobilized numerous calls to prevent similar pandemics in the future. Appeals have ranged from advocacy for the permanent closure of markets where wild animals may be sold, banning all commercial use of wildlife, significantly stepping up sanitary measures, and monitoring all food value chains.

Encroachment of human activities and destruction of ecosystems increase the risk of emergence and spread of zoonotic diseases (UNEP and ILRI 2020). In particular, deforestation, the degradation and fragmentation of habitats, and the unsustainable expansion of agriculture bring humans and livestock into closer contact with wildlife. To reduce the risk of future zoonotic diseases, both the immediate pressures of biodiversity loss and ecosystem degradation and the underlying drivers must be addressed through an integrated approach that works across disciplines, sectors, value chains, and spatial scales (UNEP and ILRI 2020).

Under the above circumstances, this book attempts to address all the above issues, from growth and environment, biodiversity and ecosystem services loss, climate change and nature conservation, waste management, energy, and ecology, thereby linking the environment and sustainable economic development. The book provides theory and applied tools of environmental economics that address the environmental challenges of developing economies.

## Environmental Economics in South Asia and the Contribution of Professor Rabindra N. Bhattacharya

Most of the South Asian countries, including India, followed a path of development in the immediate post-independence period with a goal of import substitution and self-sufficiency. Science and technology dominated the education structure, with engineers created to build the country. Building dams and factories were given top priority. Environmental destruction was never considered to be an issue. However, the environment became a big issue with mass movements and accidents in the region.

The first significant environmental movement against such development occurred in India and is commonly known as the *Chipko movement,* which originated in 1973 in the Himalayan region of Uttarakhand (then part of Uttar Pradesh) and went on to become a rallying point for many future environmental movements all over the world. The name of the campaign 'Chipko' comes from the word 'embrace', as the villagers hugged the trees and encircled them to prevent trees from being hacked. It created a precedent for starting non-violent protests in India. It was Sunderlal Bahuguna, a Gandhian activist, who passed away very recently, who gave the movement a proper direction. Its success meant that the world immediately took notice of this non-violent movement, which was to inspire in time many similar eco-groups by helping to slow down the rapid deforestation, expose vested interests, increase social awareness and the need to save trees, increase ecological awareness, and demonstrate the viability of people power.

The other environmental movement that had a significant impact on the country was the *Narmada Bachao Andolan* in 1985 spearheaded by native tribals, or *Adivasis*, and later joined by farmers and human rights activists such as Medha Patkar and Baba Amte, against several large dam projects across the Narmada River, which flows through the states of Gujarat, Madhya Pradesh, and Maharashtra. Sardar Sarovar Dam in Gujarat is one of the biggest dams on the river and was one of the first focal points of the movement.

In the early hours of 3 December 1984, methylisocyanate (MIC) gas leaked from a plant owned, managed, and operated by Union Carbide India Limited (UCIL) in the central Indian city of Bhopal. According to government figures, approximately 5,200 people died, and several thousand other individuals suffered permanent or partial disabilities. This terrible tragedy continues to evoke strong emotions even 37 years later.

The above-mentioned three events shook the international world, and governments were forced to control pollution and promote nature conservation. One of the environmentalists whose passion, vision, and immense energy brought environmental concerns from the margins of the public sphere into the mainstream was Anil Agarwal.[4] By asserting that ecological sustainability and social justice are two sides of the same coin, Agarwal helped establish a distinctive identity and direction for environmentalism in the country. The staggering breadth and depth of Agarwal's concerns were demonstrated first in The State of India's Environment: A Citizens' Report. Published in 1982 by the Centre for Science and Environment (CSE), the non-governmental organization (NGO) that Agarwal founded and directed along with Sunita Narain, this monumental document presented, for the first time, an overview of India's ecological problems. After a decade of rising environmental awareness in the West, the Indian media had begun to cover environmental issues sporadically.

Both South and East Asia have enjoyed growth in GDP at a sufficient pace to have substantial impacts on natural environments. According to one estimate (ADB 2013), more than half of Asia's last frontiers are under moderate to high threat. At risk is the Sundarbans, the world's largest mangrove forest and the habitat for the largest and only viable population of the Royal Bengal tiger, located in Southwest Bangladesh and Southeast West Bengal, India. Economic production dominates most Asian economies as they increasingly become interdependent market economies. This is reflected in the pace of investment in infrastructure in Asia for such items as roads, communication systems, electricity generation, water supply and irrigation, safe water, and sanitation (ADB 2017). While such developments often improve human welfare in terms of modernization and human-made environments, their impact on the natural environments has been far from benign. Human activity critically impacts the physical environment. South Asia faces many environmental problems, including urban and rural settings.

It is in this background that the South Asian Network for Development and Environmental Economics (SANDEE) evolved as a direct response to geo-political circumstances in South Asia.[5] There are several reasons for the origin of SANDEE. First, it was well known that due to geo-political constraints, countries across South Asia did not have much academic interaction though they faced similar economic and environmental problems. Moreover, the interdisciplinary approach that was necessary to address issues of environment and development were absent in most academic institutions (Lele 2009). Most importantly, the distrust among scientists and academicians prevailed due to the geo-political tensions, which did not allow them to interact freely. The state was sceptical towards such interactions.

However, countries in South Asia share many common property resources such as rivers, forests, biodiversity, and climate. They must act together to fight common issues such as flood mitigation, forest and biodiversity conservation, river water sharing, and fighting against climate change. Given the gravity of the situation, some common platform needed to be created where interdisciplinary research support could be continuously backed by skill-building through training, repeat interactions, and mentoring. Unfortunately, due to the geo-political conditions, it was challenging to build such a platform from within (Mukhopadhyay et al. 2014).

Beijer Institute of Ecological Economics, Stockholm, under the guidance of Karl Goran Maler and Sir Partha Dasgupta, took the initiative to form such a platform for environment development economics interaction among scholars and researchers of South Asia. The first institutionalized environmental economics regional network emerged in 1993 in East Asia in the form of the Economy and Environment Programme for Southeast Asia

(EEPSEA), following which SANDEE was founded in 1999. The objective of SANDEE is

> a regional network that uses economic tools and analyses to address South Asia's environmental challenges. It is based on the premise that solutions to economic development concerns and environmental problems are integrally linked. Thus, SANDEE brings South Asian researchers and institutes interested in the inter-connections among development, poverty, and the environment. Its main goal is to build the professional skills required to enable South Asians to address local and global environmental concerns. SANDEE works in seven countries in South Asia – Bangladesh, Bhutan, India, Maldives, Nepal, Pakistan, and Sri Lanka.[6]

The impact of SANDEE towards research in environmental economics and capacity building in the subject has been tremendous. The institute has enhanced research and teaching capacity among South Asian scholars. Its research mandate covers local, regional, and global sustainability concerns. Research topics have changed over the years, and the current focus is on ecosystems management, the economics of climate change, and policies and programmes for greener development. The network draws in regional and international talent to help local researchers address questions identified by them. Many researchers trained by SANDEE have been placed at universities, research institutes, and administrative positions in government and non-governmental organizations.

This book takes pride in having several chapters written by resource persons and researchers of SANDEE. Professor Rabindra N. Bhattacharya, in whose honour this book is published, was himself a resource person of SANDEE for many years. Sir Partha Dasgupta, one of the founding members of SANDEE and a pioneer in environmental economics, has written the Foreword for this book. Many contributors to this book are actively involved with SANDEE.

The contribution of another organization in the field of environmental economics worth mentioning is that of the Indian Society for Ecological Economics (INSEE), which was established in 1998 and registered as a society in 1999 and whose office is based in New Delhi, India. Around 1998, the World Bank initiated a capacity-building programme in environmental economics for faculty and researchers in India. Two nodal agencies responsible were the Madras School of Economics (MSE) and the Institute of Economic Growth (IEG). The project was termed the *World Bank Aided India: Environmental Management Capacity Building Technical Assistance Project*. This project equipped many faculty members and researchers of various universities, research institutes, and colleges to teach the subject of environmental economics. The subject was included in the syllabus at the postgraduate programmes of different universities. Professor Rabindra N. Bhattacharya, in whose honour this book is published, was instrumental in introducing and teaching a master's level course in North Bengal University in 1987, perhaps for the first time in the country (Bhattacharya 2001).

Within a brief period and due to the capacity-building programme, many academicians started teaching or doing research in Environmental Economics. It was felt that a common platform was necessary for discussion and dialogue.

INSEE was initially presided over by Professor Kanchan Chopra, the Director of the Institute of Economic Growth. She pioneered the organization to new heights and was instrumental in establishing INSEE as an institution of repute in environmental economics. Subsequently, over time, famous academicians in the subject became directors of the institute.

Professor Kanchan Chopra, Professor M.N. Murty, and many other academicians associated with INSEE have contributed to the present volume. The objective of INSEE is to encourage multidisciplinary, scientific, and technological research on the integration of ecology, economics, and related disciplines.

SANDEE and INSEE have played a significant role in the Indian subcontinent to spread the subject of environmental economics. Most of the universities in South Asia now have environmental economics as part of their syllabus. A large number of research on various issues have been done in this region by the people living in the region itself. Such micro-level studies have enabled policy decisions on environment and development, keeping the stakeholders in mind.

## Contribution of Professor Rabindra N. Bhattacharya in the Field of Environmental Economics

The year was 1998. I was in the second year of my postgraduation in economics at the University of Calcutta. During the second year of our postgraduation, we were offered a new subject to study for the first time. The subject was called 'Natural Resource and Environmental Economics'. Out of the growing concern about the environment and guided by the thought that since the subject is in discussion, if we opt for this subject, our probability of getting a job or doing research after postgraduation would be high, many of us decided to opt for studying 'Natural Resource and Environmental Economics'. This choice introduced us to Professor Rabindra N. Bhattacharya, perhaps the only formally trained environmental economist in Calcutta during that time. Professor Bhattacharya would teach us natural resource economics.

Perhaps for the first time in India, Professor Bhattacharya had introduced the subject of natural resource economics in North Bengal University at the postgraduate level, way back in 1987, where he taught the subject for several years. Later, when he shifted to Kalyani University in 1995, he introduced and taught there the same subject. He helped in formulating the syllabus and taught for the inaugural semester when environmental economics was introduced as a compulsory paper for students doing master's in quantitative economics at Indian Statistical Institute (ISI), Kolkata, in 1999. He also helped the Department of Economics, Jadavpur University, by formulating the syllabus on environmental economics and also taught the subject there for a couple of years.

After obtaining a PhD from Utah State University, where he won the 'Outstanding Achievement Award', and leaving the offer of teaching in another American University, Professor Bhattacharya joined the University of North Bengal in West Bengal, where he taught for almost ten years before shifting to University of Kalyani, another University in West Bengal from where he retired as Professor in 2004. During his career, he has published many papers on environmental economics in topmost journals. His most noted paper, written jointly with Professor Donald L. Snyder, was titled 'A More General Dynamic Economic Model of the Optimal Rotation of Multiple Use Forests', published in *Journal of Environmental Economics and Management*'. Professor Bhattacharya was a resource person for SANDEE for more than ten years and has imparted his knowledge on environmental economics to many students from South Asia. These students have gone on to become big names in environmental economics, some becoming faculties in universities and colleges as also researchers. He has undertaken several research projects at both national and international levels. He was also a visiting faculty at various universities and research institutes in the country, including the Indian Statistical Institute (Kolkata), Jawaharlal Nehru University (JNU), Indira Gandhi Institute of Development Research (IGIDR), University of Calcutta (Department of Economics), Jadavpur University, etc. His edited book on environmental economics, titled 'Environmental Economics: An Indian Perspective', published by Oxford University Press, is one of the earliest and most popular textbooks in the country on the subject (Bhattacharya 2001).

Professor Bhattacharya introduced us to the world of environmental economics and the economy–ecology interaction. Many of us were inspired by Professor Bhattacharya's lectures. He would explain very slowly and convincingly. He was of the more traditional type. He would come by public bus with a cloth bag on his shoulder, which in Bengali we traditionally call the 'jhola'. It would be difficult to distinguish him in public; such was his simplicity. Although India was moving into the world of fast money and fast life, it did not affect Professor Bhattacharya. His only job was to teach and do research. This attracted many like me to him, and many of us went on to do our PhDs under his supervision. Any new academic paper, any novel idea would excite him. However, this did not stop him from the regular Sunday morning Coffee House 'adda' in Jadavpur. He is a social and amiable person, and everyone in Coffee House loves him. The partition of India would always haunt him. His family moved from Faridpur (now in Bangladesh) to Kolkata when he was six. He had to struggle to survive. However, even in this entire struggle, and with all the academic achievements, he has remained the Bengali 'Bhadralok' (gentleman). He is much like nature. He is silent, perhaps invisible, but like the shadow of a tree, has given shelter to an innumerable number of students, many of whom have achieved success as teachers and academicians because of him.

### *About the Book*

The book is divided into four parts, with each part discussing different but pertinent issues on the economics of the environment. The book covers the following themes: Environment, Ecology, and Development; Economics of Nature Conservation; Climate Change and Development; and Economics of Environmental Policy. There are 15 chapters in this book. Part I, Environment, Ecology, and Development, has four chapters. Part II, Economics of Nature Conservation, has four chapters. Part III, Climate Change and Development, has three chapters. Part IV, Economics of Environmental Policy has four chapters. Each part has been given equal importance with a balanced distribution of the chapters under each theme. Contributions within each theme engage with policy issues and practice, as well as with both macro and micro aspects. The contributors are mostly economists. The approach is interdisciplinary, both in spirit and content, which goes beyond the mainstream ideology of economics.

Some of the chapters are conceptual and reflective essays, and some are case studies. The book has been written by various national and international experts in the field of different branches of environmental economics. Most of the contributors are or were connected to SANDEE, with whom Professor Rabindra N. Bhattacharya was involved as a resource person for more than ten years.

The other organization with which Professor Rabindra N. Bhattacharya was closely involved was INSEE. Many contributors in this volume were actively involved in the foundation of INSEE.

Although Professor Rabindra N. Bhattacharyya contributed to various areas of environmental economics, his major contribution was in the economics of forestry. One of his most well-known papers is on forestry (Snyder and Bhattacharyya 1990). One of the parts of this book (Part III) is on nature conservation and forestry. In all, 35 authors have contributed to this volume. The contributions are from across the world, with authors from diverse racial, ethnic, and cultural backgrounds. This book would benefit advanced undergraduate and postgraduate level students and researchers who work on environment and development economics, faculty members in universities and colleges and young researchers in South Asia doing research in related areas. It would also be helpful for the interested trying to know about contemporary issues in development and environmental economics.

## Chapter-wise Layout

### Part I: Environment, Ecology, and Development

Part I introduces us to the interrelationship between ecology, environment, and development. The term 'sustainable development' gained wide international currency with the growth of ecological understanding at local, national, and international levels among the communities and movements and nation-states and governments. Ensuring environmental sustainability with economic growth for developing countries requires them to achieve sustainable development patterns and preserve natural ecosystems' productive capacity for future generations. There are four chapters in this part.

Widening income disparity and environmental deterioration in relation to economic growth have increasingly become pressing issues of concern for developing nations. In this context, the Environmental Kuznets Curve (EKC) defines the changing relationship between income per capita and environmental degradation, that is, environmental quality declines in the early stage of economic growth, but beyond a certain level of income per capita, the trend reverses as income rises, generating the EKC inverted U-curve. Since the introduction of the EKC hypotheses, numerous studies have been undertaken by applying the samples of countries and regions of varied sizes and with varied types of pollutants surveyed over different periods. In his chapter titled 'Three Theories of Growth, Environment and Poverty Nexus' (Chapter 1), Professor M.N. Murty discusses the three theories of growth, environment, and poverty nexus. The first theory predicts that due to market failure and free-rider problems in developing countries, there will be a fall in environmental quality and a rise in poverty. The second theory, following EKC, identifies income growth as a key factor in determining poverty and environment nexus and predicts that a downward spiral of environment and poverty will break after income reaches a certain threshold level when people will be conscious about the environment. The third one proposes that with appropriate micro- and macro-level institutions in the economy, the downward spiral may break even at low levels of income. The Ramsey optimal growth model is used to analyze the three theories. The author concludes that the powerful models of participatory development and the theory of environmental entitlements break the traditional notion of a downward spiral of environment and poverty as also the trade-off between environment and growth even at low levels of per capita income in developing countries, thereby giving hope of a new way of thinking about environment and poverty.

The COVID-19 pandemic has highlighted the vulnerabilities of our socio-economic systems globally and exposed the risks that natural capital degradation imposes on human health, our economy, and society. Yet, natural capital, in particular the biodiversity and ecosystem services upon which we depend, is rapidly deteriorating. The deterioration of natural capital threatens the productivity of several economic sectors, ranging from agriculture and fisheries to tourism and industry. At the same time, the drivers of biodiversity loss, such as deforestation, land use change, overexploitation of natural resources, wildlife trade, and climate change, are helping to create the conditions for pathogens to leap from animals to humans. The recent spread of new diseases from livestock and the homogeneity of farmed species underlines the importance of enhancing the resilience and security of our food system. How to build resilience and sustainability in the recovery phase of this pandemic is becoming an overwhelmingly important topic for policymakers. Low-income countries and developing countries face a more challenging situation than others due to their limited health infrastructure, limited financial and human resources, and limited capacity of governments to respond. The interconnected nature of the COVID-19 pandemic crisis demands an integrated approach and coordinated action, which complicates decision-making even more. Chapters 2 and 3 discuss the impact of COVID-19 on the economy. In Chapter 2, titled 'Natural Capital, Pandemic and Development: Exploration of Nexus and Solutions', Pushpam Kumar, Amelia Holmes, and Samia Islam discuss how the depletion of natural capital, including biodiversity, affects poverty, inequality, and wealth distribution in developing countries. This chapter highlights the linkages of declining natural capital and zoonotic impacts through a pandemic and attempts to understand and map out the impact on the development agenda like poverty and economic inequality, and then attempts to find some workable solutions. The authors suggest that the knowledge and tools derived from research on the issue be made accessible to national governments, businesses, the health sector, local communities, and others to reduce the risk of future pandemics. Their study suggests that a financial accounting of the societal effects of zoonotic diseases can be a guiding policy in solving the problem.

In order to achieve sustainable development, it is important to understand the interlinkage between ecology, economy, and human health. If one gets affected, a chain reaction will follow in the others. Under the circumstances, it is also important that humans rethink their pattern of consumption, especially with respect to the consumption of animals.

The late 18th-century theory that the geometric progression of the population would outstrip the arithmetic progression of food production is not really a concern today, even if the world's population has increased from one billion to more than seven billion in the interim. Malthus (1798) believed that natural catastrophes and human disasters could correct the imbalance between food supply and population growth. He was also convinced that higher levels of food would lead to higher population levels, with supply creating demand. This reasoning could be applied to any item other than food if we consider the supply to be limited. When production factors are supposed to be at least partially fixed, the capacity of supply to address growing demand leads to the law of diminishing returns. One of the key theoretical answers to this problem has been Ricardo's competitive advantage theory, which made a convincing case for an economic system based on free trade, international flows, and specialization. Indeed, technological progress and globalization have provided above-average historical growth. Nevertheless, with climate change and the COVID-19 crisis, it is now obvious that the negative externalities created by this economic structure are starting to outweigh its advantages.

In Chapter 3, titled 'COVID-19: A Neo-Malthusian Event? Ecological links, Challenges and Opportunities', the authors Ramprasad Sengupta and Chetana Chaudhuri, carrying the message from Chapter 2, warn us on the Neo-Malthusian consequences of continuous biodiversity loss leading to the destruction of life and livelihood for a highly populated country like India. They highlight the adverse economic impact of the pandemic on economic growth and social well-being and show how the pandemic has revealed the weakness in managing ecosystem resources that point to the need to maintain the ecological balance through sustainable development and considering the limitations of nature. The authors suggest a change in cultural legacy.

It is universally accepted that electrification enhances the quality of life at the household level and stimulates the economy at a broader level. The immediate benefit of electrification comes through improved lighting, which promotes extended hours of study and reading and other household chores, and in turn contributes to better educational achievements. Lighting can also benefit many other household activities, such as sewing by women, social gatherings after dark, and many others. Electronic devices such as radios and television also improve access to information by rural households and can provide entertainment to family members. In addition, households' economic activities benefit tremendously from electricity, both inside and outside the home. However, access to electricity is still a problem for many poor households. Also, whether electricity provides large or small benefits is debatable and depends on the condition of the household. In this light, Ujjayant Chakravorty and Martino Pelli, in Chapter 4, titled 'Electrification and Development: Empirical evidence on the effect of electricity provision on household welfare', highlight the state of current knowledge on the costs and benefits of electrification by reviewing the recent empirical literature. The selective review shows that grid connections have significant impacts on poor households in developing countries. However, in very poor areas, such as sub-Saharan Africa, the immediate benefit of electrification is small. In areas where credit is available, improvement in life and livelihood is significant.

A growing body of impact studies has shown that access to electricity programmes in developing countries has brought mixed effects. Several challenges still prevent universal access to electricity: (i) high investment and operation costs, (ii) limited demand given market conditions, (iii) technical implementation and maintenance issues, and (iv) regulatory and political issues. Even with expanded access, other factors like quality of connection and equity may have limited the development impacts. Important evidence gaps remain for future studies to address. Understanding what works and what does not is important for policy planning and decision-making.

Moreover, the sources of electricity production in developing countries are mainly coal, oil, and natural gas, which contribute to one-third of global greenhouse gas emissions, leading to climate change and other human hazards. Therefore, it is essential to raise the standard of living by providing cleaner and more reliable electricity to ensure sustainable development without the destruction of natural resources.

*Part II: Economics of Nature Conservation*

In the Foreword to this book, Sir Partha Dasgupta mentions that 'Nature is our most precious asset'. Economic behaviour is arguably the most accurate expression of national, corporate, community, and individual values. No conservation effort can long endure without an intimate connection to value. And no expression of value in conservation can endure with vitality unless it finds expression in economic behaviour, either through what we spend to acquire what is needed by other species or what we do without in order that what is needed by other species is not consumed and destroyed. Conservation of nature might 'pay' from an economic perspective: it may be rational to conserve natural capital rather than convert it into alternative forms of capital or consume it today. Some forms of natural resource use leave natural habitats more or less intact, such as the conservation of forests. To observe that nature conservation pays does not imply there are no incentives for resource managers to destroy it (or to convert it into other forms of capital). An important reason nature may be destroyed is that many of the valuable services and benefits nature provides are 'free' in the sense that they are not marketed. This is an obvious case of market failure. Even if nature is valuable, if it does not command a flow of money, its value tends to be ignored by private parties. Examples include the air purifying qualities of ecosystems and non-use values associated with biodiversity conservation.

In recent decades, concern has grown globally over threats to natural resources and corresponding rates of species extinction. Nowhere is the concern greater than in developing countries, which represent much of the world's biological diversity. Changing social and economic conditions, because of rapid population growth, technological advancements, poverty, and the pressure to exploit natural resources, have substantial implications on the state of the environment of the developing countries. In the subsistence economy of rural communities, conservation plays an important role in ensuring that essential natural resources are available in the future amid the constraints presented by changing social and economic conditions. Consequently, conservation efforts in developing nations are perceived to be essential, but to be implemented in a practical sense requires a delicate balance between satisfying the social and economic needs of rural communities while ensuring ecological balance.

Environmental economists have developed methods to attach monetary values to ecosystem services, but that is different from money in the bank. The point is that even if the social returns to conservation and sustainable management are high, from the perspective of a private individual, it may be better to ignore these benefits (i.e., those accruing to others) and focus on the small subset of tradable benefits only. Hence the conversion of nature into alternative forms of capital may be privately optimal and socially non-optimal at the same time. In the above light, four chapters have been included in Part III, Economics of Nature Conservation.

Incentive-based policy instruments have long been argued by economists to be a more efficient means of achieving environmental goals such as reductions in polluting emissions and fostering the delivery of ecosystem services. Over the last few decades, governments worldwide have begun to make increasing use of policy instruments such as 'green' taxes and tradable pollution permits in an attempt to achieve environmental targets in a more cost-effective manner.

In Chapter 5, titled 'Incentive-Based Approaches to Nature Conservation', the author E. Somanathan talks about how, through the policy of incentive-based approaches to conservation, the administration can motivate local users to modify their land use in ways that are compatible with nature conservation. Since such modifications will typically impose costs on local users, hence, the government needs to give incentives to local users if they are to adapt to such modifications. The various kinds of incentives are discussed in detail, such as command and control, tax and fees, local governance, subsidies, and direct payments for conservation with various examples and case studies. While various approaches to conservation have their strengths and weaknesses, the author suggests a portfolio of conservation strategies for the effective conservation of nature.

Chapter 6, written by R. David Simpson titled 'Forests, Carbon Sequestration and Ecosystem Services: Are There "Two-for-One" Deals?', explores the conditions under which it would be optimal to reforest an area and then never harvest it again, as opposed to harvesting it on a cycle of set rotations. Rotational harvesting depends on several factors, the most important being the 'pickling rate', the fraction of carbon from harvested material that is permanently sequestered in building materials or other 'sinks'. Recently, significant importance has been given to bio energy with carbon capture and storage. Using Faustmann's classic model (1849) of optimal forest management, the above discussion has been developed in a simple derivative model. The model highlights the trade-offs between the objectives of carbon sequestration and the provision of other ecosystem services since carbon is sequestered in growing forests.

In contrast, ecosystem services are provided by grown forests. The opportunity cost of allowing a forest to mature to the point that its ecosystem service provision is greatest implies forgoing opportunities to sequester carbon more rapidly over time. While carbon is sequestered in growing forests, ecosystem services are provided most prolifically by grown forests. The opportunity cost of allowing a forest to mature to the point that its ecosystem service provision is greatest may be forgoing opportunities to sequester carbon more rapidly over time. The author suggests more research in the area from different perspectives before coming to any conclusion.

Chapter 7, written by Stella Z. Schons, Gregory S. Amacher, Kelly M. Cobourn, Nilesh Shinde, and Haripriya Gundimeda titled 'Incentives for Rural Households to Establish Tree Cover on Agricultural Land in Andhra Pradesh, India', in continuation of the theme of Chapter 6, explores the incentives of farmers to establish forest cover on agricultural land based on field level survey of a large number of farm households in the east and west Godhavari regions in the state of Andhra Pradesh, India. The authors use the multi-level mixed effect probit method to account for unobserved variation across clusters of villages, as well as unobserved variation within villages. Their estimates identify the key drivers of tree planting decisions on land that can also provide agricultural returns. Based on econometric models, their empirical results establish that length of land tenure and land ownership constitute significant and positive factors for the tree planting decision. This is an especially important result for future policy decisions on forestry for the government in framing the National Forest Policy and could lead to the transformation of the region. Their results also provide scope for 'public–private participation models' for Andhra Pradesh in India. Their results also suggest that any long-term forest policy should involve all the stakeholders, incentives, and laws in conjunction.

Road networks form the basic transportation system for most of the world's inhabitants, stimulating local and regional economies. Scientific advances in recent years have revealed that this vast, growing, planetary construction boom has been occurring mostly in non-urban environments and most aggressively in developing frontiers of tropical regions. However, even in highly urbanized countries, road networks consist mostly of roads outside of urban areas. To produce a reliable, comprehensive picture of the global road network, scientists have taken advantage of improvements in mapping technologies, including automated detection from satellite imagery and real-time mapping on the ground. Because the extent of the global road network is increasing at a rapid, unprecedented pace, the pervasive and sometimes dramatic impacts on ecosystems and their services in rural areas will continue. These include destruction of habitat, including fragmentation of plant and animal populations, as also traffic disturbance, including animal–vehicle collisions that reduce populations and habitat quality to the point of causing local extinctions.

Several strategies exist for mitigating the adverse effects of roads in rural landscapes. Satellite imagery can be applied advantageously in transportation policy, planning, and decision-making to reduce the impacts of roads by evaluating development alternatives, including whether to build a road, where to build, as well as how and when to build. Such strategies can be applied at continental, regional, or local scales, contributing to the discussion of trade-offs within a framework of sustainable development.

Chapter 8, by Susmita Dasgupta and David Wheeler, titled 'Minimizing Ecological Damage from Road Improvement in Tropical Forests' with respect to the above discussion, develops and applies a spatial econometric model that links road upgrading to forest clearing and biodiversity loss in the tropical forests of Bolivia, Cameroon, and Myanmar. Information on forest clearing, biodiversity and protected areas, digital road maps and elevation maps, and agricultural opportunity values are used. A specified econometric model is used to estimate the effects of the above-mentioned variables on the cumulative percent of forest cleared. The econometric measurement of road quality effects enables estimation of the deforestation impact of programmes that upgrade secondary roads to primary status.

The results to identify priority areas with high expected losses, along with ecologically critical road corridors within those areas, are mapped. Highly diverse patterns of expected forest clearing and biodiversity loss are found from the analysis. Explicit identification of ecologically vulnerable areas and road corridors can help steer road upgrading programmes towards corridors where expected biodiversity losses will be minimized and can inform the adoption of appropriate protection measures in vulnerable road corridors and neighbouring areas.

### *Part III: Climate Change and Development*

High population density, degrading natural resources, water scarcity and water pollution, and high levels of poverty and food insecurity make South Asia one of the most vulnerable regions with respect to the impact of climate change. The changes in precipitation, sea-level rise, glacial cover reduction, and incidence of extreme events associated with climate change are likely to result in large-scale internal migration of people and render about 125 million migrants homeless. In the face of the environmental crisis, the states of South Asia will need to cooperate with a new commitment and sense of urgency. Part III has three chapters relating to climate change and its impact on development. South Asia, home to about 1.5 billion people, nearly a third of whom are still living in poverty, faces a major challenge of achieving rapid economic growth to reduce poverty and attain the SDGs in an era of accentuated risks posed by global climate change. The impacts of climate change are likely to result in huge economic, social, and environmental damage to the South Asian countries, compromising their growth potential and poverty-reduction efforts.

Countries in the Greater Himalayan region, which includes Bangladesh, Bhutan, northern India, and Nepal, are facing increased frequency and magnitude of extreme weather events resulting in flooding, landslides, damage to property and infrastructure, the devastation of agricultural crops, reduction of hydropower generation, and negative impact on human health. The coastal areas of Bangladesh, India, the Maldives, and Sri Lanka are at high risk from projected sea-level rise, which may result in displacement of human settlements, loss of agricultural land and wetlands, saltwater intrusion, and negative impacts on tourism and fisheries. Accelerating climate adaptation is critical to building resilience to the rapidly warming climate in the region. Recovery from the COVID-19 pandemic offers South Asian countries a unique opportunity to adapt to and mitigate climate change by massively investing in resilient infrastructure, re-skilling their populations for high-productivity jobs, and rebuilding their economies around cleaner energy.

Chapter 9, titled 'Regional Climate Vulnerabilities in South Asia: A Development Perspective' and written by Anil Markandya, Muthukumara Mani, Vaideeswaran Sankaran, and Prema Sai Narasimhan, talks about the issues mentioned above. The chapter emphasizes the important task of understanding how climate change is influencing development through the above-mentioned effects and what actions are needed to mitigate the impact through a global path of de-carbonization by addressing proactively the challenges that are arising in different sectors of the economy. It starts by talking about the regional climate impacts, which can be divided broadly into temperature, precipitation, frequency, and intensity of extreme events and sea-level rise and its effects on people and the economy of the region.

The wide range of adverse effects of climate change must be countered through a programme of country-specific national and sub-national actions that include gearing the institutional settings in governments towards actions against climate change, taking climate predictions to the end user by downscaling of climate models, interlinking of sectors on climate-related issues, making funds available to address climate change, and having a vision of sustainable long-term economic growth.

Climate change is expected to have negative impacts on agriculture and food security in many regions, particularly in developing countries highly dependent on rainfed agriculture. The fifth assessment report of the Intergovernmental Panel on Climate Change (IPCC) released in 2014 found that climate change effects are already being felt in agriculture and food security. The negative impacts are most pronounced in tropical zones where most of the world's poor and agriculture-dependent populations are located (IPCC 2012). And yet, in the next 20 years, increasing the rate of agricultural growth in these regions is essential to reach the goals of eradicating poverty and meeting the growing food demand associated with population growth and dietary transitions. Understanding the potential impacts of climate extremes and shifting climate patterns, and evaluating how different options and strategies can best address these is a complicated process.

As a beginning step, the climate-smart agriculture (CSA) concept was developed to address the complex issue of achieving sustainable agricultural growth for food security under climate change (FAO 2009, 2010; Lipper et al. 2014). The concept calls for integrating the need for adaptation and the possibility of GHG mitigation in agricultural growth and poverty-reduction strategies. CSA is an approach for transforming and reorienting agricultural systems to support food security under the new realities of climate change. Widespread changes in rainfall and temperature patterns threaten agricultural production and increase the vulnerability of people dependent on agriculture for their livelihoods, including most of the world's poor. Climate change disrupts food markets, posing population-wide risks to the food supply. Threats can be reduced by increasing the adaptive capacity of farmers as well as increasing resilience and resource use efficiency in agricultural production systems. CSA promotes coordinated actions by farmers, researchers, private sector, civil society, and policymakers towards climate-resilient pathways through four main action areas: (1) building evidence; (2) increasing local institutional effectiveness; (3) fostering coherence between climate and agricultural policies; and (4) linking climate and agricultural financing.

Chapter 10, titled 'Climate-Smart Agriculture in Developing Economies: An Analysis of Strategies and Policies', discusses the above issues concerning developing countries in South Asia and sub-Saharan Africa. The chapter analyzes various policies, actions, investments, and partnerships that have been initiated in the region to put the idea of CSA into the application. Many of those efforts are in early stages, and their impacts cannot yet be fully quantified; however, some general lessons are often drawn to ensure the success of those efforts. The experiences from sub-Saharan Africa and South and Southeast Asia show that regional cooperation and knowledge exchange between countries is one of the major keys to success. The aim to promote regional cooperation, especially through South–South cooperation, should be aimed further.

Although we do not have direct evidence that climate change is influencing the spread of COVID-19, we know that climate change alters how we relate to other species on Earth and that matters to our health and our risk for infections. Many of the root causes of climate change also increase the risk of pandemics. Deforestation, which occurs mainly for agricultural purposes, is the largest cause of habitat loss worldwide. Loss of habitat forces animals to migrate and potentially contact other animals or people and share germs. Large livestock farms can also serve as a source for spillover of infection from animals to people. Less demand for animal meat and more sustainable animal husbandry could decrease emerging infectious disease risk and lower greenhouse gas emissions.

As COVID-19 batters the world and its economy, it is time to rethink sustainable pathways for our planet. Rosy hopes that globalization and economic growth will bankroll waves of green investment and development are no longer realistic. It is unlikely there will be enough money or attention to banish poverty and inequality, expand healthcare, and overturn biodiversity loss and climate change, all by 2030. The success of the Sustainable Development Goals depends on two big assumptions: sustained economic growth and globalization. COVID-19 has torn these to shreds.

Chapter 11, written by Jyoti K. Parikh and titled 'Pandemic, Climate Change and Sustainable Development', discusses the above issues and seeks answers to our future lifestyle. COVID-19 has taught us quite a few lessons. We are now more aware of diseases, and many are trying to adopt a healthy lifestyle. In this context, the author takes stock of what is already happening in our societies due to the pandemic. She looks at the scenario from climate-positive and climate-negative aspects. Climate-positive aspects include technology substitution and increased efficiency as well as technology transformation through the use of smartphones and acceptance of online shopping, working, communicating, and conferencing that would surely have a positive impact in reducing GHGs. Among the climate-negatives due to the pandemic, one could think of increased waste generation, reduced public transport, and increased air travel that can increase pollution and GHGs. The pandemic showed us how important it is to ensure digital connectivity for all to be a functional society. This could address the essential aspects of human well-being such as health, education, and basic supply services like food and medicines. The digital infrastructure is from the beginning with the private sector. Therefore, on the supply side, the government's push and budgets are needed for expediting decisions about spectrum allocation, ensuring standardization, quality control, etc. The author concludes that increased institutional capacity and awareness-building measures will be required to maximize the potential for cooperation of our lifestyle under climate change.

### *Part IV: Economics of Environmental Policy*

Governments have gradually adopted more stringent environmental policies to tackle challenges associated with rising environmental issues, such as climate change, air pollution, waste management, or biodiversity loss. The ambition of these policies is, however, often shaped by their perceived adverse effects on the economy. Indeed, environmental regulations require polluting facilities to undertake abatement activities, which imposes costs on businesses. Despite their small negative effects on the economy, implementation of stringent environmental policies remains politically tricky because the localized effects can be significant (e.g., in terms of employment or competitiveness losses), even if small overall, which can generate strong opposition. Therefore, from an efficiency, distributional and political standpoint, it is essential to design environmental policies in a way that emphasizes their positive net effects for the economy without sacrificing their impact on the environment while also helping those individuals working in the most polluting companies. In this respect, an advantage of market-based policies is that they generate additional public revenues. These can be used to address potential adverse distributional impacts of environmental policies, fund environmental innovation and investments, reduce the tax burden elsewhere in the economy, or reduce public deficits. Nevertheless, market-based approaches can be administratively more demanding to implement because of monitoring requirements and can also be socially less acceptable. Combining environmental policies with other policies (such as trade, education, employment, and fiscal policies) can also play a vital role to deal with the challenges associated with the unavoidable adverse effects of environmental policies on the least-efficient, most-polluting companies.

In the above context, the last section of the book contains four chapters that discuss various issues related to the economics of environmental policy. Chapter 12, by Kanchan Chopra, titled 'Environmental Policy in India: Retrospect and Recent Developments', discusses environmental policy issues concerning India. The author looks at environmental policy from two imperatives. One is the international imperative to reduce GHG and take strict environmental policies, while the other imperative is the flexible environmental policy for more economic growth. The politics of environmental regulation everywhere turn on the debate over whether cleaner technologies cost jobs. Economic growth is frequently seen as the major imperative facing governments in developing countries that often point to industrialized countries' polluting past as an argument against domestic environmental regulation. Over the past decade, India's annual economic growth rate has averaged around 6%, led by the industrial and manufacturing sectors. Hundreds of thousands of new jobs have been created in these sectors, and the domestic marketplace now offers an array of goods that middle-class consumers would not have imagined only ten years ago. However, such rapid economic gains come at a cost: industrial pollution and its ramifications are features of that progress.

India, in the last six years since July 2014, has approved over 270 projects in and around its most protected environments, including biodiversity hotspots and national parks, and at the same time has watered down environmental safeguards, prompting stakeholders to warn that such interference not only imperils habitat and ecosystems but also endangers public health. In this light, the author cautions us about the early warning signals of a degrading environment. This early warning went unheeded, and the world moved relentlessly towards higher and higher levels of production and consumption, ignoring the natural capital stock. Urbanization, an integral part of the above process, has brought with it its own set of environmental disasters and problems. The framework for conceptualization provided by the Millennium Ecosystem Assessment (MA) has led to understanding the limitations of the environment concerning planetary boundaries. The author mentions three dilemmas to demonstrate the problem India is facing concerning environmental policy and economic growth. The first involves preferences of current and future generations; the second with the treatment of agents situated unequally with respect to wealth, power, or knowledge; and the third that concerns the nature of governance, partly following from and overlapping with the first two. The author concludes that in India, with a preference for present growth and with unequal entities coming together as decision-makers, the governance of environmental laws will leave much to be desired.

Segregating household waste at the source means the involvement of household members in waste management. Women are an integral part of the home, or else it can be said that they are the epicentre of all the household activities. Due to their imperative nature, they can do the work with efficacy. Household waste is one thing that is generated by each household, and much of its disposal lies in the hands of a homemaker. However, there is a lack of understanding of the gender dynamics involved in at-source segregation, composting of biodegradable waste and recycling of useful materials. Chapter 13, titled 'Household waste management and the role of gender in Nepal' by Mani Nepal, Marina Cauchy, Apsara Karki Nepal, and Chanda Gurung Goodrich, examines whether women and men manage household waste differently at the household level, especially at-source segregation, managing recyclable waste and composting degradable waste by using a household survey data from a metropolitan city in Nepal, where urbanization is increasing at an alarming rate, thereby putting enormous pressure on municipal services, particularly for managing the growing amount of waste generated. To properly manage solid waste (MSW), segregation of several types of waste at the source is the initial work. Without segregation at the source, the three key principles of MSW management – reduce, reuse, and recycle (3Rs) – cannot be implemented properly. In this context, the chapter focuses on the role of gender on at-source segregation of household waste and recycling behaviour using relatively large size of gender-disaggregated household survey data from one of the metropolitan cities in Nepal (Bharatpur). Studies by the authors reveal that the gender of the household waste manager has differential impacts on waste disposal and degradable waste management approach. Women waste managers tend to segregate household waste and compost the degradable waste more frequently as compared to the situation where men are the managers of the household waste. Thus, gender roles, norms, and practices significantly shape the different behaviours of men and women when it comes to managing household waste. Such behavioural change at the source of segregation of waste and its management not only helps generate resources for sustainable financing of the municipal solid waste management but also appreciates housing property value in cleaner neighbourhoods. For the municipality to reduce the volume of the municipal solid waste at the source, the authors suggest providing training to women waste managers since they form the majority of the total waste managers in the sample and will have more effect in comparison to providing such training to men. To achieve this, it is necessary to raise awareness about the policies and provide economic incentives for women to take such training.

The relationship between humans and wildlife is a challenging one. While people place boundaries around their homes, communities, and countries, wildlife does not recognize them. As people and wildlife increasingly find themselves living in competing spaces, a continual struggle for resources leads to human–wildlife conflict. The conflict between people and wildlife has been widely recognized as one of the most challenging issues for wildlife conservation. While Bhutan's conservation efforts have been hailed globally, the increasing incidences of encroachment in the agricultural territory of humans by wild animals are seen as a big challenge for the survival of the rural economy. In this context, Chapter 14, written by Jamyang Choda, Heman Das Lohano, and Priya Shyamsundar and titled 'Fabricated Electric Fencing: A Promising Strategy for Reducing Crop Damages from Wildlife in Bhutan', is an essential contribution to the existing literature. The authors examine the economic returns of fabricated electric fencing (FEF) used by the Bhutanes government, which is a low-cost mitigation strategy against wildlife-related destruction of crops, livestock, and property. To calculate the economic returns from such fencing, a cost–benefit analysis of the use of FEF is done based on primary data from 110 households in eastern Bhutan by considering the probability of crop damages from wildlife with and without fencing. An econometric model using plot-level data from household surveys is being used to examine the effect of FEF on the probability of crop damage by wildlife, as also using plot-level data from farms without FEF to estimate the average damages per acre on the plots that were damaged by wild animals. Results from the analysis show that locally fabricated electric fencing is a cost-effective and economically viable option to reduce wildlife predation and indicates that the probability of crop damage reduces significantly in plots with FEF, thereby proving that FEF is an economically viable investment that can be scaled up.

Developing countries rely heavily on their environmental resources and associated services for their economic prosperity and societal well-being. With countries facing increasing environment and climate-related risks, there is increasing realization that they must integrate sound and locally relevant economic governance into current environmental discussions. In response to this need, in Chapter 15, titled 'Revisiting the Regional Environmental Economics Networks: Some Lessons and Reflections', the authors make a convincing case for capacity building for environmental sustainability that has been made in countries in the Global South to analyze environmental issues from an economic standpoint and knowledge-action networks (KAN). The chapter focuses on analyzing the effectiveness of the capacity-building model used by the four regional networks, namely, (i) EEPSEA, (ii) South Asian Network for Development and Environmental Economics (iii) Centre for Environmental Economics and Policy in Africa (CEEPA), and (iv) Latin American and Caribbean Environmental Economics Program (LACEEP), in creating locally relevant environmental economics (EE) knowledge and their capacity for fostering knowledge dissemination and intake by policymakers for change. The four networks share several similarities with other knowledge networks such as IPCC, Third World Network, Global Development Network, or the Climate and Development Knowledge Network, and provide a platform for multidisciplinary and multi-stakeholder work; allow expertise to be pooled and enable communication and information sharing. The networks are funded on the principle of social learning. They aim to improve a certain practice of application of environmental economics in policy decisions and put a strong emphasis on participation and boundaries, peripheries, linkages, and interaction. From the in-depth study of the effectiveness and outcome of the above-mentioned networks, it is clear that all four of the presented networks have made a significant contribution not only in EE capacity building but also in the development of a local leadership trained in addressing local sustainability issues. A strong emphasis has been made, since the creation of these networks, on the capacity building for early career researchers. These networks have funded research that provided the necessary evidence to create strong policies that address environmental issues in countries across each of their region of action. Further efforts should be made by the networks to be not only inclusive and geographically representative but also pursue new strategic directions that will help in addressing the ever-evolving nature of climate change and environmental degradation.

### *Concluding Observations*

The 15 chapters discussed above cover every aspect of the current discourse in environmental economics, starting from the environment and economic growth, impact of COVID-19 on environment and ecology, especially concerning zoonotic relationships, economic policies for nature conservation, such as forestry, as also minimizing ecological damage from economic development. Issues related to climate change and development, including discussion on the impact of the pandemic on climate change and sustainable development for developing countries and climate-smart agriculture for developing countries, have been discussed. Case studies relating to household waste management and the role of gender, and the impact of fabricated electric fencing have been covered. The book's last chapter makes a case for the tremendous role that environmental economics networks have played in capacity building, framing of policies using ecological economics tools, and developing a local leadership trained in addressing local sustainability issues.

This book holds the legacy that Professor Rabindra N. Bhattacharya started, in whose honour this book is written and who is a pioneer in introducing the subject of environmental economics in India. The book would serve students, researchers, faculty members, and the average reader interested in learning about the contemporary issues in development and environmental economics.

## Notes

1 For a detailed discussion on how environmental thinking can be integrated into development economics, please read the article published in *Economic and Political Weekly* (EPW) by Sir Partha Dasgupta titled "The Nature of Economic Development and the Economic Development of Nature" (Dasgupta, 2013).
2 Jawaharlal Nehru, public address "in Hindustani," Calcutta, 14 July 1949, Selected Works of Jawaharlal Nehru, 2nd ser., vol.12, edited by S. Gopal et al. (New Delhi: Jawaharlal Nehru Memorial Fund, 1991), 241.
3 For more on environment and development, one can look at the two volumes titled *Environment and Emerging Development Issues*, edited by Partha Dasgupta and Karl Goran Maler and published from Oxford University Press (Dasgupta and Maler 2000).
4 To understand Anil Agarwal's work, one may read his obituary written by Ramchandra Guha (Guha R. 2002).
5 For more details on SANDEE and Regional Environmental Economics Networks in South Asia, see this book, chapter 15, written by Bhim Adhikari and Lowine Hill.
6 See http://www.sandeeonline.org/about_us.php (accessed on 25 May 2021).

## References

Acharyya, Achiransu. 2009. "Valuing Health Damages from Arsenic Contamination: A Willingness to Pay and Dose Response Approach". In *Water, Agriculture and Sustainable Well-Being*, edited by Unai Pascual, Amita Shah and Jayanta Bandopadhyay, 19–41. New Delhi: Oxford University Press. ISBN 0-19-806175-7.

Acharyya, Achiransu. 2014. "Groundwater, Climate Change and Sustainable Well Being of the Poor: Policy Options for South Asia, China and Africa".

*Procedia – Social and Behavioral Sciences* 157: 226–235. doi: 10.1016/j.sbspro.2014.11.025.

Asian Development Bank (ADB). 2013. *The rise of natural disasters in Asia and the Pacific: Learning from ADB's experience.* Mandaluyong City, Philippines. https://www.adb.org/sites/default/files/evaluation-document/36114/files/rise-natural-disasters-asia-pacific.pdf (accessed on 12 March 2021)

Asian Development Bank (ADB). 2017. Meeting Asia's Infrastructure Needs. Mandaluyong City, Philippines. https://www.adb.org/sites/default/files/publication/227496/special-report-infrastructure.pdf (accessed on 14 May 2021)

Bhattacharya, Rabindra N. (ed.) 2001. *Environmental Economics: An Indian Perspective.* New Delhi: Oxford University Press.

Brundtland, G.H. 1987. *Our Common Future: Report of the World Commission on Environment and Development.* Geneva, UN-Dokument A/42/427. http://www.un-documents.net/ocf-ov.htm (accessed on 7 September 2021)

Chakrabarty, Dipesh. 2021. *The Climate of History in a Planetary Age.* The University of Chicago Press. Chicago, USA.

Coase, Ronald H. 1937. "The Nature of the Firm". *Economica* 4 (16): 386–405. doi:10.1111/j.1468-0335. 1937.tb00002.x.

Coase, Ronald H. 1960. "The Problem of Social Cost". *Journal of Law and Economics* 3 (1): 1–44. doi:10.1086/466560. S2CID 222331226.

Copeland, B.R., and M.S. Taylor. 1994. "North-South Trade and the Environment". *The Quarterly Journal of Economics* 109 (3): 755–787. doi:10.2307/2118421.

Copeland, B. R, and M.S. Taylor. 2004. "Trade, Growth, and the Environment". *Journal of Economic Literature* 42 (1): 7–71. doi:10.1257/.42.1.7.

Daly H. 1977. *Steady State Economics.* San Francisco: Freeman

Dasgupta, P. 1982. *The Control of Resources.* Oxford: Basil Blackwell.

Dasgupta, P. 2013. "The Nature of Economic Development and the Economic Development of Nature" *Economic and Political Weekly* 48 (51): 38–51.

Dasgupta, P. 2021. *The Economics of Biodiversity: The Dasgupta Review.* London: HM Treasury. https://www.gov.uk/government/publications/final-report-the-economics-of-biodiversity-the-dasgupta-review (accessed on 21 June 2021).

Dasgupta, P. and G. Heal. 1980. *Economic Theory and Exhaustible Resources (Cambridge Economic Handbooks).* Cambridge. Cambridge University Press. doi: 10.1017/CBO9780511628375.

Dasgupta, P. and K.G. Maler. 1991. *The Environment and Emerging Development Issues.* WIDER Study Group Report No. 7. http://dlc.dlib.indiana.edu/dlc/bitstream/handle/10535/7980/The%20Environment%20and%20Emerging%20Development%20Issues.pdf?sequence=1 (accessed on 8 May 2021).

Dasgupta, P. and K.G. Maler (ed.). 2000. *The Environment and Emerging Development Issues Vol.1 and Vol 2.* New Delhi: Oxford University Press.

FAO. 2009. *Food Security in Agricultural Mitigation in Developing Countries: Options for Capturing Synergies.* October 2009. Rome: FAO.

FAO. 2010. *Climate-Smart Agriculture: Policies, Practices and Financing for Food Security, Adaptation and Mitigation.* Rome: FAO.

Faustmann, M. 1849. [Linnard (tr.) and Gane (ed.)1968]. "On the Determination of the Value Which Forest Land and Immature Stands Possess for Forestry". English Translation in: Martin Faustmann and the Evolution of Discounted Cash Flow (Translated by W. Linnard; with editing and introduction by M. Gane).

Commonwealth Forestry Institute Paper No. 42. University of Oxford: Oxford, England. [Translation republished with permission from Commonwealth Forestry Association in Journal of Forest Economics 1: 1 (1995).] https://www.worldcat.org/title/martin-faustmann-and-the-evolution-of-discounted-cash-flow-on-determination-of-the-money-value-of-bare-forest-land-calculation-of-the-value-which-forest-land-and-immature-stands-possess-for-forestry-two-articles-from-the-original-german-of-1849/oclc/888569197 (accessed on 16 July 2021)

Georgescu-Roegen, N., 1971. *The Entropy Law and the Economic Process. [Erscheinungsort nicht ermittelbar]*. Harvard University Press.

Guha, R. 2000. *Environmentalism: A Global History*. New Delhi: Oxford University Press.

Guha, R. 2002. "Environmentalist of the Poor". *Economic and Political Weekly*, 37(3): 204–207.

Hardin, Garrett. 1968. "The Tragedy of the Commons". *Science* 162 (3859): 1243–1248. doi:10.1126/science.162.3859.1243.

IPCC. 2012. Managing the Risks of Extreme Events and Disasters to Advance Climate Change Adaptation. A Special Report of Working Groups I and II of the Intergovernmental Panel on Climate Change [Field, C.B., V. Barros, T.F. Stocker, D. Qin, D.J. Dokken, K.L. Ebi, M.D. Mastrandrea, K.J. Mach, G.-K. Plattner, S.K. Allen, M. Tignor, and P.M. Midgley (eds.)]. Cambridge, UK, and New York: Cambridge University Press

IPCC. 2014. *Climate Change 2014: Synthesis Report. Contribution of Working Groups I, II and III to the Fifth Assessment Report of the Intergovernmental Panel on Climate Change* [Core Writing Team, R.K. Pachauri and L.A. Meyer (eds.)], 151 pp. Geneva, Switzerland: IPCC. https://www.ipcc.ch/report/ar5/syr/ (accessed on 5 October 2021)

Jodha, N.S. 1966. "The Scarcity Oriented Growth Pattern of Arid Agriculture". *Indian Journal of Agricultural Economics* XXI (4): 1–10.

Jodha, N.S. 2002. *Life on the Edge: Sustaining Agriculture and Community Resources in Fragile Environments*. New Delhi: Oxford University Press.

Jones, K.E., Patel, N.G., Levy, M.A., Storeygard, A., Balk, D., Gittleman, J.L., and Daszak, P. 2008. Global trends in emerging infectious diseases. *Nature*, 451 (7181): 990–993. https://doi.org/10.1038/nature06536

Kenneth, Boulding E. 1966. "The Economics of the Coming Spaceship Earth". In *Environmental Quality in a Growing Economy*, edited by H. Jarrett, 3–14. Baltimore: Resources for the Future/Johns Hopkins University Press.

Lele, S. 2009. "Reflections on Interdisciplinarity in Environmental Economics in India". In *Handbook of Environmental Economics*, edited by Kanchan Chopra and Vikram Dayal, 305–325. New Delhi: Oxford University Press.

Lipper, L., P. Thornton, B.M. Campbell, T. Baedeker, A. Braimoh, M. Bwalya, P. Caron, A. Cattaneo, D. Garrity, K. Henry, R. Hottle, L. Jackson, A. Jarvis, F. Kossam, W. Mann, N. McCarthy, A. Meybeck, H. Neufeldt, T. Remington, P. Thi Sen, R. Sessa, R. Shula, A. Tibu, and E. Torquebiau. 2014. Climate-smart agriculture for food security. *Nature Climate Change*, 4(12): 1068–1072. DOI: https://doi.org/10.1038/nclimate2437

Mukhopadhyay, P., M. Nepal, and P. Shyamsundar. 2014. Building skills for sustainability: a role for regional research networks. *Ecology and Society* 19(4): 45. http://dx.doi.org/10.5751/ES-07105-190445.

NITI Aayog. 2019. *Composite Water Management Index*. New Delhi: Niti Aayog in association with Ministry of Jal Shakti and Ministry of Rural Development. https://www.niti.gov.in/sites/default/files/2019-06/Final%20Report%20of%20the%20Research%20Study%20on%20%20Composite%20Water%20Resources%20Management%20Index%20for%20Indian%20States%20conducted%20by%20Dalberg%20Global%20Development%20Advisors%20Pvt.%20Ltd_New%20Delhi.pdf (accessed on 20 May 2021).

Nordhaus, William D., 1982. "How Fast Should We Graze the Global Commons?" Cowles Foundation Discussion Papers. 851. https://elischolar.library.yale.edu/cowles-discussion-paper-series/851 (accessed on 9 September 2021).

Ostrom, Elinor.1990. *Governing the Commons: The Evolution of Institutions for Collective Action*. Cambridge [England]; New York: Cambridge University Press, 1990.

Porter, Michael E, and Claas van der Linde. 1995. "Toward A New Conception of the Environment-Competitiveness Relationship". *Journal of Economic Perspectives* 9 (4): 97–118. doi:10.1257/jep.9.4.97.

Rachel, Carson. 1962. *Silent Spring*. Boston, USA: Houghton Miffin .

Smith, K.F., M. Goldberg, S. Rosenthal, L. Carlson, J. Chen, C. Chen, and S. Ramachandran. 2014. "Global Rise in Human Infectious Disease Outbreaks". *Journal of the Royal Society Interface*, 11 (101): 20140950. doi:10.1098/rsif.2014.0950

Snyder, Donald L, and Rabindra N Bhattacharyya. 1990. "A More General Dynamic Economic Model of the Optimal Rotation of Multiple-Use Forests". *Journal of Environmental Economics and Management* 18 (2): 168–175. doi:10.1016/0095-0696(90)90046-2.

Stern, David I. 2004. "The Rise and Fall of the Environmental Kuznets Curve". *World Development* 32 (8): 1419–1439. doi: 10.1016/j.worlddev.2004.03.004.

Stern, David I. 2018. "The Environmental Kuznets Curve". *Reference Module in Earth Systems and Environmental Sciences*. Elsevier. doi:10.1016/B978-0-12-409548-9.09278-2.

Thomas, Malthus R. 1798. *An Essay on the Principle of Population. Reeves and Turner*. London.

UNEP and ILRI. 2020. "Preventing the Next Pandemic: Zoonotic Diseases and How to Break the Chain of Transmission". Nairobi, Kenya. https://wedocs.unep.org/bitstream/handle/20.500.11822/32316/ZP.pdf?sequence=1&isAllowed=y (accessed on 4 September 2021).

WHO. 2020. "Coronavirus Disease (COVID-19) Pandemic". In *World Health Organization* [online] Geneva. https://www.who.int/emergencies/diseases/novel-coronavirus-2019 (accessed on 24 September 2020).

# Part I

# Environment, Ecology and Development

Chapter 1

# Three Theories of Growth, Environment, and Poverty Nexus

*M.N. Murty*

## Introduction

Natural resource stocks, especially environmental resource stocks, are now recognized as constraints on the rate of growth of the economy along with the conventional man-made capital stock. The contribution of natural resource stocks to well-being measured either as flow (income) or stock (wealth) is well recognized now.[1] The environmental capital provides direct and indirect inputs to various production processes creating income and wealth in the economy (Heal and Kristrom 2005). Environmental capital is renewable or regenerative, and depletion of it below a threshold level affects the services it provides. In a developing country aiming at increased income and growth, the difficult problem is to maintain the environmental capital at its threshold level while carrying out its developmental plan.

Planning of allocation of resources, including environmental resources for achieving a sustainable growth path of the economy, has to address the effects of planning on equity (income distribution), poverty (incomes of people not having endowments and capabilities), and the environment. The well-known Kuznets[2] hypothesis in development economics about the relationship between growth (income growth) and equity (income distribution) and its extension to consider the relationship between growth and environmental pollution could explain the growth, environment, and poverty nexus (Simonis 1992). In the beginning stages of development in a poor country, resource allocations to increase income could result in increased inequalities in income distribution and increased poverty and, at the same time, increased environmental pollution. After per capita income reaches a threshold level, further increases in income result in reduced inequality in income distribution and reduced pollution. Therefore, in this orthodox view emanating from the Kuznets hypothesis, growth, poverty, and pollution move together in the initial stages of the development of a country. Therefore, it is important to examine whether this orthodox view is correct if we consider some recent developments in the literature leading to new thinking about growth, environment, and poverty.

DOI: 10.4324/9781003253884-3

The standard Ramsey optimal growth model[3] predicts the trade-off between growth and equity. An extended model considering constraints of environmental resource stocks to the development predicts a positive relationship between growth and pollution. These model predictions about growth, pollution, and equity nexus show a downward spiral of poverty and environment in the economy. It is useful to study whether a further extended model introducing pollution abatement and considering individuals and society's preferences for consumption and pollution could predict an inverse U-shape type of relation between the growth of income and growth of pollution.

There are three powerful models in environmental economics literature predicting theoretically the orthodox view of growth, environment, and poverty nexus. These are the well-known tragedy of commons, prisoners' dilemma, and logic of collective action models.[4] They predict that in a free-market situation, efficient cooperative solutions are not possible for the sustainable use of environmental resources. The theory of environmental entitlements and other recent related theories predict that voluntary collective action of a group of individuals is possible in a free-market setting for efficient management of environmental resources in the presence of certain micro- and macro-level institutions.[5] This theory espouses new thinking about poverty and the environment. The new thinking about poverty considers that poverty is not simply due to a lack of private income or consumption but it is due to a lack of endowments and capabilities for individuals. Similarly, the environment has to be understood in a larger socio-economic context rather than considering it simply as an aggregate environment to which society relates (Leach et al. 1997)

The rest of the chapter is planned as follows. The following section discusses considering environmental resources as stocks of capital. Section 1.3 presents a standard optimal growth model with environmental extensions and examines the model's predictions about growth, equity, environment, and poverty nexus. Section 1.4 discusses the model's predictions about the relationship between the rate of growth of income and the rate of growth of pollution. Section 1.5 explains the orthodox view of poverty and environment or a paradigm of the downward spiral of environment and poverty. Section 1.6 describes a new paradigm of growth, environment, and poverty nexus. Finally, Section 1.7 provides some conclusions.

## 1.1 Natural Capital and Growth

Environmental resource stocks are contributing factors as well as limiting factors of growth. Environmentally sustainable growth is the maximum possible growth maintained in the country given constraints on man-made physical and human skill capital and natural capital consisting of environmental and exhaustible resource stocks. Millennium Ecosystem Assessment

(2005) points out that the services provided by environmental capital could be grouped as (a) provisioning, (b) regulating, (c) cultural, and (d) supporting. These services provide direct and indirect inputs to various production processes creating income and wealth in the economy. These include global life support functions, water regulation, pollution filtering, waste sink, soil retention, nutrient retention, and waste decomposition. There could be a sustainable supply of these services in the economy, provided environmental resource stocks are kept at regenerative or threshold levels (United Nations 2002). The need to maintain resource stocks at threshold levels acts as a constraint on growth, resulting in the possible trade-off between growth and the environment.

Resource allocation in the economy to achieve the simple objective of growth could create a problem of equity, resulting in a skewed distribution of income favouring the rich. Using environmental resources, particularly by industry, agriculture, and households, to achieve growth objectives could also create the problem of distribution of income in the economy resulting in the rich getting benefits of resources while the poor suffer. Unsustainable use of resources to achieve growth objectives could lead to forest degradation and air and water pollution, to which the poor are more vulnerable than the rich. With limited resources and choices for adaptation to environmental changes, poverty-ridden people look for resources like forests and unsustainable agricultural practices for their livelihood, which in turn may further degrade the environment. Poor will be caught in a vicious circle of poverty–environment–poverty.

In developing economies with already higher levels of poverty and population growth and aiming at resource allocation for achieving a higher rate of growth of income, as is the case of India, the environmental footprints could far exceed the carrying capacity of the natural resources (Davidson 2000). In such economies where a large proportion of the population already relies on natural resource-based livelihoods, including agriculture, grazing, forest products, and fishing for income and subsistence on marginal lands and less productive natural ecosystems, poverty is exacerbated by poor households having very restricted access to natural resources. Situations like this demand adequate safeguards for the poor, ensuring decent livelihood, the absence of which may result in degraded social order contributing to further problems for the environmental management and strain on the poor.

## 1.2 Standard Optimal Growth Model: Growth, Equity, and Environment Nexus[6]

We consider in this section the standard Ramsey optimal growth model with environmental extensions to study the relationship between growth, equity in poverty, and the environment. The environmental extensions of the model are attempted by considering pollution abatement in production and the disutility from pollution in consumption. We assume no population growth and exogenous technical change.

Consider an economy producing a commodity $X_t$ using capital $K_t$ and labour $L_t$ at time *t*. The production function of $X_t$ is given by

$$X_t = F(K_t, L_t) \tag{1.1}$$

*F* is concave and an increasing and continuously differentiable function of each of its variables with $\partial X_t / \partial K_t \geq 0$ and $\partial K_t / \partial L_t \geq 0$

Dividing (1) throughout by $L_t$, we have

$$x_t = f(k_t) \text{ with } \partial f(k_t) / \partial k_t = f'(k_t) \geq 0 \tag{1.2}$$

where $x_t$ and $k_t$ represent output-labour and capital-labour ratios.

Let $C_t$ represent aggregate consumption and $c_t$ represent per capita consumption at time *t*. Assume pollution generation at each point of time is described by a function $v(k_t, a_t)$, with pollution increasing with capital ($v_k > 0$) and decreasing with abatement ($v_a < 0$), where $a_t$ denotes abatement at time *t*. The net accumulation of man-made capital ($\dot{k}$) and change in environmental capital ($\dot{E}$) therefore satisfy the conditions (1.3) and (1.4), respectively.

$$\dot{k} = f(k) - c - a - \mathrm{d}\,\mathrm{k} \tag{1.3}$$

$$\dot{E} = v(k, a) - mE \tag{1.4}$$

where *E* is pollution as a stock, *d* is the rate of depreciation of man-made capital, and *m* is the natural rate of decay of pollution.

The planner's problem is

$$Maximize \int_0^\infty e^{-rt} U(c, E) dt \tag{1.5}$$

with respect to *c* and a subject to the conditions

$$\dot{k} = f(k) - c - a - \mathrm{dk}$$

$$\dot{E} = v(k, a) - mE$$

The current value Hamiltonian of the problem is

$$H = U(c, E) + q(f(k) - c - a - dk) + \lambda(v(k, a) - mE) \tag{1.6}$$

where $c_t$ and $a_t$ are control variables, $k_t$ and $E_t$ are state variables, and $q$ and $\lambda$ are co-state variables.

The first-order conditions for maximizing $H$ with respect to control variables are

$$U_c(c,E) = q \tag{1.7}$$

$$\lambda v_a(k,a) = q \tag{1.8}$$

Equations (1.7) and (1.8) indicate that marginal utility of consumption is equal to the marginal cost of pollution abatement in utility terms. The canonical equations of Hamiltonian (6) defining the time paths of co-state variables are given as

$$\dot{q} = q\left(r + d - \mathrm{f}'(\mathrm{k})\right) - \lambda v_k \tag{1.9}$$

$$\dot{\lambda} = \lambda(r + m) - U_E(c,E) \tag{1.10}$$

where $f'(k) = \partial f / \partial k$

Taking the time differential of (1.7) and substituting for $\dot{q}$ from (1.9) we have

$$\frac{\dot{C}}{C} = 1/\mu\left[\left(f'(k) - r - d\right) + \frac{v_k}{v_a} + € \frac{\dot{P}}{P}\right] \tag{1.11a}$$

where

$\mu = -(U_{cc} / U_c)c$, elasticity of marginal utility of consumption with respect to consumption;

$€ = (U_{cP} / U_c)P$, elasticity of marginal utility of consumption with respect to pollution.

If there is spending on pollution abatement and there are no environmental concerns, Equation (1.11a) becomes

$$\frac{\dot{C}}{C} = 1/\mu\left[\left(f'(k) - r - d\right) + \frac{v_k}{v_a}\right] \tag{1.11b}$$

If there is no spending on pollution abatement and there are no concerns of environmental problems in the economy, Equation (1.11a) becomes

$$\frac{\dot{C}}{C} = 1/\mu\left[f'(k) - r - d\right] \tag{1.11c}$$

Higher values of $\mu$ imply a relatively higher valuation of reduced consumption for increasing rate of growth. That means in countries with lower levels of per capita consumption, the reduced current consumption levels to achieve higher rates of growth could result in higher utility or welfare losses to the poor. Thus, there is a trade-off between equity and growth as seen in Equation (1.11c) of a simple growth model without pollution abatement and environmental concerns. In this equation, there is an inverse relationship between the rate of growth of per capita consumption ($\frac{\dot{C}}{C}$) and the elasticity of marginal utility of consumption ($\mu$). Also, Equation (1.11b) shows that the rate of growth of consumption is low when there is pollution abatement in the economy since $\frac{v_k}{v_a}$ is negative, with $v_k > 0$ and $v_a > 0$ showing trade-off between growth and environment.

The elasticity of marginal utility of consumption with respect to pollution € could be positive or negative depending upon whether consumption and pollution are complements or substitutes. Equation (1.3) shows that higher expenditures on pollution abatement results in either reduced consumption or reduced investment or both. Therefore, both consumption and pollution in the economy increase (decrease) as abatement expenditures decrease (increase). Equation (1.11a) shows that without pollution abatement there is a positive relationship between the rate of growth of consumption and the rate of growth of pollution if € > 0. However, with abatement, the rate of growth of consumption could increase or decrease accordingly as $\left(\frac{v_k}{v_a} + €\frac{\dot{P}}{P}\right)$ > 0 or < 0. If $c$ and $E$ are substitutes in the utility function $U$ ($c$, $E$), we have € < 0, and hence $\left(\frac{v_k}{v_a} + €\frac{\dot{P}}{P}\right) < 0$. In this case, increase in the rate of growth of pollution results in a fall of the rate of growth of per capita consumption in the economy. As the growth of pollution increases, defensive expenditures in terms of the cost of illness of individuals may increase, resulting in reduced consumption.

## 1.3 Society's Choices between Consumption and Pollution and Environmental Kuznets Curve

The simple model of growth, described in Section 1.3, explains the relationship between growth, equity, and environment. In the initial phase of economic development in a poor country with lower levels of consumption and growth, individuals' or societal choices of consumption and pollution may show them as complements in consumption. Preferences for consumption dominate preferences for environment during this phase. This phenomenon may reveal a positive relationship between the rate of growth of consumption and the rate of growth of pollution during this phase of development. Given the low levels of income and poverty and concerns for equity during this phase of development, society's preferences are to attend to these concerns making unsustainable use of natural resources. Given this preference pattern, there may not be any abatement expenditures during this phase of development. Equation (1.12a) expresses a positive relationship between the rate of growth of consumption and the rate of growth of pollution if pollution and consumption are complements (€ > 0) and there are no abatement expenditures.

$$\frac{\dot{P}}{P} = \frac{1}{€}\left[\mu\frac{\dot{C}}{C} - \left(f'(k) - r - d\right)\right] \tag{1.12a}$$

where

$$€ > 0 \frac{\dot{P}}{P} = \frac{1}{€}\left[\left(f'(k) - r - d\right) + \frac{v_k}{v_a} - \mu\frac{\dot{C}}{C}\right] \tag{1.12b}$$

where € < 0 and devoid of sign.

There could be a reversal of society's preferences for consumption and environment, considering them as substitutes after a country reaches the threshold level of development, by which time the problems of low income, poverty, and equity are addressed properly. Also, given this preference pattern, there will be abatement expenditures during this penultimate phase of development process. Equation (1.12b) explains the negative relationship between the rate of growth of consumption and the rate of growth of

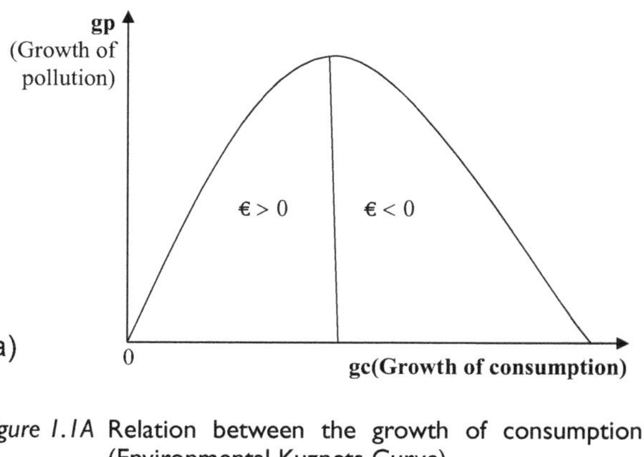


(a)

*Figure 1.1A* Relation between the growth of consumption and growth of pollution (Environmental Kuznets Curve).

pollution in the economy if pollution and consumption are substitutes ($\epsilon < 0$). Equations (1.12a) and (1.12b) explain the well-known Environmental Kuznets Curve-type of relationship between the rate of growth of per capita consumption and the rate of growth of pollution, as shown in Figure 1.1A.

However, the empirically observed the environmental Kuznets curve explains the relationship between per capita income and pollution, unlike the one we derived here.

The question of whether poverty is the cause of environmental degradation or the concern about the environment is the cause of poverty has to be examined in the context of theoretically predicted relationship between growth, equity, and the environment by the model described above.

## 1.4 Conventional View of Poverty and Environment

Growth could be a cause of environmental degradation and could also be the cause of poverty, as the model predicts. Increasing rates of growth could be at the cost of unsustainable use of environmental resources affecting the environmental services they offer to the poor. Given the trade-off between growth and equity, as the model predicts, non-inclusive growth could benefit the rich while affecting the poor. Some earlier discussions on this subject have focussed on the issues of population growth and economic growth affecting the environment (Panayotou 2000). The equation I = PAT summarizes this position in which 'I' represents environmental impacts, 'P' represents population growth, 'A' represents growth of Gross Domestic Product (GDP), and 'T' represents changes in technology. In the same vein, poverty could be considered a result of population growth and environment.

In the context of population and environment contributing to poverty, it is important to know how different people depend on environment for their livelihoods and how they are affected by environmental changes. Population growth and high economic growth with associated technological changes could lead to economic marginalization of certain sections of people who eventually get caught in a downward spiral of poverty–environment–poverty trap. This orthodox view of poverty assumes that[7] (a) there is an aggregate 'population' or 'community' which interacts with an aggregate 'environment'; (b) people's livelihoods are based more or less exclusively on the use and management of environmental resources; (c) poverty and environmental change have a direct causal relationship, and can feed each other in some kind of cumulative causation process, and that (d) poverty is the principal or only cause of environmental change, and vice versa.

This conventional view of poverty and environment was widely accepted earlier in the literature, considering many of the environmental resources such as forests, water resources, and atmosphere that are open-access resources without well-defined property rights. In such a resource regime, people try to overexploit the resources to maximize their individual benefits.

There are three powerful models in the literature explaining this phenomenon. They are the tragedy of the commons (Hardin 1968), the prisoner's dilemma game, and the logic of collective action (Olson 1965). Considering pasture as an open-access resource, Hardin (1968) writes

> Each man is locked into a system that compels him to increase his herd without limit – in a world that is limited. Ruin is the destination toward which all men rush, each pursuing his own best interest in a society that believes in the freedom of the commons.

The problem of the tragedy of commons of Hardin has often been formalized in the literature as a prisoner's dilemma game, which explains that individually rational strategies lead to collectively irrational outcomes. Olson (1965) argues in his *Logic of Collective Action* that voluntary collective action by individuals to achieve their group interest is not possible and there is a need for coercion by an outside agency to achieve the group interest. In his own words, his main proposition is

> unless there is coercion or some other special device to make individuals act in their common interest, rational, self-interested individuals will not act to achieve their common or group interest.

These models thus provide the analytical base for the conventional view of population, environment, and poverty nexus.

## 1.5 Environmental Entitlement Approach: A New Thinking on Poverty and Environment

It is important to investigate whether the predictions of the above-mentioned analytical models about the downward spiral of environment and poverty hold true as an exception or as a general rule. These have to be understood in the context of very diverse ways environmental changes happen, affecting different groups of people differently, different ways poverty is understood, and the ways in which institutional factors determine the relationship between poor people and environmental resources. Poverty has to be understood in the wider context rather than as a measure based simply on private income or consumption. It has to be understood in the context of private income, access to common property resources, state-provided commodities, personal assets, and subjective assessment of dignity and autonomy.[8] The environment has to be understood in a larger socio-economic context rather than considering it simply as an aggregate environment to which society relates and assuming that methods of assessing environmental change are neutral and value-free. There could be a coexistence of a number of perspectives on a particular environmental issue upheld by people belonging to different social and political groups. People belonging to different social groups use and value different elements of environment in different ways.

Literature shows that the prediction of models mentioned above of the downward spiral of poverty and environment in a free-market situation may not be correct in the context of a new way of looking at poverty and environment (Porter and Claas van der Linde 1995). Sen's[9] endowments, entitlements, and capabilities approach to understanding poverty is helpful to knowing about possible complex institutional settings in which the relationship between poverty and environment is better understood. Ostrom (1990) writes

> An important challenge facing policy scientists is to develop theories of human organization based on realistic assessment of human capabilities and limitations in dealing with a variety of situations that initially share some or all aspects of a tragedy of the commons.

There is now a lot of empirical evidence to show that voluntary collective action of a group of individuals is possible in managing common property/environmental resources in a free-market setting in the presence of certain micro- and macro-level institutions.[10]

It is useful to know how the environmental entitlements approach explains that predictions of models espousing tragedy of commons and free-rider problem may not be correct. Consider a micro watershed consisting of local forest land of a village.[11] This forest land is an endowment of the village community with property rights provided by the laws governing panchayat raj institutions and forest conservation laws in India. If watershed is preserved, the entitlements include a sustainable supply of fodder for milch animals and also water for irrigation, with some investments made to have irrigation tanks for water harvesting. However, only those households in the village owning milch animals and irrigable land could avail these entitlements. Macro-level institutions like banks and other financial institutions of state and central governments, and NGOs, could ensure entitlements to every household by providing (a) finances for investments in irrigation tanks, (b) extending loans to households to buy milch animals, and (c) facilitating land redistribution so that every household has some irrigable land or create market for water by creating and enforcing water rights so that landless households can sell water to landed households. In this setting, there are increased capabilities of households in terms of increased incomes and well-being.

The analytical models predicting the downward spiral of poverty and environment relationship provide theoretical support for the environmental Kuznets curve hypothesis showing an inverted U-shape type of relationship between environmental pollution and per capita GDP of countries. Identifying poverty with low per capita income (orthodox definition of poverty), the pollution per unit of output (pollution GDP ratio) increases with per capita income and falls after per capita income reaches

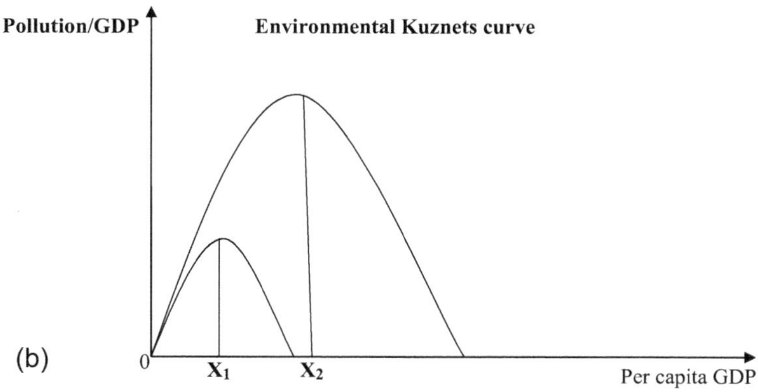


*Figure 1.1B* Environmental Kuznets curve showing the relation between per capita GDP and Pollution per GDP.

the level at which poverty is no longer there. Therefore, this hypothesis espouses that poverty or low per capita income is the cause of environmental degradation.

However, the new way of looking at poverty and environment and environmental entitlements approach described above do not subscribe to this view (Ranjan and Shortle 2007). In developing countries, low incomes may not be the reason for environmental degradation if there are micro- and macro-level institutions ensuring the poor environmental endowments and entitlements. In such situations, the capabilities of the poor may increase to protect the environment and use it for their increased well-being (Dietz 2000). Therefore, in the presence of institutions and policies securing environmental endowments and entitlements to the poor, there may not be a trade-off between environment and income growth. Even if the trade-off is there, it may not persist until a country attains a very high level of income, as predicted by the Kuznets hypothesis. The turning point may happen on an inverted U-shaped curve at a much lower level of per capita income than predicted in Figure 1.1B.

## 1.6 Conclusion

In the environmental economics literature, the analytical models predicting the growth, environment, and poverty nexus have developed in three stages. In the first stage, the theoretical models explaining market failure in the efficient management of environmental resources predict downward spiral or vicious circle of environmental and poverty relationship. These are well-known theoretical models of the tragedy of commons, prisoner's dilemma, and the logic of collective action. This is an orthodox view of growth, environment, and poverty nexus which has faced severe criticism and could not be sustained as literature further develops.

In the second stage, the analytical methods originating from the original Kuznets hypothesis explaining growth and equity nexus have partially refuted the orthodox view of the downward spiral of environment and poverty. By bringing to the forefront growth of income as a key factor in determining the environment and poverty nexus, they predicted an inverse U-shaped type of relationship between income growth and environmental degradation. This implies that the vicious circle of environment and poverty persists, resulting in increasing environmental degradation as per capita income grows up to a threshold level and breaks afterwards.

In the third stage, the powerful models of participatory development and the theory of environmental entitlements have refuted the persistence of the downward spiral of environment and poverty and equally the trade-off between environment and growth even at low levels of per capita income in especially the developing countries. These models espouse a new way of thinking about environment and poverty, as explained in this chapter.

## Notes

1 See for details UN (2002); Arrow et al. (2012); Dasgupta (2013); and Murty (2014).
2 See for details Kuznet (1955) and Grossman and Krueger (1995)
3 See for details Anastasios Xepapadeas (2005).
4 See for details Hardin (1968) and Olson (1965).
5 See for details Sen (1981) and Ostrom (1990)
6 See for details Anastasios Xepapadeas (2005) for a detailed review of models of growth and environment.
7 See for details Forsyth et al. (1998).
8 See for details Baulch (1996).
9 See for details Sen (1981).
10 See for details Ostrom (1990), Chopra, Kadekodi and Murty (1990).
11 See for details Chopra, Kadekodi and Murty (1990).

## References

Arrow, K.J., P. Dasgupta, L.H. Goulder, K. Mumford and K. Oleson. 2012. "Sustainability and the Measurement of Wealth." *Environment and Development Economics* 17 (3): 317–353. doi:10.1017/S1355770X12000137.

Baulch, B. 1996. "The New Poverty Agenda: A Disputed Consensus." *IDS Bulletin* 27 (1): 1–10. https://opendocs.ids.ac.uk/opendocs/bitstream/handle/20.500.12413/9257/IDSB_27_1_10.1111-j.1759-5436.1996.mp27001001.x.pdf?sequence=1&isAllowed=y (accessed on 27 June 2021).

Chopra, K. G. K., Kadekodi and M. N. Murty. 1990. *Participatory Development: People and Common Property Resources (Studies in Economic Development and Planning.)*. No.52.ISBN: 0803996314. Institute of Economic Growth. Delhi: Sage Publications.

Dasgupta, P. 2013. *Green National Accounts in India: A Framework A Report of Expert Group Convened by National Statistical Organization*. Ministry of Statistics and Programme Implementation. Government of India. March 2013. https://www.cbd.int/financial/hlp/doc/literature/Green_National_Accouts_in_India_1may13.pdf (accessed on 28 June 2021).

Davidson, C. 2000. "Economic Growth and the Environment: Alternatives to the Limits Paradigm." *Bioscience* 50 (5): 433. doi:10.1641/0006-3568(2000)050[0433:egatea]2.0.co;2.

Dietz S. 2000. "Does an Environmental Kuznets Curve Exist for Biodiversity?" Institut für Wirtschaftsforschung, Eidgenössische Technische Hochschule Zürich. https://www.ethz.ch/content/dam/ethz/special-interest/mtec/cer-eth/cer-ethdam/documents/working-papers/wp_00_19.pdf (accessed on 29 June 2021).

Forsyth T., M. Leach and I. Scoones.1998. "Poverty and Environment: Priorities for Research and Policy, An Overview Study." Falmer, Sussex BN1 9RE, UK: UNDP Institute of Development Studies. http://eprints.lse.ac.uk/4772/1/Poverty_and_environment-priorities_for_research_and_study.pdf (accessed on 25 June 2021).

Grossman, G.M. and A.B. Krueger. 1995. "Economic growth and the environment." *The Quarterly Journal of Economics* 110 (2): 353–377.doi: 10.2307/2118443.

Hardin, G. 1968. "The Tragedy of the Commons." *Science* 162 (3859): 1243–1248. doi:10.1126/science.162.3859.1243.

Heal G. and B. Kristrom. 2005. "National Income and the Environment." In *Handbook of Environmental Economics*, edited by Geoffrey Heal and Bengt Kristrom, Vol. 3, 1219–1271. North Holland, USA: Elsevier.

Kuznets S.1955. "Economic growth and income inequality." *American Economic Review* 49: 1–28. https://assets.aeaweb.org/asset-server/files/9438.pdf (accessed on 4 July 2021).

Leach M., R. Mearns and I. Scoones. 1997. "Environmental entitlements: a framework for understanding the institutional dynamics of environmental change." *IDS Discussion Paper No. 359*. Brighton: IDS. https://agris.fao.org/agris-search/search.do?recordID=GB9715127 (accessed on 7 July 2021).

Millennium Ecosystem Assessment. 2005. *Ecosystems and Human Well-being: Synthesis*. Washington, DC: Island Press. https://www.millenniumassessment.org/documents/document.356.aspx.pdf (accessed on 10 June 2021)

Murty, M N .2014. "Measuring Well-being and Accounting Prices of Environmental Resources." *Economic and Political Weekly* 49 (35): 64–69.

Olson, M. 1965. *The Logic of Collective Action*. Cambridge, MA: Harvard University Press.

Ostrom, E. 1990. *Governing the Commons: The Evolution of Institutions for Collective Action*. Cambridge: Cambridge University Press.

Panayotou, T. 2000. "Economic Growth and the Environment." *CID Working Papers 56*. Center for International Development at Harvard University. https://dash.harvard.edu/bitstream/handle/1/39570415/056.pdf?sequence=1&isAllowed=y (accessed on 25 June 2021).

Porter, Michael E and Claas van der Linde. 1995. "Toward A New Conception of the Environment-Competitiveness Relationship." *Journal of Economic Perspectives* 9 (4): 97–118. doi:10.1257/jep.9.4.97.

Ranjan, R. and J. Shortle. 2007. "The Environmental Kuznets Curve When the Environment Exhibits Hysteresis." *Ecological Economics* 64 (1): 204–215. doi:10.1016/j.ecolecon.2007.02.035.
Sen, A. 1981. *Poverty and Famines: An Essay on Entitlement and Deprivation.* Oxford: Oxford University Press.
Simonis, Udo E. 1992. "Poverty, Environment and Development." *Intereconomics* 27 (2): 75–85. doi:10.1007/bf02926179.
United Nations (UN). 2002. *Report of the World Summit on Sustainable Development*. New York: United Nations, 2002. https://undocs.org/pdf?symbol=en/A/Conf.199/20 (accessed on 15 August 2021).
Xepapadeas, A. 2005. "Economic Growth and the Environment." In *Hand Book of Environmental Economics*, edited by Maler K. G. and J. Vincent, 1219–1271. doi:10.1016/S1574-0099(05)03023-8k.

Chapter 2

# Natural Capital, Pandemic, and Development

## Exploration of Nexus and Solutions

*Pushpam Kumar, Amelia Holmes, and Samia Islam*[1]

### Introduction

Perturbation in the human–nature nexus can result in devastating outcomes that jeopardize development and human well-being. The ways in which the degradation of nature creates forces that are antithetical to global sustainable development goals are still being explored. Nevertheless, one of the enduring questions for natural resource economists has been to understand how the depletion of natural capital, including biodiversity, impacts the incidence of poverty and generates inequality in income and wealth distribution (Solow 1993). The impact of COVID-19 on health and the economy has made epoch-making changes in society globally. There is a scientific consensus that regardless of the exact origin of the SARS-CoV-2 virus of COVID-19, the incidence of emerging zoonotic diseases and their potential to escalate to pandemics is increasing due to global environmental changes, including biodiversity loss, habitat fragmentation, climate change, land-use change, and domestication of the wild.

In this chapter, we attempt to synthesize the state of knowledge on (1) the state of ecosystems and nature in the age of the Anthropocene, (2) nature and pandemic relationship through the mechanics of zoonosis, (3) development impacts of pandemic, (4) building nature into green recovery for sustainable and resilient societies, and (5) lessons learned and challenges ahead.

We try to highlight the linkages of declining natural capital and zoonotic impacts through a pandemic, attempt to understand and map out the implications for development agendas like poverty and economic inequality, and then propose some solutions for synergistic policies. Our effort here is to provide insights into how the conservation and restorative policies for nature can be better aligned with economic and development strategies to help achieve the prevailing consensus on 'Build Back Better'.

### 2.1 Ecosystems and Nature in the Age of the Anthropocene

The emerging scientific assessments and evidence are almost conclusive that the influences of human consumption, production, and distribution on the

DOI: 10.4324/9781003253884-4

biosphere are so significant that we have entered a new geological epoch: the Anthropocene (Ellis 2018: Crutzen 2000: Lewis 2015). Compounding anthropogenic pressures, such as land- and sea-use change, monoculture food systems, overexploitation of species, pollution, and climate change, are causing a detrimental decline in the life-supporting natural systems we depend upon. Anthropogenic environmental change at the broadest level can be attributed to ever-increasing material consumption, human population growth, and outdated economic indicators of progress focused on output rather than well-being (UNEP 2019b: Dagnet et al. 2020: Dasgupta 2021). The emergence of new infectious zoonotic diseases – such as that which resulted in the COVID-19 pandemic – is just one example of the types of existential challenges we face in the Anthropocene.

From the genetic scale to the loss of species to the collapse of entire ecosystems, global change is having a negative impact across all dimensions of nature, with trends of decline projected to continue to 2050 and beyond. The environmental decline is pervasive, and ecosystems of all types – freshwater, forests, wetlands, polar, marine, and coastal – suffer losses in quantity and quality due to various and compounding pressures. Between 1970 and 2016, global wildlife populations fell by an alarming 68% on average (WWF 2020). In the absence of significant transformational change, we may witness the demise of around one million species currently facing the threat of extinction – many within decades (IPBES 2019).

In 2017, global warming reached approximately 1°C above pre-industrial levels, and the damage may become irreversible if the temperature rise exceeds a threshold of 2.5°C (UNEN 2020). Climate change has become so prolific that it is now considered a powerful driver of environmental change and is flagged as an increasingly dominant influence on biodiversity trends in the ensuing decades (UNCCD and CBD 2019: CBD 2020). In the Arctic Circle, positive feedback loops may be triggered by the thawing of the permafrost in boreal peatlands, which has alarming projections for the acceleration of carbon emissions (UNEP 2019a).

The net rate of global forest loss has halved since 1990. Still, biodiversity-rich tropical forests continue to decline, now covering a land area that is approximately 68% of the estimated pre-industrial levels. The Amazon Rainforest, for instance, has lost 17% of its land area in the past 50 years and now absorbs a third less carbon than it did a decade ago, mainly due to expansion in commercial agriculture (UNEP 2019a: FAO 2016). Habitat fragmentation by deforestation increases the risk of ecosystem decline by disturbing ecological balance. One-fifth of the Earth's surface is at risk of plant and animal invasions, a notorious disrupter of ecosystem function, as well as potentially benefiting vectors of emerging diseases.

Anthropogenic drivers have particularly impacted inland waters and freshwater ecosystems due to the intensity of human dependence on wetlands, marshes, rivers, lakes, and peatlands. River systems face ongoing pressures from dam building and water diversion due to an ever-increasing demand for water availability. Aquifers are thus becoming an increasingly important source of water, but poor management of groundwater supplies is already resulting in salinity problems, land subsidence, and pollution. Damming and groundwater extraction contribute to the decline of wetlands, which are experiencing compounding stressors from plastic and chemical pollution and nutrient overload from agricultural inputs and industrial activities (UNEP 2019a).

Pollution is a growing global environmental problem, with no country unaffected by its impacts. Organic and chemical pollution in the form of pathogens, pesticides, heavy metals, and microplastics have contributed to worsening water and soil contamination and quality. E-waste leaches hazardous toxins as it breaks down and is the fastest growing waste stream globally. Along with plastics, marine plastic pollution remains one of the most difficult challenges of our times. Air pollution is so significant that in some places it is among the leading causes of morbidity and mortality – globally, between six and seven million premature deaths are attributed to air pollution (UNEN 2020).

## 2.2 COVID-19 Pandemic and Zoonotic Diseases

COVID-19 is the disease caused by a new strain of coronavirus called SARS-CoV-2, with the first cluster of cases identified on 31 December 2019 in Wuhan, the People's Republic of China (WHO 2020). The specific chain of events leading to the emergence of COVID-19 is not yet fully understood. However, with near certainty, the SARS-COV-2 virus is thought to originate in insectivorous bats, as it is part of a clad of closely related SARS-related coronaviruses found almost exclusively in *Rhinolophus* spp. bats in nature (Zhou et al. 2020). More than five new diseases emerge in people every year, and the risk of pandemics is increasing due to the exponentially growing anthropogenic drivers that influence zoonotic disease transmission rates. It is essential to take a broad view from attributing zoonotic emerging infectious diseases (EID) to wildlife to understand the more general patterns and key drivers that influence EID emergence and escalation (Simpson et al. 2018: IPBES 2020).

Zoonoses are a growing challenge in the global public health sphere. They are represented by well-known or newly emerging zoonotic diseases caused by bacteria, fungi, parasites, viruses, or prions (Asante et al. 2019). Microbes of animal origin cause zoonotic diseases and, due to numerous factors, may 'spill over' via contact with wildlife, livestock, and people. An estimated 73% of emerging infectious diseases (EIDs), including Ebola, Zika, and Nipah encephalitis and almost all known pandemics such as influenza (Spanish Flu), HIV/AIDS, and COVID-19, are zoonotic in origin (Jones et al. 2008: Földvári et al. 2014: IPBES 2020). Around 2.5 billion cases of zoonotic infections are recorded globally every year, resulting in 2.7 million deaths (Grace et al. 2012). Approximately 1.7 million currently undiscovered viruses are thought to exist in mammal and avian hosts, of which between 631,000 and 827,000 have been identified to potentially infect humans (IPBES 2020). The biological process of viral emergence has not changed over time, but the risk of novel disease outbreaks increases due to anthropogenic environmental changes (UNEP 2016).

## 2.3 Drivers of Zoonoses

Well-established interdisciplinary research demonstrates that human, animal, and ecosystem health are inextricably linked. Infectious diseases and vast diversity of pathogens naturally exist in ecosystems, and they contribute to biodiversity and the system's long-term dynamic stability. In the 20th century particularly, an unprecedented dramatic decline in biodiversity and equally dramatic increases in people and domestic or farmed animals had presented an increased opportunity for pathogens to pass from the biophysical environment with wild and domestic animals, in human communities and across the world. This section will explore key factors driving the transmission of disease.

There is overlap with the direct drivers of EIDs, those of biodiversity loss, including climate change, land-use change (for example, deforestation, degradation, and conversion to cropland), direct exploitation of species, pollution, etc., and invasive species (Figure 2.1). These drivers are themselves effects of the structure of economic incentives (e.g. subsidies for unsustainable farming and livestock production practices), globalized production and consumption, population pressure, and less tangible yet pervasive drivers such as social norms and values (IPBES 2019).

### *2.3.1 Ecosystem Loss and Fragmentation*

The emergence and re-emergence of zoonotic diseases are closely interlinked with the integrity, biological diversity, and resilience of ecosystems. Environmental changes are driven by human activity; they modify wildlife population structure and reduce biodiversity at rates that may be too fast to allow system adaptation, resulting in new environmental conditions that favour particular hosts, vectors, and pathogens (Jones et al. 2008). Even small changes in abiotic (e.g. climate change), biotic (e.g. invasive species), and biophysical (e.g. deforestation) aspects of an ecosystem can trigger significant changes in breeding conditions for the potential vectors of EIDs (Wilcox and Colwell 2005: Wilcox and Gubler 2005). In short, when disturbances occur or the natural ecosystem is stressed somehow, disease outbreaks may become more frequent. With such disorders, long-term negative impacts on human society will likely follow due to the disruption of

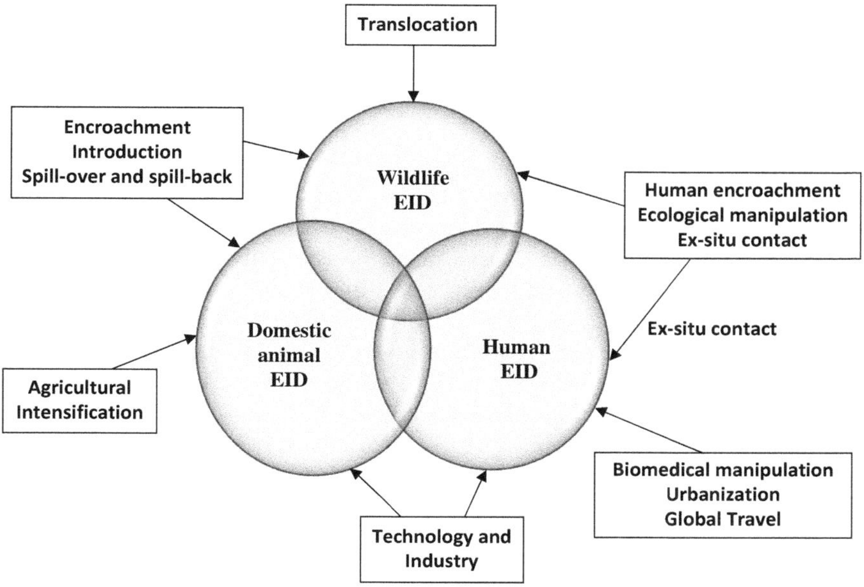


*Figure 2.1* Emerging relations across wildlife, livestock, and people linked through various anthropogenic drivers. *Source:* Author's illustration.

essential ecosystem services, including clean air and water, to the 'existence value' of biodiversity (OSI UK 2006).

Land-use change predominantly occurs from deforestation, human encroachment into a natural habitat, urbanization, and crop and livestock production. Land-use change is thought to have caused the emergence of more than 30% of new diseases since 1960 and is considered a significant factor in EID and pandemic risk (Zahouli 2017: IPBES 2020). Land-use change of all types increases the prevalence of edge-type ecosystems and ecotones, which refer to the break-in continuity between vastly different environments, causing changes in the environmental and biological conditions. Abrupt edges that may frequently occur with human encroachment in pristine areas (for example, constructing a highway or clearing for cropland) can be detrimental to species and ecosystem stability. Specific animals with common disease vectors thrive in edge ecosystems like rats in industrial plantations or mosquitoes in deforested areas. The encroachment of human settlements into natural forested ecosystems not only disrupts ecological balance but also enhances the public health risk, as it provides new pathways of pathogen spillover from wildlife and humans, driving up transmission rates (Gibb et al. 2017: IPBES 2020). Furthermore, edge effects and habitat fragmentation are primary causes of species extinction (Faust et al. 2017).

Previous EID outbreaks have been attributed to the disruption and fragmentation of biodiverse ecosystems. The abundance of the host species carrying the pathogen that causes Lassa fever (endemic in West Africa) is found in significantly higher abundance in rural homes and gardens and the surrounding agricultural fields compared to relatively low abundance in forested and urban areas. For example, in Malaysian Borneo, human movement into insect vector and wildlife reservoir habitats has been linked to a higher incidence of zoonotic malaria. The ecology and epidemiology of yellow fever have been well-documented since the 1950s. It has been established that the virus is maintained among monkey species and mosquito transmission cycles and emerges at a higher rate where human settlements have encroached along the forest fringes. The presence of fragmented ecosystems and edge effects now dominates many of the world's tropical regions, especially in developing nations where forested land is being converted for agriculture and human settlement at unprecedented rates over the last three decades (Despommier et al. 2006). Figure 2.1 shows the emerging relations across wildlife, livestock, and people linked through various anthropogenic drivers.

### 2.3.2 *Biodiversity and the Dilution Effect*

The potential mechanisms linking biodiversity with microbe transmission to humans and other animals are complex and multifaceted. Specific hosts have a higher 'competence' or capacity to transmit microbes, thereby playing a more critical role in transmission due to preferential infection, higher contact rates, and higher production and excretion of microbes (LoGiudice et al. 2003). Hosts with differing competencies for a particular microbe or pathogen means that in regions with high biodiversity, a so-called dilution effect may play a role in zoonoses dynamics. The dilution effect is observed where highly competent reservoirs represent a small proportion of the available reservoirs, and the transmission risk to people is reduced (Dobson 2004: Roche et al. 2013). The dilution effect has been observed for various zoonotic diseases, including Hantavirus (Tersago et al. 2008: Luis et al. 2018) and West Nile virus (Swaddle and Calos 2008: Ezenwa et al. 2006), and has been well-studied for Lyme disease (Ostfeld and Keesing 2012: Ostfeld 2017). The dilution effect implies that biodiversity loss due to anthropogenic environmental changes may drive higher zoonotic EID risk.

### 2.3.3 *Livestock and Animal Agriculture*

Livestock often serves as an epidemiological bridge between wildlife and human infections. Due to breeding for production rather than disease resistance, intensively reared livestock often lack the genetic diversity required to provide resilience to disease outbreaks. Where livestock rearing occurs adjacent to forested land within which enzootic diseases (those which affect animals in a particular place or season) exist, there is enhanced opportunity for pathogens to spill over to domesticated animals, followed by transmission to humans (Gibb et al. 2017). This was observed in northern Brazil in a human rabies outbreak, as well as the Nipah virus in Malaysia and Singapore, for which swine husbandry was partly responsible for setting the intermediate environment for human infection, paired with amplification via agricultural encroachment into the tropical forest to establish mango plantations (Olival and Daszak 2005). Another example of livestock acting as a 'disease bridge' was observed in avian influenza (bird flu), which first circulated in wild birds, then infected domestic poultry, and from them passed to humans (David et al. 2013: UNEP 2020).

The use of antimicrobial agents in both clinical and veterinary practice is rising and gaining global interest as a subject of concern (Dweba et al. 2018). Microorganisms can utilize various mechanisms to adapt to and thrive in the presence of antimicrobials, which makes infections increasingly challenging to treat and control (Dweba et al. 2018: Holmes et al. 2016). Resistance to antibiotics originating from humans, animals, and farms will spread to the larger environment, in that gene resistance may be facilitated by excreta contacting soils, surface, and groundwater (Holmes et al. 2016: Laxminarayan et al. 2013).

In already stressed ecosystems, such as overexploited marine systems, overgrazed grasslands, and degraded and logged forests, the effects of a disease outbreak may be aggravated, thus inhibiting their capacity to bounce back to function. Mainly where keystone species are infected by a new disease, such as top predators, impacts on ecosystems could be disastrous as they trigger trophic cascades (Silliman and Angelini 2012). In a study on the effects of the Zaire strain of the Ebola virus, gorilla mortality rates between 90% and 95% were observed in one region of 5,000 km$^2$ (Bermejo et al. 2006). This can have huge implications on ecosystem stability, as the contribution of primates is considered critically important for seed dispersal in tropical forest ecosystems (Poulsen et al. 2001: Lambert 2010). Human activities that drive zoonotic disease risk in people can also directly threaten biodiversity. The emergence of chytridiomycosis in amphibians worldwide was due to the wildlife trade, and this has heightened the risk of extinction and vulnerability of numerous amphibian species, many of which are already experiencing declines in the IUCN's red list index of extinction (IUCN 2021).

### *2.3.4 Climate Change*

Climate change is a compounding factor further complicating the changing dynamics of zoonoses. Climate-driven changes in migration patterns of people, wildlife, reservoirs, and vectors have been observed and are also expected. This may increase contact among species that would not usually interact and cause other disruptions in host–pathogen dynamics. Climate change is also projected to drive changes to the life cycles of vectors and hosts under altered climatic conditions. Climate change also creates compounding effects with land-use change and biodiversity loss such as forest loss, heat island effects, and wildfires, further driving up the risk of zoonotic EIDs. Shifts in precipitation may alter the abundance of crop plants and affect population cycles of herbivores, including rodents and other potential disease vectors, with potential for shifts in pathogen risk (Cascio 2011). The migration and movement of human and animal species may allow microbes to expand and invade new niches and infect even relatively unrelated hosts (IPBES 2020). For example, climate-induced migration of a biting midge vector of bluetongue disease was identified throughout Europe recently (Purse et al. 2008). Ticks transmit a great variety of pathogenic agents. They are thus major vectors of infection for humans and wildlife, and the geographic ranges for ticks have been expanding, primarily due to climate change (Hvidsten 2020). The climate-driven northern expansion of the black-legged tick range – the most critical vector transmitting Lyme disease – was observed in North America (Sonenshine 2018). Climate change was also implicated in studies looking at the patterns of tick-borne encephalitis in Scandinavia due to the northern migration of the vector species (Daniel 2018: Waits 2018: Smura 2019).

### *2.3.5 Bush Meat and Illegal Trade of Wildlife*

Bushmeat consumption can increase the risk of zoonotic disease emergence and it is growing in concern due to increases in human population density, heightened demand, and globalized trade (Nasi et al. 2008). The illegal trade in wildlife continues to pose a serious threat to ecosystems and wildlife populations, which not only threatens species' survival but also exposes humans to zoonotic diseases associated with the traded species.

Experts point to pandemics such as severe acute respiratory syndrome (SARS), Middle East respiratory syndrome (MERS), Avian flu, Monkeypox, and even Ebola as some of the diseases most likely to make the jump to global human populations in the future as a result of the live trade in illegal wildlife (UNEP 2016).

The last few decades have seen substantial growth in wildlife farming. The value of the legal wildlife trade (which includes the farming trade and consumption of wildlife and wildlife-derived products for food, medicine, fur, and other products) has increased fivefold since 2015, worth an estimated US$107 billion in 2019. The illegal wildlife trade poses a threat in that it is not regulated in terms of sustainability or risk of disease transmission and other risks, and the trade in mammals and birds is likely a higher risk for disease emergence than other trades because mammals and birds are important reservoirs of zoonotic pathogens. Even where regulations for legal trade exist, they tend to be limited in scope and inconsistently enforced (Salkeld et al. 2013: IPBES 2020).

### *2.3.6 Human Connectivity and Urbanization*

The rise in urbanization and the closer integration of the world economy is an important mechanism of disease transmission. By 2050, up to 68% of the human population may reside in cities – as of 2018, the proportion was estimated at around 55% (UN DESA 2019). Cities often have more enhanced disease control systems to help protect, treat, and help residents affected by EIDs, but the high density of people in urban centres increases the risk for disease outbreaks, and this is true for nations across all income levels (Lehmann 2021). In West Africa, the Ebola virus infection was amplified in urban centres, and New York City suffered one of the worst prolonged outbreaks of COVID-19 in the United States. Population dynamics of vectors of disease can be significantly influenced by urbanization, such as in northern latitudes where hedgehogs, rats, and squirrels can present known zoonotic diseases and can exist as pathogen reservoirs in city parks (Foldvari et al. 2014: Himsworth 2013: Rothenburger 2017). Cities in Southeast Asia and Africa have experienced cycles of significant outbreaks of Dengue fever attributed to urban heat-island effects that contribute to high-risk habitats for mosquito vectors (Akhtar 2016: Zahouli 2017).

## 2.4 Impact of COVID-19 on Economic Development

COVID-19 is not only a global pandemic and public health crisis: it has also severely affected the global economy and financial markets (UN 2020). Significant reductions in income, a rise in unemployment, and disruptions in the transportation, service, and manufacturing industries are among the consequences of the disease mitigation measures that have been implemented in many countries. It has become clear that most governments underestimated the risks of rapid COVID-19 spread and mainly were reactive in their crisis response. We look at the impact of COVID-19 on the different sectors of the economy.

### *2.4.1 Impact on Economic Output*

The COVID-19 pandemic has caused unprecedented shocks to economies and labour markets globally. What started as a public health emergency transformed into a deep global recession. Lockdowns and workplace closures, often at short notice, have been occurring periodically since March 2020 to minimize the spread of the disease and have resulted in reduced working hours and job losses for most countries. They have also contributed to an unprecedented halt in demand, worsening the economic downturn. The contraction and restrictions of world trade have caused significant disruptions to production, with flow-on effects felt throughout supply chains worldwide.

Governments responded to the crisis promptly through relief packages, providing financial aid to their citizens to maintain some level of consumer spending and economic activity. The United States spent 25% of their GDP on relief packages. In contrast, China spent 4.7% of its GDP, and Europe spent 10% of EU27 GDP (€750 billion/US$906 billion) on top of the €450 billion/US$652 billion allocated by the European Commission (UN DESA 2021a).

Despite often significant stimulus packages in some countries, estimates show that the global economy contracted by 3.5% in 2020 compared to the previously projected rate of 4.4% in October 2020 (average taken from estimates by IMF 2021: WEF 2021: OECD 2021: and UNDESA 2021). However, the global output is set to rise by 5.8% in 2021, making it the most robust post-recession pace in 80 years (average taken from estimates by World Bank 2021a: OECD 2021: IMF 2021: UN DESA 2021a). The world economy was supposed to remain 2% below pre-pandemic level until 2022 (World Bank 2021a) and by the first half of 2022 the world economy was predicted to recover to the pre-pandemic level (World Economic Forum 2021). Expected growth projections for China and the United States (8.7% and 6.5%, respectively) are expected to be responsible for the upward trajectory of the global output (UN DESA 2021a: OECD 2021). Following a strong rebound in 2021, the global economy is entering a pronounced slowdown amid fresh threats from COVID-19 variants and a rise in inflation, debt, and income inequality that could endanger the recovery in emerging and developing economies. Global growth is expected to decelerate markedly from 5.5% in 2021 to 4.1% in 2022 and 3.2% in 2023 as pent-up demand dissipates and as fiscal and monetary support is unwound across the world. The rapid spread of the Omicron variant indicates that the pandemic will likely continue to disrupt economic activity in the near term (World Bank 2022).

Much of the rest of the world faces a less optimistic outlook. The possibility of a resurgence of COVID-19 outbreaks, delayed vaccine rollout, increased debt levels, and other severe effects of the pandemic (e.g., low level of investments, stressed human capital with prolonged unemployment and academic institution closures) pose downside risks to economic growth overall. In addition, high trade costs incurred in 2020 significantly hampered world trade growth, which declined by 8.4% compared to 1.25% in 2019 (World Bank 2021a: OECD 2021). Generally, trade costs include transportation expenses, tedious border and customs procedures, trade agreements, and tariffs. Still, border closures, health safety measures, and prolonged debate on protectionist measures – such as the US–China trade deal – have also contributed to the increase in trade costs in 2020 (World Bank 2021a). Fortunately, the trade growth projection for 2021 is an 8.25% increase and 5.8% in 2022 (World Bank 2021a: OECD 2021).

### 2.4.2 Impact on Employment

In 2020, global employment fell by 114 million jobs, total international working hours reduced by 8.8% (approximately 225 million full-time jobs), and about 108 million workers now earn less than US$3.20 per day (ILO 2021). The economic effect of COVID-19 on businesses and employment varied across sectors, with each facing unique challenges. Small independent companies are experiencing very tough and uncertain futures, and some have filed for bankruptcy due to prolonged closures and not deemed essential services. The hospitality and tourism industry, wholesale and retail trade industry, group fitness industry, restaurant and bars, and other personal hygiene services, in particular, faced challenging disruptions and difficulties.

The effect of COVID-19 disruptions is non-uniform in the skill level of workers as well. Women and young people have been affected severely and although most of the global workforce is suffering from the pandemic, informal and low-wage workers are the most vulnerable. The decline in women's employment rate is 5% compared to the 3.9% decline in men's employment in 2020 (ILO 2021). Women's representation in essential services, health services, and caregiver services is also higher than men's, placing them in vulnerable spots while fighting against the pandemic. Additionally, 90% of women who lost their jobs in 2020 exited the labour force (ILO 2021), which suggests that their working lives are likely to be disrupted over an extended period unless appropriate measures are adopted. The burden of intensified childcare and home-schooling activities has disproportionately fallen on them, leading to a rise in unpaid working time for women that reinforces traditional gender roles. Moreover, women often work in front-line occupations, such as care workers or grocery clerks that face elevated health risks and difficult working conditions (World Economic Forum 2021).

Informal labour has 92.70% of the total labour share in low-income countries, 83% in lower-middle, 55.35% in upper-middle, and 14.43% in high-income countries. Also, most informal workers are not benefiting from the relief packages declared by the governments. The University of Oxford's COVID-19 Government Response Stringency Index places India, Pakistan, Nigeria, and Brazil at high risk of their people falling into poverty due to their higher share of the workforce in the informal economy (Hale et al. 2020).

### 2.4.3 Impact on Poverty

In countries that already have high poverty rates, the incidences of extreme poverty have increased significantly due to severe economic contractions around the globe. The World Bank (2020a: 2020b) projection in mid-2020 anticipates that several countries will observe a significant number of people drop below the extreme poverty line in 2020 (defined as living on less than US$1.9 per day) and that the majority of these (82%) will occur in middle-income countries. This fact is further enhanced by the effects of rising global inflation and the war in Ukraine. Estimates of the World Bank in early 2021 (World Bank 2021b) project extreme poverty to rise by around 100 million people, depending on the degree of economic contraction experienced and the model used for projections (World Bank 2020b: IMF 2020a: IMF 2020b: WEF 2020). These estimates translate to a worsening global poverty rate from 9.2% in 2017 to 9.4 % in 2020. Had the pandemic not occurred, the poverty rate was projected to drop to around 7.9% in 2021 (World Bank 2020b). Although revised and updated data shows a decrease of about 20 million people in poverty in 2021 than 2020, and the poverty trajectory is declining again, global poverty has been historically high for an unprecedented time. Even at the pre-pandemic level, 655 million people lived in extreme poverty. If the pace of poverty reduction is to be the same as the pre-pandemic time, tens of millions of people will still be living in poverty (World Bank 2021b). If the more pessimistic scenario plays out, 2022 could be the second-worst year in terms of progress made in reducing extreme poverty this century—behind only 2020, when there was an actual increase in global poverty.

The anticipation of severe economic devastation for South Asia and sub-Saharan Africa was extremely high in 2021 (World Bank 2020a, b: World Bank 2021a, b). Previous projections showed an increase in the poverty rate in 2021 for lower-income countries and sub-Saharan Africa, but updated estimates expect the poverty rate to more than double. The economic outlook for these regions is unclear and unstable, with recurrent waves of COVID-19 outbreaks and new variants, prolonged lockdown, and insufficient fiscal and monetary policies. Specifically, the sudden lockdown during the early stages of pandemic in 2020 and resurgence of COVID-19's delta variant in April and May 2021 in India left the people in a highly vulnerable state with casualties of almost half a million in the second wave (Al Jazeera 2021). As a result, the GDP per capita of India is expected to contract by a significant amount and push many Indians into extreme poverty (UN DESA 2021a). Although Nigeria surpassed India with the largest number of extremely poor in recent years, this pandemic again put India at the top (Kharas 2020).

Long-term poverty can leave permanent scars such as malnutrition, prolonged infections, school interruption, and severe and chronic mental health impacts. Alongside monetary or income poverty, there is also acute multidimensional poverty (impoverishment in aspects other than income). As a result, households are deprived of one-third or more of the ten indicators of health, education, and living standards set by the Sustainable

Development Goals (UNESCAP 2018; UNDP 2019). According to global Multidimensional Poverty Index (2021), across 109 countries, out of 1.3 billion people—21.7%—live in acute multidimensional poverty. About half (644 million) are children under age 18. Nearly 85% live in Sub-Saharan Africa (556 million) or South Asia (532 million) (UNDP and OPHI 2021). People experiencing acute multidimensional poverty are at incredibly high risk for COVID-19 and unable to comply with the preventative measures of social isolation (UNDP 2020). This estimated projection of global monetary poverty (US$5.5 per day) increases sets back any progress in eliminating extreme poverty by some years (World Bank 2020c).

### *2.4.4 Loss of Decades*

Studies show that the effects of the COVID-19 pandemic will unravel two decades (back to 2000) worth of progress on alleviating global poverty. For those who rely on daily wage labour and are not supported by a social safety net, sudden income losses were damaging when mobility restrictions were imposed. This is just one change in conditions that have devastatingly driven increasingly the number of people existing below the extreme poverty line in 2020 (World Bank 2020a 2020b: IMF 2020b: IMF 2020c: UN DESA 2020: Kharas 2020: Wheatley 2020).

## 2.5 COVID-19, Pandemics, and Inequality

Global inequality is a rising threat to the health, well-being, and security of all people. Epidemics in the past have triggered worsening poverty and inequality following outbreaks (Furceri et al. 2020). Recent research has warned that the COVID-19 pandemic has and will continue to exacerbate economic and gender inequalities (de Haan and Sturm 2017: Furceri et al. 2020: IMF 2020b: World Bank 2020c). Certain sectors of the economy, especially women, young people, and informal workers, have been impacted disproportionately.

### *2.5.1 Income and Sector Inequalities*

Income inequality rose significantly since the early 1990s in developed countries and current emerging economies (IMF 2020b). Inequalities arise from a combination of factors, often compounding, including a skill-biased technological change that favours the higher-educated – the decline in and absence of workers' unions, regressive tax policies, and the increase in firms' monopoly power, e.g. big grocery chains, Amazon, and Zoom (IMF 2020b). The economic burden of the pandemic falls unevenly across different sectors, with workers from the accommodation, food services, tourism, transportation, retail, and wholesale among the worst affected as their job descriptions cannot be carried out online (Brussevich, Dabla-Norris and Khalid 2020). Informal workers, most of whom reside in developing countries, and many of whom are women, are more likely to lose their jobs, as are those with limited flexibility in 'working from home', such as those with market stalls. This drives income inequalities within but almost between countries, as digitally advanced developed countries can more effectively cope with lockdowns and physical distancing (Jain et al. 2020). COVID-19 has demonstrated the vulnerability of those with inadequate housing, including the 1.2 billion people who currently reside in urban slums and informal settlements (UNEN 2020). Stay-at-home requirements are unsafe or practical for those in precarious and shared confined-space living. Patterns of social and economic inequality have been driven by globalization and the cultural, economic, and political aspects of increased global interdependency (Chan et al. 2020). Exponential growth in product demand, often driven by developed countries, affects land-use change and globalized trade.

### 2.5.2 Gender and Age Inequalities

Over half of those estimated to have slid into extreme poverty are women and girls (World Economic Forum 2021). As women are the primary caregivers of children in many cultures, the gaps in childcare often restrict women's ability to work. Mckinsey and colleagues (2020) reported that women are disproportionately exposed to COVID-19 (1.8 times more than men) because around 70% of the healthcare workforces are women (World Bank 2020b). Furthermore, women share 38% of the global employment but account for 54% of overall job losses globally and decline in jobs in all countries (ILO 2020a: ILO 2020b). Gender-based violence has increased due to lockdown measures, and opportunities to escape abuse have been severely minimized.

Children have been affected by prolonged school closures during the pandemic, leading to increased screen time and a lack of playing time amongst peers. Many students, particularly girls, will not return to school as they are required to contribute to keeping the household afloat. The return to school rate for girls after an EID outbreak is lower than for boys, as found in evidence from the Ebola outbreak in the Democratic Republic of Congo (World Bank 2020b). More than 1.6 billion global learners have been affected by academic institution closures (UNESCO 2020). From an economic standpoint, the human capital of future generations is projected to be severely impacted by the closure of schools and ill-equipped homeschooling set-ups. Underprivileged students from developing and developed worlds are not receiving the appropriate learning instructions as those with highly educated parents. Younger workers often hold less job security and are thus more vulnerable to job and income losses than experienced senior workers in the industry. Young people aged 16–25 years experienced job losses (one in every ten) and a decline in their salaries (six in every ten) during the early stages of the COVID-19 pandemic (LSE 2020). The younger and less skilled workforce is especially missing out on many professional development endeavours, including networking opportunities that are hard to re-create in remote and fragmented office culture.

### 2.5.3 Environmental and Health Inequalities

Ecosystem goods and services such as quality topsoil, availability of water, nutrient cycling, timber resources, and many other non-marketed goods make up between 50% and 90% of the total source of livelihoods among poor rural and forest-dwelling households. It is well established that affluent people and nations have a greater carbon and ecological footprint in terms of total resources used and waste created (Global Footprint Network 2021). However, poor, particularly rural communities, rely on the environment in more direct ways and, therefore, any declines in quality, access, and benefits from ecosystem services are felt profoundly. Such disturbances may be caused by logging concessions to foreign entities, mining permits, overexploitation of species, or climate-driven land desiccation. The 'GDP of the poor' is a concept that arose from the need to estimate and recognize the contribution of natural resources and ecosystem services to livelihoods and well-being, given that much of the developing world's poor draw directly on natural assets for employment and survival (TEEB 2008).

The burden of zoonotic disease is significantly more significant in developing countries, particularly in tropical and subtropical regions. Zoonotic diseases comprise 25% of the infectious disease burden in low-income nations due to a generally higher incidence of close contact with livestock and wildlife (Grace et al. 2012). A combined disease burden may occur where there is the likelihood of zoonotic diseases, co-infection with other pathogenic or infectious diseases, such as malaria, tuberculosis, and HIV (Asante et al. 2019). Current hotspots of EID incidence have been identified and are particularly prevalent in some areas of Africa and Southeast Asia. Much of the vast block of tropical rainforest extending across equatorial, central, and East Africa has been affected by human encroachment to the point where all but the core of central Africa can essentially be described as a regional-scale edge-type ecosystem. Similarly, population growth and pressure on natural resources have transformed Southeast Asia in recent decades, such that anthropogenic edge ecosystems cover far more land area than entire blocks of forest (Wilcox and Colwell 2005).

The disparity in COVID-19 vaccination distribution between countries and regions poses additional pressure on an already uneven and precarious global economic recovery. Notably, the vaccine scarcity in the global south is hindering the public health and economic recovery of countries and prolonging plans to reopen to worldwide trade and tourism (WEF 2021).

### 2.5.4 Recovery Strategies

There have been mixed approaches to post-COVID-19 economic stimulus, and the idea that monetary stimulus should be centred on the green economy and sustainability is unfortunately not unanimous (Pelenc et al. 2015). The European Union has allocated around 30% of its US$891 billion EU-wide stimulus package towards climate-friendly investments. France and Germany are leading the way and announcing the highest investments in green projects (Neumayer 2003, 2012: Dedeurwaerdere 2014). On the other side of the spectrum, the United States announced the most significant fiscal support package of any country – US$3 trillion – with support focused on the fossil fuel industry and wholly lacking any considerations of sustainability. Most national economic plans sit somewhere in the middle – making green investments while also supporting fossil fuels as part of their economic recoveries, such as South Korea, China, and India (Chan et al. 2020). The pandemic has disproportionately burdened least developed countries (LDCs) and small island states, and up to US$2.5 trillion in additional economic support may be needed to support developing countries to overcome the unprecedented crisis.

## 2.6 Green Recovery for Resilient and Sustainable Society

The post-COVID-19 world has made starkly apparent the interconnectedness of nature, economies, and human well-being (*The Economist* 2020). Nations seek guidance to create policies that will nurture economic recovery and improve resilience to future novel disease outbreaks and other global shocks (Rockström et al. 2009). There are excellent opportunities to safeguard ecosystems and biodiversity and build sustainable energy futures with governments and policymakers creating stimulus packages (Deutz et al. 2020: IRP 2020). Natural capital must form a key role in creating the scaffolding that will enable all countries, particularly low- and middle-income countries, to thrive economically post-pandemic (Noël and O'Connor 1998: Ekins et al. 2003: Brand 2009: ELD Initiative 2015: Natural Capital Coalition 2016).

To tap into the synergistic power of cross-cutting policy initiatives, multifaceted approaches such as the One Health Initiative, circular economy model, natural capital accounting, Nature-based Solutions (NbS), and land degradation neutrality principle can form the cornerstone of sustainable development in the future (De Groot et al. 2003: Cleaveland et al. 2017: Frantzeskaki et al. 2017: UNEN 2020).

In 2021, a review was published by the HM Treasury – the United Kingdom's Economic and Finance Ministry – to understand the relationship between biodiversity and economics. *The Economics of Biodiversity: The Dasgupta Review* was led by Professor Sir Partha Dasgupta and sets out key economic and scientific concepts, and the messages are clear and profound.

i. The devastation that COVID-19 is causing underscores the importance of biodiversity for our health and that of the global economy, as well as the need for the human enterprise to live within the 'safe operating space' of the biosphere.
ii. Since the advent of the Anthropocene and particularly since the 1950s, the phenomenal rise in economic growth has been achieved at the cost of biodiversity, climate, and nature in general.
iii. Biodiversity is a key determinant of the productivity and resilience of nature. Just as diversity within a portfolio of financial assets reduces risk and uncertainty, so diversity within a portfolio of natural assets increases nature's resilience to shocks, including major natural disasters, human-made environmental damage, and the emergence and spread of infectious diseases.
iv. Ecosystems are like capital assets providing more than a 19% rate of return, but they remain unacknowledged as their contributions do not get captured by the conventional metrics of the economy.
v. Fundamentally, we have to get to a point where we operate within the limits of the regenerative capacity of the Earth's ecosystems.

As part of its recommendations, *The Dasgupta Review* calls for better accounting for natural capital and more holistic measures of economic progress that can be used as a complement to GDP. It is particularly important to focus on a nation's wealth – their capacity to provide income and prosperity long term – rather than income and output (as GDP does), which is more appropriately used as a 'snapshot' indicator of progress.

The UN Environment Programme's Inclusive Wealth Index (IWI) is one such indicator. It is a wealth-based indicator calculated by estimating the stocks of a nation's human, natural, and produced capital. The inclusive wealth biennial report tracks these stocks of capital for 140 countries to provide an overall picture of the wealth base of nations. It is a multipurpose indicator capable of measuring not only traditional stocks of wealth but also those less tangible, such as skill sets, healthcare, and environmental assets that form the backbone of human progress (Managi and Kumar 2018: Raworth 2017).

The current IWI methodology components included in the calculation of natural capital include both renewable resources (agricultural land, forests, and fisheries) and non-renewable resources (fossil fuels and minerals). As of now, comparable data for countries on ecosystem services are not available for incorporation into the IWI. Progress is being made in this space, however, particularly through the System of Environmental-Economic Accounting Experimental Ecosystem Accounting (SEEA-EA), which was recently updated in 2021 after a comprehensive review and consolidation for methodologies of accounting for ecosystems (UN DESA 2021b).

According to the most recent iteration of the Inclusive Wealth Report (2018), the annual global growth rate of inclusive wealth (taking the net growth of all capital types into one measure) between 1990 and 2014 averaged 1.8% – only around half the 3.4% average growth rate of global GDP for the same period. Disaggregating this by country, growth in inclusive wealth per capita (after adjustments for carbon damages, oil prices, and total factor productivity) has been observed in only 96 of 140 countries since 1998. This suggests that 32% of countries' income is being generated unsustainably, as their wealth base is being depleted as a result of their current production and consumption patterns. In short, although produced capital has grown impressively, the potential in health, education, and natural assets is not being realized. An intuitive interpretation is that produced capital (and to a lesser extent, human capital) has been enhanced at the cost of undermining critical natural capital.

At the national level, a large number of countries have undertaken wealth-based assessments. Countries including India, Morocco, Canada, China, and Pakistan have produced their estimates of national and regional wealth following UNEP's IWI approach. Additionally, Thailand, St Lucia, Barbados, Botswana, and Vietnam began working with the index in 2020 (UNEP 2021).

Developing countries have a particular advantage over developed countries in sustainable development agendas because they do not need to rebuild extensive networks of infrastructure or institutions: nature-centric economic growth can be incorporated directly into their economic planning. Shifts in energy systems, water use, and conservation are more sustainable than using traditional industrial practices which degrade natural capital by design (Faucheux and O'Connor 1998).

## 2.7 Conclusion

The links between biodiversity, emerging infectious diseases, and inequalities are complex and need to be considered carefully in national and global governance as we face some of the greatest challenges of our time. Natural capital and the resilience of ecosystems continue to decline around the world, with loss of wildlife populations and extinction of species, land degradation, depleted resources, and climate-induced extreme weather. The COVID-19 pandemic has deepened the existing inequalities among and within countries, with those most vulnerable bearing the brunt of the pandemic damages and are at great risk of being left behind (UNEN 2020).

The role of ecosystem integrity in preventing and mediating zoonotic outbreaks had been scientifically well-established for some time. Global alarm bells have been ringing for urgent action on zoonotic disease and emerging infectious disease threats for more than a decade, with not enough attention given to integrative environmental health initiatives such as One-Health and

Eco-Health in developing global zoonoses control programmes. In 2006, *Infectious Diseases: Preparing for the Future* was produced by the UK government's Foresight Project. As well as calling for better early detection and warning systems, the report noted that degrading natural ecosystems continues to be a major source of zoonotic diseases that may threaten agricultural systems and human health. Additionally, the four most recent iterations of the UN Environment Programme's biannual *Frontiers Report* series have dedicated a chapter highlighting the threat of increased risk of emerging infectious zoonotic disease. In 2014, the UN Frontiers report warned that environmental factors (e.g. land conversion and climate change) play a major role in the development and transmission of infectious diseases. A triple threat was identified in the combination of (i) new infectious diseases, (ii) the re-emergence of infectious diseases, and (iii) increasing antibiotic resistance. The report warned: "Along with changes in society and technology – and in the microorganisms themselves – these factors are contributing to a 'perfect storm' of vulnerability."

In the wake of the devastation caused by COVID-19, numerous intergovernmental agencies have called for the urgent need for prioritizing a One-Health, interdisciplinary approach to preventing pandemic- and epidemic-scale zoonotic EIDs, as well as creating resilient, thriving human societies into the future (IPBES 2020: UNEP 2020). As part of 'building back better' for resilient economies and societies after COVID-19, we need improved governance in biosafety, and pathogen and ecosystem management, at the national and global levels.

The knowledge gap needs to be addressed and the knowledge and tools derived from research made accessible to national governments, businesses, the health sector, local communities, and others to reduce the risk of future pandemics. Full-cost financial accounting of the societal impacts of zoonotic diseases can be a helpful addition for guiding policy in this space (Watson 2020). Inter-sectoral approaches which have been developed on the premise of 'healthy environment – healthy people' have had notable successes, ultimately improving human health such as controlling rabies in the Serengeti ecosystem, understanding brucellosis in Mongolia, and controlling leishmaniasis in Tunisia (UNEP 2016).

To ensure long-term positive outcomes to sustainable development, we can no longer consider ecological, economic, and human health as isolated issues. What affects one will inevitably directly or indirectly affect the other. Several factors have been identified as influencing the increased threat of zoonotic emerging infectious diseases, including the rising demand for animal protein, and associated agricultural intensification, the increased use and exploitation of wildlife, and the unsustainable use of natural resources exacerbated by land-use change. These same factors are also driving the biodiversity and climate crises, which are global challenges that require integrated approaches.

Biodiversity conservation needs to become a national priority and can be improved and enhanced through nature-based solutions and rewinding frameworks. For co-benefits to be realized for mitigating and adapting to climate change, it needs to include restoration of carbon-rich habitats and climate-resilient agriculture. Post-COVID-19 pandemic, economic activities must revolve around job creation from the green sector, the key to which is ecosystem restoration. In many countries, building back better involves investing in jobs within the green economy, both rural and urban, and the COVID-19 pandemic has shown us that working from home is possible and productive, and investments in broadband networks are as important as infrastructure investments as expanding road and rail networks. Economic recovery activities should refrain from bolstering extractive sectors and polluting industries, and direct investments should be made to transition to renewable energy systems.

Economic systems require transformative change, including moving from the take-make-waste linear model towards circular production and consumption. Systems of national accounts should urgently integrate natural capital and wealth accounting to ensure ecosystem management has a seat at the policy table and that nature is properly valued in decision-making. Pursuing growth for the sake of growth (in GDP) alone is an outdated and inadequate approach to development, and indicators such as the Inclusive Wealth Index and those centred on human and environmental health can help re-centre economic progress on sustainability and human well-being, rather than output alone.

The recovery from the COVID-19 pandemic must show that we have learned lessons in the type of investments and stimulus needed in the economy and jobs, to promote improved human health, cleaner air, and greener landscapes.

## Note

1 The views expressed in this chapter are not necessarily those of the organization where the author works. Other disclaimers apply as well.

## References

Akhtar R., P.T. Gupta and A.K. Srivastava 2016. "Urbanization, Urban Heat Island Effects and Dengue Outbreak in Delhi". In: *Climate Change and Human Health Scenario in South and Southeast Asia*, edited by Akhtar R, 99–111. Advances in Asian Human-Environmental Research. Cham: Springer. https://doi.org/10.1007/978-3-319-23684-1_7

Al Jazeera. 2021, July 02. India COVID Death Toll Crosses 400,000: Half Died in Second Wave. Retrieved from https://www.aljazeera.com/news/2021/7/2/india-covid-death-toll-400000-black-fungus. (accessed on 3 July 2021).

Asante, J., A. Noreddin, and M. El Zowalaty. 2019. "Systematic Review of Important Bacterial Zoonoses in Africa in The Last Decade in Light of the "One Health" Concept". *Pathogens* 8 (2): 50. doi:10.3390/pathogens8020050.

Bermejo, M., J. D. Rodriguez-Teijeiro, G. Illera, A. Barroso, C. Vila, and P. D. Walsh. 2006. "Ebola Outbreak Killed 5000 Gorillas". *Science* 314 (5805): 1564–1564. doi:10.1126/science.1133105.

Brand, F. 2009. "Critical Natural Capital Revisited: Ecological Resilience and Sustainable Development". *Ecological Economics* 68 (3): 605–612. doi: 10.1016/j.ecolecon.2008.09.013.

Brussevich, M., E. Dabla-Norris, C. Kamunge, P. Karnane, S. Khalid, and K. Kochhar. 2018. *Gender, Technology, and the Future of Work*. IMF Staff Discussion Note 18/07. Washington, DC: International Monetary Fund. https://www.imf.org/en/Publications/Staff-Discussion-Notes/Issues/2018/10/09/Gender-Technology-and-the-Future-of-Work-46236. (accessed on 11 February 2021).

Cascio, A., M. Bosilkovski, A.J. Rodriguez-Morales, and G. Pappas. 2011. "The Socio-Ecology of Zoonotic Infections". *Clinical Microbiology and Infection* 17 (3): 336–342. doi:10.1111/j.1469-0691.2010.03451.x.

CBD. Convention on Biological Diversity. 2020. *Biodiversity and the 2030 Agenda for Sustainable Development. Policy Brief*. Montreal: Secretariat of the Convention on Biological Diversity. https://wedocs.unep.org/bitstream/handle/20.500.11822/11300/Biodiversity-2030-agenda.pdf?sequence=1&isAllowed=y (accessed on 14 June 2021).

Chan, Kai M. A., D. R. Boyd, R. K. Gould, J. Jetzkowitz, J. Liu, B. Muraca, and R. Naidoo et al. 2020. "Levers And Leverage Points for Pathways to Sustainability". *People and Nature* 2 (3): 693–717. doi:10.1002/pan3.10124.

Cleaveland, S., J. Sharp, B. Abela-Ridder, K. J. Allan, J. Buza, J. A. Crump, and A. Davis et al. 2017. "One Health Contributions Towards More Effective and Equitable Approaches to Health in Low- And Middle-Income Countries". *Philosophical Transactions of the Royal Society B: Biological Sciences* 372 (1725): 20160168. doi:10.1098/rstb.2016.0168.

Crutzen, Paul J. and E. F. Stoermer. 2000. "The 'Anthropocene'". In *The Future of Nature: Documents of Global Change*, edited by Libby Robin, Sverker Sörlin and Paul Warde, 479–490. New Haven: Yale University Press, 2013. doi:10.12987/9780300188479-041.

Dagnet, Y., and J. Jaeger. September 15, 2020. *Not Enough Climate Action in Stimulus Plans*. Retrieved October 27, 2020, from https://www.wri.org/blog/2020/09/coronavirus-green-economic-recovery (accessed on 15 June 2021).

Daniel, M., V. Danielová, A. Fialová, M. Malý, B. Kříž, and P. A. Nuttall. 2018. "Increased Relative Risk of Tick-Borne Encephalitis in Warmer Weather". *Frontiers in Cellular and Infection Microbiology* 8: 1–11. doi:10.3389/fcimb.2018.00090.

Dasgupta Review. 2021. *The Economics of Biodiversity: The Dasgupta Review*. Retrieved from https://www.gov.uk/government/publications/final-report-the-economics-of-biodiversity-the-dasgupta-review (accessed on 1 August 2021).

David, Aaron S., J. M. Kaser, A. C. Morey, A. M. Roth, and D. A. Andow. 2013. "Release of Genetically Engineered Insects: A Framework to Identify Potential Ecological Effects". *Ecology And Evolution* 3 (11): 4000–4015. doi:10.1002/ece3.737.

De Groot, R., J. Van der Perk, A. Chiesura, and A. van Vliet. 2003. "Importance and Threat as Determining Factors for Criticality of Natural Capital". *Ecological Economics* 44 (2–3): 187–204. doi:10.1016/s0921-8009(02)00273-2.

de Haan, Jakob, and Jan-Egbert Sturm. 2017. "Finance and Income Inequality: A Review and New Evidence". *European Journal of Political Economy* 50: 171–195. doi: 10.1016/j.ejpoleco.2017.04.007.

Dedeurwaerdere, T. 2014. *Sustainability Science for Strong Sustainability*. Northampton: Edward Elgar.

Despommier, D., B. R. Ellis, and B. A. Wilcox. 2006. "The Role of Ecotones in Emerging Infectious Diseases". *Ecohealth* 3 (4): 281–289. doi:10.1007/s10393-006-0063-3.

Deutz, A., G. M. Heal, R. Niu, E. Swanson, T. Townshend, L. Zhu, A. Delmar, A. Meghji, S.A. Sethi, and J. laT. Puente, 2020. *Financing Nature: Closing the global biodiversity financing gap*. The Paulson Institute, The Nature Conservancy, and the Cornell Atkinson Center for Sustainability. https://www.paulsoninstitute.org/wp-content/uploads/2020/09/FINANCING-NATURE_Full-Report_Final-Version_091520.pdf (accessed on 23 August 2021).

Dobson, A. 2004. "Population Dynamics of Pathogens with Multiple Host Species". *The American Naturalist* 164 (S5): S64–S78. doi:10.1086/424681.

Dweba, C. C., O. T. Zishiri, and M. E. El Zowalaty. 2018. "Methicillin-resistant *Staphylococcus aureus*: livestock-associated, antimicrobial, and heavy metal resistance". *Infection and Drug Resistance*, *11*, 2497–2509. https://doi.org/10.2147/IDR.S175967

Ekins, P., S. Simon, L. Deutsch, C. Folke, and R. De Groot. 2003. "A Framework for The Practical Application of The Concepts of Critical Natural Capital and Strong Sustainability". *Ecological Economics* 44 (2–3): 165–185. doi:10.1016/s0921-8009(02)00272-0.

ELD Initiative. 2015. *Report for Policy and Decision Makers: Reaping Economic and Environmental Benefits from Sustainable Land Management*. www.eld-initiative.org. (accessed on 21 June 2020).

Ellis, E. C. 2018. *Anthropocene. A Very Short Introduction*. Kettering: Oxford University Press.

Ezenwa, V. O., M. S. Godsey, R. J. King, and S. C. Guptill. 2006. "Avian Diversity and West Nile Virus: Testing Associations Between Biodiversity and Infectious Disease Risk". *Proceedings of the Royal Society B-Biological Sciences* 273: 109–117, doi:10.1098/rspb.2005.3284.

Faucheux, S., and M. O'Connor. 1998. *Valuation for Sustainable Development*. Cheltenham: Elgar.

Faust, C. L., A. P. Dobson, N. Gottdenker, L. S. P. Bloomfield, H. I. McCallum, T. R. Gillespie, M. Diuk-Wasser, and R. K. Plowright. 2017. "Null Expectations for Disease Dynamics in Shrinking Habitat: Dilution or Amplification?" *Philosophical Transactions of The Royal Society B: Biological Sciences* 372 (1722): 20160173. doi:10.1098/rstb.2016.0173.

Földvári, G., S. Jahfari, K. Rigó, M. Jablonszky, S. Szekeres, G. Majoros, M. Tóth, V. Molnár, E. C. Coipan, and H. Sprong. 2014. "Candidatusneoehrlichia Mikurensis Andanaplasma Phagocytophilumin Urban Hedgehogs". *Emerging Infectious Diseases* 20 (3): 496–498. doi:10.3201/eid2003.130935.

FAO Food and Agriculture Organization of the United Nations. 2016. *Commercial Agriculture Accounted for Almost 70 Percent of Deforestation in Latin America.* Available from http://www.fao.org/americas/noticias/ver/en/c/425600/. (accessed on 2 July 2020).

Frantzeskaki, N. S. Borgström, L. Gorissen, M. Egermann, F. Ehnert. 2017. “Nature-Based Solutions Accelerating Urban Sustainability Transitions in Cities: Lessons from Dresden, Genk and Stockholm Cities”. In *Nature-Based Solutions to Climate Change Adaptation in Urban Areas. Theory and Practice of Urban Sustainability Transitions. Linkages between Science, Policy and Practice*, edited by N. Kabisch, H. Korn, J. Stadler, A. Bonn, 65–88. Cham: Springer International Publishing. doi:10.1007/978-3-319-56091-5_5.

Furceri, D., P. Loungani, J. D. Ostry, and P. Pizzuto. May 08, 2020. “COVID-19 Will Raise Inequality If Past Pandemics Are a Guide”. Retrieved October 27, 2020, from https://voxeu.org/article/covid-19-will-raise-inequality-if-past-pandemics-are-guide (accessed on 3 January 2021).

Gibb, R., L. M. Moses, D. W. Redding, and K. E. Jones. 2017. “Understanding the Cryptic Nature of Lassa Fever in West Africa”. *Pathogens And Global Health* 111 (6): 276–288. doi:10.1080/20477724.2017.1369643.

Global Footprint Network. 2021. *Earth Overshoot Day*. https://www.overshootday.org/ (accessed on 15 June 2021).

Grace, D., J. Gilbert, T. Randolph, and E. Kang’ethe. 2012. “The Multiple Burdens of Zoonotic Disease and an Ecohealth Approach to Their Assessment”. *Tropical Animal Health and Production* 44 (S1): 67–73. doi:10.1007/s11250-012-0209-y.

Hale, T, A. Petherick, T. Phillips, and S. Webster. 2020. *Variation in Government Responses to COVID-19(Working Paper, 31)*. Oxford, UK: Blavatnik School of Government, University of Oxford. http://www.bsg.ox.ac.uk/covidtracker (accessed on 2 February 2021).

Himsworth, C. G., K. L. Parsons, C. Jardine, and D. M. Patrick. 2013. “Rats, Cities, People, And Pathogens: A Systematic Review and Narrative Synthesis of Literature Regarding the Ecology of Rat-Associated Zoonoses in Urban Centers”. *Vector-Borne and Zoonotic Diseases* 13 (6): 349–359. doi:10.1089/vbz.2012.1195.

Holmes, A. H, L. S P Moore, A. Sundsfjord, M. Steinbakk, S. Regmi, A. Karkey, P. J Guerin, and L. J V Piddock. 2016. “Understanding the Mechanisms and Drivers of Antimicrobial Resistance”. *The Lancet* 387 (10014): 176–187. doi:10.1016/s0140-6736(15)00473-0.

Hvidsten, D., K. Frafjord, J.S. Gray, A.J. Henningsson, A. Jenkins, B.E. Kristiansen, and M. Lager et al. 2020. “The Distribution Limit of the Common Tick, Ixodes Ricinus, and Some Associated Pathogens in North-Western Europe”. *Ticks and Tick-Borne Diseases* 11 (4): 101388. doi: 10.1016/j.ttbdis.2020.101388.

IPBES. 2020a. *Workshop Report on Biodiversity and Pandemics of the Intergovernmental Platform on Biodiversity and Ecosystem Services*. Daszak, P., C. das Neves, J. Amuasi, D. Hayman, T. Kuiken, B. Roche, C. Zambrana-Torrelio, P. Buss, H. Dundarova, Y. Feferholtz, G. Foldvari, E. Igbinosa, S. Junglen, Q. Liu, G. Suzan, M. Uhart, C. Wannous, K. Woolaston, P. ReidlMosig, K. O'Brien, U. Pascual, P. Stoett, H. Li, H. T. Ngo. Bonn, Germany: IPBES Secretariat. doi:10.5281/zenodo.4147317.

IPBES. 2020b. *Workshop Report on Biodiversity and Pandemics of the Intergovernmental Platform on Biodiversity and Ecosystem Services.* Intergovernmental Science-Policy Platform on Biodiversity and Ecosystem Services (IPBES). https://ipbes.net/sites/default/files/2020-12/IPBES%20Workshop%20on%20Biodiversity%20and%20Pandemics%20Report_0.pdf (accessed on 8 February 2021).

ILO. 2020a. *International Labour Organization. (2020, April 7). ILO Monitor 2nd Edition: COVID-19 and the World of Work.* https://www.ilo.org/wcmsp5/groups/public/@dgreports/@dcomm/documents/briefingnote/wcms_740877.pdf. (accessed on 20 April 2020).

ILO. 2020b. *International Labour Organization. (2020, October). ILO Monitor Sixth Edition: COVID-19 and the World of Work.* https://www.ilo.org/wcmsp5/groups/public/---dgreports/---dcomm/documents/briefingnote/wcms_755910.pdf. (accessed on 25 October 2020).

ILO. 2020c. *ILO Monitor: COVID-19 and the World of Work. 6th edition.* http://www.ilo.org/global/topics/coronavirus/impacts-and-responses/WCMS_755910/lang--en/index.htm. (accessed on 26 October 2020).

ILO. 2021. *World Employment and Social Outlook: Trends 2021.* https://www.ilo.org/global/research/global-reports/weso/trends2021/WCMS_794452/lang--en/index.html. (accessed on 2 June 2021).

IMF. 2020a. *International Monetary Fund. World Economic Outlook, April 2020:Chapter 1: The Great Lockdown.* https://www.imf.org/en/Publications/WEO/Issues/2020/04/14/weo-april-2020. (accessed on 20 April 2020).

IMF. 2020b. *International Monetary Fund. World Economic Outlook, October 2020 -- Chapter 1: Global Prospects and Policies.* https://www.imf.org/en/Publications/WEO/Issues/2020/09/30/world-economic-outlook-october-2020. (accessed on 25 October 2020).

IMF. 2020c. *World Economic Outlook, October 2020: A Long and Difficult Ascent.* https://www.imf.org/en/Publications/WEO/Issues/2020/09/30/world-economic-outlook-october-2020. (accessed on 26 October 2020).

IMF. 2021. *World Economic Outlook, April 2021: Managing Divergent Recoveries.* (2021, April). Retrieved from https://www.imf.org/en/Publications/WEO/Issues/2021/03/23/world-economic-outlook-april-2021 (accessed on 28 October 2021)

Intergovernmental Science-Policy Platform on Biodiversity and Ecosystem Services (IPBES). 2019. *Global Assessment Report on Biodiversity and Ecosystem Services.* Available from https://ipbes.net/global-assessment-reportbiodiversity-ecosystem-services. (accessed on 26 October 2020).

IRP. 2020, August 13. *Building Resilient Societies after the Covid-19 Pandemic.* International Resource Panel (IRP). https://www.resourcepanel.org/reports/building-resilient-societies-after-covid-19-pandemic (accessed on 20 October 2020).

IUCN. International Union for the Conservation of Nature. 2021. *IUCN Red List – Amphibian Stats. IUCN Red list of Threatened Species.* https://www.iucnredlist.org/search/stats?query=amphibian&searchType=species. (accessed on 29 June 2021).

Jain, R., J. Budlender, R. Zizzamia, and I. Bassier. 2020. "The Labor Market and Poverty Impacts of COVID-19 in South Africa". *CSAE Working Paper*

*WPS/202014*. Cambridge, MA: Center for the Study of African Economies, Harvard University.

Jones, K. E., N. G. Patel, M. A. Levy, A. Storeygard, D. Balk, J. L. Gittleman, and P. Daszak. 2008. "Global Trends in Emerging Infectious Diseases". *Nature* 451 (7181): 990–993. doi:10.1038/nature06536.

Kharas, H. 2020. The Impact of COVID-19 on Global Extreme Poverty. https://www.brookings.edu/blog/future-development/2020/10/21/the-impact-of-covid-19-on-global-extreme-poverty/.(accessed on 26 October 2020).

Lambert, Joanna E. 2010. "Primate Seed Dispersers as Umbrella Species: A Case Study fromKibale National Park, Uganda, With Implications for Afrotropical Forest Conservation". *American Journal of Primatology* 73 (1): 9–24. doi:10.1002/ajp.20879.

Laxminarayan, R., A. Duse, C. Wattal, A. K M Zaidi, H. F L Wertheim, N. Sumpradit, and E. Vlieghe et al. 2013. "Antibiotic Resistance—The Need for Global Solutions". *The Lancet Infectious Diseases* 13 (12): 1057–1098. doi:10.1016/s1473-3099(13)70318-9.

Lehmann, S. 2021. "Growing Biodiverse Urban Futures: Renaturalization and Rewilding as Strategies to Strengthen Urban Resilience". *Sustainability* 13 (5): 2932. doi:10.3390/su13052932.

Lewis, Simon L., and Mark A. Maslin. 2015. "Defining the Anthropocene". *Nature* 519 (7542): 171–180. doi:10.1038/nature14258.

LoGiudice, K., R. S. Ostfeld,K. A. Schmidt, and F. Keesing. 2003. "The Ecology of Infectious Disease: Effects of Host Diversity and Community Composition on Lyme Disease Risk. "*Proceedings of the National Academy of Sciences* 100: 567–571. doi:10.1073/pnas.0233733100.

LSE, Major, L., A. Eyles, and S. Machin. 2020. *Generation COVID: Emerging Work and Education Inequalities*. Economic and Social Research Council. https://cep.lse.ac.uk/pubs/download/cepcovid-19-011.pdf. (accessed on 21 June 2021).

Luis, A. D., A. J. Kuenzi, and J. N. Mills. 2018. "Species Diversity Concurrently Dilutes and Amplifies Transmission in a Zoonotic Host-pathogen System Through Competing Mechanisms". *Proceedings of the National Academy of Sciences* 115, 7979–7984. doi:10.1073/pnas.1807106115.

Managi, S., and P. Kumar, (Eds.). 2018. *Inclusive Wealth Report 2018: Measuring Progress Towards Sustainability* (1st ed.). London: Routledge. https://doi.org/10.4324/9781351002080.

Mckinsey, Madgavkar, A., White, O., Krishnan, M., Mahajan, D., and Azcue, X. 2020, July 17. *COVID-19 and Gender Equality: Countering the Regressive Effects*. https://www.mckinsey.com/featured-insights/future-of-work/covid-19-and-gender-equality-countering-the-regressive-effects# (accessed on 20 October 2020).

Nasi, R., D. Brown, D. Wilkie, E. Bennett, C. Tutin, G. van Tol, and T. Christophersen. 2008. *Conservation and Use of Wildlife-based Resources: The Bushmeat Crisis*. Montreal: Secretariat of the Convention on Biological Diversity, and Bogor: Center for International Forestry Research (CIFOR). Technical Series no. 33, 50 pages. https://www.cbd.int/doc/publications/cbd-ts-33-en.pdf (accessed on 25 August 2021).

Natural Capital Coalition. 2016. *The Path Towards the Natural Capital Protocol: A Primer for Business*. https://naturalcapitalcoalition.org/wp-content/uploads/2016/07/NCC_Primer_WEB_2016-07-08.pdf (accessed on 26 August 2021).

Neumayer, E. 2003. *Weak Versus Strong Sustainability: Exploring the Limits of Two Opposing Paradigms*. Northampton: Edward Elgar.

Neumayer, E. 2012. "Human Development and Sustainability". *Journal Of Human Development and Capabilities* 13 (4): 561–579. doi:10.1080/19452829.2012.693067.

Noël, J-F., O'Connor, M. 1998. "Strong Sustainability and Critical Natural Capital". In: *Valuation for Sustainable Development: Methods and Policy Indicators*, edited by S. Faucheux, and M. O'Connor, 75–99. Cheltenham: Edward Elgar Publisher.

OECD. OECD Economic Outlook. 2021, May. https://www.oecd.org/economic-outlook/may-2021/ (accessed on 20 October 2020).

Olival, Kevin J, and Peter Daszak. 2005. "The Ecology of Emerging Neurotropic Viruses". *Journal of Neurovirology* 11 (5): 441–446. doi:10.1080/13550280591002450.

OSI UK. 2006. *Foresight. Infectious Diseases: Preparing for the Future. Executive Summary*. London: Office of Science and Innovation. https://assets.publishing.service.gov.uk/government/uploads/system/uploads/attachment_data/file/294762/06-761-infectious-diseases-futures.pdf (accessed on 11 September 2021)

Ostfeld, Richard S. 2017. "Biodiversity Loss and the Ecology of Infectious Disease". *The Lancet Planetary Health* 1 (1): e2–e3. doi:10.1016/s2542-5196(17)30010-4.

Ostfeld, Richard S., and F. Keesing. 2012. "Effects of Host Diversity on Infectious Disease". *Annual Review of Ecology, Evolution, and Systematics* 43 (1): 157–182. doi:10.1146/annurev-ecolsys-102710-145022.

Pelenc, J., J. Ballet and T. Dedeurwaerdere. 2015. "Weak Sustainability versus Strong Sustainability". https://sustainabledevelopment.un.org/content/documents/6569122-Pelenc-Weak Sustainability versus Strong Sustainability.pdf (accessed on 1 July 2021).

Poulsen, John R., C. J. Clark, and T. B. Smith. 2001. "Seed Dispersal by a Diurnal Primate Community in the Dja Reserve, Cameroon". *Journal of Tropical Ecology* 17 (6): 787–808. doi:10.1017/s0266467401001602.

Purse, B.V., H.E. Brown, L. Harrup, P.P.C. Mertens, and D.J. Rogers. 2008. "Las Invasiones De Lengua Azul Y Otras Infecciones Por Orbivirus En Europa: Papel De Los Procesos Biológicos Y Climáticos". *Revue Scientifique Et Technique De L'oie* 27 (2): 427–442. doi:10.20506/rst.27.2.1801.

Raworth, Kate (2017). *Doughnut Economics: Seven Ways to Think Like a 21st Century Economist*. Vermont: White River Junction. ISBN: 9781603586740.

Roche, B., P. Rohani, A. P. Dobson, and Jean-François Guégan. 2013. "The Impact of Community Organization on Vector-Borne Pathogens". *The American Naturalist* 181 (1): 1–11. doi:10.1086/668591.

Rockström, J., W. Steffen, K. Noone, Å. Persson, F. S. Chapin, III, E. Lambin, T. M. Lenton, M. Scheffer, C. Folke, H. Schellnhuber, B. Nykvist, C. A. De Wit, T. Hughes, S. van der Leeuw, H. Rodhe, S. Sörlin, P. K. Snyder, R. Costanza, U. Svedin, M. Falkenmark, L. Karlberg, R. W. Corell, V. J. Fabry, J. Hansen, B. Walker, D. Liverman, K. Richardson, P. Crutzen, and J. Foley. 2009. Planetary Boundaries: Exploring the Safe Operating Space for Humanity. *Ecology and Society* 14(2): 32. online URL: http://www.ecologyandsociety.org/vol14/iss2/art32/ (accessed on 20 October 2020).

Rothenburger, J. L., C. H. Himsworth, N. M. Nemeth, D. L. Pearl, and C. M. Jardine. 2017. "Environmental Factors and Zoonotic Pathogen Ecology In Urban Exploiter Species". *Ecohealth* 14 (3): 630–641. doi:10.1007/s10393-017-1258-5.

Salkeld, D. J, K. A Padgett, and J. H. Jones. 2013. "A Meta-Analysis Suggesting that the Relationship Between Biodiversity and Risk of Zoonotic Pathogen Transmission is Idiosyncratic". *Ecology Letters* 16 (5): 679–686. doi:10.1111/ele.12101.

Silliman, B. R. and C. Angelini. 2012. Trophic Cascades Across Diverse Plant Ecosystems. *Nature Education Knowledge* 3(10): 44. https://www.nature.com/scitable/knowledge/library/trophic-cascades-across-diverse-plant-ecosystems-80060347/ (accessed on 9 September 2021).

Simpson, Gregory J.G., V. Quan, J. Frean, D. L. Knobel, J. Rossouw, J. Weyer, T. Marcotty, J. Godfroid, and L. H. Blumberg. 2018. "Prevalence of Selected Zoonotic Diseases and Risk Factors at a Human-Wildlife-Livestock Interface in Mpumalanga Province, South Africa". *Vector-Borne and Zoonotic Diseases* 18 (6): 303–310. doi:10.1089/vbz.2017.2158.

Smura, T., E. Tonteri, A. Jääskeläinen, G. von Troil, S. Kuivanen, O. Huitu, and L. Kareinen et al. 2019. "Recent Establishment of Tick-Borne Encephalitis Foci with Distinct Viral Lineages in the Helsinki Area, Finland". *Emerging Microbes & Infections* 8 (1): 675–683. doi:10.1080/22221751.2019.1612279.

Solow, R. 1993. "An Almost Practical Step toward Sustainability". *Resources Policy* 19 (3): 162–172. doi:10.1016/0301-4207(93)90001-4.

Sonenshine, D. 2018. "Range Expansion of Tick Disease Vectors In North America: Implications for Spread of Tick-Borne Disease". *International Journal of Environmental Research and Public Health* 15 (3): 478. doi:10.3390/ijerph15030478.

Swaddle, John P., and S. E. Calos. 2008. "Increased Avian Diversity Is Associated with Lower Incidence of Human West Nile Infection: Observation of the Dilution Effect". *Plos ONE* 3 (6): e2488. doi: 10.1371/journal.pone.0002488.

TEEB. 2008. *The Economics of Ecosystems and Biodiversity: An Interim Report.* https://ec.europa.eu/environment/nature/biodiversity/economics/pdf/teeb_report.pdf (accessed on 27 October 2020).

Tersago, K., A. Schreurs, C. Linard, R. Verhagen, S. Van Dongen, and H. Leirs. 2008. "Population, Environmental, And Community Effects on Local Bank Vole (Myodes Glareolus) Puumala Virus Infection in An Area with Low Human Incidence". *Vector-Borne and Zoonotic Diseases* 8 (2): 235–244. doi:10.1089/vbz.2007.0160.

The Economist. 2020. *The Epidemic Provides a Chance to do Good by the Climate* (2020, March 26). https://www.economist.com/science-and-technology/2020/03/26/the-epidemic-provides-a-chance-to-do-good-by-the-climate. (accessed on 20 April 2020).

UN. 2020. *Coronavirus "Grim Reality": World Economy to Shrink by 3.2 percent, New UN Report Project UN News*. United Nations, 13 May 2020, www.news.un.org/en/story/2020/05/1064032. (accessed on 20 October 2020).

UNCCD and CBD. 2019. *Land Degradation Neutrality for Biodiversity Conservation: How Healthy Land Safeguards Nature*. Technical Report. Bonn, Germany. https://www.unccd.int/publications/land-degradation-neutrality-biodiversity-conservation-how-healthy-land-safeguards (accessed on 2 September 2021).

UN DESA. 2019. United Nations, Department of Economic and Social Affairs, Population Division (2019). World Urbanization Prospects: The 2018 Revision (ST/ESA/SER.A/420). New York: United Nations. https://population.un.org/wup/Publications/Files/WUP2018-Report.pdf (accessed on 3 August 2021)

UN DESA. 2020. *Impact of COVID-19 on SDG Progress: A Statistical Perspective-Policy Brief no 81*. https://www.un.org/development/desa/dpad/wp-content/uploads/sites/45/publication/PB_81.pdf (accessed on 27 October 2020).

UN DESA. 2021a. *World Economic Situation and Prospects as of mid-2021 | Department of Economic and Social Affairs*. (2021, May). https://www.un.org/development/desa/dpad/publication/world-economic-situation-and-prospects-as-of-mid-2021/. (accessed on 21 June 2021)

UN DESA. 2021b. United Nations Department of Economic and Social Affairs: Statistics Division (UN DESA SD) (2021b). System of Environmental-Economic Accounting— Ecosystem Accounting: Final Draft. https://unstats.un.org/unsd/statcom/52nd-session/documents/BG-3f-SEEA-EA_Final_draft-E.pdf. (accessed on 2 July 2021)

UNDP (2019). "Global Multidimensional Poverty Index 2019: Illuminating Inequalities". Oxford Poverty & Human Development Initiative, 2029, https://ophi.org.uk/wp-content/uploads/G-MPI_Report_2019_PDF.pdf. (accessed on 13 August 2021).

UNDP. 2020. "Multidimensional Poverty in Times of COVID-19". UNDP, 28 Apr. 2020, www.latinamerica.undp.org/content/rblac/en/home/blog/2020/pobreza-multidimensional-en-tiempos-del-covid-19.html (accessed on 3 August 2021).

UNDP and OPHI. 2021. Global Multidimensional Poverty Index 2021 – Unmasking disparities by ethnicity, caste and gender. United Nations Development Programme and Oxford Poverty and Human Development Initiative. https://ophi.org.uk/global-mpi-report-2021/ 9accessed on 7 August 2022)

UNEN. 2020. "Report of the UN Economist Network for the UN 75th Anniversary: Shaping the Trends of Our Time | Multimedia Library - United Nations Department of Economic and Social Affairs". United Nations, 16AD, 2020, https://www.un.org/development/desa/publications/report-of-the-un-economist-network-for-the-un-75th-anniversary-shaping-the-trends-of-our-time.html (accessed on 3 July 2021).

UNEP. 2016. *UNEP Frontiers 2016 Report: Emerging Issues of Environmental Concern*. United Nations Environment Programme, Nairobi. https://www.unep.org/resources/frontiers-2016-emerging-issues-environmental-concern (accessed on 18 August 2021).

UNEP. 2019a. Frontiers 2018/2019 Emerging Issues of Environmental concern. Nairobi: United Nations Environment Programme. https://www.unep.org/resources/frontiers-201819-emerging-issues-environmental-concern (accessed on 15 August 2021).

UNEP. 2019b. *Global Environmental Outlook 6*. Nairobi: United Nations Environment Programme. https://www.unep.org/resources/global-environment-outlook-6 (accessed on 15 August 2021).

UNEP. United Nations Environment Programme. 2021. Inclusive Wealth of Pakistan: The case for Investing in Natural Capital and Restoration. Nairobi. https://www.unep.org/resources/report/inclusive-wealth-pakistan-case-investing-natural-capital-and-restoration (accessed on 16 August 2021).

UNEP. 2018. Inclusive Wealth Report. Nairobi, Kenya. https://www.unep.org/resources/inclusive-wealth-report-2018

UNESCAP. 2018. Inequality in Asia and the Pacific in the Era of the 2030 Agenda for Sustainable Development (UNESCO). https://www.unescap.org/publications/inequality-asia-and-pacific-era-2030-agenda-sustainable-development (accessed on 16 August 2021).

Waits, A., A. Emelyanova, A. Oksanen, K. Abass, and A. Rautio. 2018. "Human Infectious Diseases and the Changing Climate in the Arctic". *Environment International* 121: 703–713. doi: 10.1016/j.envint.2018.09.042.

Watson, R. (2020) The World's Banks Must Start to Value Nature and Stop Paying for Its Destruction. *The Guardian: Environment.* https://www.theguardian.com/environment/commentisfree/2020/oct/28/the-worlds-banks-must-start-to-value-nature-and-stop-paying-for-its-destruction-aoe (accessed on 19 August 2021)

WEF. World Economic Forum. 2020. *New Nature Economy Report II: The Future of Nature and Business.* Cologne, Switzerland: WEF. https://www.weforum.org/reports/new-nature-economy-report-ii-the-future-of-nature-and-business (accessed on 19 May 2021)

WEF. 2021. Chief Economists Outlook: weforum.org. http://www3.weforum.org/docs/WEF_Chief_Economists_Outlook_June_2021.pdf. (accessed on 14 July 2021)

Wheatley, J. 2020, October 07. Covid-19 Will Push Millions in Middle-income Nations into Poverty, Warns World Bank. https://www.ft.com/content/2a41fa8b-e5d1-4102-b14f-7ec5820a5d7d (accessed on 27 October 2021).

WHO. World Health Organisation. 2020. Origins of SARS-CoV-2. WHO Reference Number: WHO/2019-nCoV/FAQ/*Virus Origin*/2020.1. https://apps.who.int/iris/bitstream/handle/10665/332197/WHO-2019-nCoV-FAQ-Virus_origin-2020.1-eng.pdf (accessed on 19 June 2021).

Wilcox, B. A., and R. R. Colwell. 2005. "Emerging and Reemerging Infectious Diseases: Biocomplexity as an Interdisciplinary Paradigm". *Ecohealth* 2 (4): 244–257. doi:10.1007/s10393-005-8961-3.

Wilcox, B. A., and D. J. Gubler. 2005. "Disease Ecology and the Global Emergence of Zoonotic Pathogens". *Environmental Health and Preventive Medicine* 10 (5): 263–272. doi:10.1265/ehpm.10.263.

World Bank. 2020a. Mahler, D. G., Lakner, C., Aguilar, R. A. C., & Wu, H. (2020, April 20). The Impact of COVID-19 (Coronavirus) on Global Poverty: Why Sub-Saharan Africa Might be the Region Hardest Hit. https://blogs.worldbank.org/opendata/impact-covid-19-coronavirus-global-poverty-why-sub-saharan-africa-might-be-region-hardest (accessed on 27 April 2020).

World Bank. 2020b. Updated Estimates of the Impact of COVID-19 on Global Poverty: The Effect of New Data. https://blogs.worldbank.org/opendata/updated-estimates-impact-covid-19-global-poverty-effect-new-data?token=d3c7288f257b662e819adb237c06033e (accessed on 26 October 2020).

World Bank. 2020c. Gender Inequality Exacerbates the COVID-19 Crisis in Fragile and Conflict-affected Settings. https://blogs.worldbank.org/dev4peace/gender-inequality-exacerbates-covid-19-crisis-fragile-and-conflict-affected-settings (accessed on 3 October 2020).

World Bank. 2021a. *Global Economic Prospects, June 2021.* The World Bank. doi:10.1596/978-1-4648-1665-9.

World Bank. 2021b. Updated Estimates of the Impact of COVID-19 on Global Poverty: Turning the Corner on the Pandemic in 2021? https://blogs.worldbank.org/opendata/updated-estimates-impact-covid-19-global-poverty-turning-corner-pandemic-2021 (accessed on 15 May 2021)

World Bank. 2022. *Global Economic Prospects, January 2022*. Washington, DC: World Bank. doi: 10.1596/978-1-4648-1758-8. License: Creative Commons Attribution CC BY 3.0 IGO. https://www.worldbank.org/en/news/press-release/2022/01/11/global-recovery-economics-debt-commodity-inequality (accessed on 7 August 2022)

WWF. 2020. *Worldwide Fund for Nature (WWF) (2020) Living Planet Report 2020 - Bending the Curve of Biodiversity Loss*. Edited by Almond, R.E.A., Grooten M. and Petersen, T. Gland, Switzerland: WWF. https://www.zsl.org/sites/default/files/LPR%202020%20Full%20report.pdf (accessed on 18 July 2021).

Zahouli, J.B.Z., B.G. Koudou, P. Müller, D. Malone, Y. Tano, and J. Utzinger. 2017. "Urbanization is a Main Driver for the Larval Ecology of *Aedes* Mosquitoes in Arbovirus-endemic Settings in South-eastern Côte d'Ivoire". *PLoS Negl Trop Dis* 11(7): e0005751. https://doi.org/10.1371/journal.pntd.0005751

Zhou, P., Xing-Lou Yang, Xian-Guang Wang, B. Hu, L. Zhang, W. Zhang, and Hao-Rui Si et al. 2020. "A Pneumonia Outbreak Associated With A New Coronavirus Of Probable Bat Origin". *Nature* 579 (7798): 270–273. doi:10.1038/s41586-020-2012-7.

Chapter 3

# COVID-19: A Neo-Malthusian Event?

## Ecological links, Challenges, and Opportunities

*Ramprasad Sengupta and Chetana Chaudhuri*

### Introduction: Coincidence of Extreme Events and Coronavirus Disease 2019

Humanity is currently facing a substantial existential crisis due to the coronavirus disease pandemic caused by the highly infectious nature of the disease. Although the world is still amid the pandemic, we cannot as yet make a total assessment of its impact and sustainability policy implications; all the countries of the world are already affected by this pandemic in a manner that their socio-economic life has been derailed from its normal course of movement. The cumulative number of cases of infection worldwide (with a base on 22 January 2020) due to COVID-19 reached 56,713,594 as of 19 November 2020, out of which 39,495,825 people recovered and 1,357,672 died. There have been worldwide 15,860,097 active cases as of 19 November 2020. Figure 3.1A shows the daily new cases of infection and the same for the number of deaths as on the date indicated worldwide. Figure 3.1B shows the cumulative number of infections (in millions) and the total number of active cases (in millions) globally as of 19 November 2020.[1] Figure 3.1C highlights the prevalence rate per million population and incidence of COVID-19 infections across different countries as of 19 November 2020.

India is at the second position among the countries in the world in terms of a cumulative number of cases as of 19 November 2020. Table 3.1 presents a state-wise number of active cases, cured/discharged/migrated cases, deaths, and a cumulative number of confirmed cases of COVID-19 for India as of 19 November 2020 vis-à-vis 15 July 2020. At the start of lockdown, i.e., on 25 March 2020, a cumulative number of confirmed cases in India stood at 563, which spiked to 8,958,483 by 19 November 2020. As of 19 November 2020, there were 131,578 cumulative deaths in India due to COVID-19, among which 35% of deaths occurred in Maharashtra (46,202 deaths), followed by Karnataka (9%) and Tamil Nadu (9%). These reveal the prevalence and pattern of regional concentration of risk of life involved in the disease.

DOI: 10.4324/9781003253884-5

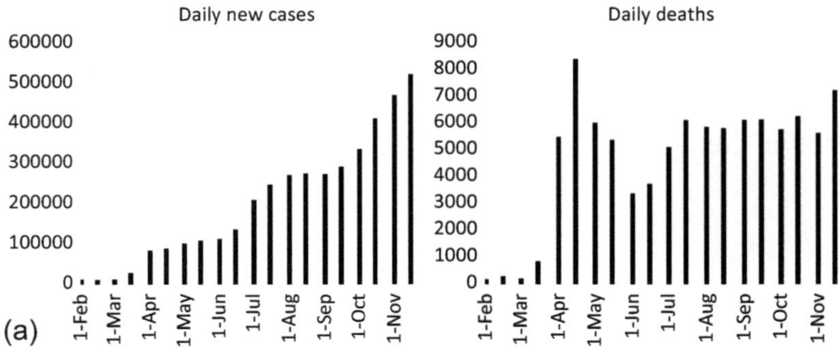


*Figure 3.1A* Number of daily new COVID-19 cases and daily new deaths due to COVID-19 worldwide from February to November 2020. *Source:* https://www.worldometers.info.

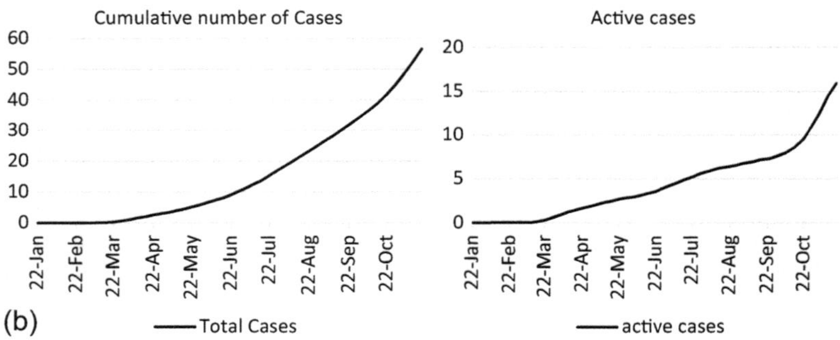


*Figure 3.1B* Cumulative number of COVID-19 cases (in millions) and the total number of active COVID-19 cases (in millions) in the world as of 19 November 2020. *Note:* Cumulative number of cases refers to the cumulative number of cases with a base on 22 January 2020. *Source:* https://www.worldometers.info. Data is accessed on 19 November 2020.

From the data for the spread of COVID-19 infection across different states in India, we have estimated the doubling time, which is defined as the number of days required for the number of cases of the infection (here COVID-19 pandemic) to double, based on the rate of increase in a cumulative number of cases. Doubling time, in this study, is estimated by dividing the number of cases at the initial date of analysis by the per day growth in a cumulative number of confirmed cases (between the initial and final date of analysis) and multiplying them by 2. We have taken two time intervals for the analysis: from 10 May to 15 July 2020; and from 15 July to 19 November 2020. We started our analysis on 10 May 2020 since the infection was limited to a very few states before that, and considering those dates would not be appropriate for state-wise analysis. Any increase in doubling the time between the two time

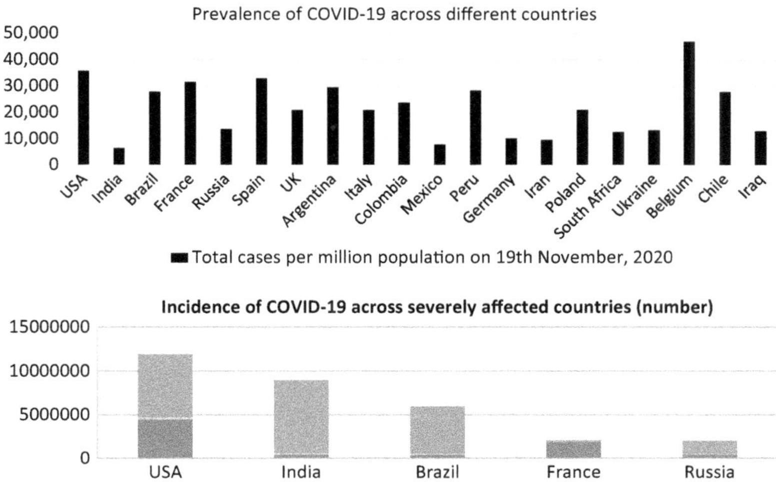


(c)

*Figure 3.1C* Prevalence and incidence of COVID-19 infection across different countries as of 19 November 2020. *Source:* https://www.worldometers.info. Data is accessed on 19 November 2020.

periods would signify that state governments have been able to overpower the spread of the virus through proactive measures for controlling the virus-like strict implementation of lockdown, social distancing, etc. On the contrary, any reduction in doubling time would show that the strength of the virus has increased over time in those regions, and there is an urgent need for state governments to take plausible measures to control the virus. It can be seen from the data that doubling time has increased substantially between the two periods in states/UTs like Delhi, Gujarat, Tamil Nadu, and Maharashtra, and it has decreased in states/UTs like Andaman and Nicobar Islands, Chhattisgarh, Punjab, Kerala, and Madhya Pradesh (see Figure 3.2).

As we shall see in our more detailed description and analysis of the impact of this pandemic across the world, from India to the United States, the poor and economically marginalized sections of the population, irrespective of if they are black or brown, have been disproportionately hit by the pandemic caused by the virus by losing both life and livelihood, i.e., job and income.

It is also noticeable that India has faced several cyclonic storms with catastrophic impacts in the recent past. The frequency of such extreme events has been growing not only in India but also globally (Andharia 2019). India, in fact, experienced one super cyclone hitting the eastern coasts of West Bengal and Orissa in May 2020, which has been unprecedented in terms of wind speed and devastation in the years since 1737 for the region.

*Table 3.1* COVID-19 statistics across states in India

| *Name of state/UT (in descending order in terms of cumulative confirmed cases)* | *Active cases* | | *Cured or discharged or migrated* | | *Deaths* | | *Cumulative* confirmed cases* | |
|---|---|---|---|---|---|---|---|---|
| | *15 July 2020* | *19 November 2020* | *15 July 2020* | *19 November 2020* | *15 July 2020* | *19 November 2020* | *15 July 2020* | *19 November 2020* |
| 1 Maharashtra | 107,963 | 81,207 | 149,007 | 1,630,111 | 10,695 | 46,202 | 267,665 | 1,757,520 |
| 2 Karnataka | 25,845 | 25,165 | 17,390 | 829,188 | 842 | 11,578 | 44,077 | 865,931 |
| 3 Andhra Pradesh | 15,144 | 16,516 | 17,467 | 833,980 | 408 | 6,899 | 33,019 | 857,395 |
| 4 Tamil Nadu | 47,915 | 14,470 | 97,310 | 737,281 | 2,099 | 11,531 | 147,324 | 763,282 |
| 5 Kerala | 4,458 | 69,516 | 4,438 | 468,460 | 34 | 1,943 | 8,930 | 539,919 |
| 6 Uttar Pradesh | 13,758 | 21,954 | 24,983 | 487,221 | 983 | 7,441 | 39,724 | 516,616 |
| 7 Delhi | 18,664 | 42,458 | 93,236 | 452,683 | 3,446 | 7,943 | 115,346 | 503,084 |
| 8 West Bengal | 11,927 | 26,296 | 19,931 | 407,769 | 980 | 7,820 | 32,838 | 441,885 |
| 9 Odisha | 4,342 | 7,568 | 9,864 | 301,777 | 74 | 1,575 | 14,280 | 310,920 |
| 10 Telangana | 12,530 | 12,682 | 24,840 | 246,733 | 375 | 1,419 | 37,745 | 260,834 |
| 11 Rajasthan | 5,885 | 19,478 | 19,161 | 210,779 | 525 | 2,101 | 25,571 | 232,358 |
| 12 Bihar | 6,261 | 5,349 | 12,849 | 221,272 | 174 | 1,201 | 19,284 | 227,822 |
| 13 Chhattisgarh | 1,084 | 18,770 | 3,275 | 193,997 | 20 | 2,646 | 4,379 | 215,413 |
| 14 Assam | 6,351 | 3,285 | 11,416 | 206,611 | 40 | 969 | 17,807 | 210,865 |
| 15 Haryana | 5,226 | 19,543 | 17,090 | 185,403 | 312 | 2,093 | 22,628 | 207,039 |
| 16 Gujarat | 11,065 | 12,457 | 30,503 | 175,362 | 2,069 | 3,823 | 43,637 | 191,642 |
| 17 Madhya Pradesh | 4,757 | 9,338 | 13,575 | 174,202 | 673 | 3,115 | 19,005 | 186,655 |
| 18 Punjab | 2,635 | 5,937 | 5,663 | 132,917 | 213 | 4,541 | 8,511 | 143,395 |
| 19 Jharkhand | 1,628 | 2,637 | 2,427 | 103,171 | 36 | 934 | 4,091 | 106,742 |
| 20 Jammu and Kashmir | 4,755 | 5,570 | 6,223 | 96,972 | 195 | 1,613 | 11,173 | 104,155 |
| 21 Uttarakhand | 769 | 4,147 | 2,867 | 64,032 | 50 | 1,128 | 3,686 | 69,307 |
| 22 Goa | 1,128 | 1,364 | 1,607 | 44,310 | 18 | 670 | 2,753 | 46,344 |
| 23 Puducherry | 684 | 705 | 829 | 35,152 | 18 | 608 | 1,531 | 36,465 |
| 24 Tripura | 630 | 997 | 1,538 | 30,856 | 2 | 364 | 2,170 | 32,217 |

| | | | | | | | | |
|---|---|---|---|---|---|---|---|---|
| 25 Himachal Pradesh | 347 | 6,901 | 951 | 24,025 | 11 | 475 | 1,309 | 31,401 |
| 26 Manipur | 702 | 2,828 | 970 | 19,259 | 0 | 231 | 1,672 | 22,318 |
| 27 Chandigarh | 144 | 1,081 | 446 | 14,833 | 10 | 253 | 600 | 16,167 |
| 28 Arunachal Pradesh | 306 | 1,182 | 153 | 14,715 | 3 | 48 | 462 | 15,945 |
| 29 Meghalaya | 250 | 753 | 66 | 10,014 | 2 | 103 | 318 | 10,870 |
| 30 Nagaland | 550 | 1,255 | 346 | 9,057 | 0 | 54 | 896 | 10,366 |
| 31 Ladakh | 146 | 924 | 946 | 6,605 | 1 | 94 | 1,093 | 7,623 |
| 32 Andaman and Nicobar Islands | 57 | 154 | 109 | 4,378 | 0 | 61 | 166 | 4,593 |
| 33 Sikkim | 122 | 300 | 87 | 4,182 | 0 | 95 | 209 | 4,577 |
| 34 Mizoram | 79 | 487 | 159 | 3,021 | 0 | 5 | 238 | 3,513 |
| All India | 319,840 | 443,303 | 592,032 | 8,383,602 | 24,309 | 131,578 | 936,181 | 8,958,483 |

Source: Ministry of Health and Family Welfare accessed on 15 July 2020 and 19 November 2020.

Note: * Represents cumulative number with base on 30 January 2020, when the first case was reported in India. Active cases, cured or discharged or migrated and confirmed cases (cumulative) include foreign nationals. Cumulative confirmed cases = Active cases + cured or discharged or migrated + deaths.

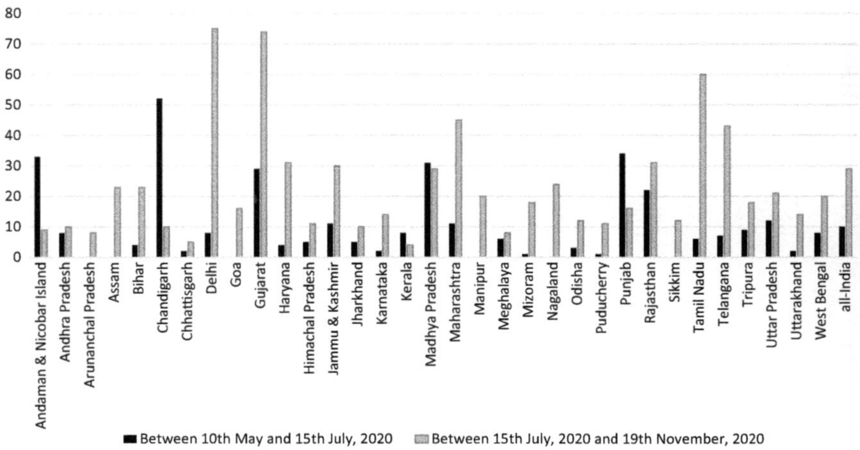


*Figure 3.2* Doubling time of COVID-19 infections (days). *Source:* Author's estimation from data collected from Ministry of Health and Family Welfare, Government of India.

Another such cyclone hit the western coast near Mumbai on 2 June 2020. The cyclones with extreme characterization, and their rapidification, and rising frequency of incidences of excessive rainfall arise mainly because of changes in temperature on land and sea. Such extreme events render millions of people homeless, destroy standing crops and valuable plants, and wipe away the dividend of development of infrastructure over the past many years for improving the lives of the people, ending up with colossal destruction or wasting of our environmental and man-made capital.

India is also now witnessing forest fires in the Himalayan state of Uttarakhand. Thousands of people were battling the fire, which had burnt more than 1,900 hectares in that state with more than 400 burning sites. Such events are also attributable to the exceptionally dry nature of the region caused by the low rainfall in the area. Globally, satellite data show that the frequency and scale of forest fires have been increasing over time in recent years. Vast tracts of land in Brazil, Russia, Indonesia, and Africa have been burning for quite some time. While Siberia in Russia, one of the coldest places on earth on the one hand, and the Amazon rain forest – one of the wettest places – are constituting one of the major carbon storages of the planet on the other, the wildfires in the Siberian Forests and the Amazon rain forests are causing deep anxiety for our survival and sustainability. Indonesian forests, which are also experiencing fires, are the most bio-diverse and oldest tropical forests globally. The fires produce smoke and haze, causing health hazards and loss of biodiversity, contributing to the erosion of both biodiversity and the environmental capital stock of the planet.

However, this is not all. There were swarms of locusts devouring vast tracts of our crop fields in western India. These locusts originating from Africa travelled across the Middle East, entered India on 11 April 2020 via Pakistan's Sind province, and had damaged 90,000 hectares as of 2 June 2020 in districts of Rajasthan alone. These locusts threatened to do much more damage as their inexorable flight continued across the states of our subcontinent and other countries.

The combined impact of all these extreme events is likely to be huge, if not disastrous or devastating, in terms of loss of life, asset, and livelihood. Does an underlying common causality or driving factor as experienced in India, accidental or otherwise, connect such coincidence of pandemic virus-borne disease, forest fire, cyclones, and locust attack? Even if these events are coincidental by accident, the coincidence itself constitutes a message sent by nature warning about the deep malady with potent dangerous and devastating impact in the contingent event of such coincidence. However, the commonality among the driving factors of all these events that can be traced is that they are all caused by human interventions in the form of overuse of resources or bio-capacity of the local and global ecosystems. The *Guardian*, London, 25 March 2020 issue, reported the observation of the United Nations Environment Chief Inger Anderson as 'humanity was placing too many pressures on the natural world with damaging consequences and warned that failing to take care of the planet meant not taking care of ourselves'.[2]

The global heating and the destruction of the natural world for farming, mining, infrastructure construction, and housing have driven wildlife into contact with humans. The destruction of wildlife habitats and the ongoing climate change are hurting humanity, COVID-19 being a 'clear warning shot'. It is, in fact, the concern of zoologists and medical scientists that far more deadly diseases than COVID-19 exist in wildlife (Settele et al. 2020: Johnson et al. 2020) and that today's civilization was 'playing with fire'. They think that it was always human behaviour responsible for diseases that spill over to humans from zoonotic sources (*The Guardian*, 25 March 2020).[2]

## 3.1 Deforestation, Biodiversity Loss, Globalization, and COVID-19

According to the United Nations, a substantial total natural forest area of 290 million hectares was lost between 1990 and 2015. This deprived billions of large or small animals, birds, insects, and other micro-organisms who lost their habitats. This deforested area compares land size almost with India's (328 million hectares) (FAO and UNEP 2020). The consequent current rate of loss of biodiversity on land in this age of *Anthropocene* is now estimated to be 100–1,000 times faster than during any preceding *geological* age before the arrival of *Homo sapiens* (Dogra 2020). However, it should also be noted that apart from deforestation, climate change has also forced animals to come close to humans who created opportunities for pathogens in animal bodies to get new hosts in the human body (Bernstein of Harvard School of Public Health as quoted in *The Guardian*, 25 March 2020).

It may be noted that since the turn of the century, many new diseases have been linked to the transmission of microbes from animals, birds, and other life forms to human beings. A Middle Eastern Respiratory Syndrome (MERS), severe acute respiratory syndrome (SARS), COVID-19, the avian flu, Swine flu, Zika virus, West Nile virus, etc. are examples of such zoonotic diseases caused by pathogens of various kinds jumping from animals to humans. These viruses often emerge in one country and place and mutate and get transmitted and established in other regions and continents. Increased interactions between the human population and these pathogens (containing these viruses) from zoonotic sources due to deforestation, economic growth, and climate and socio-cultural changes have increased the possibility of the outbreak of virus-related diseases among the human population (Wong et al. 2020, Ye et al. 2020, Everard et al. 2020). Experts like Anderson of the United Nations Environment Programme (UNEP) opined that 75% of all emerging infectious diseases come from wildlife. The fatality rates in such diseases are often very high (much higher than COVID-19), like 50% for Ebola, and 60–70% for Nipah virus, which is transmitted from bats in South Asia. But the serious problem is that we do not have an adequate understanding of the source or origin of these viruses or the nature of their mutation and their fatality implications for humans. It is like the throw of a dice to get the answer to any question. The phenomenon is not only random but also so uncertain that the latter cannot be modelled using the calculus of probability (Andrew Cunningham of the Zoological Society of London).[3]

It is to be noted further that habitat destruction is not the only reason for biodiversity loss and the transmission of pathogens from animals to humans. The shift of human preferences in some countries and cultures favouring consuming meat of exotic wild animals resulted in the wet market of butchering, transporting, and selling live wild animals. Globalization has further promoted the transportation of such animals to far and wide places across countries in cramped and unhygienic conditions. Such animals are often transported in stressed and immune-suppressed conditions, causing the excretion of pathogens from their bodies. When people are visiting and working in such markets and coming into intimate contact with the body fluids of animals, it leads to an ideal situation for the emergence of a mixing bowl for the origin of diseases (Andrew Cunningham as quoted in *The Guardian*, 25 March 2020). The ease of fast travel makes the spread of such diseases possible, which are most highly infectious from human to human and pose the threat of emergence of a pandemic. Sub-Saharan Africa and several Asian countries have developed such wet markets that have led to the fast spread of virus-related diseases. A wet market in China's Wuhan province is suspected to be the source of COVID-19.

Besides, the profit motive across developed countries often drives the behaviour of the people involved in the concerned production and trade activities to keep farm animals, including poultry chickens, etc. in cruel and unhygienic conditions to reduce costs. To cater to the rapidly changing food habits of developing countries and meet growing demand in the meat industry, the animals are being fed with products and chemicals to fatten them quickly. This leads to a high-risk situation that may cause the spread of some diseases through the harmful elements flowing from domesticated animal bodies (including poultry products) into humans along the food chain.

The market-driven forces induced by globalization have further caused the harvest and trade of many birds, animals, fruits, and vegetables for their meat or exotic value (including medicinal ones) and their sowing or replantation in new locations. However, once they are outside their native habitat, of which they were intrinsic parts, such biotic species of plants and animals can no longer be part of the natural ecosystem. Such interventions can disturb the natural ecosystem cycles, leading to unpredictable consequences concerning the health of humans or the ecosystem (Dogra 2020).

## 3.2 Human Intervention, Nonlinearity of Ecosystem's Functioning, and Ecological Link of the Current Pandemic

The destruction of forests, fast loss of species – both plants and animals – and the market-driven trade of biotic species and their artificial cultivation led to the erosion of the biosphere and emergence and spread of various diseases in this era, as outlined above. However, humans are embedded in the biosphere as an integral part of it. One may ask how human behaviour can so evolve that it may be held responsible for the loss and exacerbation of the process of biodiversity loss. This can, however, happen because of two reasons: (a) human intervention to change in land use pattern of the ecosystem for economic development, and (b) nonlinearity of the ecosystem's functioning (Dasgupta 2021, Report on the Economics of Biodiversity).

Most human activities of appropriation of resources, particularly those involving land use changes, cause fragmentation of ecosystems. The sum of productivities of such fragmented ecosystems would be less than that of the integrated, undivided one. Most of the deforestation by way of clearing of strips of forest land for agriculture and human settlements, setting up of fences fragmenting grassland preventing migration of animals, development of mines, township or building up of linear infrastructures like railways and road systems, etc. cause fragmentation of the forest ecosystem.

In the water areas too, freshwater habitats of vertebrates, including fishes, are also adversely affected in their reproduction and growth by constructing dams for irrigation and electricity, which disturbs and fragments water flows, adversely affecting hydrological cycles. The living planet index[4] shows that dams have altered 50% of existing water flows worldwide. This share will go up to 90% if future dam projects are implemented, fragmenting freshwater hydrology further. Fragmentation obstructs fish migration routes critical for spawning and feeding, and dispersal, leading to biodiversity loss.

The impact of all such fragmentations falls heavily on the habitats of a variety of animal species, including birds, insects, and tree-dwelling and other bigger animals, all of which play a crucial role through their interdependences in the integrity and functioning of the ecosystem. Paleobiologists warn us about the implications of such habitat loss as early signals of biodiversity loss.

The nonlinearity of the ecosystem's functioning makes, on the other hand, its processes quite complex, leading to the emergence of several niches of locally stable eco-regimes along its dynamic path. Once caught in one of these locally stable regimes, the ecosystem would remain there until a big shock comes to displace it, depending on its resilience. The nonlinearity also causes segmentation of the population of species across eco-regimes as might have unfolded over time and spatially separated places which result in the extinction of the species. The accumulation of erosion of bio-capacity of an ecosystem through fragmentation of ecosystems, habitat loss and extinction of species because of human interventions push the ecosystem to a tipping point beyond which it would flip on to a new eco-regime (moving from one niche to another of locally stable eco-regime) representing irreversible changes of its characteristics and processes (The Economics of Biodiversity: The Dasgupta Review 2021. Dasgupta 2021).

However, the erosion of the biosphere in terms of its biodiversity reduces fundamentally the resilience of its ecosystems and makes them vulnerable when exposed to any exogenous shocks through human interventions, as referred to above. There may be a shift in the regime of the ecosystem, which may be catastrophic in nature and lead to disruption of supplies of our food, water, and climate, raising serious concerns about our health and life support sustainability. The coronavirus pandemic is an illustrative case of a fallout of such shift of eco-regime as fundamentally driven by the fast loss of biodiversity and erosion of bio-capacity.

Moreover, the processes driving the spread of infectious diseases like COVID-19 are also nonlinear. With globalization, humans' ability to intrude into any ecological niche occupied by various organisms with which we have not evolved has exposed us to new, unfamiliar pathogens. The biodiversity loss creates niches for pathogens waiting on the side wings in small numbers to explode into a large population and creates conditions for new pathogens to evolve through mutations as part of a nonlinear process. The continuous or too frequent mutations of the strains of viruses like COVID-19 make the situation highly challenging for the virologists and epidemiologists to precisely pinpoint the nature of origin or cause of the disease and the process of its spread. The nonlinearity of behaviour of COVID-19 is such that it is becoming extremely challenging to remove uncertainty regarding the future evolution of the spread, the invention of vaccine, and its control and treatment, explaining the currently unacceptable fatality rate of the disease. Besides, the quantitative studies regarding the transmission of infectious disease point to the fact that the wide-scale movement of people and goods has made the socio-ecological system quite fragile. The human economies in this era of global integration through the mobility of goods and people have eroded the modularity of our socio-economic system and facilitated the emergence of the current pandemic from the invasion of coronavirus from zoonotic sources on cells of the human body in one part of the world, the disturbance soon reverberating around the globe. In view of all these originating from human pressure and nonlinearity of behaviour of ecosystem, one may wonder: can this current pandemic of COVID-19 be described as a Malthusian event?

## 3.3 Malthusianism and COVID-19

Human society is embedded in the biosphere as part of the totality of the ecosystem of the planet. The coronavirus pandemic, as a fallout of the loss of biodiversity, is causing such fast spread of the disease and such high rate of fatality (ratio of deaths to cases of virus infection) that it shows the fragility of our ecosystem and signs of erosion of its resilience with reference to the protection of human health. The famous book authored by Malthus, *An Essay on the Principle of Population* (1798), had a great influence on the development of the classical political economy and even on Darwin's theory of evolution. The essential idea of the book was that the growth of population in an economy would be limited by the carrying capacity of nature in terms of bounds on food supply. According to Malthus, the natural fertility of women under the condition of long-run equilibrium subsistence wage rate and the environmental socio-cultural condition of that time put up such resistance as would contribute towards the realization of some underlying exogenous base rate of growth of population in geometric progression. On the other hand, he considered that the growth of food production and supply would be in arithmetic progression due to the fixity and scarcity of land of good quality, which is responsible for the diminishing returns to land.

As the growth of the population is to outpace that of food supply, the environmental resistance factors would result in acute scarcity of food, soaring food prices, rise in poverty, famine, war, diseases, and pestilence. These would exercise positive checks on Malthusian population growth in the form of its crash. The most cited examples of Malthusian checks have been the black deaths brought about by bubonic and pneumonic plague that ravaged late medieval Europe from the 14th century for about 150 years. These had been preceded by overpopulation in Western Europe, while the Mongol invasion from Asia had already resulted in population trauma a century earlier, i.e., in the 13th century. The positive checks of Malthusianism created conditions of underpopulation, greater productivity growth, and lower economic inequality in society, creating conditions for the emergence of early capitalism in 15th-century Europe. Some historians even argue that World War I was a Malthusian event driven by the conditions of too many unsustainably large families in large parts of Europe (although not in France) (Keith Rankin in *Scoop*, 27 March 2020).[5]

However, Malthus's principle was good analytics but bad futurology. Malthus's prediction did not come true because of migrations from Europe to North and Latin America, New Zealand, and Australia, on the one hand, and the advancement of science and technology leading to both agricultural and industrial revolutions from the 17th century to the 18th century onwards on the other. The latter gave fossil fuels, electricity, rail and road transport, and new agricultural technology. All these raised land and labour productivity and efficiency of energy use dramatically and led to revolutionary changes in the facility of transportation and communication, facilitating food security through the higher food supply. As a fallout of all these, humankind developed preventive checks on population growth which became more important and led to the development of a new culture where the normative living standard for the masses became substantively higher than the Malthusian subsistence minimum. The emerging industrial capitalism required the emergence of a free labour market, more egalitarian distribution of income and consumption than as prevailing in the preceding feudal era so that the mass production of manufacturing industries could be supported by mass spending. These led to a demographic transition induced by the rise of consumption norms above the subsistence one and its influence on reproductive preferences regarding family size and choice. The emergence of the welfare state of the 20th century has been the culmination of the socio-economic process, which ensured adequate preventive checks on population growth and protection of human life and living.

There was, however, a return of Malthusianism in the late 1960s and early 1970s with the publications of neo-Malthusian writings like *Tragedy of Commons* (Hardin 1998), *Population Bomb* (Ehrlich 1968), and the *Club of Rome Report: Limits to Growth* (Meadows et al. 1972). All these writings focused on how the interrelated issues of human numbers, overuse of natural resources, and use of the commons of a society play a role in determining the sustainability of life support and the livelihood and economic well-being of people of an economy. They point out that it is not merely the relation between population size and food supply but the relationship among population, resource use, pollution, and the state of environmental capital stock which would be critical for the vulnerability of the common mass. This induced the scientists to take initiatives to develop measures of environmental stress (ecological footprint or carbon footprint) and its relationship with both human number and human activities and particularly consumption patterns.

How would we situate the COVID-19 pandemic in the wider context of sustainability and development? We made some empirical investigation to find out if the total number of cases of infection per million population and its fatality per million population have any relationship with some variables (on a priori ground) like per capita GDP, population density, the share of the urban population, the share of elderly and young population, tests per million population, health infrastructure as indicated by per capita health expenditure, and international tourist arrivals. The results of pairwise correlations using global cross-country data of 214 number countries for 2020[6] between the rate of prevalence and that of fatality of the disease with each of these causal variables (estimates of the correlation coefficients along with the level of statistical significance) are reported in Table 3.2.

We find no statistically significant correlation between cases of infection or cases of fatality with population density. However, it is found that both the number of cases and the number of deaths per million population are significantly positively correlated with the share of the urban population in the total population of a country.

However, it is also important to note that per capita GDP, the share of the urban population, tests per million population, and per capita health expenditure have all significant positive correlations with both the cumulative number of cases and death per million population. Again, the share of the elderly population is found to have a significant positive correlation (and the share of the younger population (children) to have a significant negative correlation) with the number of cases and number of deaths per million population and with GDP per capita. On the other hand, health expenditure per capita is found to be positively and significantly related to the rate of prevalence of the disease, the rate of death per million population, GDP per capita, tests per million population, and the share of the elderly population. That such a positive correlation as obtained at cross-country level is not surprising since the coverage of data of the present pandemic shows that the highly advanced high-income countries with high per capita GDP and better health infrastructure were earlier adversely affected and suffered physically more given the history of travel or spread of the virus-borne disease across countries. Besides, some of the results of correlations, though counter-intuitive, can be explained by the inter-correlation of some explanatory variables, given the history of the spread of the pandemic across the countries. These correlations cannot explain the cause or origin of the outbreak of the disease but only reflect the degree of cross-section association among the concerned variables as revealed by the data on the state of spread and fatality in the period and the countries covered. The proper explanation of the dynamics of the pandemic requires, in fact, more

*Table 3.2* Correlation matrix for countries

| | *Cumulative number of cases per million population* | *Cumulative number of deaths per million population* | *GDP per capita, PPP§* | *Population density* | *Urban share of population* | *Share of elderly population (%) #* | *Share of children in total population (%) @* | *Tests per million population* | *Health expenditure per capita, 2017 @@* | *International tourist arrival 2018 ##* |
|---|---|---|---|---|---|---|---|---|---|---|
| Cumulative number of cases per million population | 1 | | | | | | | | | |
| Cumulative number of deaths per million population | 0.732$^{***}$ (0.000) | 1 | | | | | | | | |
| GDP per capita, PPP* | 0.474$^{***}$ (0.000) | 0.256$^{***}$ (0.001) | 1 | | | | | | | |
| Population density | −0.0295 (0.687) | −0.0825 (0.259) | 0.472$^{***}$ (0.000) | 1 | | | | | | |
| Urban share of population | 0.432$^{***}$ (0.000) | 0.373$^{***}$ (0.000) | 0.655$^{***}$ (0.000) | 0.207$^{**}$ (0.004) | 1 | | | | | |
| Share of elderly population (%) # | 0.404$^{***}$ (0.000) | 0.433$^{***}$ (0.000) | 0.542$^{***}$ (0.000) | 0.0597 (0.431) | 0.448$^{***}$ (0.000) | 1 | | | | |
| Share of children in total population (%) @ | −0.519$^{***}$ (0.000) | −0.413$^{***}$ (0.000) | −0.676$^{***}$ (0.000) | −0.182$^{*}$ (0.016) | −0.573$^{***}$ (0.000) | −0.814$^{***}$ (0.000) | 1 | | | |
| Tests per million population | 0.391$^{***}$ (0.000) (0.289) | 0.154$^{*}$ (0.024) (0.147) | 0.674$^{***}$ (0.000) (0.000) | 0.0983 (0.178) (0.374) | 0.453$^{***}$ (0.000) (0.833) | 0.401$^{***}$ (0.000) (0.000) | −0.496$^{***}$ (0.000) (0.000) | 1 (0.175) | | |
| Health expenditure per capita, 2017 @@ | 0.563$^{***}$ (0.000) | 0.444$^{***}$ (0.000) | 0.872$^{***}$ (0.000) | 0.141 (0.070) | 0.614$^{***}$ (0.000) | 0.688$^{***}$ (0.000) | −0.641$^{***}$ (0.000) | 0.595$^{***}$ (0.000) | 1 | |
| International tourist arrival 2018 ## | 0.149 (0.064) | 0.287$^{***}$ (0.000) | 0.325$^{***}$ (0.000) | 0.0797 (0.327) | 0.269$^{***}$ (0.001) | 0.411$^{***}$ (0.000) | −0.369$^{***}$ (0.000) | 0.103 (0.202) | 0.431$^{***}$ (0.000) | 1 |

Source: https://www.worldometers.info/coronavirus/ and World Development Indicators as accessed on 19 November 2020.

Note: § constant 2017 international $ for 2018, # population ages 65 years and above, 2018, @ population ages 0–14 years, 2018, @@ PPP (current international $), ## in thousands. Figures in the parenthesis show the level of significance. * $p < 0.05$, ** $p < 0.01$, *** $p < 0.001$. Data on the cumulative number of cases per million population, cumulative number of deaths per million population, and tests per million population are collected on 19 November 2020. Cumulative number refers with base on 22 January 2020. Urbanization represents the urban population as % of the total population. Population density represents people per square kilometre of land area in 2018.

epidemiological analysis at both the micro and macro public health levels. Finally, the international tourist arrival is found to be positively correlated with the rate of fatality as well as with GDP per capita, which is supported by intuition on a priori ground.

Since multiple factors might have influenced the infection and fatality rates, multiple regression models were also estimated based on the same cross-section data whose coverage also included some possible determining variables other than population density like per capita GDP, share of urban population, share of the elderly population, and share of children in the population, health expenditure per capita, and international tourist arrival. The results of the models which were significant with reasonable explanatory power are presented in Table 3.3. The results show that the

*Table 3.3* Estimated coefficients from the multiple regression models

| | *Coefficient* | *P > \|t\|* |
|---|---|---|
| **Equation 1: Cumulative number of cases per million population** | | |
| GDP per capita, PPP (constant 2017 international $) 2018 | 0.0753 | 0.125 |
| Urban population (% of total population) | 122.4* | 0.011 |
| Share of elderly population (%) (age 65 and above) | –447.0 | 0.057 |
| Share of children in total population (%) (age 14 or less) | –368.0* | 0.034 |
| Dummy variable for region (Omitted: sub-Saharan Africa) | | |
| Europe and Central Asia | –8626.1** | 0.006 |
| East Asia, Pacific, and South Asia | 9355.7** | 0.006 |
| Middle East and North Africa | 3330.3 | 0.25 |
| Latin South America | 5580.1 | 0.103 |
| Middle East and North Africa | 9087.7 | 0.195 |
| North America | 1678.3 | 0.666 |
| Constant | 12499.6 | 0.123 |
| Number of observations | | 167 |
| Adjusted $R^2$ | | 0.482 |
| **Equation 2: Cumulative number of deaths per million population** | | |
| GDP per capita, PPP (constant 2017 international $) 2018 | –0.00189 | 0.085 |
| Urban population (% of total population) | 3.935** | 0.001 |
| Life expectancy at birth, total (years) 2018 | 3.719* | 0.023 |
| International tourist arrival (in thousands) 2018 | 0.00385** | 0.003 |
| Dummy variable for region (Omitted: sub-Saharan Africa) | | |
| Europe and Central Asia | –149.5* | 0.032 |
| East Asia, Pacific, and South Asia | 154.0* | 0.015 |
| Middle East and North Africa | 194.5** | 0.002 |
| Latin South America | –56.66 | 0.487 |
| Middle East and North Africa | 181.5 | 0.286 |
| North America | 12.36 | 0.907 |
| Constant | –358.4** | 0.002 |
| Number of observations | | 143 |
| Adjusted $R^2$ | | 0.404 |

Source: *Author's estimation.*

Note: *** represents the level of significance at 1%, ** represents the level of significance at 5% and, * represents the level of significance at 10% level. Cumulative number of cases and deaths refers to the data collected on 19 November 2020 with base on 22 January 2020.

*Table 3.4* Correlation results for Indian states

| | *Cumulative number of confirmed cases per thousand population* | *Cumulative number of deaths per thousand population* | *Population density* | *Share of urban population* | *Total public health expenditure as % of GSDP (2016–2017)* | *HDI* |
|---|---|---|---|---|---|---|
| Cumulative number of confirmed cases per thousand population | 1 | | | | | |
| Cumulative number of deaths per thousand population | 0.896*** (0.000) | 1 | | | | |
| Population density | 0.520** (0.003) | 0.519** (0.003) | 1 | | | |
| Share of urban population | 0.734*** (0.000) | 0.730*** (0.000) | 0.798*** (0.000) | 1 | | |
| Total public health expenditure as % of GSDP (2016–2017) | –0.204 (0.280) | –0.335 (0.070) | –0.341 (0.070) | –0.365* (0.047) | 1 | |
| HDI | 0.628*** (0.000) | 0.572*** (0.001) | 0.393* (0.029) | 0.686*** (0.000) | –0.121 (0.522) | 1 |

Source: Author's estimation based on data accessed from Ministry of Health and Family Welfare, Government of India, Census 2011, RBI state finances and Global Data Lab, Radboud University. Data related to COVID-19 is accessed on 19 November 2020.

Note: $p$-values in parentheses; * $p < 0.05$, ** $p < 0.01$, *** $p < 0.001$

cumulative number of cases per million population can be explained using cross-country data in terms of the share of urban population having a positive significant partial regression coefficient and share of children in population with a significant negative population, and the dummies representing the fixed effects of the regions of Europe and Central Asia with significant negative and those of East Asia, Pacific, and South Asia which have positive significant partial regression coefficient with overall adjusted $R$-square 0.482 (the omitted region as the base of comparison for regional fixed effect in the model being sub-Saharan Africa).

For the model explaining the cumulative number of deaths per million population, it is the share of the urban population, the life expectancy at birth, and international tourist arrivals, which have all significant positive partial regression coefficients. In contrast, the regional dummy for Europe and Central Asia on the one hand and those of (a) East Asia, Pacific, and South Asia, and (b) of the Middle East and North Africa on the other have negative and positive partial effects, respectively (with sub-Saharan Africa being the omitted dummy variable as the base of regional comparison), adjusted $R$-square being 0.404.

We also made an empirical investigation to explore the determining factors of the prevalence and fatality of the disease in India. We, however, could only get some results on simple pairwise correlations between prevalence rate or the fatality rate per thousand population and the possible determining factors like population density, and share of the urban population in total, and the share of public health expenditure in the gross state domestic product for the year 2016–2017. The results are presented in Table 3.4. However, we have not attempted to make any multiple regression analysis with the state-level data for India because of the limitedness of cross-section sample size in the context of our analysis.

## 3.4 COVID-19: A Neo-Malthusian Message

Our limited empirical study points out that the current pandemic of COVID-19 is not a Malthusian event. Although population pressure is not a significant explanatory factor for COVID-19 or its scale, the event still has a neo-Malthusian message. Malthus's major concern had been that the population size would exceed the carrying capacity of the ecosystem where the latter is defined in terms of the capacity of the land to produce food, i.e., the maximum size of the population that can be fed with a subsistence food basket. The fixity of land and the Ricardian law of diminishing returns can explain the population size without preventive checks to overshoot the carrying capacity. Neo-Malthusians do not define the carrying capacity of the ecosystem in terms of the capacity of food production but in terms of the ecosystem's potential capacity of resource supply to support human consumption of various kinds of goods and services and waste absorption, including change of land use for building up fixed infrastructure or changing product mix of the economy as per the changing preference structure of the people with the growth of income and change in technology. This should also include the requirement of land use change for carbon sequestration of the carbon dioxide that is unabsorbed by the ocean or existing photosynthetic green cover. The concept of an ecological footprint as defined and estimated globally and country-wise by the Global Footprint Network[7] captures this appropriation of all such demand for resources and eco-services expressed in units of land use of various types as normalized aggregate in terms of per capita cropland of average photosynthetic productivity. Given the availability of land for various types of uses, the regenerative capacity or bio-capacity of a country or the earth can be taken to be the aggregate of availabilities of crop land, pasture, forest, water area (both inland and coastal) of fisheries, etc. in a similar normalized unit for meeting the need of resource supply for the humans. In case the ecological footprint exceeds bio-capacity, the measure of excess can be called the bio-deficit of our ecosystem. Emergence and growth of bio-deficit would lead to the erosion of our biosphere with the following possible consequences:

(a) Overharvesting of resources of biosphere, leading to depletion of the biotic stock of plants and animals in the land and water area and loss of biodiversity.
(b) Enlargement of carbon footprint due to rise in the concentration of unabsorbed carbon dioxide in the atmosphere, causing global warming and climate change.
(c) Deprivation of livelihood and basic needs for the poor and marginalized section of the population who do not have the property right over land and other natural resources and therefore can share only disproportionately very small share of the benefit of bio-capacity of the ecosystem, thus limiting of their share of total ecological footprint. Such people will suffer from poverty, hunger, malnutrition, disease, and premature death, as experienced in many poor developing countries of Afro-Asia. The market-driven neoliberal regime in these countries ensures the struggle for ultimately limited finite natural resources of this planet, ending up with the Darwinian survival of the fittest.

It is to be noted here that these consequences are interactive with each other. For example, climate change resulting in extreme events of cyclones, floods, and sea-level rise and submergence of coastal areas would lead to the destruction of habitats of wildlife, plants, and animal species and their eventual extinction. Sustainable development would thus require the human system to operate within the operational limit of the biosphere's capacity. As the world population exceeded the 6 billion mark around the year 2000, and the ecological footprint as per the Global Footprint Network's demonstration overshot the bio-capacity of the earth in the late 1960s itself, the ecological footprint of humanity reached a value of 1.7 of our planet in 2016.[7] We have been therefore heavily drawing down the stock of our biosphere resources since the date of overshoot in the 1960s. COVID-19, as we have seen in the earlier sections, is a fallout of such a heavy loss of biotic resource stock.

As sustainable development would require social intervention to reverse the trend, it has been important to examine the economics of the linkage of ecological footprint and bio-capacity gap with major developmental variables of an economy. As biodiversity loss is at the core of the current problem of the unsustainability of our development process, Dasgupta (2021) has addressed this important issue in his report on the Economics of Biodiversity for the Government of the United Kingdom.

Dasgupta (2021) takes the measure of ecological footprint to represent the impact of humanity on the biosphere per unit of time. He represents essentially the same measure as defined by the global ecological footprint network alternatively as the ratio of the GDP, or 'Y', to the rate of conversion of resources of the biosphere for supplying inputs to production and absorbing wastes, into GDP denoted by, say '$\alpha$'. However, GDP underestimates the value of contribution of resources to biosphere as there are non-market resources and eco-services which provide human life support and support to economic activities. In any case, we can take ecological footprint to be $Y/\propto = y.N/\propto$ where $N$ is the size of the population of the economy and $y$ per capita GDP or income per unit of time, following Dasgupta (2021).

On the supply side, eco-service is determined by the stock of ecological resources of the biosphere, which grows over time as these resources are regenerative, the size of growth per unit of time, depending on the size of the stock $S$ and can be represented by $G(S)$, $G$ being the rate of regeneration. The excess of ecological footprint over $G(S)$ is the bio-deficit yielded by the impact inequality $N.y/\alpha > G(S)$ (as Dasgupta 2021 called it). The measure of gap causes depletion of the biotic resource stock $S$, which would lower the value of $G(S)$, contributing to the further rise of the bio-deficit if the size of the footprint remains the same. Since $S$ and $G(S)$ are bounded from above as earth is a finite place and entropy law[8] governs the ecological system, the erosion of $S$ is unfolded in the form of deforestation, destruction of habitats of other species, and biodiversity loss. These fundamentally drive the degradation of both human health and the health (regenerative ability) of the ecosystem. The emergence and alarming rate of spread of the infectious disease COVID-19 thus gives a warning signal of humanity's crossing the safe operational limits of functioning of the biosphere.

For the long-term durable solution to preventing such pandemic diseases as COVID-19, it is important that we attain the condition of sustainable development. This implies the requirement that the impact inequality

($\frac{N.y}{\alpha} > 1.7G(S)$), as existing in 2019 (Dasgupta 2021), be converted into impact equality ($\frac{N.y}{\alpha} = G(S)$) over a chosen time horizon. If we assume that the United Nations prescribed Sustainable Development Goal is to be attained by 2030,[9] Dasgupta's report points out that given the growth rate of global GDP per capita at the rate of 3.4% and the rate of decline of global natural capital stock at the rate 0.3% per annum as experienced over the period 1992–2014, such conversion of impact inequality into equality would require 'α' to grow at the rate of 9.1% per annum. This is going to be a tall order given the fact that the historical rate of growth of such economic productivity of bio-resources has been 2.5% per annum. Dasgupta's report also points out that even in a situation of zero growth of global GDP and no decline of natural capital stock from now onwards, the growth requirement of the productivity parameter would be 5.4% per annum. One can generate alternative scenarios of dynamics of impact inequality depending on the alternative growth rate of global GDP and pace of conservation of bio-resources and bio-capacity. At the same time, the ultimate choice will have to be left to be political. In any case, the conversion of impact inequality into equality would require massive investment in the coming days in science and technology, research and development for both restructuring the economy and conservation of resources and raising the productivity of our ecosystems. Such measures will have to include measures for biodiversity conservation by containing all fragmentation of ecosystems and controlling the impact of non-linearity in their behaviour. These are supposed to be required to address the problems of health of both the humans and of the ecosystems of biosphere.

## 3.5 Challenges of Meeting the Existential Crisis: Economic Impact of COVID-19 and Future Opportunities for Sustainability

The different countries of the world are now facing a huge challenge of sustainability because of the existential problem arising from the highly infectious nature of the fast-spreading disease COVID-19. As the virus from the zoonotic source spreads among humans at an exponential rate through contacts and droplets once the virus has jumped onto a new host of the human body, an immediate measure for the control of the spread has required social distancing among people and lockdown of the society ensuring cessation of all movements of people, all assemblages, and therefore that of all production or economic activities. Such measures have led everywhere to loss of employment and income, disrupting demand for goods and services on the one hand and disruption of the supply chain due to stoppage of production activities on the other. The two disruptions further have caused, in turn, disruption of the capital market, which is plagued by various types of uncertainties. The economies are thus pushed into recession due to a fall in effective demand, investments, and growth propagated through inter-sectoral input–output linkages caused by such disturbances and turmoil. The policy for saving life thus inevitably leads to a situation of a trade-off between life and livelihood or economic survival of the people. However, the purpose of such measures of physical control of normal human activities is supposed to be of short run-in nature. They are supposed to be meant to buy time for the preparedness of the health and social service infrastructure to cope with the unprecedented and unexpected fast-growing demand for their services. These included facilities on a large scale for testing infection, discovering, and introducing vaccines for the viral disease, treatment in hospital, supply of medicines and personal protection equipment (like masks, gloves, face shields, lab overcoats, etc.), life support oxygen supply equipment, ventilators, etc.

The sudden outbreak of the disease as it first broke out in most countries warranted such drastic measures of command and control, resulting in substantial economic loss. IMF has projected initially minus 3% growth for the global economy for 2020. This describes a far worse situation than that of the 2009 financial crisis. While for the advanced countries the growth rate slumped to minus 6%, the developing countries may experience a growth of minus 1% in the same year of 2020. However, if China is excluded, the growth of developing economies together slumped to minus 2.2% as per IMF projections.[10]

For the Indian economy, the impact of the lockdown of eight weeks from 25 March 2020, as analyzed by Panda (2020), was estimated to cause an overall loss of income of 8% compared to the pre-pandemic 2020–2021 income level. He used a multi-sector input–output model to project the losses of sectoral gross outputs and factor income or GVAs[11] for the shock effects of a reduction in final demand for the products of various sectors due to the lockdown and other precautionary measures for the control of the spread of the disease. His projection implied a slump in the growth rate of 2020–2021 over 2019–2020 to be minus 2.7% per annum. As the GVA data for quarters 1 and 2 are now available in both constant (2011–2012) and current prices for 2020–2021, we have estimated the loss of sectoral and aggregate GVA as per the business-as-usual scenario on the assumption of extrapolation of growth of income for the quarters 1 and 2 of 2020–2021 at the same past rate of the growth rate of GVA as historically realized between 2018–2019 and 2019–2020 for the concerned sectors, and then comparing them with the actual sectoral GVAs in the first two-quarters of 2020–2021. Table 3.5 gives the sector-wise and aggregate percentage loss of income and the estimated rate of decline of income on an annual basis. It is thus found that the loss of income as estimated due to pandemic, among other exogenous factors between the first half of 2019–2020 and the same first-half period 2020–2021, has been overall 18.1%. This has implied the rate of growth of GVA to be minus 14.9% on an annual basis. Table 3.5 further shows that natural resource extraction, manufacturing industry, construction, trade, transport, and hospitality sector are the most adversely

*Table 3.5* Sectoral losses of first half yearly income, decline in growth and employment between 2019–2020 and 2020–2021 (estimates on the basis of constant 2011–2012 prices) due to pandemic and other extraneous factors

| | *Actual GVA of 2019–2020 for Q1+Q2 Rs. Crore** | *Actual GVA of 2020–2021 for Q1+Q2 Rs. Crore** | *BAU GVA of 2020–2021 for Q1+Q2 Rs. Crore** | *% loss of GVA in 2020–2021 Q1 + Q2vis-à-vis BAU sc.* | *% point drop of actual growth rate of GVA of 2020–20 21 Q1 +Q2 vis-à-vis BAU sc. growth* |
|---|---|---|---|---|---|
| 1 Agriculture, forestry, and fishing | 807,601 | 834,897 | 839,905 | 0.6% | 0.6 |
| 2 Natural resources | 161,785 | 133,883 | 166,800 | 19.7% | 20.3 |
| 3 Manufacturing | 1,155,048 | 931,079 | 1,155,395 | 9.4% | 19.4 |
| 4 Construction | 506,920 | 35,3871 | 513,510 | 31.1% | 31.5 |
| 5 Electricity and water supply | 161,153 | 158,928 | 167,760 | 5.3% | 5.5 |
| 6 Trade, Hotels, transport and communication | 1242,469 | 850,784 | 1,287,198 | 33.9% | 35.1 |
| 7 Financial, real estate and professional services | 1,668,296 | 1,555,486 | 1,745,038 | 10.9% | 11.4 |
| 8 Public administration, defence and other services | 882,579 | 782,982 | 970,837 | 19.3% | 21.3 |
| All sectors | 6,585,851 | 5,601,910 | 6,842,699 | 18.1% | 18.8 |

Source: Estimates are based on Press Release by Ministry of Statistics and Programme Implementation (MoSPI) for Q1 and Q2 GVA for 2020–2021 and 2019–2020. Employment elasticity is taken from Misra and Suresh (2014).

Note: * at constant 2011–2012 prices. Q1 and Q2 are Quarters 1 and 2 of the financial year, respectively.

affected sectors in India, suffering percentage losses of 19.7, 19.4, 31.1, and 33.9, respectively.

The impact of the decline in growth rate would have an effect on employment. The projection of the estimated growth rate of income in the first half year of 2020–2021 over the same period of 2019–2020 would imply a decline of overall employment of 2.8% in 2020–2021 over 2019–2020, using the employment elasticity with respect to GVA on the above-estimated rates of growth (Misra and Suresh 2014). This, along with employment estimates from PLFS (Periodic Labour Force Survey), implies that the job loss due to the pandemic during this one year would be a magnitude of around 11.7 million in India.

So far as the impact of lockdown in India is concerned, it is important to further mention the effect on particularly the migrant labourers who have been the worst sufferers. In India, there existed an inter-state migrant population of 5.47 crores as per the 2011 census. Of this migrant population, migrant labourers (including petty self-employed ones) are engaged in unorganized sectors with subsistence income and no social security. They live mostly in slums or slum-like living conditions, entire family mostly living in one-room accommodation with a poor water supply, and sanitary conditions. These people became very vulnerable to all infectious diseases like COVID-19. However, with the announcement of the lockdown, these labourers almost instantly lost their jobs, income, and rented accommodation as they were immediately evicted by their landlords. With their family members, these labourers were forced to return to their homes in different states. At the same time, the government had no planning and preparedness to facilitate the return of these people. The central government announced lockdown thoughtlessly at 4 hours' notice, without having any preparedness for transportation of such a substantial migrant population estimated by the World Bank to be 40 million (World Bank 2020) left in the lurch initially (*Economic Times* 25–26 June 2020).[12] As a result of such a desperate situation, such people began to walk or take a ride by truck or any motorized vehicle paying excessive charges in order to return to their respective homes. Many of them suffered from hunger and exhaustion and fell ill or collapsed to death on the way, as reported widely in the media. The government was ultimately forced to arrange buses and trains to transport these migrant labourers because of adverse media reporting revealing the truth. However, these migrants had to be herded into these transports throwing the social distancing norms to the wind. This resulted in many returning migrants reaching their destination with COVID-19 infections. This has aggravated the disease situation in the destination home state, although the situation varied across the states.

### *3.5.1 What Is the Way Ahead?*

First of all, how deep or prolonged is the current economic depression caused by the pandemic of COVID-19 going to be? This will depend on two factors:

1. Exit policies of lockdown of the countries depending on their assessment of trade-off between life and livelihood.
2. What kind of fiscal and monetary incentives or reliefs are provided by the governments of the concerned countries? As we are aware, the governments of Japan, the United States, China, Sweden, Germany, and India, among others, have offered financial packages of relief amounting to 21.1%, 13%, 12%, 10.7%, and 10% of GDP, respectively.

These reliefs would be helpful in recovering of the economies by alleviating the suffering of losing jobs by the common people in the pandemic by the provision of reliefs in various forms and incentivizing the business to restart operations and spending both on current and capital accounts.

However, as the social security, health, and social infrastructural conditions are much worse in developing countries than the advanced industrialized ones, the overall human development impact of the current pandemic, despite such relief packages, would be worse for the former. This would underline the need for vast improvement of the social security condition of the Indian common people and health and other social infrastructural condition by raising the share of spending on these sectors as a share of GDP to be able to better withstand the impact of any such extreme event in future. These issues have been long neglected as the business-as-usual suffering of common people due to poverty, and health insecurity is politically acceptable to be normal in India despite our political democracy. This pandemic has revealed our weaknesses and makes the provision and improvement in social security imperative for the survival of our people and the improvement of both robustness and resilience of our health and socio-economic system in the event of external shocks in future due to extreme natural and disease-related event.

We in India and people in many other countries are still in the various stages of the pandemic COVID-19. Table 3.6 shows how the growth of confirmed cases of infection per day has risen from the period 25 March to 15 July 2020 to the period 15 July to 19 November 2020 for different states in India. It shows that the growth of cases per day for all India was 8,353.7 in the first period (25 March to 15 July) to 63,669.1 per day between the periods 15 July and 19 November 2020. As the trend of infection and fatality is still not declining due to mutation of the virus and emergence of new strains, we are confronted with a hard choice between saving life by isolating people and easing restrictions to save the livelihood and income of the poor.

## 3.6 Concluding Remarks

The preceding sections of this chapter have pointed out that the COVID-19 pandemic and other extreme natural events that India is experiencing have disrupted the ecological balance between human appropriation of resources of the biosphere and bio-capacity of our ecosystem. This has resulted in biodiversity loss and climate change, which are again interactive. These events

*Table 3.6* Per day growth of cumulative number of confirmed cases of COVID-19 infection per day during 25 March–15 July 2020 and 15 July–19 November 2020

| | *Per day growth in cumulative number of confirmed cases of COVID-19 infections in India* | |
|---|---|---|
| | *Between 25 March 2020 and 15 July 2020* | *Between 15 July 2020 and 19 November 2020* |
| Andaman and Nicobar Island | 1.5 | 35.1 |
| Andhra Pradesh | 294.7 | 6,542.7 |
| Arunachal Pradesh | 4.1 | 122.9 |
| Assam | 159.0 | 1,532.2 |
| Bihar | 172.1 | 1,655.1 |
| Chandigarh | 5.3 | 123.5 |
| Chhattisgarh | 39.1 | 1,674.9 |
| Delhi | 1,029.6 | 3,077.3 |
| Goa | 24.6 | 346.0 |
| Gujarat | 389.3 | 1,174.6 |
| Haryana | 201.9 | 1,463.6 |
| Himachal Pradesh | 11.7 | 238.8 |
| Jammu & Kashmir | 99.6 | 738.0 |
| Jharkhand | 36.5 | 814.7 |
| Karnataka | 393.2 | 6,522.7 |
| Kerala | 78.8 | 4,214.2 |
| Madhya Pradesh | 169.6 | 1,330.6 |
| Maharashtra | 2,388.8 | 11,824.2 |
| Manipur | 14.9 | 1,63.9 |
| Meghalaya | 2.8 | 83.7 |
| Mizoram | 2.1 | 26.0 |
| Nagaland | 8.0 | 75.2 |
| Odisha | 127.5 | 2,354.3 |
| Puducherry | 13.7 | 277.3 |
| Punjab | 75.7 | 1,070.5 |
| Rajasthan | 228.0 | 1,641.2 |
| Sikkim | 1.9 | 34.7 |
| Tamil Nadu | 1,315.3 | 4,888.6 |
| Telangana | 336.8 | 1,770.5 |
| Tripura | 19.4 | 238.5 |
| Uttar Pradesh | 354.4 | 3,784.9 |
| Uttarakhand | 32.9 | 520.8 |
| West Bengal | 293.1 | 32,46.4 |
| All India | 8,353.7 | 63,669.1 |

Source: Author's estimation from data collected from Ministry of Health and Family Welfare, Government of India.

posed a challenge to us. Today, we are confronted with a tough choice between life and livelihood and between economic growth and halting erosion of environmental capital stock of the biosphere. This further takes us to the fundamental question: how do we reduce the requirement of growth of the scale of our economy to operate within the safe operating limits of the biosphere system without affecting social well-being? This, in other words, asks for such change in preference structure of the people of society and distribution of their income and wealth that the resulting aggregate demand can limit the demand for the biosphere resources to be used within such bound of the regenerative capacity of the biosphere. The feasibility of such change would depend on our sense of values and ethics concerning the growth, well-being, and sustenance of other species. These would imply our long-run policies to ensure adjustment of our system as described by the people (population with demographic characteristics and reproductive and other health conditions) on the one hand, and the scale, composition, technology, and the architectural design of human organization of economic activities on the other.

Apart from the development of science and technology with a special thrust on the genome and bio-medical research for facilitating the development of vaccine and medicinal treatment, this would require a shift of regime of working practices and reforms of the law, administration, regulatory system, and socio-cultural norms of society. The COVID-19 pandemic has revealed the weakness of our socio-economic system, which involved inefficiencies and wasteful practices and provided us at the same time with the opportunity of introducing such structural changes and reforms which can lead to a more efficient health-wise safe and qualitatively improved new regular post-pandemic socio-economic system. These would correct our old weaknesses and ensure greater robustness and resilience of the new system and order in the event of any future external shock to our system caused by extreme events.

## Acknowledgements

The authors would like to thank Professors Kanchan Chopra and Manoj Panda, former directors of the Institute of Economic Growth, Delhi, for their valuable comments and suggestions on an earlier draft of the chapter. They also thank Dr Achiransu Acharya of Visva-Bharati University, Santiniketan, for his help in providing valuable references on COVID-19.

## Notes

1 Cumulative number refers with a base on 22 January 2020.
2 For more details, please see https://www.theguardian.com/world/2020/mar/25/coronavirus-nature-is-sending-us-a-message-says-un-environment-chief (accessed on 2nd July 2021).
3 For more details, please see https://www.zsl.org/blogs/science/covid-19-the-wildlife-facts (accessed on 3 August 2021).
4 The Living Planet Index (LPI) measures the state of the world's biological diversity based on population trends of vertebrate species from terrestrial, freshwater, and marine habitats. The LPI has been adopted by the Convention of Biological Diversity (CBD) as an indicator of progress towards its 2011–2020 targets to 'take effective and urgent action to halt the loss of biodiversity'. For more details, please see https://livingplanetindex.org/home/index (accessed on 5 August 2021).

5 For details, please see https://www.scoop.co.nz/stories/HL2003/S00228/coronavirus-a-malthusian-event.htm (accessed on 1 September 2021).
6 Country-level data for different socio-economic and demographic indicators depends on data availability. Data is collected for the latest year available. Data related to COVID-19 is for 19 November 2020.
7 For details, see https://www.footprintnetwork.org (accessed on 15 August 2021).
8 In analyzing economy–environment interactions, for example, resource extraction, energy use, production, and generation of wastes, entropy is a useful concept. The entropy law states that with every energy-based transformation, a system loses part of its ability to perform useful mechanical work.
9 For details, see https://sdgs.un.org/goals (accessed on 16 August 2021).
10 For details, see https://blogs.imf.org/2020/04/20/a-global-crisis-like-no-other-needs-a-global-response-like-no-other (accessed on 18 August 2021).
11 Gross value added (GVA) is an economic productivity metric that measures the contribution of a corporate subsidiary, company, or municipality to an economy, producer, sector, or region. GVA is the output of the country less the intermediate consumption, which is the difference between gross output and net output.
12 For details, see https://economictimes.indiatimes.com/news/politics-and-nation/lockdown-in-india-has-impacted-40-million-internal-migrants-world-bank/articleshow/75311966.cms (accessed on 1 September 2021).

## References

Andharia, J. 2019. "Disaster Management: Institutionalizing the Risk Informed Planning." In *The Crisis of Climate Change, IIC Quarterly, Winter 2019*. ISSN No.: 0376-9771. https://almashines.s3.dualstack.ap-southeastamazonaws.com/assets/media/files/266_1590735039_a55c5e5e74c1dd69b00f1488ddfdd49c.pdf (accessed on 24 June 2021).

Dasgupta Review. The Economics of Biodiversity: The Dasgupta Review. 2021. Retrieved from https://www.gov.uk/government/publications/final-report-the-economics-of-biodiversity-the-dasgupta-review (accessed on 1 August 2021).

Dogra, B. 2020. "How Pandemics are linked with Ecological Crises." *Newsclick*. 11 May, 2020. https://www.newsclick.in/COVID-Crisis-Pandemic-Linked-to-ecological-crisis (accessed on 14 June 2021).

Ehrlich, P. 1968. *The Population Bomb*. New York, USA: Ballentine Books.

Everard, M., P. Johnston, D. Santillo, and C. Staddon. 2020. "The Role of Ecosystems in Mitigation and Management of Covid-19 and Other Zoonoses." *Environmental Science & Policy* 111: 7–17. doi:10.1016/j.envsci.2020.05.017.

FAO, and UNEP. 2020. *The State of the World's Forests 2020. Forests, Biodiversity and People*. Rome: FAO and UNEP. https://doi.org/10.4060/ca8642en

The Guardian. 25 March 2020 "Coronavirus: "Nature is Sending us a Message", Says UN Environment Chief." By D. Carrington. .https://www.theguardian.com/world/2020/mar/25/coronavirus-nature-is-sending-us-a-message-says-un-environment-chief. (accessed on 24 June 2021).

Hardin, G. 1998. "The Tragedy of the Commons." In *Managing the Commons*, edited by Baden and Noonan, 3–15. Indiana University Press. https://www.mohfw.gov.in/ https://www.worldometers.info/coronavirus/

Johnson, C. K., P. L. Hitchens, P. S. Pandit, J. Rushmore, T. S. Evans, C. C. Young, and M. M. Doyle. 2020. "Global Shifts in Mammalian Population Trends Reveal Key Predictors of Virus Spillover Risk." *Proceedings of the Royal Society B* 287 (1924): 20192736. doi:10.1098/rspb.2019.2736.

Malthus, T. 1798. *An Essay on the Principle of Population*. London: St. Paul's Church-Yard. http://www.esp.org/books/malthus/population/malthus.pdf (accessed on 11 July 2021).

Meadows, D. H., D. L. Meadows, J. Randers, and W. W. Behrens. 1972. *The Limits to Growth*. New York: Universe Books. ISBN: 0-87663-165-0.

Misra, S., and A. K. Suresh. 2014. "Estimating Employment Elasticity of Growth for the Indian Economy." *RBI Working Paper Series No. 06*. Mumbai: Department of Economic and Policy Research, Reserve Bank of India. https://rbidocs.rbi.org.in/rdocs/Publications/PDFs/06WPSN240614.PDF (accessed on 18 June 2021).

MOSPI. 2020a. Press Note on Estimates of Gross Domestic Product for the Second Quarter (July to September, 2020-2021) http://mospi.nic.in/sites/default/files/press_release/PRESS_NOTE-Q2_2020-21.pdf (accessed on 24 June 2021).

MOSPI. 2020b. Press Note on Provisional Estimates of Annual National Income 2019–2020 and Quarterly Estimates of Gross Domestic Product for the Fourth Quarter (q4) of 2019–2020. http://mospi.nic.in/sites/default/files/press_release/PRESS%20NOTE%20PE%20and%20Q4%20estimates%20of%20GDP.pdf (accessed on 24 June 2021).

Panda, M. 2020. "Growth Scenarios during COVID-19 Pandemic." In *Fighting COVID-19: Assessments and Reflections*, 4–13. Delhi: Institute of Economic Growth. http://iegindia.org/upload/uploadfiles/insight_covid_2.pdf (accessed on 18 June 2021).

Rankin, K. 2020. "Coronavirus – A Malthusian Event?" *Scoop*. 27 March, 2020. https://www.scoop.co.nz/stories/HL2003/S00228/coronavirus-a-malthusian-event.htm (accessed on 24 June 2021).

Settele, J et al. 2020. "COVID-19 Stimulus Measures Must Save Lives, Protect Livelihoods, and Safeguard Nature to Reduce the Risk of Future Pandemics."*The Intergovernmental Science-Policy Platform on Biodiversity and Ecosystem Services*. https://ipbes.net/covid19stimulus (accessed on 24 June 2021).

Wong, G, Y. H. Bi, Q. H. Wang, X. W. Chen, Z.-G. Zhang, and Y. G. Yao. 2020. "Zoonotic Origins of Human Coronavirus 2019 (Hcov-19 / SARS-Cov-2): Why Is This Work Important?" *Zoological Research* 41 (3): 213–219. doi:10.24272/j.issn.2095-8137.2020.031.

World Bank. 2020. *World Development Indicators*. https://databank.worldbank.org/source/world-development-indicators (accessed on 10 May 2020).

Ye, Zi-Wei, S. Yuan, K. S. Yuen, S. Y. Fung, C. P. Chan, and D. Y. Jin. 2020. "Zoonotic Origins of Human Coronaviruses." *International Journal of Biological Sciences* 16 (10): 1686–1697. doi:10.7150/ijbs.45472.

Chapter 4

# Electrification and Development

## Empirical Evidence on the Effect of Electricity Provision on Household Welfare

*Ujjayant Chakravorty and Martino Pelli*

### Introduction

Nearly a billion people do not have access to grid electricity despite significant increases in access in the last few decades.[1] Providing these large numbers of people with electricity has major implications. First, it is costly, especially for developing countries with limited budgets and the ability of the consumer to fully pay for these services.[2] Moreover, if electricity is generated by fossil fuels such as coal or even cleaner natural gas, there will be significant adverse impacts on the environment in terms of increased carbon emissions. This is why a focus of recent research in environment and development economics has been to disentangle and study the causal effect of electricity access at the household level. This chapter reviews the current literature on this topic.

In order to interpret the results of the different studies presented here, it is important to clarify what is meant by access to electricity. There are different definitions in circulation. For instance, the Government of India declares a village to be electrified if the following three conditions are met: (i) provision of basic infrastructure such as distribution of transformers and lines in the inhabited locality, (ii) provision of electricity in public places like schools, panchayat offices, health centres, dispensaries, and community centres, and (iii) at least 10% of the total number of households in the village is electrified.[3] On the other hand, the International Energy Agency (IEA) defines access by setting a minimum level of electricity consumption of 250 kWh per year for rural households and 500 kWh for urban households.

China has been at almost 100% access since early this century, yet per capita average consumption started growing only after the year 2000. In India, by 2018, over 90% of the population was considered connected to the grid, yet average consumption per capita has increased only from roughly 272 kWh in 1990 to 804 kWh in 2014. In the same period, mean Chinese per capita consumption went from 511 kWh to 3,927 kWh. The increase in consumption in India is still a remarkable 195%, yet it pales when compared to the 545% increase experienced in China (World Bank Global Electrification Database 2020).

DOI: 10.4324/9781003253884-6

There are various reasons why researchers and policymakers link electrification to development. Observations relating to the average per capita electricity consumption since the mid-1970s for the same three regions as before and the per capita GDP over the same period tell us that the increase in electricity consumption is strongly correlated with an increase in GDP (World Bank Global Electrification Database 2020). The only way to properly answer this question is to adopt a micro perspective. The literature needs to focus on individuals and households and see whether electrification causes an improvement in their socio-economic status.

Access to electricity may have many impacts at the household level. Individuals may increase their labour supply since various tasks can now be performed at night. Food can be stored in a refrigerator, requiring fewer trips to the market. Children can study at night as well, which may affect educational outcomes. On the other hand, increased opportunities to provide labour or participate in household income-generating activities may draw them away from schooling. School instruction may improve if there is access to electricity. Agricultural productivity may increase if irrigation pumps are run using electricity. Firms can produce more efficiently and offer newer products with reliable access to power. Electricity access may also boost entrepreneurship and artisanal activity. At the regional level, these channels can lead to changes in employment, income, and, more broadly, higher levels of economic development. Access to electricity can also help reduce indoor air pollution, one of the leading causes of death and morbidity in the developing world. The possibility of generating light, heating, and cooking energy with electricity reduces the need to use solid fuels.

The identification of a causal effect of access to electricity is a challenging task from an empirical perspective. The placement of an electric grid and the availability of electric power may be endogenous for a variety of reasons. Access to electricity may be affected by reverse causality, especially if we are trying to capture its effect on income, as seen earlier. Regions that are wealthier may be better at lobbying for an extension of the electric grid. Areas that are flat and easy to access may be attractive as candidates for grid extension but for the same reason may exhibit faster economic growth, which may be confounded with electricity provision. Governments do not randomly electrify villages, and their choice of villages to electrify can be dictated by a variety of arguments: they could start with the poorest villages or households, or the richer areas, or with the least costly to connect, or again with neighbourhoods that are closer to urban areas or the transportation network. The availability of electricity may be jointly determined together with other outcomes of interest through numerous potentially omitted variables.

There may be important network effects, e.g., a household, even if not connected to the grid, could be impacted if neighbouring households get electricity. For instance, the spillover may be positive – if village residents can watch television at the home of the household that has electricity. On the other hand, electrified households may increase their productivity, which may reduce local crop prices and hurt those not able to do the same.

## 4.1. Findings from the Literature

In this section, we review a few selected studies of the effect of electrification on household outcomes. We will first present the studies that find a positive impact of access to electricity and then those that do not find any statistically significant effect. We will then discuss some of the factors that may contribute to this diversity of results. For instance, one of the issues when studying electrification in developing countries, a recent phenomenon, is that we only have access to short-term impacts, so these effects may only tell part of the story. We also have to keep in mind that the results obtained are highly dependent on the subsample of the population studied, on whether we are estimating an average or a local treatment effect, on the level of aggregation of the outcomes studied, and on many other factors. As pointed out by Lee and colleagues (2020a), often, a set of complementary factors must be in place in order to allow a population to reap the full benefits of electrification. If these factors are not in place, electrification should be accompanied by complementary programmes. Table 4.1 presents a summary of the papers presented in this chapter and their results.

### *4.1.1 Statistically Significant Impacts*

Dinkelman (2011) was among the first papers trying to identify the causal effect of electrification. She focuses on the effect of a mass electricity roll-out in rural South Africa on labour market outcomes. Her choice of an instrument for placement of the electricity grid is the gradient of the land in which the community is located. The intuition is that a sloped terrain significantly increases the cost of electrification. She shows using a placebo experiment[4] that gradient is unlikely to affect employment outcomes directly. She finds that electrification increases female employment by 30–35% within five years. It also increases female wages and the number of hours worked: male employment also increases but not in a statistically significant sense. The impact of electrification on females works through a re-organization of the labour supply and a boost in entrepreneurship. One mechanism through which electrification works is by shifting households from using wood towards electric cooking and lighting.

Thus, electricity works as a labour-saving technology. Dinkelman finds evidence that there was no clear increase in labour demand in the electrified areas, and wages actually declined somewhat. These findings suggest that electricity only affected labour supply and had little effect on labour

*Table 4.1* Review of Literature

| *Article* | *Country of Study* | *Methodology* | *Results* |
|---|---|---|---|
| Dinkelman (2011) | South Africa (1996–2001) | IV, instrument: gradient | Female employment +9% to 9.5% (*N* = 1,816 communities) |
| Bensch et al. (2011) | Rwanda (2007–2008) | Propensity score matching | Positive effect on lighting hours, no effect on other outcomes (*N* = 537 households) |
| Rud (2012) | India (1965–1984) | IV, instrument: introduction of a new agricultural technology | Manufacturing output +14% (*N* = 15 states) |
| Khandker et al. (2013) | Vietnam (2002–2005) | Fixed effects | Income +28%, expenditures +23% (*N* = 1,120 households) |
| Grogan and Sadanand (2013) | Nicaragua (1998–2005) | IV, instruments: land slope and pre-civil war population density | Probability of work for females +23% (*N* = 6,882 households) |
| Lipscomb et al. (2013) | Brazil (1960–2000) | IV, instrument ideal electricity network placement | 10% increase in electrification leads to 10% increase in income per capita, 7% decrease in poverty; positive effect on education (*N* = 2,184 counties) |
| Chakravorty et al. (2014) | India (1994–2005) | IV, instrument: transmission cable density | Non-agricultural income +9% for a connection, +28.6% for a high-quality connection (*N* = 9,791 households) |
| Chakravorty et al. (2016) | Philippines (2003–2012) | IV, instrument: least-cost projected grid expansion | Income +42%, expenditures +38% (*N* = 209 villages) |
| Burlig and Preonas (2016) | India (2001–2011) | Regression Discontinuity, population of a village in order to be in the programme | No impact (*N* = 25,942 villages) |
| van de Walle et al. (2015) | India (1982–1999) | IV, instrument: proximity to power generators | Consumption +0.5% per annum for connected HH, +0.8% per annum for neighbours (*N* = 6,008 households) |
| Barron and Torero (2017) | El Salvador (2009–2013) | RCT, Intent-to-treat | Indoor $PM_{2}PM_{2.5}$ –66% (*N* = 2,269 households) |

(*Continued*)

*Table 4.1* Continued

| *Article* | *Country of Study* | *Methodology* | *Results* |
|---|---|---|---|
| Gupta and Pelli (2020) | India (2004–2009) | IV, instrument: hydro-supply shifts | Adoption of LPG –6.02%, adoption of fuelwood +5.53% (*N* = 136,221 households) |
| Thomas et al. (2020) | India (2018) | IV based on local randomization, instrument: proximity to a pole | Positive impact on expenditures (*N* = 686 households) |
| Lee et al. (2020) | Kenya (2013–2017) | RCT | No impact (*N* = 2,504 households) |

demand. She also finds some reduced-form evidence that in the electrified districts households not only supplied more labour but also engaged in creating new products and services that raised both female and male labour employment. There was limited inward migration to the electrified areas and outward migration, but it was not clear whether these effects were due to electrification. These results are similar to the one found by Grogan and Sadanand (2013) for Nicaragua. Using initial population density and the mean slope gradient as instruments for electricity placement, they find that access to electricity has no impact on male employment but increases female employment. In Nicaragua, electrification is linked to an increase (of about 23%) in the propensity of women to work outside the home.

Another study that uses geography variables as instruments for project placement is Lipscomb et al. (2013). Their focus is on long-term development over several decades (1960–2000). Based on hydropower potential in Brazil, this study produces a set of hypothetical maps that show how electrification would have evolved over time had it been based purely on the power generation potential of the rivers and the budget constraint of the government. This instrument works well for Brazil because power there is almost exclusively sourced from hydropower (over 60%). A possible concern with this instrument is that people and firms could settle following this predicted evolution of the electrification grid. Yet, most areas in Brazil were already settled by the beginning of the sample period, so this is not a major issue. The authors find large effects of electrification at the county level on the Human Development Index and on average housing values, the idea being that economic development was capitalized into housing prices. Ordinary Least Squares (OLS) estimates are lower than Instrumental Variables (IV) estimates, suggesting that either the poor areas were targeted or the IV compilers are much more efficient than the hydro power plants, which were placed for political reasons. The authors find that the impact of electrification did not occur through immigration to the electrified areas but through increased employment and salaries and investments in education, but not health. One of the issues with health is that it is not clear whether electricity should improve health because it may increase incomes and improve the productivity of the health sector but there may be negative effects on health through increased industrialization and pollution. One key conclusion of the paper is that the long-run effects of grid electricity may be quite high when one takes into account general equilibrium effects, and much of the benefits may accrue from people and resources moving to electrified areas even within the same jurisdiction.

Khandker et al. (2013) use a simple fixed effects model to identify the impact of electrification in Vietnam, which provides an improved identification strategy compared to previous papers that did not use fixed effects and simply compared households before and after electrification. This paper does not deal with the endogeneity of electrification and, therefore, establishes a correlation rather than a causal impact. Making the strong assumption that unobserved heterogeneity is time-invariant, Khandker et al. (2013) find that following electrification non-farm incomes rise by 20–30%, total income by 28%, and expenditures by 23%. The study also acknowledges the importance of spillovers and community-level connections. Community-level spillovers are analyzed in greater detail in Van de Walle et al. (2015). This paper studies the impact of electrification over the long run (17 years) and focuses on both internal (household) and external (village) effects. They use the distance from the village to the power generation source about two decades before the study period in order to instrument for electrification. The article finds a large asymmetry in the external effects between connected and unconnected households. The results show an increase in annualized consumption of roughly 0.5% for households connected to the grid and 0.8% for households not directly connected but belonging to an electrified village. These results suggest that the external effects of electrification are larger than the internal ones.

Thomas et al. (2020) use an IV approach that exploits the geographic discontinuity in legal access to electricity in the Bahraich and Lakhimpur districts of Uttar Pradesh in India. They exploit a law of the state which allows households within a 40-metre distance from an electric pole to be officially eligible to receive electricity from that pole, while those living outside that range are not eligible. The authors conducted a survey among 686 households in 120 habitations (clusters) within villages. They found that access to electricity increases household expenditures, adult household activity, and ownership and usage of appliances. This study is unique because, unlike many other micro studies, the residents had an average of four years of electricity, which is a reasonable interval of time. They measured total household expenditures and expenditures on food, kerosene, and education. They also find that in electrified households, both adults and children spend more time at home although their leisure time does not increase, suggesting that this increased time is being spent on productive activities. These households also have more appliances like bulbs, radios, and refrigerators. These results are more optimistic than other studies and may indicate that the longer-term effects of grid connections may be quite different from the short-term effects of studies that fail to find major changes at the household level.

Chakravorty et al. (2016) adopt a least-cost approach and focus on the impact of access to electricity on agricultural incomes in the Philippines. The identification in this paper is based on the projected expansion of the electricity grid under a least-cost first principle. The hypothesis is that the first villages to be electrified are those closest to the existing grid. The predicted electrification status resulting from this exercise is then used as an instrument for the actual electrification status. Access to electricity in the village raises household expenditures and total income by roughly 40%. Most of these expenditures were on energy consumption. These results suggest that the cost of the physical infrastructure needed to extend the grid may be recovered after only one year.[5]

Rud (2012) focuses on the other side of the labour market and investigates whether the supply of electricity increases labour demand using a state-level panel between 1965 and 1984. He finds that, in India, a one standard deviation increase in the rate of electrification leads to an increase in industrialization of roughly 14%. The paper uses the large disparity in electrification across regions and across time. For instance, while average village electrification was 10% in 1965, it was 50% in Tamil Nadu while being close to 3% in Assam and West Bengal. In order to solve for the endogeneity of electrification, the author uses the introduction of a new agricultural technology, intensive in irrigation (the Green Revolution) and the uneven distribution of groundwater as a natural experiment to develop an instrumental variable. Since the new high-yield varieties are water-intensive, and most irrigation in India is done by pumping groundwater to the surface with electricity, easier access to groundwater is a good predictor of electrification.

Most of the above studies focus on economic outcomes; however, access to electricity affects other household-level outcomes. Barron and Torero (2017) examine the effect of grid connection on indoor air quality using a randomized encouragement experiment in Northern El Salvador between 2009 and 2013, which offers connection subsidies to a subsample of study households. Two years after the beginning of the programme, the electrification rate of encouraged households was 19 percentage points higher than that of the rest of the sample. Barron and Torero (2017) measured indoor minute-by-minute night-time PM2.5 concentrations[6] and found that the concentration for encouraged households was 66% lower, which contributed to an important reduction in acute respiratory infections among children under the age of six. Newly electrified households changed the fuel used for lighting, switching from candles, kerosene lamps, and wood sticks to electric light, and these changes brought about measurable reductions in air pollution and morbidity.

Gupta and Pelli (2020) also look at the pollution question by focusing on the impact of electrification on cooking fuel choice. If electrification improves the socio-economic status of a household, it should contribute to pushing households up the energy ladder. They use hydro-supply shifts, developed in Allcott et al. (2016), with initial levels of electrification as an instrument. A positive shock to the availability of power in a district that historically has a higher degree of electrification results in a higher number of new connections. Using this strategy, they find that for poor households, electrification alone, without accompanying policies, has an adverse effect on cooking fuel choices in the form of increased use of biomass and less of cleaner fuels. Electrification increases expenditures, for instance on entertainment and on energy, and pushes poor households towards reducing their expenditures on other items. A relatively easy way is to switch from costly liquefied petroleum gas (LPG) to virtually free fuelwood, dung, and crop residues for cooking.

### 4.1.2 Little or No Impact

For electrification to have the expected outcome – a boost in development – certain preconditions need to be met. For instance, if the people receiving grid connections are too poor, they will not be able to take advantage of it. One place where this seems to be the case is Africa, which accounts for some of the lowest electrification rates in the world. For example, in 2016, the electrification rate in Chad was 8.83%, and in South Sudan it was just slightly higher at 8.95%.[7]

Lee et al. (2020b) study electrification in rural Kenya by randomly selecting clusters of households and offering them subsidized rates for connecting to the electric grid. By varying the subsidy offered, they can elicit the demand curve for grid electricity, and using administrative data, they also plot the average and marginal cost curves for household grid connections of various sizes. Newly connected households are found to consume very low amounts of electricity, and no impacts are found in the medium run. The study also finds low demand among the poor; a subsidy of roughly 60% on the price of a connection leads to an increase in demand by only 25%. They find that the supply cost of providing connections is higher than the demand. Estimated consumer surplus through this revealed preference approach is almost a fifth of total construction costs. Household surveys conducted 16 and 32 months after connections were completed find no significant impacts across a range of economic and non-economic outcomes.[8] The authors suggest that credit constraints may have contributed to low demand and low usage of electricity among connected households, and bureaucratic red tape and low system reliability may have driven up supply costs.

Burlig and Preonas (2016) study the Rajiv Gandhi Grameen Vidyutikaran Yojana (RGGVY) electrification programme in India, which initially targeted villages with habitations of more than 300 people for connecting to the grid. This rule allows for the execution of a Regression Discontinuity (RD) design.[9] The authors use night lights data to study villages around the cut-off and show that indeed the villages above it exhibit a higher degree of brightness. Of course, one concern is whether night-time brightness as observed from sky satellites can correctly measure electricity consumption within the household. Other studies have suggested a positive correlation between street lighting and lighting within the household (see for instance Kiran Chand et al. 2009; Min et al. 2013; Min and Gaba 2014). The authors find that despite significant increases in electrification, there was little impact of the programme on a wide range of economic outcomes such as employment, asset ownership, housing stock, and village-level variables such as school enrolment, but male agricultural employment declined somewhat, and non-agricultural employment increased by a small magnitude. Analysis conducted on the sample of villages with above-average power reliability also leads to the same conclusion, suggesting that reliability may not be an issue. These effects were measured roughly three to five years after the programme received funding. If there were large implementation delays because of administrative red tape, which are quite common in India, then it is possible that the time between being connected to the grid and the economic surveys conducted was small enough that the medium-term effects of electrification did not manifest in the surveys.

Several reasons could explain the lack of impact of electrification. First, village-level aggregation may have hidden some of the heterogeneity of the effect of access to electricity across households or habitations. Second, the sample studied by Burlig and Preonas (2016) focuses on the smallest and least developed villages, which may not be able to reap all the benefits of access to electricity (Aklin et al. 2017) as in the Kenya study.

## 4.2 Reasons for Difference in Impacts

Several reasons could explain the diversity of results obtained in the literature. Lee et al. (2020a) suggest that the results may depend on factors like the population of interest or pre-existing conditions.

A possible reason for the lack of an effect in some of these studies may be the quality of the power supply. Households connected to the grid in rural India still have power only for a fraction of the day (see for instance Desai and Vanneman 2005, 2012). Chakravorty et al. (2014) focus on the issue of reliability. The identification strategy uses the transmission network, which connects power generation to distribution as an instrumental variable. The transmission network is mainly used to transport electricity from generation plants to large consumption poles using the shortest and, therefore, cheapest route available. Once this network is installed, it is relatively cheaper to electrify neighbouring areas. The study uses a panel of over 9,000 Indian rural households and finds that the effect on non-agricultural incomes of a high-quality power supply is three times larger (roughly 30%) than the impact of a grid connection of average quality (around 9%).

Another way to shed light on the impact of electrification is to look at its impact in the long term. This is difficult for developing countries, where at best we can look at 15–20 years of data. In order to investigate the long-term effects of electrification, we need to focus on the outcomes of connecting the grid in developed countries. Lewis and Severnini (2020) look at the short- and long-run impacts of rural electrification in the United States. Access to electricity in the rural United States rose from 10% to 100% between 1930 and 1960. The paper uses a difference-in-difference approach[10] based on local access to electricity, where local access is measured by the distance from the closest power plant. This rather simple identification strategy is supported by three facts: (i) records show that location decisions were based on costs and urban demand, (ii) urban demand used up more than 90% of the production of these plants, and (iii) no statistically meaningful difference is detectable in the rural population that was electrified first or at a later stage. In the short run, electrification is not found to have an impact on income but on housing and farmland values.

Lewis and Severnini (2020) estimate that the average farmer would have to pay 24% of farm income in order to obtain an electricity connection. Electrification also had long-lasting effects in the United States. In 2000, counties that gained access to the grid earlier were on average 15% more populous relative to counties that gained access later but had similar characteristics before electrification. It is important to keep these long-term impacts in mind when analyzing the impact of electrification in developing countries, where, at best, we can observe some medium-run effects.

## 4.3 Concluding Remarks

The above review, although selective, shows that the jury is still out on whether grid connections have significant impacts on poor households in developing countries. Large effects are found in most studies, and in some studies, the effects are small or statistically insignificant. Most of the studies focusing on developing countries focus on short-term effects and only a few on the long term. In the long run, the literature seems to agree on a generally positive effect of electrification. The context is important as well, making the impact of electrification heterogeneous. In very poor areas, such as sub-Saharan Africa, the immediate benefits of connecting to the grid seem small. On the other hand, in regions where credit and other constraints are not severely binding, the effects on employment, education, and other outcomes seem to be encouraging. More research needs to be done to understand the precise mechanisms through which households benefit from electricity.

## Notes

1 For details, see https://www.visualcapitalist.com/mapped-billion-people-without-access-to-electricity/ (accessed on 14 August 2021).
2 For instance, the electrification of a village located 15 kilometres away from the grid in India costs about $150,000 (Greenstone and Weisbrod, 2014).
3 'Office memorandum: Deendayal Upadhyaya Gram Jyoti Yojana', Ministry of Power, December 3, 2014. http://powermin.nic.in/sites/default/files/uploads/Deendayal_Upadhyaya_Gram_Jyoti_Yojana.pdf (accessed on 14 August 2021)
4 In a psychology experiment, a placebo is an inert treatment or substance that has no known effects. Researchers might utilize a placebo control group, which is a group of participants who are exposed to the placebo or fake independent variable. The impact of this placebo treatment is then compared to the results of the experimental group.
5 The estimated cost for electrifying an additional household is $325, while an increase in expenditures of 38% corresponds to an increase of roughly $615.
6 There is a close, quantitative relationship between exposure to high concentrations of small particulates ($PM_{10}$ and $PM_{2.5}$) and increased mortality or morbidity, both daily and over time. Conversely, when concentrations of small and fine particulates are reduced, related mortality will also go down, presuming other factors remain the same. This allows policymakers to project the population health improvements that could be expected if particulate air pollution is reduced. For details, see https://www.who.int/news-room/fact-sheets/detail/ambient-(outdoor)-air-quality-and-health (accessed on 12 August 2021).
7 For details, see https://www.iea.org/reports/sdg7-data-and-projections/access-to-electricity (accessed on 9 July 2021).
8 Another paper focusing on an African country that does not find any statistically significant effect of electrification is Bensch et al. (2011), who use data from the EnDev rural electrification programme in Rwanda and generate probabilities of electrification by looking at a subset of already electrified households. These probabilities are then used to match electrified with non-electrified households and produce a counterfactual. The article finds a strong impact on lighting hours and a small significant effect on kids studying at home, yet the effect disappears once regional differences are taken into account. Income also shows a positive response, but again vanishes when regional differences are accounted for.
9 A regression discontinuity design allows researchers to evaluate the impact of an intervention when the assignment to the treatment and control groups is based on a cut-off using a numeric variable.
10 The difference-in-differences method is a quasi-experimental approach that compares the changes in outcomes over time between a population enrolled in a programme (the treatment group) and a population that is not (the comparison or control group). It is a useful tool for data analysis.

## References

Aklin, M., P. Bayer, S. P. Harish, and J. Urpelainen. 2017. "Does Basic Energy Access Generate Socioeconomic Benefits? A Field Experiment with Off-Grid Solar Power in India". *Science Advances* 3 (5): e1602153. doi:10.1126/sciadv.1602153.

Allcott, H., A. Collard-Wexler, and S. D. O'Connell. 2016. "How Do Electricity Shortages Affect Industry? Evidence from India". *American Economic Review* 106 (3): 587–624. doi:10.1257/aer.20140389.

Barron, M., and M. Torero. 2017. "Household Electrification and Indoor Air Pollution". *Journal of Environmental Economics and Management* 86: 81–92. doi:10.1016/j.jeem.2017.07.007.

Bensch, G., J. Kluve, and J. Peters. 2011a. "Impacts of Rural Electrification in Rwanda". IZA Discussion Paper No. 6195. SSRN Electronic Journal. doi:10.2139/ssrn.1928537.

Bensch, G., J. Kluve, and J. Peters. 2011b. "Impacts of Rural Electrification in Rwanda". *Journal of Development Effectiveness* 3 (4): 567–588. doi:10.1080/19439342.2011.621025.

Burlig, F. and L. Preonas, 2016. "Out of the Darkness and Into the Light? Development Effects of Rural Electrification". *Working Paper Number 268*. Energy Institute, HAAS. https://ei.haas.berkeley.edu/research/papers/WP268.pdf (accessed on 27 June 2021).

Chakravorty, U., M. Pelli, and B. U. Marchand. 2014. "Does The Quality Of Electricity Matter? Evidence from Rural India". *Journal of Economic Behavior & Organization* 107: 228–247. doi:10.1016/j.jebo.2014.04.011.

Chakravorty, U., K. Emerick, and M.-L. Ravago, 2016. "Lighting up the Last Mile: The Benefits and Costs of Extending Electricity to the Rural Poor". *Resources for the Future Discussion Paper*, 16–22. https://www.rff.org/documents/1721/RFF-DP-16-22-REV.pdf (accessed on 27 June 2021).

Chand, T. R. K., K. V. S. Badarinath, C. D. Elvidge, and B. T. Tuttle. 2009. "Spatial Characterization of Electrical Power Consumption Patterns over India Using Temporal DMSP OLS Night Time Satellite Data". *International Journal of Remote Sensing* 30 (3): 647–661. doi:10.1080/01431160802345685.

Desai, S., and R. Vanneman. 2005. *India Human Development Survey (IHDS), 2005*. National Council of Applied Economic Research, New Delhi. Inter-university Consortium for Political and Social Research [distributor], 2018-08-08. doi:10.3886/ICPSR22626.v12.

Desai, S., and R. Vanneman. 2011–12. *India Human Development Survey-II (IHDS-II)*. New Delhi: National Council of Applied Economic Research. Inter-university Consortium for Political and Social Research [distributor], 2018-08-08. doi:10.3886/ICPSR36151.v6.

Dinkelman, T. 2011. "The Effects of Rural Electrification on Employment: New Evidence from South Africa". *American Economic Review* 101 (7): 3078–3108. doi:10.1257/aer.101.7.3078.

Greenstone, M. and A. Weisbrod. 2014. *Energy, Growth and Development*. International Growth Center. Evidence Paper. https://www.theigc.org/wp-content/uploads/2014/09/IGCEvidencePaperEnergy.pdf (accessed on 27 June 2021).

Grogan, L., and A. Sadanand. 2013. "Rural Electrification and Employment in Poor Countries: Evidence from Nicaragua". *World Development* 43: 252–265. doi:10.1016/j.worlddev.2012.09.002.

Gupta, R. and M. Pelli. 2020. "Electrification and Cooking Fuel Choice in Rural India". *Working Paper Number: SAUFE-WP-2020-010*. http://www.sau.int/fe-wp/wp010.pdf (accessed on 27 June 2021).

Khandker, S. R., D. F. Barnes, and H. A. Samad. 2013. "Welfare Impacts of Rural Electrification: A Panel Data Analysis from Vietnam". *Economic Development and Cultural Change* 61 (3): 659–692. doi:10.1086/669262.

Lee, K., E. Miguel, and C. Wolfram. 2020a. "Does Household Electrification Supercharge Economic Development?" *Journal of Economic Perspectives* 34 (1): 122–144. doi:10.1257/jep.34.1.122.

Lee, K., E. Miguel, and C. Wolfram. 2020b. "Experimental Evidence on the Economics of Rural Electrification". *Journal of Political Economy* 128 (4): 1523–1565. doi:10.1086/705417.

Lewis, J., and E. Severnini. 2020. "Short- And Long-Run Impacts of Rural Electrification: Evidence from the Historical Rollout of the U.S. Power Grid". *Journal of Development Economics* 143: 102412. doi:10.1016/j.jdeveco.2019.102412.

Lipscomb, M, A. M. Mobarak, and T. Barham. 2013. "Development Effects of Electrification: Evidence from the Topographic Placement of Hydropower Plants in Brazil". *American Economic Journal: Applied Economics* 5 (2): 200–231. doi:10.1257/app.5.2.200.

Min, B., and K. Gaba. 2014. "Tracking Electrification in Vietnam Using Nighttime Lights". *Remote Sensing* 6 (10): 9511–9529. doi:10.3390/rs6109511.

Min, B., K. M. Gaba, O. F. Sarr, and A. Agalassou. 2013. "Detection of Rural Electrification in Africa Using DMSP-OLS Night Lights Imagery". *International Journal of Remote Sensing* 34 (22): 8118–8141. doi:10.1080/01431161.2013.833358.

Rud, J. P. 2012. "Electricity Provision and Industrial Development: Evidence from India". *Journal of Development Economics* 97 (2): 352–367. doi:10.1016/j.jdeveco.2011.06.010.

Thomas, D. R., S. P. Harish, R. Kennedy, and J. Urpelainen. 2020. "The Effects of Rural Electrification in India: An Instrumental Variable Approach at the Household Level". *Journal of Development Economics* 146: 102520. doi:10.1016/j.jdeveco.2020.102520.

Van de Walle, Dominique, M. Ravallion, V. Mendiratta, and G. Koolwal. 2015. "Long-Term Gains from Electrification in Rural India". *The World Bank Economic Review*, lhv057. doi:10.1093/wber/lhv057.

World Bank Global Electrification Database. 2020. *From "Tracking SDG 7: The Energy Progress Report" led jointly by the custodian agencies: the International Energy Agency (IEA).* The International Renewable Energy Agency (IRENA), the United Nations Statistics Division (UNSD), the World Bank and the World Health Organization. https://data.worldbank.org/indicator/EG.ELC.ACCS.ZS (accessed on 27 June 2021).

# Part II

# Economics of Nature Conservation

Chapter 5

# Incentive-Based Approaches to Nature Conservation

*E. Somanathan*

## Introduction

> Pragmatism seems a better approach to saving the diversity and integrity of life than does a pursuit of a single universal ethic based in a sense of moral superiority or virtue. If we take the narrow—mostly western—view that nature is harmonious unless disturbed by humanity and that protected areas are necessary to ensure the survival of wildlife, there can be no hope for wildlife outside parks. Today, on the basis of biological insights, we know that protected areas themselves are far too small and scattered to avert mass extinction. Take the broader view of nature in continual flux and humans as part of it, and there is far more space for wildlife, if we can rediscover the art of coexistence.
>
> David Westernin, *In the Dust of Kilimanjaro*, p xv

Protected areas (wildlife sanctuaries and national parks) cover some 161,000 sq km in India (Morales-Hidalgo et al., 2015), which is about 23% of an area under forest and tree cover of some 712,000 sq km (Government of India, 2019).[1] These areas are under fairly strict protection, which means that local residents' rights to extract forest produce from them have been extinguished or severely restricted. Extending this strict level of protection to cover larger areas will be expensive and time-consuming since the rights of local residents will have to be acquired through a process of compensation. Moreover, it will, of course, be simply infeasible to extinguish residents' rights to use the forests over the entire remaining 550,000 sq km.

Therefore, such lands will have to be protected in other ways if they are to be protected at all. A failure to protect and preserve biodiversity in these lands will jeopardize the entire project of conserving India's biodiversity. It is unlikely that the fragmented 'islands' constituted by the protected areas will be able to prevent their uncommon species from going extinct if the surrounding landscapes are hostile to their preservation. Multiple uses of these forest lands outside the protected areas are inescapable. Incentive-based approaches to conservation are those that seek to motivate local users

DOI: 10.4324/9781003253884-8

to modify their land use in ways that are compatible with conservation. Such modifications will typically impose costs on local users. Therefore, the government needs to give incentives to local users if they are to adopt these modifications. It is useful to classify these incentives into the following kinds:[2]

i. Restrictions or prohibitions on land uses and activities that harm biodiversity (the standard approach in protected areas, reserved forests, etc.).
ii. Taxes or fees on land uses and activities that harm biodiversity (no examples from India of which I am aware).
iii. The allocation of rights to revenue streams from biodiversity to local residents who are well-placed to conserve biodiversity, together with the allocation of rights of control (for example, Van Panchayats, Joint Forest Management).
iv. Subsidies to activities that lead to biodiversity conservation as a side effect (eco-development, eco-tourism).
v. Direct payments for the conservation of biodiversity.

Of course, these approaches may be used in combination. Nevertheless, it will be enlightening to consider them separately. We shall discuss these approaches one by one in some detail below. It is worth noting that local residents would clearly prefer the last three approaches to the first two approaches because the last three approaches *compensate them for modifying their behaviour in ways that promote conservation*, while the first two *force them to modify their behaviour or penalize them if they do not modify it.*

## 5.1 Restrictions and Prohibitions

This approach to conservation is still the dominant one in India. It arose out of the assertion of the colonial state in the 19th century that forests were state property, not the property of village communities (Guha 1983). The colonial state was, of course, primarily motivated by considerations of revenue, not the welfare of the people, in taking this approach. It accordingly created an Indian Forest Service and forest departments in each province for the efficient generation of revenue from forests. This revenue maximization included measures for forest protection to ensure that revenue continued to flow. These measures were to restrict or prohibit hunting and the extraction of timber, firewood, and other forest produce by local residents. They were enforced by the staff of the provincial forest departments.

This approach to protection was inherited by independent India and has remained the primary method of forest and wildlife protection. It has been supported by non-government conservationists, perhaps because it has been the 'only game in town' for conservation. There is another attraction of this approach for conservationists and government managers, but it is misleading. The approach appears to be relatively cheap (or it did, before the costs of policing national parks, wildlife sanctuaries, and reserved and protected forests rose to their current levels). This perception is misleading because the costs of conservation were not really as low as they appeared from some perspectives. They were simply shifted to local residents who were denied the use of forest resources enjoyed by them and their ancestors in the past.

The approach seems to have been at least partially successful. It is clear that, by and large, the densest forests and wildlife populations are in the protected areas, generally followed by the reserved and protected forests administered by state forest departments as described above. Areas not given such protection were largely converted to agriculture. However, some forest areas administered by villages and tribes have been protected. These will be discussed in Section 5.4.

The increasing population and economic growth have increased pressure on forest resources from hunting, woodcutting, grazing, and cultivation by local residents, as well as larger-scale threats from dam construction, road construction, and mining. In this chapter, I do not discuss policies that may reduce the demand for conversion of natural ecosystems to human uses, such as agriculture and mining. Such policies operate indirectly, and in this chapter, I discuss only those policies that operate directly.

Nevertheless, it is worth bearing in mind that *none of the policies discussed in this chapter is likely to succeed in the long run* if the underlying demand for land conversion continues to increase indefinitely. Reducing this demand involves, first and foremost, a fall in food prices that would induce a decline in the demand for cultivated land, thus allowing some land to revert to a more natural eco-system. Food prices can fall because agricultural productivity increases via agricultural research and development or because the population declines with an increase in education and access to health and contraception. Increasing agricultural productivity and education and health levels are both desirable for their own sake, of course. Still, conservationists would do well to bear in mind that they are vital for conservation as well. Policies to reduce the use of fossil fuels and new dams would also make a big difference in conservation outcomes. The fact that renewable electricity is now cheaper than coal-fired electricity in India is a direct outcome of such policies (and also of policies in other countries) (IRENA 2020) and will greatly reduce the growth of coal mining that happens in forest areas. Conversely, misguided policies to promote coal mining may cause devastation in forest areas. The willingness on the part of the general public to bear the costs of conservation in the form of foregone mining and industrial projects is also related to the economic security of the people. An economically secure population will be more willing to give up narrowly defined economic gains for the sake of a better environment. Thus, the promotion of economic security is, in the long run, also important for the conservation of the natural environment.

Since it is legally easier to divert reserved and protected forests than protected areas for industrial purposes, and since the level of patrolling by the state forest departments in reserved and protected forests has proved inadequate for wildlife protection, in particular, there are increasing calls by conservationists for expansion of the protected areas to safeguard wildlife populations.

This expansion has, however, run into the problem that the formerly politically weak residents of forests, many of the Scheduled Tribes, have gradually become more politically conscious and electorally significant. In 1961, the literacy rate among Scheduled Tribes, who are concentrated in states with the most forest cover, was about 10%, only about one-third of the national literacy rate of 30%. In 2011, the literacy rate of Scheduled Tribes had increased to 59%, which was about four-fifths of the national literacy rate of 73%.[3] This kind of social change, among other causes, has led to the passing of the Forest Rights Act of 2006, making it more difficult for forest residents to be evicted or for their customary rights of forest produce extraction to be extinguished without compensation. These political trends are unlikely to reverse themselves, given the strong socio-economic trends that underlie them. Thus, the expansion of the protected area network without adequate compensation for residents of the areas concerned is now a non-starter.

In fact, the future of the dominant approach to conservation, restrictions on forest resource use without compensation for those living in and around forests, is itself in doubt. Thus, the standard approach to conservation, at least in so far as it concerns wildlife, which is harder to monitor and protect than trees, is now confined to the wildlife sanctuaries and national parks, and even in these, it has suffered some notable setbacks, for example, the recent extinctions of tigers in the Sariska and Panna Tiger Reserves.[4]

I conclude that while strict protection of wildlife sanctuaries and national parks seems to be necessary for the conservation of wildlife and other biodiversity in India, it has become increasingly clear that it is, by itself, insufficient to do the job. Shifting the cost of conservation to those living in and around forests has always been unjust. It is also increasingly inefficient and infeasible.

## 5.2 Taxes and Fees

The idea behind this approach is simple. If you want to discourage an activity, raise its price by taxing it or charging for it so as to deter people from engaging in it. This approach has not been tried in India. The colonial government had grazing fees, but it is not clear whether these were intended to prevent damage to the forests and grasslands or only to raise revenue.

This approach is attractive in contexts where a total ban on some activity is unnecessary or too costly, but it is beneficial if the activity is reduced. A concrete example is a disturbance to wildlife from road traffic. In the

Shencottah Gap in the southern Western Ghats, between the Periyar and Kalakkad-Mundanthurai Tiger Reserves, the National Highway 208 runs from Kerala to Tamil Nadu. Heavy and noisy traffic on the road tends to scare off animals like gaur and elephants. Thus, the populations to the south, centred in Kalakkad-Mundanthurai and adjoining wildlife sanctuaries, are cut off from those centred at Periyar in the north, with the absence of gene flow raising the risk of extinction of the isolated southern populations. Banning road traffic at night has been suggested. But it has the drawback that those who genuinely need to use the road urgently will suffer unduly.

Imposing a high enough toll, on the other hand, will allow those who have to use the road urgently to go ahead while deterring more price-conscious users enough for them to postpone their use to the daytime. At the same time, the toll will raise some revenue, which can be used to help build overpasses and underpasses for animals to use at night.

Another example where a fee can be usefully used to reduce overuse is the entry fee for national parks and sanctuaries. It is clear that some of our national parks and sanctuaries suffer from excessive tourist traffic that causes congestion, disturbs wildlife, and reduces the utility of the experience for tourists. Raising the entry fee in such cases will reduce use while bringing in revenue that can be used for conservation purposes. Of course, indiscriminately high entry fees may not always be a good idea for a number of reasons. For example, public support for conservation is likely to wane if the public is priced out of national parks altogether. Thus, reducing numbers has to be balanced against other considerations. For example, discounts for Indians, students, senior citizens, and residents of the locality during off-seasons may be a sensible compromise. It is by visiting national parks and enjoying nature that young people will develop a taste for nature and the outdoors and be more motivated to conserve it.

## 5.3 Devolution of Management and Control to Local Communities

The third approach, devolving rights of use and control to local communities, can be beneficial for conservation because local users, once they are given secure rights to exploit forest produce, have a reason to conserve forests. However, unlike the case with private ownership, community ownership is subject to the problem of the commons. This arises because individual incentives to conserve common property are weakened by the possibility that other rights holders in future may reap the benefits of an individual's restraint in harvesting today. This problem can be overcome if there is good local governance. Good governance, of course, cannot be taken for granted, as the large literature on commons management has shown.[5]

State management of forests has been the traditional solution to the common problem. But it is not without its problems. Delegating the responsibility for forest management to the agents of the state will work well only if the political system is capable of ensuring that they are accountable to the people at large. It is clear that the political system has been less than successful at this task. The question of whether governance of forests is better at the state or the local level has no obvious answer.

Local management of forests has been tried in the case of the Van Panchayats of Kumaun and, more recently, in Joint Forest Management in most of India. It has also been the practice all along in most of the hill areas of north-eastern India. The Van Panchayats of Kumaun (in the Uttarakhand Himalaya) are the most studied example of legally sanctioned community management in India (Somanathan 1991; Agrawal 2001).

The system began in 1930 and has expanded to cover more than a third of the forest area. It has resulted in lower lopping damage than in adjacent comparable reserved forests and equivalent canopy cover, biomass, and regeneration (Baland et al. 2010) at a small fraction of the cost (Somanathan, Prabhakar et al. 2009). What this shows is that a well-designed system for local management of forests can result in far more cost-effective conservation than management by state forest departments.

Guidelines for Joint Forest Management by state forest departments and community groups were issued by the Government of India in the 1990s. The idea was to restore degraded reserved or protected forests by forming forest user groups from local communities and giving them some user rights if they protected the forest. The devolution of management has been much more limited than in the case of the Van Panchayats of Kumaun, and forest user groups generally have less security of tenure and less control of the forests they manage. Unlike the case of the Van Panchayats, there do not appear to be any systematic studies that compare Joint Forest Management with management by the state forest departments while controlling for confounding factors. My subjective assessment of the case study literature is that Joint Forest Management is generally seen as less effective at forest conservation and provision of benefits to local people than are the Van Panchayats of Kumaun. In many cases, they appear to have made no substantive difference to the system of forest management by state forest departments.

The hill areas of north-eastern India make an interesting contrast with the rest of the country in that the state forest departments administer only a minority of the forest lands, with the rest being administered by communities in diverse ways. Again, there are no studies comparing conservation outcomes between state and community-managed forests that carefully control for confounding factors.

While appropriately designed local institutions for forest management may improve upon the management of reserved and protected forests, they will generally not have sufficient incentives to conserve biodiversity. This is because while the local community gains from some aspects of conservation, such as assured nearby supplies of fodder, firewood, and timber, they do not benefit from all the external benefits of conservation. These include hydrological benefits at the regional scale and biodiversity and carbon sequestration benefits at the global scale. In particular, it appears to be the case that communities are not good managers of faunal resources. Instances of active wildlife management by local forest management institutions in India are rare. The protection of certain species by a few communities for religious reasons, such as the blackbuck by the Bishnois of Rajasthan, tends to be exceptions that prove the rule. It doesn't help that existing legislation makes no provision for community management of wildlife.

This is only to be expected from an economic point of view because it is difficult to perceive wildlife numbers and, therefore, difficult to know whether it is one's own hunting that is causing wildlife populations to fall. Moreover, wildlife tends to stray outside local boundaries, so its protection today will not guarantee its availability tomorrow to any particular village. The benefit of wildlife conservation tends to be largely external to small communities.

Thus, when there is management by local communities, additional policies will usually be needed to provide sufficient motivation for them to conserve all aspects of natural resource values. This brings us to the relatively new approaches to conservation: explicit attempts by the state to subsidize or pay people who live in the vicinity of forests to conserve biodiversity.

## 5.4 Subsidies to Activities That Are Complementary to Conservation

There are many possible policies that fall under this description. I mention two prominent ones here. The first is subsidies for alternatives to firewood or to more efficient stoves that use less wood. This could help forest conservation in situations where firewood collection is a significant contributor to forest degradation. Such is the case in the western and central Himalayas (Baland, Bardhan et al. 2006–07). Baland et al.'s econometric estimates based on their survey data from Himachal Pradesh and Uttarakhand are that a 100-rupee subsidy to a cylinder of cooking gas (assuming a base price of Rs 300/cylinder) would reduce firewood use by 22%, while a 200-rupee subsidy would reduce usage by 40%. Such a policy would have other important benefits as well. It would reduce indoor air pollution, which more than doubles the risk of acute respiratory infections and other serious diseases.

Subsidies to gas (over-and-above the usual central government subsidy) have been tried in some 'eco-development' programmes of the Government of India, but their effects on forest preservation have not been properly measured and documented. The Pradhan Mantri Ujjwala Yojna has recently greatly expanded access to subsidized Liquid Petroleum Gas (LPG) cylinders, with 80 million new households enrolled for household LPG cylinders in just over three years. However, usage of LPG by newly enrolled users averages less than four cylinders per month, which is about half the average usage and only 40% of what would be required to give up firewood entirely.

Whenever an intervention is carried out, it is important to conduct trials that build in the measurement of effects in their design so that the impact of such policies can be measured. This is really crucial as the example of the national programme for improved *chulhas* (cookstoves) shows. Launched in 1985, the programme was said to have resulted in the installation of 35 million cookstoves before it was closed in 2002. Independent evaluations, however, suggested that improved stoves often did not reduce pollution emissions (Smith 1989). The programme also suffered from low adoption and high rates of disuse (Venkataraman, Sagar et al. 2010) and was discontinued in 2002. Finally, it is not clear if the programme succeeded in its primary aim of reducing fuel wood use. Field tests conducted by the Tata Energy and Research Institute in Rajasthan, Tamil Nadu, and West Bengal showed, on average, greater consumption of fuel wood by the improved stoves in the former two states, and less in West Bengal, with the average fuel wood saving from the three being negative (Kishore and Ramana 2002). If evaluation and monitoring had been built in from the start, these problems might have been avoided.

Starting about 25 years ago, the Government of India launched 'eco-development' programmes with World Bank funding. These have not had very clearly stated objectives. Propaganda in favour of conservation in villages surrounding national parks appears to be a significant component of most eco-development programmes. Common sense suggests that we should not expect much from this.

Support for livelihoods that do not involve extractive use of forests appears to be another major component of the programmes, at least as stated. Most of such programmes appear to involve infusions of loans or small amounts of capital for investments in non-forest-related businesses. Again, a hard-headed economic view suggests that such attempts are likely to fail because such small amounts of capital tied to particular sectors may not be the sole constraint (or even one of the constraints) that prevents people from entering occupations with higher returns. Moreover, it is very difficult for outsiders to evaluate business opportunities and the one-size-fits-all model in which governments are constrained to work, implying a very high probability of failure. Eco-development is thus not likely to be much of 'eco' or 'development'. Casual observation from sites in Kerala suggests that the principal benefit that local people actually derive from the programme is employment. This sort of unemployment insurance is of value in itself but is unrelated to conservation.

One component of these programmes that does make sense, at least in theory, is the subsidization of LPG as an alternative to fuel wood in areas where fuel wood pressure is a significant component of forest degradation.

However, any evaluations of such programmes are hard to find in practice. In fact, the so-called integrated conservation and development programmes have been tried in many developing countries, but we have little reliable evidence on their efficacy because not enough attention has been paid to constructing appropriate control groups (groups that were not included in the programme but nevertheless monitored to provide a benchmark against which to assess the effects of a programme). To illustrate this difficulty, Ferraro and Pattanayak (2006) cite a study by Struhsaker et al. (2005). The latter conclude that the success of a protected area is not correlated with the presence of integrated conservation and development programmes. Ferraro and Pattanayak (2006) point out that this could be because integrated conservation and development programmes tend to be tried in areas where human pressures on parks are high. Thus, they are tried in an adverse environment, and this could be masking the positive impact that they produce when a cross section of parks is examined.

A second major policy that falls under the heading of subsidies to activities that are complementary to conservation is the promotion of eco-tourism. Here the idea is that eco-tourism will give people residing around forests a stake in conserving biodiversity and that this will lead to better protection of biodiversity. For this to actually be the case, several conditions need to be met. First, eco-tourism itself has to be a viable business proposition. If it is not, then its promotion will fail in the absence of continuing subsidies. Continuing subsidies cannot be ruled out; after all, if we want conservation, then we as taxpayers had better be willing to pay for it. But they do raise the question, then why subsidize eco-tourism, why not pay forest residents directly to conserve biodiversity? Promoting eco-tourism requires that it be a viable business proposition and that only temporary barriers like information, training, and access to capital prevent forest residents from taking to it. Next, it has to be the case that the government or conservation NGOs are able to supply the missing capital and training. Finally, it has to be true that those residing near forests and benefitting from eco-tourism actually feel that biodiversity conservation will maintain their incomes and are able to take actions such as reporting poaching or engaging in local political activity to ward off threats to biodiversity. Or revenues from eco-tourism may be taxed to raise revenue for protective activities.

Eco-tourism has become a big business in several African countries. In many cases, it clearly has helped protect wildlife by giving ranchers and communities who benefit from tourism a strong incentive to conserve wildlife on their lands. In India, we need to experiment with eco-tourism as a deliberate strategy to conserve wildlife on the outskirts of national parks and sanctuaries that already attract large numbers of visitors.

Unfortunately, overcentralized government policymaking deters experimentation. In the current policy framework, forest areas adjoining wildlife sanctuaries and parks are usually reserved or protected forests in which local community management is ruled out. An experiment that allowed such an area to be governed by a local consortium of villages in order that the residents profit from tourism revenue might result in effective protection of the forest at a much lower cost than the government could achieve.

## 5.5 Direct Payments for Conservation

Rather than indirectly motivating communities to protect wildlife by subsidizing infrastructure for eco-tourism or providing them with sources of livelihood that remove their reasons to extract forest resources, economists have advocated directly paying private landowners and communities for the eco-system services that they provide by maintaining natural vegetation on their lands (Ferraro 2002). This approach, most commonly called 'Payments for Eco-system Services' (PES), avoids the problems associated with integrated conservation and development projects mentioned above. Paying for conservation directly may enable funding agencies to get more conservation from any given budget because money will not be spent on programmes that are not directly related to conservation.

Of course, this approach will only work if it is feasible to monitor conservation outcomes so that payments are made only when conservation is achieved and not made when it is not. Thus, there are two conditions necessary for such an approach to work. It must be technically and economically feasible to monitor conservation outcomes and condition payments on those outcomes, and the programme must be designed well so that land managers, whether individuals or communities, have the incentive to actually engage in conservation.

Payments for eco-system services have been used in developed countries such as the United States and the Australian state of Victoria. They work by paying landowners to take actions on their land that help preserve native vegetation. The programmes are designed to be cost-effective by employing auctions. Farmers are invited to place sealed bids for conservation actions that they will take, specifying how much they would like to be paid for the actions. The bids are ranked on the basis of conservation value for money, and the highest bids that exhaust the budget or meet a minimum cut-off are accepted. The attractiveness of the auction design is that it minimizes the cost of achieving any given level of conservation since those farmers for whom it is least costly to carry out conservation actions will be the ones selected to carry them out. Thus, any given conservation budget will be able to go further and achieve more conservation.

These programmes involve relatively easy monitoring of vegetation protection and payments to individuals. A more ambitious programme to protect carnivores (wolverines and lynxes) from poaching in northern Sweden has existed for a few years (Zabel and Holm-Muller 2008). In this programme, large, fixed payments are made to indigenous communities of Sami reindeer herders whenever a government biologist verifies a carnivore reproduction on a community's land, with lesser (but still substantial) payments being made for the confirmed regular presence of adults of the endangered species. The Swedish government programme replaced compensation payments made by the government when reindeer were killed by predators.

A few developing countries – Colombia, Mexico, China, and Costa Rica – have government-sponsored PES programmes. An independent study found that the Mexican Payments for Hydrological Environmental Services programme resulted in participating landowners deforesting their properties 10% less on average than matched control farmers and accounting for increased deforestation in non-enrolled properties (Alix-Garcia, Shapiro et al. 2010). Pattanayak et al. (2010), after reviewing several studies, concluded that the Costa Rican programme appeared to be poorly designed, with a minimal impact on conservation, mainly because payments went to farmers who had no intention of deforesting their lands in any case. In China, the Sloping Lands Conversion Program that paid farmers to convert fields on steep slopes to tree plantations has had a large impact (Yang and Xu, 2013).

The PES approach to conservation has begun in India in a small way. Small soil conservation programmes in which downstream buyers paid upstream sellers are reported to be proposed or ongoing in a few valleys in some states (Huang and Upadhyaya 2007). These are essentially payments for hydrological services.

The Nature Conservation Foundation (NCF), based in Mysore, has taken the lead on payments for wildlife conservation in Himalayan meadows. In 1999, in the Spiti valley in Himachal Pradesh, the NCF reached an agreement with the village of Kibber to set aside about 5 sq km or 6% of the village's total rangeland to be free from grazing in exchange for payment. The use of the set-aside land by wild sheep (*bharal*) tripled in four years (Mishra, Allen et al., 2003). By 2007, the area set aside had tripled (Bhatnagar, Seth et al. 2007). The NCF has entered into a similar arrangement with villagers in Ladakh for conservation of the Tibetan gazelle (Bhatnagar, Seth et al. 2007).

Ultimately, funding for these programmes would have to come from governments since only they can guarantee the continuing funding necessary for their maintenance. On smaller scales in locales with high conservation value, NGOs could establish trust funds that would ensure a sustainable source of funds to maintain such a programme in perpetuity. However, as yet, NGOs have not been willing or able to make the necessary long-run financial commitments, although the examples given above show those efforts have begun on an experimental basis. There are many areas in which private lands are interspersed with forests or other habitats of high conservation value but which have no easily observed charismatic species that would attract tourists in large enough numbers for tourism to be a source of funding for conservation. In such areas, eco-tourism would be unworkable or insufficient by itself to generate the necessary incentives for conservation. Direct payments would appear to be the only way that the value that society places on biodiversity could be transferred to the people in a position to take conservation actions.

If such payments for wildlife conservation to communities turn out to be feasible, effective, and economical, then this raises exciting possibilities, not only for conservation in the larger landscape outside national parks and wildlife sanctuaries but also within them. A substantial part of the government budget for national parks is being devoted to pay the costs of resettling inhabitants to locations outside the parks. It may well turn out to be cheaper and lead to better conservation to instead make incentive payments to some or parts of these communities to preserve wildlife within the parks. This argument has been made for the particular case of the Himalayas by Bhatnagar (2008), but it very likely applies more widely.

## 5.6 Conclusion

Different approaches to conservation all have strengths and weaknesses, and these are context dependent. It is unlikely in the extreme that a single approach to conservation will constitute the best one all over India. Thus, a portfolio of conservation strategies is required. Conservation policy in India has been dominated by a single approach: regulation by the state. Although Joint Forest Management has been adopted as a part of the official policy all over the country, in most states, governments have been unwilling to grant tenure security, autonomy, and revenue flows to local managers, thus undercutting the incentives of local organizations to put effort into conservation. Lessons need to be learned from relatively successful instances of local management, such as the Van Panchayats of Kumaun, and these institutions adapted as necessary to other parts of India. These can be tried and monitored on a trial basis before expanding them to larger areas. This is true for the other incentive-based approaches mentioned above as well. What is critical in this process is that the trials be carefully designed and transparently monitored and documented so that learning from them can proceed. Most integrated conservation and development projects in India have suffered from insufficient documentation and monitoring and poor design.

Establishing the impacts of a programme on carbon sequestration through careful monitoring and putting it on a solid scientific basis could draw in international funds from carbon markets. This is another good reason to involve non-government scientists in the design of any trial programme from the start. It is necessary to credibly establish impacts so that international funding for programme expansion can be secured. For example, establishing the sequestration benefits from providing access to clean fuels in lieu of firewood could secure funding for the expensive but enormously productive task, from the point of view of human health, air pollution, regional climate change and agricultural productivity, and forest conservation, of replacing firewood with modern fuels.

## Notes

1 Forest and tree cover is thus somewhat more than one-fifth of the total land area of India.
2 In fact, this list is quite comprehensive, and covers all approaches to conservation. (i) and (iii) in this list are not usually thought of as incentive-based approaches, but of course, all approaches, if they are to be effective, have to provide some kind of incentive, whether negative or positive. It is useful to compare all of them, in order to understand what the 'new' incentive-based approaches (ii), (iv), and (v) have to offer.
3 For details, see https://timesofindia.indiatimes.com/india/sc/sts-take-rapid-strides-close-literacy-gap/articleshow/25536193.cms (accessed on 15 August 2021).
4 For details, see https://www.indiatoday.in/magazine/cover-story/story/20050523-indian-tiger-in-danger-of-becoming-extinct-as-wildlife-poaching-makes-deadly-revival-787672-2005-05-23 (accessed on 18 July 2021).
5 One of the winners of the Nobel Memorial Prize in Economics, Elinor Ostrom, received the award for her research on the commons.

## References

Agrawal, A. 2001. "State Formation in Community Spaces? Decentralization of Control Over Forests in the Kumaon Himalaya, India." *Journal of Asian Studies* 60 (1): 9–40. doi: 10.2307/2659503.

Alix-Garcia, J., M. Shapiro, et al. *The Environmental Effectiveness of Payments Forecosystem Services in Mexico: Preliminary Lessons for REDD*. University of Wisconsin,Madison.2010.https://www.amherst.edu/system/files/media/Policy%2520Brief-REDD%2520PES%2520Mexico-English-2010.pdf (accessed on 23 June 2021).

Baland, J.-M., P. Bardhan, S. Das and D. Mookherjee. 2010. "Forests to the People: Decentralization and Forest Degradation in the Indian Himalayas." *World Development* 38 (11): 1642–1656. doi:10.1016/j.worlddev.2010.03.007.

Bhatnagar, Y. V. 2008. "Relocation From Wildlife Reserves in The Greater and Trans-Himalayas: Is It Necessary?" *Conservation and Society* 6 (3): 263. doi:10.4103/0972-4923.49219.

Bhatnagar, Y. V., C. Seth, et al. 2007. "A Strategy for Conservation of the Tibetan Gazelle Procapra picticaudata in Ladakh." *Conservation and Society* 5 (2): 262–276. https://www.conservationandsociety.org.in/temp/ConservatSoc52262-7028868_193128.pdf (accessed on 23 June 2021)

Ferraro, P. J. 2002. "ECOLOGY: Direct Payments to Conserve Biodiversity." *Science* 298 (5599): 1718–1719. doi:10.1126/science.1078104.

Ferraro, P. J. and S. Pattanayak.2006. “Money for Nothing? A Call for Empirical Evaluation of Biodiversity Conservation Investments.” *PLoS Biology* 4 (4): 482–488. doi:10.1371/journal.pbio.0040105.

Government of India. 2019. *State of Forest Report*. Dehradun: Forest Survey of India (Ministry of Environment Forest and Climate Change). http://www.indiaenvironmentportal.org.in/files/file/isfr-fsi-vol1.pdf (accessed on 24 June 2021).

Guha, R.1983. “Forestry in British and post-British India: A Historical Analysis.” *Economic and Political Weekly18* (44): 1882–1896.

Huang, M. and S. Upadhyaya. 2007. “Watershed-based Payment for Environmental Services in Asia.” Sustainable Agriculture and Natural Resource Management Collaborative Research Support Program (SAMREM)/Office of International Research, Education, and Development (OIRED) Working Paper: 06ñ07. https://sanremcrsp.cired.vt.edu/wp-content/uploads/2013/11/Sept.2007.PESAsia.pdf (accessed on 25 June 2021).

IRENA. 2020. *Renewable Power Generation Costs in 2019*. Abu Dhabi: International Renewable Energy Agency. https://www.irena.org/publications/2020/Jun/Renewable-Power-Costs-in-2019 (accessed on 20 July 2021).

Kishore, V. V. N. and P. V. Ramana 2002. “Improved Cook Stoves in Rural India: How Improved Are They? A Critique of the Perceived Benefits from the National Programme on Improved Chulhas (NPIC).” *Energy* 27 (1): 47–63. doi:10.1016/S0360-5442(01)00056-1.

Mishra, C., P. Allen, T. McCarthy, M. D. Madhusudan, A. Bayarjargal and H. H. T. Prins. 2003. “The Role of Incentive Programs in Conserving the Snow Leopard.” *ConservationBiology*17(6):1512–1520.doi:10.1111/j.1523-1739.2003.00092.x.

Morales-Hidalgo, D., S. N. Oswalt and E. Somanathan. 2015. “Status and Trends In Global Primary Forest, Protected Areas, And Areas Designated For Conservation Of Biodiversity From The Global Forest Resources Assessment 2015.” *Forest Ecology and Management* 352: 68–77. doi:10.1016/j.foreco.2015.06.011.

Pattanayak, S. K., S. Wunder and P. J. Ferraro. 2010. “Show Me the Money: Do Payments Supply Environmental Services in Developing Countries?” *Review of Environmental Economics and Policy* 4 (2): 254–274. doi:10.1093/reep/req006.

Smith, K. 1989. “Dialectics of Improved Stoves.” *Economic and Political Weekly* 24 (10): 517–522.

Somanathan, E.1991. “Deforestation, Property Rights and Incentives in Central Himalaya.” *Economic and Political Weekly* 26 (4):37–46.

Somanathan, E., R. Prabhakar, et al. 2009. “Decentralization for Cost-effective Conservation.” *Proceedings of the National Academy of Sciences* 106 (11): 4143–4147. doi:10.1073/pnas.0810049106.

Struhsaker, T. T., P. J. Struhsaker and K. S. Siex. 2005. “Conserving Africa’s Rain Forests: Problems in Protected Areas and Possible Solutions.” *Biological Conservation* 123 (1): 45–54. doi:10.1016/j.biocon.2004.10.007.

Venkataraman, C., A. D. Sagar, G. Habib, N. Lam and K. R. Smith. 2010. “The Indian National Initiative for Advanced Biomass Cook stoves: The Benefits of Clean Combustion.” *Energy for Sustainable Development* 14 (2): 63–72. doi:10.1016/j.esd.2010.04.005.

Western, D. 2001. *In the Dust of Kilimanjaro. Shearwater Books*. Island Press. ISBN 10: 1559635347 / ISBN 13: 9781559635349.

Yang, X. and J. Xu. 2013. "Program Sustainability and the Determinants of Farmers' Self-Predicted Post-Program Land Use Decisions: Evidence from the Sloping Land Conversion Program (SLCP) In China." *Environment and Development Economics* 19 (1): 30–47. doi:10.1017/s1355770x13000259.
Zabel, A. and K. H. Muller. 2008. "Conservation Performance Payments for Carnivore Conservation in Sweden." *Conservation Biology* 22 (2): 247–251. doi:10.1111/j.1523-1739.2008.00898.x.

Chapter 6

# Forests, Carbon Sequestration, and Ecosystem Services

## Are There 'Two-for-One' Deals?

*R. David Simpson*

## Introduction

Considerable enthusiasm has been expressed for forest policies designed to meet multiple objectives. The amount of carbon held in the world's extant forests is equal to some 50 times current global $CO_2$ emissions (Garzuglia and Saket 2005). Adding to this stock could significantly help in forestalling climate change. Re-afforestation and afforestation[1] in areas where trees are not now growing could offset a sizable fraction of current emissions (Houghton and Nassikas 2018) and, in many places, do so at an attractive cost relative to alternative approaches (Griscom et al. 2017).

Forests may also provide a host of other ecosystem services. They may provide habitat for pollinators (Ricketts and Lonsdorf 2013), purify contaminated water (Emerton et al. 1999), provide protection against coastal storms (Barbier et al. 2008), cool urban and peri-urban environments (Bowler et al. 2010; Kabisch et al. 2017), and provide a host of other agricultural, residential, recreational, and aesthetic benefits (Daily 1997). Several researchers and commentators have suggested that forests ought to be preserved to provide 'nature-based solutions' to problems of both climate change mitigation (reducing net additions of greenhouse gases to the atmosphere) and adaptation (compensatory measures against higher temperatures, more extreme storms, droughts, etc.), as well as to continue to provide other ecosystem services (Seddon et al. 2019; Walters 2016; Monbiot 2020; *Nature* 2017). Reforestation may seem, then, to provide an attractive two-for-one deal: sequestering carbon while providing a suite of other valuable ecosystem services as well.

There may be problems with this prescription, however. While it seems a compelling case might be made for maintaining old-growth forests in the increasingly rare and remote areas where they are still found, it is less clear that reforesting unforested areas presently and allowing them to mature will prove to be more efficient. While forest lands can take up carbon at impressive rates in some places, the inherent photosynthetic potential is limited in many areas (Baldocchi and Penuelas 2019). Moreover, to make a

DOI: 10.4324/9781003253884-9

truly significant impact, vast areas of the globe might need to be devoted to forests, with attendant societal and ecological consequences (Houghton and Nassikas 2018; Burns and Nicholson 2017). Also, even carbon stored in old-growth forests may not be truly secure; mature stands may be more vulnerable to fire and decomposition from epidemic disease or infestation (Baldocchi and Penuelas 2019; Griscom et al. 2017).

At the heart of the problem is an inherent trade-off. Forests sequester carbon while they are *growing*. They are likely to provide ecosystem services most effectively when they are *grown*. Older forests are likely to be dense and diverse, and hence both store more carbon *in total* and provide more ecosystem services than recently planted ones. However, it is also likely that more carbon could be stored *over time* by harvesting and replanting forests (Lin et al. 2013; Pannell et al. 2006; Favero et al. 2017).

This chapter attempts to explore the conditions under which it would be optimal to reforest an area and *then never harvest it again*, as opposed to harvesting it on a cycle of set rotations. The desirability of rotational harvesting depends on several factors. Perhaps the most important technologically is the 'pickling rate' (van Kooten et al. 1995): the fraction of carbon from harvested material that may be permanently sequestered in building materials or other 'sinks'. In recent years, a great deal of hope has been placed in bioenergy with carbon capture and storage, or 'BECCS', in which trees (or other crops) would be grown and burned for energy, with their carbon content captured and permanently sequestered either pre-or post-combustion.[2] The pickling rate is unlikely ever to approach one, however, as harvest residues and, perhaps more importantly, disturbed soils will release some carbon into the atmosphere. Other factors that determine whether rotational harvesting would be preferable to a reforest-and-never-harvest-again policy include the discount rate, the forest growth rate, and the value of other ecosystem services relative to that of carbon sequestration. The opportunity cost of land is also an important consideration. The same factors that might favour adopting a policy of reforesting and not replanting might also lead to a choice not to reforest at all.

The above implications are developed in a simple and, frankly, highly derivative model. The objective here is not so much to derive novel results as to place known results in context. The basic approach derives from Faustmann's classic model (1849) of optimal forest management. Hartman (1976) was the first to expand the Faustmann model to consider the values of standing forests. I am deeply indebted to van Kooten et al. (1995) for their seminal and still highly pertinent depiction of rotation forestry with carbon sequestration values. Other important sources include Hoel et al. (2014) and Favero et al. (2017); van Kooten and Johnston (2016) provide an authoritative overview of issues in forestry management for both timber production and carbon sequestration.

In the next section, I introduce and develop a model of forestry rotations with both carbon sequestration and ecosystem service benefits; if my approach does differ in any real respect from the previous work from which I have borrowed so heavily, it is largely abstracting from the trade-off between timber production and carbon sequestration and focusing instead on that between carbon sequestration and the provision of other ecosystem services. I focus not on the length of harvest rotations per se but rather on the limiting case in which the optimal rotation period would be infinite: when a reforested area would never be harvested again. In Section 6.3, I consider how different factors would affect whether or not harvesting should ever occur. I offer some concluding comments in the final section.

## 6.1 A Simple Model

In this section, I develop a simple model of forestry rotation in the spirit of Faustmann (1849), Hartman (1976), and van Kooten et al. (1995). I will largely ignore the role of harvested timber products (other than carbon) and focus on carbon sequestration and ecosystem services. I will denote the volume of carbon stored in a forest area $t$ years after its most recent harvest as $C(t)$ and suppose that volume increases at a rate $dC(t)/t = C'(t)$. For analytical convenience in developing an illustrative calculation, I will adopt the assumption that carbon price is constant over time and normalize the prices of carbon to one.

Let me also suppose that, first, the quantity of other ecosystem services provided is proportional to the amount of carbon sequestered in the forest providing them, and second, that the value of ecosystem services may be expressed as a multiple $s$ of the volume of carbon sequestered. The first assumption is, of course, a radical simplification but is made to reflect the stylized fact that more mature ecosystems are denser and more diverse. As the system approaches maturity and carbon storage approaches an upper bound, I suppose the ecosystem services provided do so as well. It is also heroic to say, as I implicitly am doing, that the *value* of ecosystem services is proportional to the carbon sequestered in the system, but again, as a rough stylized depiction, the assumption may be serviceable.

Following van Kooten et al. (1995), let $\beta$ be the 'pickling rate' at which carbon is stored in harvested forest products. That is, $\beta$ is the fraction of carbon contained in harvested products that is permanently prevented from re-entering the environment through combustion or decomposition. Finally, let $\delta$ be the discount rate.

We may then write the value of harvesting carbon on a repeated $T-$year harvesting cycle, $V(T)$, in iterative form as

$$V(T) = \int_0^T \left[C'(t) + sC(t)\right] e^{-\delta t} dt - (1-\beta)C(T)e^{-\delta T} + V(T)e^{-\delta T}. \qquad (6.1)$$

The integrand reflects the two values of carbon storage. First, the *additional* carbon storage realized at any point in time, $C'(t)$ is credited at a price of one per unit added. Second, the *stock* of storage at any given time gives rise to $C(t)$ units of ecosystem services, which are valued at $s$. Under common assumptions on biological growth functions (for example, the logistic function $C(t) = C_\infty / \left(1 + \frac{C_\infty - C_0}{C_0} e^{-gt}\right)$), the rate of growth, $C'(t)$, will first rise and then fall, while the total accumulation, $C(t)$, may have a sigmoid ('$S$') shape, asymptotically approaching a steady-state level I will denote as $C_\infty$.

Rearranging Equation (6.1) we have

$$V(T) = \frac{\int_0^T \left[C'(t) + sC(t)\right] e^{-\delta t} dt - (1-\beta) C(T) e^{-\delta T}}{1 - e^{-\delta T}}. \tag{6.2}$$

Integrating the first term in the numerator on the right-hand side of Equation (6.2) by parts,[3]

$$\int_0^T C'(t) e^{-\delta t} dt = C(T) e^{-\delta T} + \delta \int_0^T C(t) e^{-\delta t} dt$$

We may restate Equation (6.2) as

$$V(T) = \frac{\int_0^T (\delta + s) C(t) e^{-\delta t} dt + \beta C(T) e^{-\delta T}}{1 - e^{-\delta T}} \tag{6.3}$$

Differentiating, the optimal rotation period will satisfy

$$V'(T) = \frac{\left(1 - e^{-\delta T}\right)\left[(\delta + s) C(T) - \delta\beta C(T) + \beta C'(T)\right] - \delta\left[\int_0^T (\delta + s) C(t) e^{-\delta t} dt + \beta C(T) e^{-\delta T}\right]}{\left(1 - e^{-\delta T}\right)^2} \geq 0$$

or

$$\left(1 - \frac{\delta}{\delta + s} \frac{\beta}{1 - e^{-\delta T}}\right) C(T) + \frac{\beta C'(T)}{\delta + s} \geq \frac{\int_0^T \delta C(t) e^{-\delta t} dt}{1 - e^{-\delta T}} \tag{6.4}$$

with strict inequality obtaining if, in the limit as $T$ is unbounded, the left-hand side exceeds the right.

It will sometimes be useful to adopt an analogy in interpreting the expression on the right-hand side of Equation (6.4). Note that $\delta e^{-\delta t}$ is positive on the interval $[0,\infty]$ and its integral over that interval is 1: $\delta e^{-\delta t}$ is the exponential probability distribution with mean $1/\delta$. While there are no random elements in this simple model, and it does not make sense to talk about 'the probability that the time period is $t$', the analogy to probability can be useful, as I will argue below. Another way of writing Equation (6.4) is then to say that the first-order condition with respect to the harvesting rotation is

$$\left(1-\frac{\delta}{\delta+s}\frac{\beta}{1-e^{-\delta T}}\right)C(T)+\frac{\beta C'(T)}{\delta+s}\geq E\left[C(t)\,|\,t\leq T\right], \tag{6.5}$$

where $E\left[C(t)\,|\,t\leq T\right]$ is the expectation of carbon volume conditional on accumulation being curtailed before time $T$, again, under the analogy of treating $\delta e^{-\delta t}$ *as if* it were a probability distribution.

I am particularly interested in the conditions under which Equation (6.5) would be a strict inequality. In the limit, as $T$ is unbounded, $e^{-\delta T}$ approaches zero, as does $C'(T)$, and the volume of carbon accumulated would approach $C_\infty$. So, using these facts and rearranging Equation (6.5), it would be optimal *never* to harvest a reforested area if

$$\frac{\delta+s}{\delta}\left[\frac{C_\infty-E(C)}{C_\infty}\right]\geq\beta \tag{6.6}$$

Note also from Equation (6.3) that if it were never optimal to harvest a reforested area, the value of the area at the time it is established would be

$$V_\infty=\int_0^\infty(\delta+s)C(t)e^{-\delta t}dt=\frac{\delta+s}{\delta}\int_0^\infty\delta C(t)e^{-\delta t}dt=\frac{\delta+s}{\delta}E(C). \tag{6.7}$$

## 6.2 Discussion

Equation (6.6) describes the conditions under which it would be optimal never to harvest a reforested area. We may think of this condition as depending on the realization of several parameters. They are

the pickling rate or fraction of the volume of carbon that is stored permanently following harvest;
$\delta$ the discount rate; and
$s$ the value of ecosystem services associated with a unit of stored carbon, expressed as a multiple of the climate-protection value of a unit of stored carbon.

In addition, the achievement of Equation (6.6) will be determined by two other parameters that have not been explicitly introduced yet. I will denote them as

$g$ the intrinsic growth rates. Suppose that carbon accumulation at time $t$ can be written as $C=C(g,t)$, where $g$ is a constant and the partial derivatives $C_g$ and $C_t$ are both positive. The canonical example is the logistic growth function,

$$C(g,t) = C_0 \frac{C_\infty}{C_0 + (C_\infty - C_0)e^{-gt}}.$$

$V_A$ the opportunity cost of land. From Equation (6.7) the value of a unit of land that is reforested and never harvested again is $V_\infty = \frac{\delta + s}{\delta} E(C)$. Implicit in the assumption that reforestation, in fact, the profit-maximizing land use, is that $V_\infty$ exceeds whatever the net present value of the best alternative use of the land is. Let me denote this opportunity cost as $V_A$, and now require explicitly that $V_\infty = \frac{\delta + s}{\delta} E(C) \geq V_A$ if reforesting and never harvesting is optimal.

Let me now consider the implications of each parameter in turn.

*A higher pickling rate, β, makes harvesting and replanting more attractive.* The greater is the amount of harvested carbon that is permanently removed from the environment with each harvesting cycle, the more attractive it becomes to harvest and replant rather than merely store a fixed volume of carbon in a standing forest.

It may seem reasonable to suppose that $0 \leq \beta \leq 1$. If $\beta$ were negative, it would mean that more carbon would be released into the atmosphere than had been stored in the forest since it was established. While net releases of soil carbon at the time *existing* forests are harvested have been a concern (Searchinger et al. 2008), net sequestration ought not to be negative over a one-harvest-to-the-next time frame. Perhaps more interesting is the possibility that $\beta$ might be greater than 1. While this would not be literally true (more carbon could not be *permanently* stored than had been *temporarily* stored up to the time of harvest),[4] we might subsume into $\beta$ any additional payments made for the products (e.g., building materials) or co-products (e.g., fuel pellets) into which the harvested materials might be converted.

*A higher unit value of ecosystem services, s, makes harvesting and replanting less attractive.* While an area of the forest provides more carbon storage value during periods of growth, the ecosystem services provided by a standing forest is likely to increase as the forest matures. The more important the other ecosystem service values relative to the value of carbon storage, the more attractive it becomes to retain standing forests rather than replanting and starting over.

This is unexceptionable so far as it goes, but at this point another dimension should be considered in the analysis. I have not been explicit about the area of forest under consideration. While carbon sequestration in growing forests around the globe might be substantial enough to make an important contribution to climate mitigation, it is doubtful that many individual reforestation efforts would have a large enough impact to affect the social cost of carbon – the marginal value attached to a ton of additional sequestration. Put another way, demand for forest-based carbon sequestration is likely to be highly elastic.

This is not likely to be true of other ecosystem service values, however. A wide variety of work testifies to rapidly diminishing returns in the amount of land devoted to the production of ecosystem services such as pollination (Ricketts and Lonsdorf 2013; Simpson 2018), coastal storm protection (Barbier et al. 2008), pollution treatment (Mayer et al. 2007; Mander 2008; Simpson 2016), and both the support of species diversity per se and of new product development from diverse natural sources (MacArthur and Wilson 1967; Losos and Ricklefs 2009; Simpson et al. 1996). Restored forests that might provide very valuable ecosystem services *in total*, or which might have high marginal values when only small areas are maintained, may provide little *additional* ecosystem service values when their areal extent increases.

Similarly, context is crucial in the valuation of many ecosystem services (see, e.g. Plummer 2009). A narrow area of riparian forest adjoining a stream or a narrow strip of coastal forest might provide high values for pollution treatment or storm protection, respectively, but each is only valuable if it is placed in a situation in which there are pollutants to be treated or lives and properties to be protected. It may well be that *some* sensitive lands should be permanently reforested to provide other ecosystem services as well as carbon storage, but it might still be optimal to rotate adjacent forests.

There has been some speculation as to whether there might also be some feedback from ecosystem diversity – which is in itself likely to increase with the area extent of a system – to its carbon storage potential. A large literature considers how and why ecological productivity varies with the diversity of an ecosystem (see, e.g., Tilman et al. 2014). More recently, some authors have suggested that indigenous megafauna such as elephants and rhinoceroses may promote carbon storage by seed distribution (Bello et al. 2015), fire suppression (Waldram et al. 2007), and other mechanisms. This has led some to call for 'trophic rewilding' – re-establishing the original suite of species on a landscape – as a carbon mitigation strategy (Cromsigt et al. 2018).

While there likely is such a feedback mechanism from the size of a landscape to its carbon storage potential through its species diversity, one has to wonder how significant it might prove to be. To give some sense of the magnitude, suppose that the amount of carbon stored per hectare in a habitat of size $A$ in a long-run steady state is $f(S)\cdot A$, where $S$ is the species diversity in the habitat, which itself depends on the size $A$. A common assumption is that the species–area relationship is a power function $S = \alpha A$, with $\gamma$ often supposed to be a number on the order of 0.25 (MacArthur and Wilson 1967). Then the increase in steady-state carbon storage per unit area planted might be a number on the order of

$$f(S)\left(1+\gamma\frac{f'(S)\cdot S}{f(S)}\right). \tag{6.8}$$

The elasticity expression in Equation (6.8) would likely be less than 1 and, I would hazard to guess, substantially less than 1, and, as noted, $\gamma$ is often found to be on the order of one-quarter in empirical studies. It seems unlikely, then, that any decreasing returns to scale in the provision of ecosystem services would be offset by increasing returns in carbon storage.

*A higher discount rate, $\delta$, has an ambiguous effect on the choice of whether to harvest and replant.* Recall Equation (6.6): it will be optimal never to harvest a reforested area if

$$\frac{\delta+s}{\delta}\left[\frac{C_\infty - E(C)}{C_\infty}\right] \geq \beta .$$

Differentiating the left-hand side of Equation (6.6) with respect to $\delta$, we have

$$-\frac{s}{\delta^2}\left[\frac{C_\infty - E(C)}{C_\infty}\right] - \frac{\delta+s}{\delta}\frac{\partial E(C)/\partial\delta}{C_\infty} .$$

The first term is negative. Note that if $s$, the value of ecosystem services relative to carbon storage, were zero, it would vanish. If $s$ were positive, however, a higher discount rate means less weight will be assigned to ecosystem service benefits, which are larger when the forest matures, relative to those of carbon sequestration, which are more important when the forest is growing.

The interpretation of $\delta e^{-\delta t}$ *as if* it was a probability distribution is helpful in signing the second term. As the corresponding cumulative density function is $1-e^{-\delta t}$, the cumulative density is *increasing* in the discount rate at all times. Carbon volume is an increasing function of time, and so the expectation, $E(C)$, is *decreasing* in the discount rate.[5] The effect of a higher discount rate through this term is, then, to make harvesting and replanting *less* attractive. This result may seem counterintuitive, as we often think that a higher discount rate – less regard for the future – would induce fewer conservative actions and harvesting and replanting may seem inherently less conservative. In a sense, though, cutting, *placing more carbon in permanent storage*, and renewing the cycle might be seen as the more conservative course. Why, then, would a higher discount rate mitigate against it? Because, first, it would mean paying an *immediate* penalty of $(1-\beta)C$ for any carbon that is not secured at the time of harvest, and second, because the immediate benefits of higher ecosystem service payments would be forgone in favour of an expectation of later carbon storage and ecosystem service benefits. With a higher discount rate, the immediate penalties loom larger than the longer-term benefits.

It is tempting to make inferences about how different discount rates might affect outcomes in practice, particularly in as much as the nations of the developing world – in which much of the reforestation contemplated might be intended to take place – are often felt to apply higher discount rates to their investments. Here, however, it might be appropriate to take the assumption that reforestation policy is considered in a steady state more literally. The widely accepted framework of Ramsey discounting[6] holds that the discount rate is comprised of three elements: the intrinsic rate of time preference, the elasticity of the marginal utility of consumption, and the expectation of the consumption growth rate. If we assume (regrettably, perhaps, in contradiction to much of the available evidence) that all nations will converge to the same level of consumption or, perhaps, *a lá* endogenous growth models, to the same rate of consumption growth, we ought not to apply different rates in different settings. Perhaps as much as anything, this calls into question the assumption I have made in developing such a simple model that reforestation decisions will be made in a stable setting over generations.

*A higher growth rate, g, makes harvesting and replanting more attractive.* The growth rate enters Equation (6) only through $E(C)$. The greater the growth rate, the greater the integrand in $E(C) = \int_0^\infty \delta C(t) e^{-\delta t} dt$ for all values of $t$. Heuristically, the faster the forest grows, the less there is to be gained by maintaining it when it has reached maturity, as opposed to harvesting it and realizing the benefits of re-growth sooner.

*The higher the opportunity cost, $V_A$, the more attractive is cutting a reforested area.* This result is obvious, but perhaps it bears mentioning in the context of some of the factors considered above. While a lower growth rate, $g$, would make cutting and replanting less attractive relative to maintaining a reforested area in perpetuity, and the effect of the discount rate may be ambiguous, both factors may also have the effect of dissuading landowners from reforesting *at all*. Generally speaking, factors that might dissuade a landowner from harvesting an area that has been reforested may also reflect circumstances under which reforestation is less profitable relative to alternative uses.

## 6.3 Conclusion

Forests may serve as both substantial sinks for carbon and as providers of a host of other valuable ecosystem services. This has led a number of commentators to suggest that reforestation presents a sort of two-for-one/win–win 'nature-based solution' to climate change and other societal challenges.

There is, however, often an inherent contradiction between the objectives of carbon sequestration and the provision of other ecosystem services. Carbon is sequestered in *growing* forests; ecosystem services are provided most prolifically by *grown* forests. The opportunity cost of allowing a forest to mature to the point that its ecosystem service provision is greatest may be forgoing opportunities to sequester carbon more rapidly over time.

The simple model I have presented highlights these trade-offs and suggests some of the factors which may determine their resolution. The take-away point is not necessarily that one or another objective ought to be emphasized so much so that we should not leap to the conclusion that carbon sequestration and other conservation goals are necessarily consonants. Much more sophisticated models than I have proposed have been developed for resolving these questions (see, e.g., Hoel et al. 2014, Favero et al. 2017, and the work surveyed in van Kooten and Johnston 2016). Perhaps the main observation I would offer is that work should be extended in a few other directions. One is to consider a wider range of services associated with mature forests. The other, which I only began to touch upon above, concerns ways in which the spatial extent of forests, as well as the timing of their harvests, might affect optimal forest management. While it seems likely that some areas should optimally be maintained in perpetuity because they are more valuable as sources of ecosystem services than as 'carbon farms', the very different spatial scales at which carbon and ecosystem service value accrue suggest that such areas may be relatively small.[7] These considerations suggest that the findings of another seminal contribution to forest management policy might obtain in this context as well: not all forests should be managed to provide all things (Vincent and Binkley 1993). Rather, some should be devoted to carbon sequestration on finite rotations, while others are maintained for the provision of broader suites of ecosystem services.

Finally, the assumption that forestry management decisions are made in a world of essentially stable prices and opportunity costs greatly simplifies modelling, but as the old saying has it, simplifying our models does not simplify the reality they are intended to inform. The great attraction of forest carbon sequestration is that it may provide a cost-effective alternative to more expensive alternatives to emissions reductions through alternative energy sources or curtailment of fossil fuel use. To the extent that the costs of alternative energy or energy conservation do – or do not – decline in future years, the incentives for forest-based carbon sequestration policies may look very different in future decades than they do now. This is between the objectives of carbon sequestration and provision of other ecosystem services. Carbon is sequestered in growing forests; ecosystem services are provided most prolifically by grown forests. The opportunity cost of allowing a forest to mature to the point that its ecosystem service provision is greatest may be forgoing opportunities to sequester carbon more rapidly over time.

## Notes

1 Reforestation is growing trees where trees used to grow but are not currently planted. Afforestation is growing trees where trees have not grown in historical memory, but where they could. To avoid the awkward repetition of "re- and afforestation" I will use "reforestation" in what follows, but generally intend the term to encompass both possibilities.

2 Several nations have relied heavily on BECCS in their Paris Climate Accord commitments (Burns and Nicholson 2017; Creutzig et al. 2019), though the technology has not been demonstrated at scale, and some authors suggest reforestation efforts might render it superfluous (Hausfather 2018).

3 I will assume in evaluating the integral that $C(0)$ the carbon stock at the time the area is first reforested is zero.

4 There is also an issue of whether carbon storage from forest products might also be credited with offsets from displacement of building materials whose production is carbon intensive, such as concrete or steel, or of fossil-fuel-generated energy (see, e.g., van Kooten and Johnston 2016). I will ignore this possibility here, on the argument that the effect should be measured as a *decrease* in negative externalities in the other-building-product or other-fuel sectors, not as an *increase* in positive externalities in forestry.

5 This is a straightforward application of a fundamental result in statistical decision theory. The expectation of a monotonical function is increasing in a parameter of the distribution function of its argument if and only if the cumulative distribution function is weakly declining in the parameter across its entire support. Formally, such a situation is referred to as one in which increasing the parameter induces *first-order stochastic dominance*.

6 Ramsey's social discount rate is calculated as follows: $r = d + n \times\times g$, where $d$ is time preference, $n$ is the elasticity of marginal utility of consumption, and $g$ is the growth rate.

7 Even absent any contributory ecosystem service values, it might be optimal to maintain some reforested areas in perpetuity rather than harvesting them. Returning to Equation (6.6), when $s = 0$, would be optimal never to reharvest an area if $1-\beta \geq E(C)/C_{\infty}$. This condition would only hold if the pickling rate, $\beta$ were low.

## References

Baldocchi, D., and J. Penuelas. 2019. "The Physics and Ecology of Mining Carbon Dioxide from the Atmosphere by Ecosystems." *Global Change Biology* 25 (4): 1191–1197. doi:10.1111/gcb.14559.

Barbier, E. B, E. W Koch, B. R. Silliman, S. D Hacker, E. Wolanski, J. Primavera, E. F Granek, et al. 2008. "Nonlinear Ecological Functions and Values." *Science* 319: 321–323. doi:10.1126/science.1150349.

Bello, C., M. Galetti, M. A. Pizo, L. Fernando, S. Magnago, M. F. Rocha, R. A. F. Lima, C. A. Peres, O. Ovaskainen, and P. Jordano. 2015. "Defaunation Affects Carbon Storage in Tropical Forests." *Science Advances* 1 (11): e1501105. doi:10.1126/sciadv.1501105.

Bowler, D. E., L. Buyung-Ali, T. M. Knight, and A. S. Pullin. 2010. "Urban Greening to Cool Towns and Cities: A Systematic Review of the Empirical Evidence." *Landscape and Urban Planning* 97 (3): 147–155. doi:10.1016/j.landurbplan.2010.05.006.

Burns, W., and S. Nicholson. 2017. "Bioenergy and Carbon Capture with Storage (BECCS): The Prospects and Challenges of an Emerging Climate Policy Response." *Journal of Environmental Studies and Sciences* 7 (4): 527–34. doi:10.1007/s13412-017-0445-6.

Creutzig, F., C. Breyer, J. Hilaire, J. Minx, G. P. Peters, and R. Socolow. 2019. "The Mutual Dependence of Negative Emission Technologies and Energy Systems." *Energy and Environmental Science* 12 (6): 1805–1817. doi:10.1039/c8ee03682a.

Cromsigt, Joris P. G. M., M. te Beest, G. I. H. Kerley, M. Landman, E. le Roux, and F. A. Smith. 2018. "Trophic Rewilding as a Climate Change Mitigation Strategy?" *Philosophical Transactions of the Royal Society B: Biological Sciences* 373 (1761): 20170440. doi:10.1098/rstb.2017.0440.

Daily, G. C. 1997. *Nature's Services: Societal Dependence on Natural Ecosystems.* Washington, DC: Island Press. doi:10.1023/a:1023307309124.

Emerton, L., L. Iyango, P. Luwum, and A. Malinga.1999. *The Present Economic Value of Nakivubo Urban Wetland, Uganda, and National Wetlands.* Kampala: The World Conservation Union, Eastern Africa Regional Office, Nairobi and National Wetlands Programme, Wetlands Inspectorate Division, Ministry of Water, Land and Environment. https://www.iucn.org/content/present-economic-value-nakivubo-urban-wetland-uganda (accessed on 16 July 2021).

Faustmann, Martin. 1849. [Linnard (tr.) and Gane (ed.)1968]. "On the Determination of the Value Which Forest Land and Immature Stands Possess for Forestry." English Translation in: *Martin Faustmann and the Evolution of Discounted Cash Flow* (Translated by W. Linnard; with editing and introduction by M. Gane). Commonwealth Forestry Institute Paper No. 42. University of Oxford: Oxford, England. [Translation republished with permission from *Commonwealth Forestry Association in Journal of Forest Economics* 1: 1 (1995).] https://www.worldcat.org/title/martin-faustmann-and-the-evolution-of-discounted-cash-flow-on-determination-of-the-money-value-of-bare-forest-land-calculation-of-the-value-which-forest-land-and-immature-stands-possess-for-forestry-two-articles-from-the-original-german-of-1849/oclc/888569197 (accessed on 16 July 2021).

Favero, A., R. Mendelsohn, and B. Sohngen. 2017. "Using Forests for Climate Mitigation: Sequester Carbon or Produce Woody Biomass?" *Climatic Change* 144 (2): 195–206. doi:10.1007/s10584-017-2034-9.

Garzuglia, M., and M. Saket. 2005. *Wood Volume and Woody Biomass: Review of FRA 2000 Estimates 68. Forest Resources Assessment*. Rome. http://www.fao.org/3/ae153e/AE153e00.htm (accessed on 14 May 2021).

Griscom, B. W., J. Adams, P. W. Ellis, R. A. Houghton, G. Lomax, D. A. Miteva, W. H. Schlesinger, et al. 2017. "Natural Climate Solutions." *Proceedings of the National Academy of Sciences of the United States of America* 114 (44): 11645–11650. doi:10.1073/pnas.1710465114.

Hartman, R. 1976. "The Harvesting Decision When a Standing Forest has Value." *Economic Inquiry* 14 (1): 52–58. doi:10.1111/j.1465-7295.1976.tb00377.x.

Hausfather, Z. 2018. "Analysis: How 'Natural Climate Solutions' Can Reduce the Need for BECCS." *Carbon Brief*, 2018. https://www.carbonbrief.org/analysis-how-natural-climate-solutions-can-reduce-the-need-for-beccs (accessed on 1 September 2021).

Hoel, M., B. Holtsmark, and K. Holtsmark. 2014. "Faustmann and the Climate." *Journal of Forest Economics* 20: 192–210. doi:10.1016/j.jfe.2014.04.003.

Houghton, R. A, and A. A Nassikas. 2018. "Negative Emissions from Stopping Deforestation and Forest Degradation, Globally."*Global Change Biology* 24 (1): 350–359. doi:10.1111/gcb.13876.

Kabisch, N., M. van den Bosch, and R. Lafortezza. 2017. "The Health Benefits of Nature-Based Solutions to Urbanization Challenges for Children and the Elderly: A Systematic Review." *Environmental Research* 159: 362–373. doi:10.1016/j.envres.2017.08.004.

Kooten, G. C. van, C. S. Binkley, and G. Delcourt. 1995. "Effect of Carbon Taxes and Subsidies on Optimal Forest Rotation Age and Supply of Carbon Services." *American Journal of Agricultural Economics* 77 (2): 363–72. doi:10.2307/1243546.

Kooten, G. C. van, and C. M. Johnston. 2016. "The Economics of Forest Carbon Offsets." *Annual Review of Resource Economics* 8 (1): 227–46. doi:10.1146/annurev-resource-100815-095548.

Lin, Brenda B., S. Macfadyen, A. R. Renwick, S. A. Cunningham, and N. A. Schellhorn. 2013. "Maximizing the Environmental Benefits of Carbon Farming through Ecosystem Service Delivery." *BioScience* 63 (10): 793–803 doi: 10.1525/bio.2013.63.10.6.

Losos, J. B., and R. E. Ricklefs. 2009. *The Theory of Island Biogeography Revisited*. Princeton: Princeton University Press. ISBN-9780691136530. doi:10.1111/j.1442-9993.2010.02226.x.

MacArthur, Robert, and Edward O. Wilson. 1967. *The Theory of Island Biogeography*. Princeton: Princeton University Press. https://press.princeton.edu/books/paperback/9780691088365/the-theory-of-island-biogeography (accessed on 3 June 2021).

Mander. 2008. "Watershed Management." In Sven Erik Jørgensen, Brian D. Fath (ed.) *Encyclopedia of Ecology, Five-Volume Set*, 3737–3748. Cambridge, Massachusetts, USA: Academic Press. doi:10.1016/B978-008045405-4.00082-3.

Mayer, P. M., S. K. Reynolds, M. D. McCutchen, and T. J. Canfield. 2007. "Meta-Analysis of Nitrogen Removal in Riparian Buffers." *Journal of Environmental Quality* 36 (4):1172–1180. doi:10.2134/jeq2006.0462.

Monbiot, G. 2020. "Averting Climate Breakdown by Restoring Ecosystems A Call to Action." https://www.biomassmurder.org/docs/2019-04-00-natural-climate-solutions-averting-climate-breakdown-by-restoring-ecosystems-english.pdf (accessed on 18 May 2020).

Nature. 2017. "'Nature-Based Solutions' Is the Latest Green Jargon That Means More Than You Might Think." *Nature* 541 (7636): 133–134. doi:10.1038/541133b.

Pannell, D. J., G. R. Marshall, N. Barr, A. Curtis, F. Vanclay, and R. Wilkinson. 2006. "Understanding and Promoting Adoption of Conservation Practices by Rural Landholders." *Australian Journal of Experimental Agriculture* 46 (11): 1407–1424. CSIRO. doi:10.1071/EA05037.

Plummer, M. L. 2009. "Assessing Benefit Transfer for the Valuation of Ecosystem Services." *Frontiers in Ecology and the Environment* 7 (1): 38–45. doi:10.1890/080091.

Ricketts, T. H., and E. Lonsdorf. 2013. "Mapping the Margin: Comparing Marginal Values of Tropical Forest Remnants for Pollination Services." *Ecological Applications* 23 (5): 1113–23. doi: 10.1890/12-1600.1.

Searchinger, T., R. Heimlich, R. A. Houghton, F. Dong, A. Elobeid, J. Fabiosa, S. Tokgoz, D. Hayes, and T. H. Yu. 2008. "Use of U.S. Croplands for Biofuels Increases Greenhouse Gases through Emissions from Land-Use Change." *Science* 319 (5867): 1238–1240. doi:10.1126/science.1151861.

Seddon, N., A. Chausson, P. Berry, and C. A. J. Girardin. 2019. "Understanding the Value and Limits of Nature-Based Solutions to Climate Change and Other Global Challenges." *The Royal Society* 375 (1794): 1–12. doi:10.1098/rstb.2019.0120.

Simpson, R. D. 2016. "The Simple but Not-Too-Simple Valuation of Ecosystem Services: Basic Principles and an Illustrative Example." *Journal of Environmental Economics and Policy* 6 (1): 96–106. doi:10.1080/21606544.2016.1184594.

Simpson, R. D. 2018. "Conservation Incentives from an Ecosystem Service: How Much Farmland Might Be Devoted To Native Pollinators?" *Environmental and Resource Economics* 73 (2): 661–678. doi:10.1007/s10640-018-0277-1.

Simpson, R. D., R. A. Sedjo, and J. W. Reid. 1996. "Valuing Biodiversity for Use in Pharmaceutical Research." *The Journal of Political Economy* 104 (1): 163–185. doi:10.1086/262021.

Tilman, D., F. Isbell, and J. M. Cowles. 2014. "Biodiversity and Ecosystem Functioning." *Annual Review of Ecology, Evolution, and Systematics* 45 (1): 471–493. doi:10.1146/annurev-ecolsys-120213-091917.

Vincent, J. R., and C. S. Binkley. 1993. "Efficient Multiple-Use Forestry May Require Land-Use Specialization." *Land Economics* 69 (4): 370. doi:10.2307/3146454.

Walters, Gretchen Marie et al. 2016. *Nature-Based Solutions to Address Global Societal Challenges*. Gland, Switzerland: IUCN. doi:10.2305/iucn.ch.2016.13.en.

Waldram, M. S., W. J. Bond, and W. D. Stock. 2007. "Ecological Engineering by A Mega-Grazer: White Rhino Impacts on A South African Savanna." *Ecosystems* 11 (1): 101–112. doi:10.1007/s10021-007-9109-9.

Chapter 7

# Incentives for Rural Households to Establish Tree Cover on Agricultural Land in Andhra Pradesh, India

*Stella Z. Schons, Gregory S. Amacher, Kelly M. Cobourn, Nilesh Shinde, and Haripriya Gundimeda*

## Introduction

India's forest cover transitions and land-use change have been a focus of large-scale projects carried out by governmental and non-governmental agencies over the past 50 years, most often to ameliorate degraded and previously removed forests (Kohlin et al. 2001; Kohlin and Amacher 2005). The main objectives of these projects have been to improve fuel collection and opportunities for timber use in rural villages through the establishment of community forests (Kohlin et al. 2001; Kohlin and Ostwald 2001). However, a series of policies and other obstacles limiting land holding size and expansion, and the continuing abject poverty among the rural population, have prevented the large-scale establishment of forests on private non-community agricultural land (Joshi et al. 2010).

The incentives of farming households in tropical developing countries to establish tree plantations on private land (often called 'trees outside of forests' or TOF) is a relatively understudied topic. There has been some discussion of plantation establishment at a macroeconomic scale in the forest transitions literature, but this is mostly based on modelling reforestation as a replacement land use for tropical forest removal (e.g., see Barbier et al. 2017 for a recent survey). Nonetheless, understanding incentives at the household level to establish forest cover in arid areas, especially where property rights are less than formal, remains critical in predicting the performance of afforestation and reforestation programmes worldwide.

The scientific literature demonstrates that secondary forests can generate benefits at the local to a global scale by augmenting food and fibre production, reducing harvesting pressure on native forests, and supporting climate mitigation through carbon sequestration (Barbier et al. 2017; Bastin et al. 2019). Policies that seek to provide financial incentives to establish planted forests through cost sharing of seedlings or information provision programmes reflect the perceived value of investing in secondary planting (see Rudolf et al. 2020 for an Indonesian example). However, these programmes are exceptions. Generally speaking, the decision to plant trees

DOI: 10.4324/9781003253884-10

depends critically on location and income constraints, farm and market characteristics, and the economic and demographic status of households. Obstacles to planting forests arise for a host of reasons, not the least of which is the opportunity cost of reduced agricultural income or transaction costs due to a lack of knowledge or experience with tree planting and management. One would expect that transaction costs could be lowered through information programmes or social networks that develop in villages and communities; these social fabrics could be critical in predicting reforestation even on regional scales.

In this chapter, we explore the incentives of farmers to establish forest cover on agricultural land in Andhra Pradesh, India. A large body of theoretical economic work on land-use decisions examines the opportunity costs of switching land uses from agriculture to forest production (Parks and Hardie 1995; Haim et al. 2011; Amacher et al. 2009). However, there is scant empirical work that estimates the drivers of margin changes for these problems (Parks et al. 1998). We present analyses based on a large, novel dataset collected using a randomized survey of farm households in the East and West Godhavari regions, which are separated by the Godavari River, the second largest in India, and where a large number of forest processing firms are located. We use a multilevel mixed effect probit methodology to account for unobserved variation across clusters of villages, as well as unobserved variation within villages. The latter is particularly important if the social interactions between farmers within villages might be an important vehicle to provide information for tree planting. Our estimates serve to identify the key drivers of tree planting decisions on land that can also provide agricultural returns. We present estimates of farmer responses to variables that are readily observable, and which can, in principle, be used to support the design of policy by the Indian government to achieve afforestation and reforestation targets.

## 7.1 Household Decisions

Our interest in the empirical analysis is to examine the decision to establish tree cover on agricultural land while accounting for unobserved heterogeneity across and within villages. We do not consider specific planting of individual tree species in this chapter; rather, we simply seek to understand why agricultural land is taken out of production, completely or in part, to establish forest cover of any type. The decision we study is relevant to public goods production, such as carbon storage or reducing degradation of soil and pressure on native forest cover stocks.[1]

We present a simple model of decision-making by farm households to clarify the choice between planting trees versus maintaining land for alternative use, namely agricultural production. The decision to plant forest cover depends on the rents from all farm-level decisions as revealed in input use decisions (labour and capital) for the farm as a whole.[2] Given the income and food security links to farm decision-making by each household, the decision to plant trees, therefore, should also depend on the off-farm and market-access opportunities of the household, as well as input use and profitability on the farm.

In what follows, we model decision-making by a representative household *i* in region *j* but suppress subscripts for brevity (we make the subscripts explicit in the discussion of the econometric specification). A representative household faces the time constraint:

$$T - d = L_c + L_f + L_o \tag{7.1}$$

where $T$ is total time, $d$ is an (assumed) exogenous measure of travel time to markets and/or field plots,[3] $L_c$ is time the household allocates to crop production, $L_f$ is time allocated to planted tree production, and $L_o$ is time spent by the household in off-farm work. As is conventional in these models, leisure time is not specifically defined but is completely determined by a residual after labour time is determined. Let $L$ denote the total time allocated to all income-generating activities on the right-hand side of Equation (7.1), i.e., $L \equiv L_c + L_f + L_o$.

Facing the time constraint in Equation (7.1), the household makes labour and consumption decisions to maximize utility $U(l, C_h; \theta) \equiv U(T - d - L, C_h; \theta)$, which depends on total time allocated to income-generating activities $L$, household own-consumption $C_h$, and a set of exogenous variables that are important to utility, such as household demographics, captured by the vector $\theta$. We make the standard assumptions that $\partial U / \partial C_h > 0$ and that labour results in disutility (or equivalently, leisure results in utility), i.e., $\partial U / \partial L < 0$.

The household also faces a cash constraint requiring total income from all sources to equal total expenditures for farm production and household consumption. Let total household income be given by $I = I_{ex} + I_o + (Q - C_h)P_a + FP_f$, where $I_{ex}$ is exogenous income or assets owned by the household; $I_o = wL_0$ is income earned from off-farm labour work supplied at the exogenous market wage $w$; $Q$ is household crop production; $F$ is household production of trees; and $P_a$ and $P_f$ are vectors of exogenous market prices for crops and trees, respectively. The term $(Q - C_h)P_a$ represents income earned on the sale of crops produced that are not consumed by the household, if any. When $(Q - C_h)P_a > 0$, the household has positive net production of crops relative to what the household consumes. This surplus is sold at a market price $P_a$ and is part of total income. Conversely, $(Q - C_h)P_a < 0$ implies that the household is a net purchaser of crop goods at the market price.

Using these definitions, the cash constraint requires that total household income equals expenditures:

$$I = I_{ex} + wL_0 + \left(Q - C_h\right)P_a + FP_f = wL_H + rK. \quad (7.2)$$

The right-hand side of Equation (7.2) defines expenditures, including the cost of hired labour, $L_H$, paid at the market wage rate $w$, and a vector of all other inputs used in production, denoted $K$, with unit price vector $r$.

The variables $Q$ and $F$ in the expression for total household income are household production functions relating outputs to all relevant inputs (labour and nonlabour) as well as other variables that impact production:

$$Q \equiv Q\left(L_c, K, L_H, \varnothing\right) \quad (7.3)$$

$$F \equiv F\left(L_f, K, \varnothing\right) \quad (7.4)$$

In Equations (7.3) and (7.4) $\varnothing$ is a vector of variables reflecting household experience and farm characteristics important to production. Relevant farm-level variables are similar across production activities in our study region.[4]

We assume that tree planting is a valuable activity to the household through increases in income from selling products derived from trees. This is certainly true in our study area of Andhra Pradesh; because households sell palm oil, fruits and nuts, or timber from species such as casuarinas and eucalyptus. In addition, we have not modelled the dynamic nature of tree production for timber species (such as rotation age decisions), because our data can only be used to focus on the one-time decision to plant trees on the farm. As a consequence, we assume that the farm household understands that the rents from trees are a function of rotation decisions, and thus one could re-interpret $FP_f$ in Equation (7.2) as a present value.

The household's problem can now be written as one of choosing consumption, labour allocation, and the use of hired labour and other inputs, to maximize utility subject to the cash constraint:

$$\max_{L, C_h, L_H, K, C_p} U\left(T - d - L, C_h; \theta\right) \quad (7.5)$$

$$s.t.\ I_{ex} + wL_0 + \left(Q\left(L_c, K, L_H, \varnothing\right) - C_h\right)P_a + F\left(L_f, K, \varnothing\right)P_f = wL_H + rK$$

where we have substituted Equations (7.3) and (7.4) into Equation (7.2). The solution to this problem is derived by finding the first-order conditions and solving the recursive system of equations first for production decisions and then for the choice of consumption. First-order conditions and analysis of similar problems can be found in more detail in Sills et al. (2003).

## 7.2 Welfare and the Tree Planting Decision

For the purposes of the tree planting decision, the problem in (7.5) is used to define the difference in household welfare from planting trees versus not planting trees. Welfare is defined as the indirect (maximized) utility achievable by the household.[5] The indirect utility function is derived by substituting the optimal choices for consumption, labour times, farm input use, and hired labour into the utility function:

$$V \equiv U\left(T - d - L^{*}, C_{h}^{*}; I_{ex}, \theta\right). \tag{7.6}$$

In Equation (7.6), $L^{*}$ and $C_{h}^{*}$ are optimal labour and consumption decisions, respectively. Recall that total time $T$ and access $d$ are exogenous variables. From the definition of utility and Equations (7.3) and (7.4), the optimal labour and consumption decisions are functions of prices as well as farm and household characteristics, i.e., $L^{*} = L\left(P_a, P_f, r, w, \varnothing, \theta, d\right)$ and $C_{h}^{*} = C\left(P_a, P_f, r, w, \varnothing, \theta, d, I_{ex}\right)$. The optimal on-farm labour decision $L^{*}$ is a vector of time allocated to forest and crop production and hired labour; this follows from the first-order condition of the farm profit function defined as the total value of production less the total costs, $P_aQ + FP_f - wL_H - rK$. The optimal labour vector also includes off-farm time allocation. Notice in (7.6) that while exogenous income $I_{ex}$ factors into the consumption decision due to the utility maximization problem of the household, it does not factor into farm profit maximization.[6]

Substituting the expressions for $L^{*}$ and $C_{h}^{*}$ into the utility function, we arrive at a welfare expression rewritten explicitly as a function of all the variables that are elements of $L^{*}$ and $C_{h}^{*}$ and other exogenous factors of utility and production ($d, \varnothing, \theta$):

$$V \equiv U\left(P_a, P_f, r, w, \varnothing, \theta, d, I; F = 0,1\right). \tag{7.7}$$

This indirect utility function includes the argument $F$ = 1,0, which indicates that there is potentially a different welfare level for households that plant trees ($F$ = 1) versus households that choose not to plant trees ($F$ = 0). This is true because rents for agricultural production differ depending on whether the household plants trees or not; this results in different optimal choices and, therefore, household welfare. Also, the benefits of planting trees for welfare are not purely financial. Rather, the fact that the utility function drives the tree planting decision for the household implies that non-financial considerations and benefits could be important in the decision for a household to establish forest plantations.

## 7.3 Econometric Specification of the Tree Planting Decision

The household will plant trees only if doing so results in higher indirect utility than not planting. The decision to plant trees is captured by $F_{ij}$, which takes on a value of 1 or 0 depending on whether household $i$ in region $j$ plants trees or not, respectively.[7] Observation of $F_{ij}$ depends on unobserved indirect utilities through the following stochastic relationship:

$$F_{ij} = 1\, if\; V_{1ij} + e_1 > V_{0ij} + e_0;$$

$$F_{ij} = 0 \text{ otherwise.} \tag{7.8}$$

In Equation (7.8), $e_1$ and $e_0$ are errors that may or may not be household specific, as discussed below.

The indirect utilities, $V_{1ij}$ and $V_{0ij}$, in Equation (7.8) are not observable by the researcher, nor are the error terms $e_1$ and $e_0$. Therefore, we define a probability $y_{ij}$, which is the probability that household $i$ located in region $j$ will plant trees on their farm ($F_{ij}$ = 1), which is a function of observable variables, where:

$$y_{ij} = \mathbf{g}_{ij}^{'}\beta + \epsilon_{ij}, \quad \epsilon_{ij} \sim N\left(0,\sigma^2\right) \tag{7.9}$$

In Equation (7.9), $\mathbf{g}_{ij}$ is a vector of $h$ independent variables, β is a $h$ x 1 vector of corresponding coefficients to be estimated, and $\epsilon_{ij}$ is a random error term. The $\mathbf{g}_{ij}$ vector is defined more specifically as $\mathbf{g}_{ij} = \left(1, P_{aj}, P_{fj}, r_j, w_j, \varnothing_{ij}, \theta_{ij}, d_{ij}, I_{ij}\right)$ such that Equation (7.9) incorporates all (explanatory) variables in the welfare function (7.7). For completeness, note that the underlying assumption in Equation (7.9) is $y_{ij} > 0\, if\; F_{ij} = 1$, and $y_{ij} = 0\, if\; F_{ij} = 0$.

Given the structure of our data, the standard assumption in (7.9) may not be sufficient, as there is reason to believe there is a correlation between observations that are included in the same cluster (be it villages within a mandal or households within a village). We therefore decompose the error in (7.9) further into a multilevel mixed effects specification (Guo and Zhao 2000; Gibbons and Hedeker 1997).[8] This specification may be viewed as a type of random effects model that generalizes the structure of the error term

$\epsilon_{ij}$ into three elements (Oshchepkov and Shirokanova, 2020), each measuring a different unobserved effect on the probability of tree planting by household and location:

$$\epsilon_{ij} = u_{0j} + \boldsymbol{h}_{ij}^{'}\eta_i + \xi_{ij} \tag{7.10}$$

The first term on the right-hand side of Equation (7.10), $u_{0j}$ captures unobserved factors that vary systematically by location; it therefore defines a location-specific random intercept term (fixed effect). Examples of factors captured by this term include unobserved types of social organizations and government or private company influence and technical assistance within a village that lead households to make certain decisions. In the second term on the right-hand side of Equation (7.10), the vector $\boldsymbol{h}_{ij}$ is an $m$x1 subset of the vector $\boldsymbol{g}_{ij}$, where $m \leq h$. The error $\eta_i$ is a vector of random effects specific to the individual household. The product $\boldsymbol{h}_{ij}^{'}\eta_i$ therefore defines a set of random slope coefficients for a subset of the explanatory variables. The final term in Equation (7.10), $\xi_{ij}$ captures an idiosyncratic error that is independent of $u_{0j}$ and $\eta_i$.

The error structure for our problem accommodates multiple assumptions about correlation of various clusters in the data depending on the (a priori to estimation) assumed composition of $\boldsymbol{h}_{ij}$. Our data for households are collected in individual villages, and several villages are located in mandals. Depending on how the subset vector $h_{ij}$ is defined, we can address correlation between households within an individual village in the sample (we will call this the 2-level mixed effects model); or we can assume that there is correlation both among households in a village and additionally among villages in a mandal (this more general version will be called a 3-level mixed effects model).

The mixed effects models in either 2- or 3-level form improve over standard random effects or fixed effects error structures and are relatively new to economics. These approaches have been very recently argued as relevant in problems such as ours where cluster-based correlation is possible (see Oshchepkov and Shirokanova 2020 for a discussion). The argument for using mixed effects is that cluster correlation means that the variance and covariance of the error term within each cluster might be nonzero. The model in both 2-level and 3-level form can also be estimated by assuming that the structure of the variance-covariance matrix of these correlations does not have a specific a priori form, similar to general heteroskedastic estimators.[9]

For the purposes of our tree planting study, the 2-level mixed effects error can be specified where it is a priori assumed that households within a village have the error $\epsilon_{ij}$ in (10) for tree planting decisions that are correlated, but errors across villages within each mandal are independent. The 3-level mixed effects model has a priori assumption that there is correlation of the $\epsilon_{ij}$ between households in the same village, and also across villages in the same mandal. The 3-level specification captures, for example, the correlation across villages within East and West Godavari. Failure to account for these types of correlation when they are present results in biased coefficient estimates and standard errors.

In the econometric results for tree planting of the next section, we consider both 2- and 3-level mixed effects models and formally test which one is more representative of our data. However, it should be pointed out that regardless of the model chosen, the mixed effects specification of the error components uses more information than a simple probit model of tree planting because the latter would rely on assuming errors across households in a village (or across villages in a mandal) are uncorrelated. Using a model that assumes errors are simple and uncorrelated such as (7.9) would result in tree planting analyses for rural households that are biased, thus also biasing the policy interpretations of the results. Thus, it appears to us at least that the most general approach should be a new standard for estimating the probability of tree planting and identifying drivers of this probability in village-based economies.

An estimable model of tree planting decisions using the underlying error decomposition in Equation (7.10) is of the following form for the probability of tree cover planting:

$$Pr\left(F_{ij} = 1 | \boldsymbol{g}_{ij}, \boldsymbol{u}_j, \boldsymbol{h}_{ij}\right) = Pr\left(y_{ij} > 0 | \boldsymbol{g}_{ij}, \boldsymbol{u}_j, \boldsymbol{h}_{ij}\right) = \Psi\left(\boldsymbol{g}_{ij}'\beta + u_{0j} + \boldsymbol{h}_{ij}'\eta_i\right). \quad (7.11)$$

The parameter vector $\beta$ in Equation (7.11) is estimated using the maximum likelihood procedure described by Guo and Zhao (2000) and Gibbons and Hedeker (1997). Using the estimated coefficient vector, denoted as $\hat{\beta}$, the impact of a unit change in any explanatory variable on the probability that the household will plant trees can be obtained from the marginal effect, $\frac{\partial \Psi\left(\boldsymbol{g}_{ij}'\beta + u_{0j} + \boldsymbol{h}_{ij}'\eta_i\right)}{\partial \boldsymbol{g}_{ij}}$. This effect must be calculated differently depending on whether the explanatory variable of interest is discrete or continuous. These marginal effects are critical to understanding the responses of households to changes in relevant explanatory variables such as market access, costs of inputs, and household and farm characteristics.

## 7.4 Data

We use a dataset of approximately 2,000 farming households collected across 4 villages in the district of East Godavari and 16 villages in the district of West Godavari. Villages were sampled based on the extent of tree cover on surrounding farms using two groupings; specifically, we chose the number of sampled households proportional to the total land area visible using recent satellite data on tree or plant cover. This procedure was used for two groups: villages with >60 hectares of tree cover and those with <60 hectares of tree cover. This procedure yielded 18 villages from the group with >60 hectares of tree cover and two from the group with <60 hectares of tree cover. We excluded villages with <10 hectares of forest cover (many of which had almost no tree planting on land farmed by residents in the village). Table 7.1A contains a list of villages sampled and their location; Figure 7.1 shows the geographical distribution and scale of sampled households relative to natural and human landscape features.

Within each village, we randomly selected households using a simple coin flipping method. In total, we interviewed 2,069 out of 11,747 existing households in the sample villages. Village size varied between 81 households (Lankalapalli, in West Godavari) and 1,980 households (Ungurutu, also in West Godavari). The data were collected between May and July 2019 through a survey instrument containing questions on household demographics, employment and production, community organization and technical assistance, forest management decisions, and plot characteristics, among others.[10] Household production questions (for example: agriculture, grazing, forest management, etc.) were asked for the two main seasons of the year: Kharif (or monsoon season, planted in July and harvested in the months of September and October) and Rabi (planted in November and

*Table 7.1A* List of Villages and Mandals Covered in Survey Sample[a]

| *District* | *Codes* | *Village* | *Codes* | *Mandal* | *Codes* |
|---|---|---|---|---|---|
| West Godavari | 1 | Rajanagaram | 1 | Buttayagudem | 1 |
| West Godavari | 1 | Barrinkalapadu | 2 | Jeelugu Milli | 2 |
| West Godavari | 1 | Lankalapalle | 3 | Jeelugu Milli | 2 |
| West Godavari | 1 | ParimpudiNarayanapuram | 4 | Jeelugu Milli | 2 |
| West Godavari | 1 | Vadlapatlanuthanam | 5 | Kamavarapukota | 3 |
| West Godavari | 1 | Kothapalle | 6 | Dwaraka Tirumala | 4 |
| West Godavari | 1 | Malleswaram | 7 | Lingapalem | 5 |
| West Godavari | 1 | Avapadu | 8 | Nallajerla | 6 |
| West Godavari | 1 | Nyayampalle | 9 | Pedavegi | 7 |
| West Godavari | 1 | Ramasingavaram | 10 | Pedavegi | 7 |
| West Godavari | 1 | Bandivarigudem | 11 | T.Narasapuram | 8 |
| West Godavari | 1 | Tedlam | 12 | T.Narasapuram | 8 |
| West Godavari | 1 | Gopinadhapatnam | 13 | Ungutur | 9 |
| West Godavari | 1 | Unguturu | 14 | Ungutur | 9 |
| East Godavari | 2 | Billananduru | 15 | Kotananduru | 10 |
| East Godavari | 2 | Doparthi | 16 | Prathipadu | 11 |
| East Godavari | 2 | U. Jagannadhapuram | 17 | Prathipadu | 11 |
| East Godavari | 2 | Palacharla | 18 | Rajanagaram | 12 |
| East Godavari | 2 | Dondavaka | 19 | Tuni | 13 |
| East Godavari | 2 | Brahmasamedyam | 20 | Katrenikona | 14 |
| West Godavari | 1 | Erraguntapalle | 22 | Chintalapudi | 15 |
| West Godavari | 1 | Ayyaparajugudem | 23 | Lingapalem | 16 |

[a]A mandal in India is similar to a county in the United States.

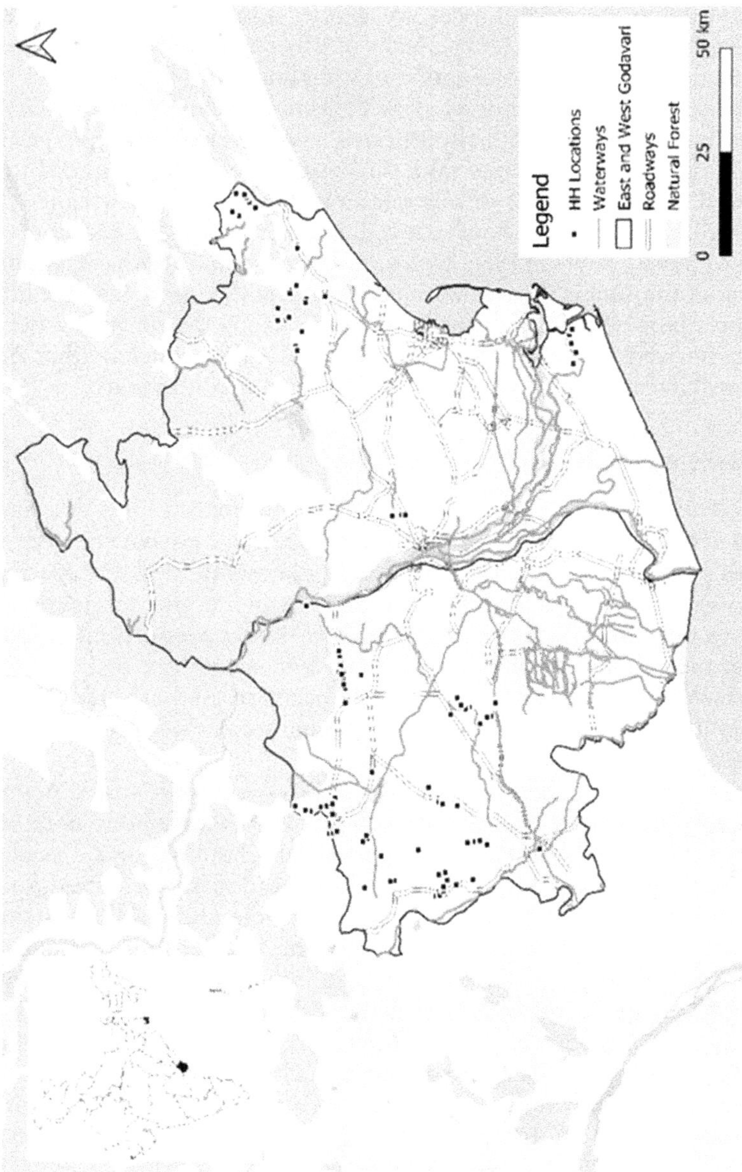


*Figure 7.1* Location of sampled villages in East and West Godavari, Andhra Pradesh. *Source:* Author.

harvested in the months of May and June). The sampling was preceded by focus group meetings with village leaders and by pretesting individual households in non-sampled villages to refine the survey instrument. In all cases, interviews were conducted with the household member who was indicated as the land-use decision-maker, although information in the survey included family-based information as well. Enumerators were hired and trained by the authors from local universities and a survey management firm in Andhra Pradesh with experience in other university research-based data collection managed coordination of sampling.

Challenges encountered during data collection included an inability to interview a few of the originally selected villages (we were not permitted by the village leaders); this said, all households sampled agreed to be interviewed, answered most of our questions, and indicated whether they planted trees or not. A few households did not provide information on the distance to plots for which there was no cultivation during Kharif. Another drawback of the data is that we were not able to gather more detailed information on a plot-by-plot basis due to time constraints. As we discuss below, however, our econometric results are robust. We thus conclude that these limitations have not had a significant impact on our conclusions.

### 7.4.1 Descriptive Statistics

Tables 7.1 and 7.2 present variables used in our analysis and descriptive statistics of the data. In total, 2,062 household heads were interviewed; 592 households (28.6% of the total sample) had planted trees of any species in at least one of their plots, with 'tree planting' including tree species planted for various purposes (for example, for fruit or timber production) in family plots that may be in conjunction with other non-woody species. This way, we can think of our analysis as one of willingness to establish tree cover on the farm rather than the choice between specific species (itself an important future research topic).

In the entire sample, there are on average 1.4 working women, 1.6 working men, and 1.5 children in each household. The average household head is 51 years of age and has gone through formal schooling for 2.8 years. A total of 1,143 (55%) of interviewed household heads are illiterate. Although discrimination on the basis of castes is illegal in India, the social hierarchical social class system in the country is still present, both in the economic and political spheres, and may for our purposes influence access to education, occupations, income, and health resources (Munshi 2004). In our sample, 16.5% are from 'scheduled caste' (SC) groups, 10.5% are from 'scheduled tribes' (ST) group, 34.07% are from 'other backward caste' (OBC) groups. Among the households that planted trees (N = 592), 13.9% of the household heads belong to SC groups, 8.9% belong to ST groups, 39.5% belong

*Table 7.1* Definition and Labels of Variables Used in the Econometric Specifications

| | *Variable name* | *Definition* |
|---|---|---|
| *Household characteristics* | Plant_tree | Households planting trees (1 = Yes; 0 = No) |
| | Schooling | Schooling of household head (n. of years) |
| | Tenure | Length of land tenure |
| | Off-farm | Number of off-farm workdays |
| | Herd | Herd size (no. of buffaloes and cows) |
| | Age | Age of household head (years) |
| | Coop | Participation in co-operatives (1=Yes; 0=No) |
| | S_group | 1 = Scheduled caste (SC)<br>2 = Scheduled tribe (ST)<br>3 = Other backward caste (OBC)<br>4 = Forward caste/other (FC) |
| *Farm characteristics* | Loan | Household head has taken loan in the past year (1 = Yes; 0 = No) |
| | Plot_avarea | Average plot area (acres) |
| | Land area | Total worked land area (acres) |
| | Elev | Elevation (metres) |
| | Plot_number | Number of plots managed |
| | Neighbour | Number of neighbours have planted tree |
| | Irrig | Irrigation availability (1 = Yes; 0 = No) |
| | Own_land | Household own the land (1 = Yes; 0 = No) |
| *Market characteristics* | Tr_market | Travel time from home to market (minutes) |
| | Tr_avplot | Average travel time from home to plot (minutes) |
| | Tr_allplots | Total travel time for all plots (minutes) |

to OBC groups, and the remaining 37.8% belong to the 'forward caste' (FC), suggesting that caste could be important to tree planting, although we will formally test this causation in the econometric results.

The average household head had been working the land for 23.4 years but reported land tenure length in our sample for a household range as high as 70 years (most likely a family measure). The average number of plots per household is 1.3, and the average total sum of landholdings per household is 3.7 acres in area (75% of the total sample holds a total of 4 acres or less). Both of these averages are higher for the group of households that planted trees *versus* households that did not plant trees. The main non-woody species cultivated by households in our sample are maize, rice, cotton, and tobacco. The main tree species planted are cashew (42.9% of households), palm tree for oil production (37.3%) or coconut (10.81%), followed by citrus species (9.9%), and timber and essential oil-producing species (for example, eucalyptus, casuarinas, etc.) at 5.6%.

A greater proportion of the group of households that did not plant trees had access to irrigation for crop production (76%) in relation to the group of households that planted trees (60%); considering our total sample, 70% of the households' have access to irrigation. The average stated

*Table 7.2* Descriptive Statistics for Continuous Variables (First Part) and Dummy Variables (Second Part)

| | *Variable name* | *Mean* | *Standard deviation* | *Min* | *Max* |
|---|---|---|---|---|---|
| Household characteristics (continuous) | Age | 51.11 | 11.79 | 22 | 86 |
| | Schooling | 2.78 | 3.81 | 0 | 17 |
| | Tenure | 24.27 | 13.26 | 1 | 70 |
| | Off-farm | 31.74 | 43.73 | 0 | 350 |
| | Herd | 1.38 | 2.66 | 0 | 53 |
| Farm Characteristics (continuous) | Plot_av area | 3.03 | 3.39 | 0 | 70 |
| | Land area | 3.72 | 4.60 | 0 | 71 |
| | Elev | 38.59 | 57.73 | 0 | 1,106 |
| | Plot_number | 1.27 | 0.62 | 1 | 7 |
| | Neighbour | 0.53 | 1.56 | 0 | 20 |
| Market characteristics (continuous) | Tr_market | 37.12 | 23.81 | 1 | 230 |
| | Tr_avplot | 25.86 | 16.28 | 0 | 120 |
| | Tr_allplots | 30.89 | 20.93 | 0 | 250 |
| | **Variable name** | **1 = Yes** | **0 = No** | | |
| Household characteristics (dummy) | Plant_tree | 592 (28.62%) | 1477 (71.39%) | | |
| | Coop | 197 (9.52%) | 1872 (90.49%) | | |
| | **Variable name** | **1 = Yes** | **0 = No** | | |
| Farm characteristics (dummy) | Irrig | 1,179 (70.35%) | 497 (29.65%) | | |
| | Own_land | 1,908 (92.22%) | 161 (7.78%) | | |

travel time from the households to the closest market (which is how we measured distance in this study) is approximately 25 minutes, whereas the average travel time from the household to one of its plots is 26 minutes. The average household income is Rs. 105,593.4 in the year immediately prior to the interview.

Table 7.3 presents the main descriptive statistics for the group of interviewed households that planted trees in at least one of their plots and for the group of households that did not plant any trees. Pairwise *t*-test statistics show that the following variables are statistically different between the two groups: land ownership and tenure length, number of plots managed, travel time to market, sum of travel time to each of the household's plots, number of days working outside of the family's land, and elevation. Although not causative, we find a correlation showing that households that planted trees have also been working their land for a longer period of time and possess a larger number of plots in relation to the households that did not plant trees. Moreover, the sum of the distances to each cultivated plot and that to the closest market are also larger for tree planting households.

The statistics are reasonable considering that, especially in developing regions, the production of food (usually annual crops) is the priority

*Table 7.3* Pairwise Differences and t-test Statistics Significance Tests for Households That Plant Trees versus Household That Do Not Plant[a]

| *Group of variables* | *Variable name* | *Households that do not plant trees* | *Households that plant trees* | *Difference (Std. error)* |
|---|---|---|---|---|
| Household characteristics | Schooling | 2.900 | 2.553 | 0.348 (0.198) |
| | Tenure | 24.05 | 24.70 | −0.649 (0.689) |
| | Off-farm | 28.91 | 37.26 | −8.343*** (2.265) |
| | Herd | 1.427 | 1.272 | 0.155 (0.138) |
| | Age | 51.13 | 51.04 | 0.0861 (0.613) |
| | Coop | 0.104 | 0.0841 | 0.0202 (0.0154) |
| | S_group | 2.896 | 3.011 | −0.115* (0.0554) |
| | SCs | 0.177 | 0.136 | 0.0415* (0.0192) |
| | STs | 0.125 | 0.0894 | 0.0359* (0.0165) |
| | OBCs | 0.321 | 0.403 | −0.0814** (0.0247) |
| | FCs | 0.376 | 0.372 | 0.0039 (0.0252) |
| Farm characteristics | Loan | 0.0961 | 0.0590 | 0.0370* (0.0144) |
| | Plot_avarea | 3.106 | 2.874 | 0.232 (0.176) |
| | Land area | 3.511 | 4.129 | −0.618** (0.239) |
| | Elev | 37.08 | 41.55 | −4.470 (3.000) |
| | Plot_number | 1.191 | 1.433 | −0.242*** (0.0317) |
| | Neighbour | 0.555 | 0.490 | 0.0652 (0.0811) |
| | Irrig | 0.755 | 0.597 | 0.157*** (0.0235) |
| | Own_land | 0.909 | 0.980 | −0.0709*** (0.0129) |
| Market characteristics | Tr_market | 35.75 | 39.78 | −4.026** (1.235) |
| | Tr_avplot | 25.78 | 26.02 | −0.245 (0.847) |
| | Tr_allplots | 28.96 | 34.69 | −5.730*** (1.079) |

[a] Standard errors in parentheses; significant levels are *** $p < 0.01$, ** $p < 0.05$, * $p < 0$.

for farmers, and it happens on the most fertile and water-abundant lands. Planting trees not only requires higher upfront costs, but it takes years before harvest can be carried out and income generated. Thus, it is common that tree planting will happen on lower quality lands that are located further away from the household and in less irrigated areas. At the same time, tree management requires little labour time after establishment, which is convenient for households with older members or with members working outside of the family's land for part of the year. Finally, we expect social status to influence a household's decision to plant trees, as they should reflect a household's wealth endowment.

## 7.5 Econometric Results

Estimation results of the tree planting probability Equation (7.11) are in Table 7.4.[11] Table 7.4 shows the estimates for four different specifications of the model: Specification 1 and Specification 2 in the first two columns of the table are 3-level mixed effects models that include random effects related to potential error correlation; as such, these specifications assume that errors are correlated among villages in a mandal and households in each village.[12] Specifications 3 and 4 in the last two columns assume errors are 2-level mixed effects models that include correlation only among households in each village. Specifications 3 and 4 are also estimated with robust standard errors as they omit the random effect related to the mandal each village is located within. We also include an interaction variable in Specifications 2 and 4 (second and fourth columns of Table 7.4) to reflect the hypothesis that there is an extra effect on the probability of planting trees for households with larger total land area managed and whose plots are on average more distant.

Referring to Table 7.4, we find statistically significant evidence that the probability that a household will decide to plant trees indeed depends on postulated error components in (7.10), including exogenous variation accommodated by the fixed effects $u_{0j}$ (which vary by location) as well as the correlation accommodated with the random effects term $h_{ij}'\eta_i$. Tests and goodness of fit measures given in Table 7.4 show that the mixed effects models fit better than a simple probit one that ignores the error components introduced into (7.10). The results are similar across the 2-level and 3-level mixed effect estimators, suggesting that the specifications are robust and that the greatest gains in estimation are from considering correlation in errors across households within a village (rather than villages within a mandal). Percent-correct predicted probabilities are also similar and relatively high (greater than 75%) across the four specifications (see Table 7.6).

Across specifications, variables that are significant and that positively affect the decision of a household in our sample to plant trees are: average travel time from home to plots, the total land area managed, whether the household head is the owner of the land, whether the household is engaged in off-farm wage work, household elevation, and the length of land tenure in years. Variables that are significant but negatively affect the decision to plant trees are: whether the household belongs to the 'scheduled tribes' social group (in relation to forward caste), whether the household has access to irrigation, whether the household has taken a loan in the past, and average plot area.

Table 7.5 contains estimated average marginal effects for each variable included in a specification, calculated at the observed levels of the

*Table 7.4* Multilevel Mixed Effects Probit Model Estimation Results for a Priori Assumed 2- and 3-level Correlation[a]

| *Explanatory Variables* | *Specification 1* | *Specification 2* | *Specification 3* | *Specification 4* |
|---|---|---|---|---|
| | *3-Level mixed effects without interaction variables* | *3-Level mixed effects with interaction variables* | *2-Level mixed effects without interaction variables and robust standard errors* | *2-Level mixed effects with interaction variables and robust standard errors* |
| Schooling | 0.0052 (0.0113) | 0.0044 (0.0113) | 0.0053 (0.0161) | 0.0045 (0.0163) |
| Tenure | 0.0107*** (0.0032) | 0.0108*** (0.0032) | 0.0108*** (0.0025) | 0.0109*** (0.0025) |
| Off-farm | 0.00349*** (0.0009) | 0.00358*** (0.0009) | 0.00348*** (0.0013) | 0.00357*** (0.0013) |
| Herd | 0.0044 (0.0155) | 0.0043 (0.0155) | 0.0043 (0.0159) | 0.0048 (0.0160) |
| Age | −0.0035 (0.0037) | −0.0035 (0.0037) | −0.0036 (0.0033) | −0.0036 (0.0033) |
| Coop | −0.161 (0.135) | −0.151 (0.135) | −0.163 (0.163) | −0.153 (0.162) |
| SC | −0.149 (0.123) | −0.154 (0.123) | −0.146 (0.116) | −0.151 (0.115) |
| ST | −0.511*** (0.146) | −0.526*** (0.146) | −0.510** (0.230) | −0.525** (0.226) |
| OBC | 0.165* (0.0957) | 0.166* (0.0958) | 0.168 (0.117) | 0.169 (0.117) |
| Loan | −0.214 (0.154) | −0.228 (0.154) | −0.211 (0.179) | −0.224 (0.178) |
| Plot_avarea | −0.115*** (0.0429) | −0.134*** (0.0451) | −0.118* (0.0717) | −0.138** (0.0692) |
| Land_area | 0.143*** (0.0391) | 0.131*** (0.0398) | 0.147** (0.0687) | 0.134* (0.0714) |
| Elev | 0.00191** (0.0007) | 0.00189** (0.0007) | 0.00188*** (0.0005) | 0.00186*** (0.0006) |
| Plot_number | 0.174 (0.158) | 0.171 (0.157) | 0.157 (0.179) | 0.154 (0.180) |
| Neighbor | 0.0142 (0.0261) | 0.0130 (0.0261) | 0.0141 (0.0224) | 0.0129 (0.0227) |
| Irrig | −0.431*** (0.107) | −0.423*** (0.107) | −0.434** (0.192) | −0.426** (0.193) |
| Own_land | 0.776*** (0.222) | 0.769*** (0.222) | 0.778*** (0.238) | 0.771*** (0.243) |
| Tr_market | −0.0016 (0.0019) | −0.0018 (0.0019) | −0.0015 (0.0029) | −0.0018 (0.003) |
| Tr_avplot | −0.0106 (0.0075) | −0.0130* (0.0077) | −0.0107 (0.0071) | −0.0131* (0.0076) |
| Tr_allplots | 0.0060 (0.0061) (0.0532) | 0.0048 (0.0062) (0.0513) | 0.0061 (0.0054) | 0.0049 (0.0054) |
| variance(villages)[b] | 0.521 (0.344) | 0.523 (0.344) | | |
| covariance (villages) | 0.0311 (0.0965) | 0.0340 (0.0949) | | |
| (Land_area)x(Tr_avplot) | | 0.00118* (0.0007) | | 0.0012 (0.0009) |
| variance (households)[c] | | | 0.0595 (0.0423) | 0.0566 (0.0405) |
| covariance (households) | | | 0.890** (0.420) | 0.897** (0.422) |

*(Continued)*

*Table 7.4* Continued

| *Explanatory Variables* | *Specification 1* | *Specification 2* | *Specification 3* | *Specification 4* |
|---|---|---|---|---|
| | *3-Level mixed effects without interaction variables* | *3-Level mixed effects with interaction variables* | *2-Level mixed effects without interaction variables and robust standard errors* | *2-Level mixed effects with interaction variables and robust standard errors* |
| Constant | −1.690*** (0.451) | −1.581*** (0.456) | −1.661*** (0.395) | −1.553*** (0.409) |
| Observations | 1,652 | 1,652 | 1,652 | 1,652 |
| Number of groups | 16 | 16 | 22 | 22 |
| Log likelihood | −695.204 | −693.747 | −695.904 | −694.460 |
| Wald chi | 122.53 | 125.35 | 2537.91 | 7206.63 |
| Prob>chi2 | 0.000 | 0.000 | 0.000 | 0.000 |
| AIC | 1440.408 | 1439.495 | 1433.81 | 1430.92 |

[a] Standard errors in parentheses; significance indicated at following levels: *** $p < 0.01$, ** $p < 0.05$, * $p < 0.1$.
[b] Significance indicates 2-level mixed effects with error correlation among villages within a mandal.
[c] Significance at household level indicates 2-level mixed effects.

*Table 7.5* Estimated Marginal Effects by Model Specification[a]

| *Explanatory variable*[b] | *Specification 1 3-Level mixed effects without interaction variables* | *Specification 2 3-Level mixed effects with interaction variables* | *Specification 3 2-Level mixed effects without interaction variables and robust standard errors* | *Specification 4 2-Level mixed effects with interaction variables and robust standard errors* |
|---|---|---|---|---|
| Schooling | 0.0012<br>(0.0027) | 0.0010<br>(0.0027) | 0.0012<br>(0.0038) | 0.0011<br>(0.0039) |
| Tenure | 0.0025***<br>(0.0008) | 0.0026***<br>(0.0008) | 0.0026***<br>(0.0006) | 0.0026***<br>(0.0006) |
| Off-farm | 0.0008***<br>(0.0002) | 0.0008***<br>(0.0002) | 0.0008***<br>(0.0003) | 0.0008***<br>(0.0003) |
| Herd | 0.001<br>(0.0037) | 0.0011<br>(0.0037) | 0.001<br>(0.0037) | 0.0011<br>(0.0038) |
| Age | −0.0008<br>(0.0009) | −0.0008<br>(0.0009) | −0.0008<br>(0.0008) | −0.0008<br>(0.0008) |
| Coop | −0.0375<br>(0.0309) | −0.0351<br>(0.0311) | −0.0378<br>(0.0372) | −0.0354<br>(0.0371) |
| SC | −0.0349<br>(0.0286) | −0.0361<br>(0.0286) | −0.0339<br>(0.0268) | −0.0350<br>(0.0267) |
| ST | −0.110***<br>(0.0327) | −0.113***<br>(0.0328) | −0.110**<br>(0.0491) | −0.113**<br>(0.0484) |
| OBC | 0.0408*<br>(0.0241) | 0.0411*<br>(0.0241) | 0.0413<br>(0.0291) | 0.0416<br>(0.0291) |
| Loan | −0.0494<br>(0.0346) | −0.0523<br>(0.0347) | −0.0485<br>(0.0403) | −0.0514<br>(0.0399) |
| Plot_avarea | −0.0273**<br>(0.0107) | −0.0319***<br>(0.0114) | −0.0281<br>(0.0172) | −0.0326*<br>(0.0167) |
| Land_area | 0.0341***<br>(0.0101) | 0.0384***<br>(0.0107) | 0.0348**<br>(0.0167) | 0.0390**<br>(0.0166) |
| Elev | 0.0004**<br>(0.0002) | 0.0004**<br>(0.0002) | 0.0004***<br>(0.000) | 0.0004***<br>(0.0001) |
| Plot_number | 0.0499<br>(0.0397) | 0.0491<br>(0.0395) | 0.0493<br>(0.0417) | 0.0484<br>(0.0418) |
| Neighbor | 0.0034<br>(0.0062) | 0.0031<br>(0.0062) | 0.0033<br>(0.0053) | 0.003<br>(0.0054) |
| Irrig | −0.106***<br>(0.0292) | −0.104***<br>(0.0291) | −0.106**<br>(0.0482) | −0.104**<br>(0.0482) |
| Own_land | 0.158***<br>(0.0427) | 0.157***<br>(0.0428) | 0.159***<br>(0.0451) | 0.158***<br>(0.0460) |
| Tr_market | −0.0004<br>(0.0004) | −0.0004<br>(0.0004) | −0.0004<br>(0.0007) | −0.0004<br>(0.0007) |
| Tr_avplot | −0.0025<br>(0.0018) | −0.002<br>(0.0018) | −0.0025<br>(0.0017) | −0.0021<br>(0.0017) |
| Tr_allplots | 0.0014<br>(0.0015) | 0.0011<br>(0.0015) | 0.0014<br>(0.0013) | 0.0011<br>(0.0013) |
| Observations | 1,652 | 1,652 | 1,652 | 1,652 |

[a] Standard errors in parentheses. All marginal effects are calculated at mean values across observations.
[b] Significance levels are as follows: *** $p < 0.01$, ** $p < 0.05$, * $p < 0.1$.

*Table 7.6* Percent Correct Predictions of Tree Planting Probability

| | | *Specification 1* 3-Level mixed effects without interaction variables | | | *Specification 2* 3-Level mixed effects with interaction variables | | | *Specification 3* 2-Level mixed effects without interaction variables and robust standard errors | | | *Specification 4* 2-Level mixed effects with interaction variables and robust standard errors | | |
|---|---|---|---|---|---|---|---|---|---|---|---|---|---|
| Model prediction | | Household[a] planted trees | | *Number observations* | Household planted trees | | *Number observations* | Household planted trees | | *Number observations* | Household planted trees | | *Number observations* |
| | | *0 = No* | *1 = Yes* | | *0 = No* | *1 = Yes* | | *0 = No* | *1 = Yes* | | *0 = No* | *1 = Yes* | |
| **0 = No** | Frequency | 972 | 179 | 1,151 | 975 | 176 | 1,151 | 974 | 177 | 1,151 | 977 | 176 | 1,153 |
| | Percentage predicted (%) | **84.45** | 15.55 | 100 | **84.71** | 15.29 | 100 | **84.62** | 15.38 | 100 | **84.74** | 15.26 | 100 |
| **1 = Yes** | Frequency | 121 | 380 | 501 | 118 | 383 | 501 | 119 | 382 | 501 | 116 | 383 | 499 |
| | Percentage predicted (%) | 24.15 | **75.85** | 100 | 23.55 | **76.45** | 100 | 23.75 | **76.25** | 100 | 23.25 | **76.75** | 100 |

[a] Stated planting of trees in a household survey

independent variables for each observation, then averaged overall sample observations. A one-year increase in land tenure length is associated with a 2.4% increase in the predicted probability of planting trees, whereas owning the land is associated with a 14.8% higher predicted probability of planting (in relation to not owning the land). Both land tenure length and land ownership are likely a feature of the perception of security with regards to property rights to land in this region. Andhra Pradesh has relatively secured property rights compared to the more frontier rural areas of India where government presence is lower. A secure property rights regime eases the uncertainty of future expropriation, resulting in higher control over the land-use decision cycle and greater likelihood of a longer-term investment such as tree planting. Long-term decisions may be more attractive if household members know that they will be the ones benefiting from the investment.

Turning to other marginal effects, we estimate, on average, that a one-hectare increase in "total land area managed" is associated with a 3.6% increase in the predicted probability that the household will plant trees. However, a one-hectare increase in "average plot area" generates a reduction in the predicted probability of a household planting a tree by 3.1%. Despite the apparent contradiction, these opposing effects are reasonable, considering that they measure different things. Total land area represents the subsistence and income production potential of the household. Households with larger land area can produce more than enough to sustain the family (food and cash income for essential needs); thus, they have greater possibilities of both reducing agricultural production costs due to economies of scale (if the plots are large enough) and diversifying the number of species cultivated. Assuming that food production and annual income are the two main objectives of the representative household in our region of study, planting trees is considered only after these two objectives are somehow fulfilled. The average size of the plot brings us information on the possibilities of commercial agricultural production for crops and as mentioned, gains of scale. A household with a larger farmland area has better possibilities or space for tree planting, whereas larger individual plots represent higher potential for production of crops on a commercial scale, making tree planting a less attractive activity.

Elevation and access to irrigation are relevant to our representative household's decision to plant trees, albeit with opposite effects. A one-metre increase in land elevation, which is significant given the topography of our village sample, increases the predicted probability that the household will plant trees in at least one of its lots by approximately 0.4% while having access to irrigation (a dummy variable) leads to a drop in the predicted probability of 9.4%. Households with access to irrigation systems are likely better off producing annual crops – the land becomes more productive (higher yields) at a relatively low cost (assuming they use flood irrigation methods).

However, farmland at relatively higher elevations is usually less productive for crops and possibly more difficult to irrigate or harder to reach and use machinery. In this case, it might make more sense for the household to plant trees on these lands as trees need less water from irrigation and labour. In the case of a more topographically diverse landscape, tree species that support non-timber products are probably preferable to timber-producing species.

We observe a negative relationship between the probability of planting trees and the average travel time to each plot (our measure of distance in this model), though this variable is significant at only the 10% level. For every one-minute increase in the average travel time from the household to a plot, the probability of planting trees decreases by 0.02%.[13] This is counter to our expectation that greater distances from the household to the plot favour planting trees versus non-woody crops since it takes longer to reach those plots and tree tending is less labour intensive than crop production. We expected that the greater opportunity cost of time in getting to further plots would be offset by the household through tree planting. However, we also find travel distance to the closest market not to be statistically significant in our model for tree planting.

There is another possibility for the unexpected distance result. We do not have data on unobserved forest industry influences in this region (in part, this is a possible reason for correlation that we allow in the model estimation). Indeed, given that most of the tree species planted by interviewed households are cashew and palm and that Andhra Pradesh presents strong and well-organized markets for these products with firms located along the Godavari River, the processing industry might be absorbing some of the production costs of these forest products for households in our study region. Further, households in our sample are likely either taking their production directly to the companies or (most commonly) to intermediaries who purchase at the farm gate rather than travelling periodically to nearby markets.

As far as caste effects are concerned, households belonging to the 'scheduled tribes' social group have a 10.6% lower probability of planting trees in relation to the base social group 'forward caste'. 'Scheduled tribes' households likely have lower exogenous income endowments and heavier reliance on farm production only for subsistence, relative to the forward caste (so that $Q(L_c, K, L_H, \varnothing) - C_h = 0$ in Equation (7.2). Planting trees as an economic activity usually requires high initial planting and opportunity costs (given the longer time that it takes for the investment to be recovered relative to annual crops), especially if the household has a small farmland area to work on and needs to produce for their own subsistence. Moreover, their ability to find credit and perhaps access to formal forest markets is lower due to the lack of collateral and contacts.

For households in our sample that have members working outside of their own farm, the probability that they will plant trees increases by 0.08% per day of off-farm work. Off-farm work is known to be a strategy to smooth out income and reduce risk exposure to extreme weather events and pests (Lamb 2003; Ito and Kurosaki 2009). If the household has members working off the farm, they will prefer to plant and cultivate species that need less attention and labour.

Finally, we should mention that we did not include input prices (for example, fertilizer, herbicides, etc.) in the model. There is very little variation in the data for these variables, which is expected given that output and input markets are complete in the region of study (see Lamb 2003 for published evidence of this). The implication of our study is that, as a consequence, all households face the same market prices.[14]

## 7.6 Discussion and Conclusions

We investigate factors determining rural household choices to plant trees on family farms in the East Godavari and West Godavari districts of Andhra Pradesh, India. We use a random utility theoretical model to develop and estimate a multilevel mixed effects probit model using a maximum likelihood procedure applied to a large survey of randomly sampled households in the region. The mixed effects probit model approach is relatively new in the economics of rural households, but it has the advantage of allowing for random effects correlations among errors in the estimation of the tree planting decision at a location scale, such as among households within villages, or among villages at a regional level. We a priori expect these correlations due to unobserved variables such as transaction costs or Forestry Company influences among households in the region.

We find evidence that the probability of tree planting is not only associated with important fixed effects, which are the same across all households in our sample but is also associated with random effects that vary from village to village and with the number of plots that the household manages. We also find that the most important positive drivers in the decision to plant trees are total land area, years of land tenure, and off-farm labour opportunity. However, factors that lower tree planting incentives are irrigation availability, average travel time to managed plots, elevation, and belonging to the scheduled tribes' social group.

There are important forest policy and development implications following these results. The establishment of secondary forest and tree cover has recently been a focused strategy of the Indian government to reduce pressure over native forests and foster rural development. Moreover, with restrictive policies on native forest harvesting and the low availability of raw material facing the forest products industry in Andhra Pradesh (Schons et al. 2020), companies have started to follow a contract farming model and are increasingly establishing agreements with private farmers to grow trees, in return for forest industry sharing in seedling cost and availability as well as providing technical assistance. Our results are suggestive of the types of households and specific characteristics of the family farm that will provide greatest traction for these agreements and meet the objective of protecting native forests.

As opposed to other regions in India and many developing countries, land tenure and ownership are relatively well defined and enforced in Andhra Pradesh, although there are still questions about the equality of land distribution and traditional rights and access of certain social groups to land. Well-defined and enforced rights to land are known to be relevant factors for long-term investment by households in their land. Tree planting constitutes such an investment and, as a direct consequence, so are commitments to carbon sequestration and avoided emissions programmes. The fact that our econometric model establishes that length of land tenure and land ownership constitute significant and positive factors for the tree planting decision represents a first step to successful income-generating tree planting farm contracting schemes and REDD+ programmes[15] (these are especially relevant for forest-dependent farmers). Such steps are already envisioned by the Indian government in a recent revision of the National Forest Policy [Draft National Forest Policy (DNFP)-2018], but our work provides evidence that this strategy is likely to be successful. In fact, based on the responses we estimate for tree planting among these households, the results suggest that this programme could be transformative, at least for Andhra Pradesh.

We also show that a greater total landholding size increases the probability that farmer households will plant trees. From the perspective that priority is given to the cultivation of cash and food-producing crops in a country as poor as India, tree planting and forest establishment would only be undertaken after subsistence needs are met using the most productive, i.e., higher-quality, land. However, considering that larger landholdings are often owned by groups with higher social status, perhaps using carbon sequestration as a complementary incentive mechanism for private planting could be a way of reducing social inequities or improving income possibilities so that subsistence-based farming is no longer a necessity. Cash transfer programmes could additionally be associated with tree planting in tribal private farmlands, perhaps through a REDD+ mechanism that includes native forest enrichment or restoration activities and encourages contracting between rural households and forest products companies. Forest products companies would not only benefit from a more available supply of timber, but households would also be able to increase the value of their final product (maybe through a price premium, but probably through greater market access) with forest management or fair-trade types of certifications.

Land quality is also the reason why households located on higher (possibly hilly) grounds present a higher probability of planting trees in our data; households with access to irrigated lands present a lower probability of engaging in the activity. Tree planting has been seen with some scepticism in drought-prone regions, especially because species such as eucalyptus are popularly known for 'drinking' all the water from the land (Tripathi and Mishra 2017). Establishment of efficient water irrigation systems that can accommodate both crop and tree production could play an important role in making wide-scale tree planting a reality.

Our results also seem to show scope for 'public-private participation models' in India as proposed in Indian policy documents surrounding DNFP-2018, at least for the case of Andhra Pradesh. Although the analysis in this chapter constitutes a first approximation of the kind of incentives for planting 'trees outside of forests' in Andhra Pradesh, further research would contribute significantly to the design of the new policy. This policy is still in the development phase and is intended to support India's responsibilities under the Paris Climate Agreement at the same time that it builds upon the current Joint Forest Management program (enacted in 1988) and the Forests Rights Act of 2006, the latter aims to give tribal communities greater traditional rights to their lands. If tree planting is to happen on a greater scale, these communities should be given greater ownership of land or management rights.

On a final note, we have discussed determinants of tree planting based on preferences that farmers have revealed to us through household surveys. Our results cannot and should not be used to debate the merits of DNFP-2018. This said, our results do hint at the fact that any long-term forest policy should consider all stakeholders, incentives, and laws in unison. Doing so would increase the likelihood that the economic development and conservation aspects related to forest management efforts are sustainable over time.

## Notes

1 A plot-based approach, where tree planting is considered on each plot, should be a goal of any future work in this area. Often such approaches are limited by quality and extent of data required for a formal econometric analysis.

2 For our study area (discussed in the next section), households are often not the owners of formal title for the land they work, but these households still make all production decisions and share income with the owners in a sharecropping system. All households we sample are identical in this regard, and this arrangement is sunk from the perspective of our sampling. As a result, it is valid to assume that the household making crop and tree planting decisions is seeking to maximize profit and thus utility from the farm.

3 Qualities of roads accessed by the households or distance to the nearest market are examples of a proxy for $d$.

4 For simplicity, we have not used separate notation for inputs other than labour. This is because, in our sample, most if not all hired labour is used in crop pro-

duction. We have also not included notation related to plot-level production on the farm. These simplifications do not detract from our main purpose but would greatly complicate the presentation. Because we focus here only on the decision to plant trees, we will not estimate Equations (7.3) and (7.4), so it does not matter here whether there is intercropping or single cropping among these outputs, nor does the pattern of input use matter for the farm as a whole. The definition of farm profit here follows from (7.2) to (7.4) and is equal to $P_aQ + FP_f - wL_H - rK$.

5 For a tree planting example of this welfare measure on a household model in different context, see Amacher et al. (2004).

6 This occurs here because the model is assumed to be separable in production and consumption decisions given that the farm economy in our sample region in Andhra Pradesh is one where labour is supplied and hired freely due to the scale of agriculture common among the villages in the data.

7 Location in our model, as described later, may have two geographical or administrative unit levels. These are the village and *mandal* locations (a mandal is equivalent to a county).

8 An alternative to specifying (7.8) is to simply use dummy variables for different villages or regions in the explanatory vector, but doing so would implicitly assume that tree planting differences across regions are constant and there is no correlation within a cluster of households in one location. Thus, to assume this a priori risks rendering estimates for and associated standard errors asymptotically inconsistent and inefficient, because it would be equivalent with assuming that the error is i.i.d.

9 That is, $\mathrm{E}\left[\left(h_{ij}'\eta_i\right)\left(h_{-ij}'\eta_{-i}\right)\right] \neq 0, for\, any\, j, ad\, i \neq -i \in j$, and thus the definition of $i$ and $j$ and the subset vector $h_{ij}$ define the type of mixed effects model.

10 The survey instrument is available upon request to the authors.

11 After accounting for missing data, we were left with 1,652 valid observations which are indicated in the results tables

12 Although the theoretical model suggests that input and output prices and costs are an important part of the tree planting decision, in our cross-sectional data at one point in time it was the case that these variables had little if any variation given the well-functioning agricultural markets or the unknown price agreements that some farmers undoubtedly have with forest industry and were unwilling to reveal to us in surveying. Two ways our analysis addresses these concerns is first to include exogenous explanatory variable proxies that are measurable and correlated with the opportunity costs and actual costs of tree planting in terms of farm and market access characteristics; and second, unknown relationships that are price-related between households and forest companies are just one important reason that the mixed effects model is needed, given the unknown correlation that likely exists in villages regarding these

13 This is exogenous for households in our sample, as there is very little choice involved in travelling to plots along the main and accepted paths leaving each village.

14 Indeed, we found that because all households faced the same regional prices, there was very little if any variation in this variable in the sample when reported. We also included herd size (number of buffaloes and cows owned) as an exogenous variable because they may be considered as a sunk asset insofar as these animals are raised to produce milk, dung, and are used for animal traction purposes in agriculture (for evidence, see Bairwa et al., 2013).

15 REDD+ is a climate change mitigation solution being developed by Parties to the United Nations Framework Convention on Climate Change (UNFCCC). REDD+ incentivizes developing countries to keep their forests standing by offering results-based payments for actions to reduce or remove forest carbon emissions.

## References


Amacher, G. S., L. Ersado, W. F. Hyde, and A. Osorio. 2004. "Tree Planting in Tigray, Ethiopia: The Importance of Human Disease and Water Micro Dams". *Agroforestry Systems* 60 (3): 211–225. doi:10.1023/B: AGFO.0000024411.22604.0a.

Amacher, G. S., E. Koskela, and M. Ollikainen. 2009. "Deforestation and Land Use under Insecure Property Rights". *Environment and Development Economics* 14 (3): 281–303. doi:10.1017/s1355770x0800483x.

ASI. Instruction Manual Annual Surveys of Industries (Concepts, Definitions and Procedures) Government of India, Ministry of Statistics & P.I. Central Statistics Office Industrial Statistics Wing NSSO, December 2016. http://mospi.nic.in/sites/default/files/publication_reports/instruction_for_filling_part-I-II_ASI_Schd16-17.pdf (accessed on 27 June 2021).

Bairwa, K. C., Varadan, R. J., Jhajhria, A., & Meena, D. K.2013. "An Economic Appraisal of Livestock Sector in India". *Indian Journal of Animal Research* 47(2): 105–112. https://arccjournals.com/journal/indian-journal-of-animal-research/ARCC106?type=onlineFirstArticle (accessed on 29 June 2021)

Barbier, E. B., P. Delacote, and J. Wolfersberger. 2017. "The Economic Analysis of the Forest Transition: A Review". *Journal of Forest Economics* 27: 10–17. doi:10.1016/j.jfe.2017.02.003.

Bastin, J.F., Y. Finegold, C. Garcia, D. Mollicone, M. Rezende, D. Routh, C. M. Zohner, and T. W. Crowther. 2019. "The Global Tree Restoration Potential". *Science* 365 (6448): 76–79. doi:10.1126/science.aax0848.

Gibbons, R. D., and D. Hedeker. 1997. "Random Effects Probit and Logistic Regression Models for Three-Level Data". *Biometrics* 53 (4): 1527. doi:10.2307/2533520.

Guo, G., and H. Zhao. 2000. "Multilevel Modeling for Binary Data". *Annual Review of Sociology* 26 (1): 441–462. doi:10.1146/annurev.soc.26.1.441.

Haim, D. "*Three Essays on the Economics of Climate Change, Land Use and Carbon Sequestration*". Doctoral Dissertation. Oregon State University. 2011. https://ir.library.oregonstate.edu/concern/graduate_thesis_or_dissertations/d791sk216 (accessed on 27 June 2021).

Ito, T., and T. Kurosaki. 2009. "Weather Risk, Wages in Kind, and the Off-Farm Labour Supply of Agricultural Households in a Developing Country". *American Journal of Agricultural Economics* 91 (3): 697–710. doi:10.1111/j.1467-8276.2009.01270.x.

Joshi, A. K., P. Pant, P. Kumar, A. Giriraj, and P. K. Joshi. 2010. "National Forest Policy in India: Critique of Targets and Implementation". *Small-Scale Forestry* 10 (1): 83–96. doi:10.1007/s11842-010-9133-z.

Köhlin, G., and G. S. Amacher. 2005. "Welfare Implications of Community Forest Plantations in Developing Countries: The Orissa Social Forestry

Project". *American Journal of Agricultural Economics* 87 (4): 855–869. doi:10.1111/j.1467-8276.2005.00774.x.

Köhlin, G., and M. Ostwald. 2001. "Impact of Plantations on Forest Use and Forest Status in Orissa, India". *AMBIO: A Journal of the Human Environment* 30 (1): 37–42. doi:10.1579/0044-7447-30.1.37.

Kohlin, G., and P. J. Parks. 2001. "Spatial Variability and Disincentives to Harvest: Deforestation and Fuelwood Collection in South Asia". *Land Economics* 77 (2): 206. doi:10.2307/3147090.

Lamb, R. L. 2003. "Fertilizer Use, Risk, and Off-Farm Labour Markets in the Semi-Arid Tropics of India". *American Journal of Agricultural Economics* 85 (2): 359–371. doi:10.1111/1467-8276.00125.

Munshi, K. 2004. "Social Learning in a Heterogeneous Population: Technology Diffusion in the Indian Green Revolution". *Journal of Development Economics* 73 (1): 185–213. doi:10.1016/j.jdeveco.2003.03.003.

Oshchepkov, A. and A. Shirokanova. 2020. "Multilevel Modeling for Economists: Why, When and How". *Basic Research Program Working Papers Series: Economics (WP BRP 233/EC/2020)*, National Research University Higher School of Economics (HSE). https://wp.hse.ru/data/2020/06/29/1610354484/233EC2020.pdf (accessed on 27 June 2021).

Parks, P. J., and I. W. Hardie. 1995. "Least-Cost Forest Carbon Reserves: Cost-Effective Subsidies to Convert Marginal Agricultural Land to Forests". *Land Economics* 71 (1): 122–136. doi:10.2307/3146763.

Park, P. J., E. B. Barbier, and J. C. Burgess. 1998. "The Economics of Forest Land Use in Temperate and Tropical Areas". *Environmental and Resource Economics* 11 (3/4): 473–487. doi:10.1023/a:1008230615436.

Rudolf, K., M. Romero, R. Asnawi, B. Irawan, and M. Wollni. 2020. "Effects of Information and Seedling Provision on Tree Planting and Survival in Smallholder Oil Palm Plantations". *Journal of Environmental Economics and Management* 104: 102361. doi:10.1016/j.jeem.2020.102361.

Sills, E. O., S. Lele, T. P. Holmes, and S. K. Pattanayak, 2003. "Non Timber Forest Products in the Rural Household Economy". In *Forests in a Market Economy*, edited by Erin O. Sills and Karen Lee Abt, 259–281. New York: Springer, Dordrecht Sills, Kluwer Academic Publishers. doi:10.1007/978-94-017-0219-5_15

Tripathi, A., and A. K. Mishra. 2017. "Knowledge and Passive Adaptation to Climate Change: An Example from Indian Farmers". *Climate Risk Management* 16: 195–207. doi:10.1016/j.crm.2016.11.002.

Chapter 8

# Minimizing Ecological Damage from Road Improvement in Tropical Forests

*Susmita Dasgupta and David Wheeler*

## Introduction

Protected-area strategies seek to conserve biodiversity in moist tropical forests by restricting infrastructure development in legally demarcated zones. However, conflicts can arise when forested areas have significant agricultural potential. Within conservation areas, regulatory enforcement may be weakened by dominant economic interests. And some areas with high biodiversity value may be left unprotected so that development can proceed. By implication, both development and conservation may be hindered by a dichotomous policy regime that treats large areas as either completely protected or completely open for development. In reality, valuable economic and ecological resources have non-uniform, overlapping spatial distributions. Therefore, policymakers should be equipped to weigh context-specific trade-offs between development and conservation objectives. This chapter seeks to contribute by focusing on the trade-offs associated with road improvement in tropical forests. For three illustrative country cases in Latin America (Bolivia), Asia (Myanmar), and Africa (Cameroon), we develop and apply a high-resolution spatial model of road improvement impacts that includes both ecological risks and the economics of forest clearing. Our empirical work makes exclusive use of globally available databases to ensure its applicability to all moist tropical forest countries.

The remainder of the chapter is organized as follows – Section 8.2 reviews prior empirical research on the economics of forest clearing. In Section 8.3, we motivate our exercise with a theoretical economic model of road improvement and deforestation. Section 8.4 describes our spatially formatted database, while Section 8.5 specifies and estimates a deforestation model that incorporates the impact of road improvement. In Section 8.6, we explore the implications of the results for our three cases. Section 8.7 develops an empirical framework for estimating the ecological impacts of road improvement, while Section 8.8 applies the framework to an assessment of local and regional impacts in Bolivia, Cameroon, and Myanmar. Section 8.9 summarizes and concludes the chapter.

DOI: 10.4324/9781003253884-11

## 8.1 Prior Research

Empirical research has provided many useful insights into the determinants of forest clearing. The results are generally consistent with an economic model in which the conversion of forested land varies with potential profitability. Nelson and Chomitz (2009) and Rudel et al. (2009) have studied this relationship across countries over multi-year intervals. Within countries, numerous econometric studies have estimated the impact of economic, social, and geographic drivers on deforestation during multi-year intervals. Some studies have used aggregate data for states, provinces, or sub-provinces (e.g., studies for Brazilian municipios by Pfaff (1997) and Igliori (2006), and Mexican states by Barbier and Burgess (1996)).

Many studies have also used GIS-based techniques to obtain multi-year estimates at a higher level of spatial disaggregation (e.g., Cropper et al. 1999, 2001) for Thailand; Agarwal et al. (2002) for Madagascar; Deininger and Minten (1999, 2002), Chowdhury (2006) and Vance and Geoghegan (2002) for Mexico; Kaimowitz et al. (2002) for Bolivia; and De Pinto and Nelson (2008) for Panama). In rare cases, studies have used annual national or regional aggregate time series for extended periods (e.g., Zikri (2009) for Indonesia; Ewers et al. (2008) for Brazil).

While econometric work on long-run deforestation drivers is well advanced, previous data problems limited treatments of economic dynamics to theoretical work and simulation. Arcanda et al. (2008) and others studied the theoretical relationships between macroeconomic drivers and forest clearing. Notable simulation exercises include Cattaneo (2001) for Brazil and San et al. (2000) for Indonesia.

Recently, the advent of monthly and annual remote sensing databases has led to the first spatial estimation exercises that explicitly incorporate economic dynamics (Wheeler et al. 2011; Dasgupta et al. 2014). Direct impact studies in Latin America using the new databases have included high-resolution work on new road construction and deforestation in Brazil, where satellite monitoring has been available for a longer period (Laurance et al. 2009) and Bolivia, Panama, Paraguay, and Peru (Reymondin et al. 2013).

More recently, Li et al. (2014) have investigated the potential impact of decreased travel time from the improvement of road links in the DRC, but their cross-sectional analysis employs land use information (JRC 2003) that predates the new high-resolution satellite data. Damania and Wheeler (2015) have advanced state of the art by estimating the potential impact of road upgrading on forest clearing and biodiversity in eight Congo Basin countries. Their deforestation model incorporates the latest high-resolution satellite data on forest cover changes, as well as quality estimates for specific links in the regional road system. They also create a biodiversity threat index that combines and synthesizes several measures of potential biodiversity loss.

This chapter builds on the approach of Damania and Wheeler (2015) while extending it in several ways. First, we broaden the research domain to include Latin America and Asia. Second, we gain precision by operating at higher spatial resolution. Third, we generalize the methodology by substituting globally available road quality estimates for the Africa-specific estimates employed in the previous work. Finally, we expand the previously developed biodiversity indices for the Congo Basin countries into a global database that includes a larger set of biodiversity measures.

## 8.2 Modeling the Economics of Road Improvement and Deforestation

From a formal analytical perspective, this research treats road improvement as a problem of competitive selection among corridors that traverse the same region. The corridors differ in length, construction cost conditions, biodiversity value, and potential agricultural income. The optimum corridor choice reflects maximization of a social utility function that values both income and biodiversity, subject to a fixed budget constraint, feasible road quality improvement in each corridor (reflecting the budget constraint), and the corridor-specific impacts of road quality improvement on potential biodiversity loss, expected income growth in the corridor and expected income growth from increased trade between areas connected by the corridor.

We motivate the following econometric analysis with a model that specifies the basic determinants of road improvement impacts and explores their economic and ecological dimensions.[1] For expositional clarity and simplicity, we use the Cobb-Douglas (constant-elasticity) specification for all profit and cost functions. This specification is linear in the logs of equation variables and is a first-order approximation to more general specifications (CES, translog, etc.). To simplify the theoretical analysis of alternatives, we assume a constant road improvement budget. Applied assessments of road improvement alternatives might also consider cases where road quality is held constant, and improvement expenditures differ because corridors differ in length. In such cases, estimated improvement costs would be subtracted from estimated income gains to provide the appropriate comparison.

### 8.2.1 Interregional Trade

We specify the economic value of trade between areas connected by a road corridor with a standard gravity model, augmented by a measure of road quality. For a prior application of this approach to overland trade expansion, see Buys, Deichmann, and Wheeler (2010).

$$T_{ij} = \propto_0 E_i^{\propto 1} E_j^{\propto 2} d_{ij}^{-\propto 3} q_{ij}^{\propto 4} \tag{8.1}$$

where $\alpha_0, \alpha_1, \alpha_2, \alpha_3, \alpha_4 > 0$

$T_{ij}$ = Value of trade between areas *i* and *j*
$E_i$, $E_j$ = Economic scale of areas *i* and *j*
$d_{ij}$ = Road distance between areas *i* and *j*
$q_{ij}$ = Quality of the road linking areas *i* and *j* ($0 \leq q \leq 1$, where $0 \rightarrow$ forest track and $1 \rightarrow$ paved 1st class road)

An improvement in road quality (q) lowers transport costs and increases the potential profitability of agricultural production in the road corridor. The budget for maintaining a particular road quality level is given by:

$$B = \gamma_0 q^{\gamma_1} d \quad (\gamma_1 > 1) \tag{8.2}$$

For a fixed road quality budget *B*:

$$q = \left[\frac{B}{\gamma_0}\right]^{\frac{1}{\gamma_1}} d^{-\frac{1}{\gamma_1}} \tag{8.3}$$

In Equation (8.3), given a fixed road quality budget, road quality declines with road length. The rate of decline depends on the cost elasticity of road quality. Substituting Equation (8.3) into Equation (8.1) and simplifying, an increase in the road improvement budget ($B_1 \rightarrow B_2$) has the following impact on trade between areas i and j:

$$\frac{T_{ij2}}{T_{ij1}} = \left[\frac{B_2}{B_1}\right]^{\frac{\alpha_4}{\gamma_1}} \tag{8.4}$$

The interpretation of Equation (8.4) is straightforward: Trade between areas i and j will expand more or less proportionately with the road improvement budget, depending upon whether the road quality elasticity of trade is greater than or less than the cost elasticity of road quality.

### 8.2.2 Local Profitability and Forest Clearing

An improvement in road quality lowers transport costs and increases the expected profitability of agricultural production in a road corridor. The expected profitability of agricultural production increases with the size of a cleared parcel, which is determined by the distance of the forest clearing limit from the road. With both factors taken into account, the expected profit function for each unit of road frontage is[2]

$$\pi = \beta_0 v^{\beta_1} q_{ij}^{\beta_2} h^{\beta_3} \tag{8.5}$$

where $\beta_0, \beta_1, \beta_2 > 0$, $0 < \beta_3 \leq 1$

$\pi$ = Potential profit from land clearing
$v$ = Potential agricultural value per hectare
$h$ = Distance of forest-clearing limit from the road

The proprietor of each road-front parcel also confronts incremental forest clearing costs that are constant or increasing with distance from the road and, for agricultural production, incremental commodity transport costs that increase with distance from the road. The proprietor's composite cost function is:

$$C = \delta_0 h^{\delta_1} \quad (\delta_1 > 1) \tag{8.6}$$

With Equations (8.5) and (8.6) specified as present values, the optimal clearing distance from the road is determined by the equality of marginal expected profits and clearing costs. Optimising the profit function for each unit of road frontage with respect to forest clearing cost and by taking appropriate derivatives, substituting, and simplifying, the optimal clearing distance is given by:

$$h^* = \theta B^{\left(\frac{\mu}{\delta_1 - \beta_3}\right)} v^{\left(\frac{\beta_1}{\delta_1 - \beta_3}\right)} d^{-\left(\frac{\mu}{\delta_1 - \beta_3}\right)} \tag{8.7}$$

where $B = \beta_2 / \gamma_1$, $\delta_1 - \beta_3 > 0$ (from Equations (8.5) and (8.6)) and $\theta$ is a composite of equation constants.

In Equation (8.7), the composite elasticities of $B$, $v$, and $d$ are positive, positive and negative, respectively. Responsiveness increases in each case as the difference narrows between the cost and profit elasticities of forest clearing ($\delta_1$ and $\beta_3$). The responsiveness of forest clearing to greater spending on road quality and greater road distance increases with the ratio of the profit and cost elasticities of road quality.

Appropriate substitution and simplification yield the following expression for total profit in the road corridor:

$$\Pi = 2d\pi\left(h^*\right) = PB^{\rho\mu} v^{\rho\beta_1} d^{1-\rho\mu} \tag{8.8}$$

where $P$ is a composite of equation constants and $\rho = \dfrac{1+\beta_3}{\delta_1 - \beta_3}$ $(> 1)$

In Equation (8.8), total expected profits rise less than proportionally with road distance since expected profits for each roadside land parcel fall as road distance increases. The sign of the distance elasticity in Equation (8.8) is ambiguous since $\rho\mu$ can be greater or less than one. In the former case, total profits will actually fall as road distance increases. From Equation

(8.8), an increase in the road improvement budget ($B_1 \rightarrow B_2$) has the following impact on total profits in a road corridor:

$$\frac{\Pi_2}{\Pi_1} = \left[\frac{B_2}{B_1}\right]^{\rho\mu} \tag{8.9}$$

In Equation (8.9), total road corridor profits increase more or less proportionately with the road quality budget, depending upon whether $\rho\mu$ is greater or less than one. The overall interpretation of Equation (8.9) is as follows: For a road corridor, the responsiveness of total profits to an increase in the road quality budget is positively related to the ratio of profit and cost elasticities of road quality, positively related to the profit elasticity of forest clearing, and negatively related to the difference between the cost and profit elasticities of forest clearing.

### 8.2.3 Biodiversity Loss

Substituting from Equation (8.7), total biodiversity loss in a road corridor is given by:

$$L = 2d\varepsilon h^{*} = 2\varepsilon\theta B^{\left(\frac{\mu}{\delta_1-\beta_3}\right)} v^{\left(\frac{\beta_1}{\delta_1-\beta_3}\right)} d^{1-\left(\frac{\mu}{\delta_1-\beta_3}\right)} \tag{8.10}$$

where $\varepsilon$ = Measured biodiversity intensity

In Equation (8.10), the relationship between total biodiversity loss and road distance depends on whether the ratio of the profit and cost elasticities of road quality is greater than the difference between the cost and profit elasticities of forest clearing. If this is the case (given a fixed budget for road quality), total biodiversity loss will decline with road distance. If the converse is true, increasing road distance will increase biodiversity loss.

From Equation (8.10), the relationship between a road budget increase and total biodiversity loss is given by:

$$\frac{L_2}{L_1} = \left[\frac{B_2}{B_1}\right]^{\left(\frac{\mu}{\delta_1-\beta_3}\right)} \tag{8.11}$$

As above, biodiversity loss will increase more than proportionately with a road budget increase if the ratio of profit and cost elasticities of road quality is greater than the difference between the cost and profit elasticities of forest clearing.

For a fixed road quality budget, the relative profit and biodiversity loss equations for two competitive road corridors (A and B) are as follows:

$$\frac{\Pi_A}{\Pi_B} = \left[\frac{v_A}{v_B}\right]^{\rho\beta_1} \left[\frac{d_A}{d_B}\right]^{1-\rho\mu} \tag{8.12}$$

$$\frac{L_A}{L_B} = \frac{\varepsilon_A}{\varepsilon_B}\left[\frac{v_A}{v_B}\right]^{\left(\frac{\beta_1}{\delta_1-\beta_3}\right)} \left[\frac{d_A}{d_B}\right]^{1-\left(\frac{\mu}{\delta_1-\beta_3}\right)} \tag{8.13}$$

Ceteris paribus (i.e., for identical road budgets and biodiversity intensities), the corridor with greater potential agricultural value per hectare will have both higher total profits and greater total biodiversity loss. The effects of road distance are more complex for two reasons. First:

$$\rho\mu - \frac{\mu}{\delta_1 - \beta_3} = \frac{1+\beta_3}{\delta_1 - \beta_3}\mu - \frac{1}{\delta_1 - \beta_3}\mu = \frac{\beta_3}{\delta_1 - \beta_3}\mu \; (>0) \tag{8.14}$$

Given Equation (8.14), Equations (8.12) and (8.13) incorporate three possibilities. Let $\eta_1 = \rho\mu$ and $\eta_2 = \mu/(\delta_1\text{-}\beta_3)$. If $\eta_1$ and $\eta_2$ are both less than one, the corridor with the longer road will have greater total profits and greater biodiversity loss. If $\eta_1$ and $\eta_2$ are both greater than one, the corridor with the longer road will have lower profits and lower biodiversity loss. In the third possible case – $\eta_1 > 1$ and $\eta_2 < 1$ – the corridor with the *shorter* road will be favoured unambiguously because it will have higher profits and lower biodiversity loss. It is important to note that this is a ceteris paribus result since the corridor with the shorter road could have sufficiently greater biodiversity intensity to reverse the result. A complete calculation would also have to include consideration of trade-related regional income, which would favour the shorter road. Given the relatively complex set of factors that affect these results, the impacts of road improvement on income gains, forest clearing, and biodiversity loss seem likely to vary significantly across countries and across regions within countries. In this chapter, we focus on the forest clearing and biodiversity components of the problem.

## 8.3 Data

### *8.3.1 Road Networks*

Table 8.1 summarizes 2014 road network information for Bolivia, Cameroon, and Myanmar. As Table 8.1 shows, there are 4,607 road links in Bolivia, 2,951 in Cameroon and 6,980 in Myanmar. Network links are graded by status: secondary roads, primary connector roads, and primary highways.

*Table 8.1* Road Links by Network Status: Bolivia, Cameroon, and Myanmar

| *Road Links* | *Bolivia* | *Cameroon* | *Myanmar* |
|---|---|---|---|
| Secondary Roads | 3,760 | 2,162 | 4,879 |
| Primary Roads | 847 | 789 | 2101 |
| Total | 4,607 | 2,951 | 6,980 |

### 8.3.2 Forest Clearing

Hansen et al. (2013) publish annual high-resolution estimates of global forest clearing. The data are currently available at 30 m spatial resolutions for 2000–2014. For this research, we have created annual files in which cleared pixels are assigned the value one in the year when most clearing occurred. Unclear pixels are assigned the value zero. We focus on areas defined as moist tropical forest eco-regions by World Wildlife Fund (Sections 8.6 and 8.8).[3]

We use the Hansen estimates to compute forest clearing rates in 250 m cells.[4] Edge effects, non-forest areas and other factors cause Hansen pixel counts to vary somewhat by cell. We standardize by computing the annual cumulative percent cleared in each cell through 2014.[5]

Figure 8.1 displays our estimates for representative moist forest areas in Bolivia, Cameroon, and Myanmar. Each cell is colour coded by cumulative percent cleared in 2001–2014. The figure reveals a striking pattern of deforestation along some of the roads in the Delorme database. Along other roads, however, deforestation is much less pronounced. Figure 8.1 also identifies road segments that we use to illustrate the relationships between clearing activity and distance from the nearest road.

In order to illustrate the relationships between clearing activity and distance from the nearest road, Figure 8.1 displays two overlapping graphs for each country. The first is a scatter diagram of changes in percent cleared (2000–2014) vs. distance from the road segment, produced using 5,000 randomly selected 250 m cells within 20 km of the road. To produce the second graph, we round to the nearest kilometre of distance for all cells within 20 km of the road; calculate the mean change in percent cleared (2000–2014) for each km; and draw connecting lines.

The mean line provides a clear interpretation of the information in the scatter diagrams. As distance from the road increases, all three graphs reveal a steep fall in mean percent cleared for the first 5 km, a declining slope through 10 km, and approximate flattening near zero beyond 10 km. Although the shapes of change/distance relationships are similar for the three countries, it is worth noting that the magnitudes are quite different. From 2000 to 2014, mean clearing within half a kilometre of the road increased by nearly 20 percentage points in Bolivia and 15 points in Myanmar, but only 5 points in Cameroon.

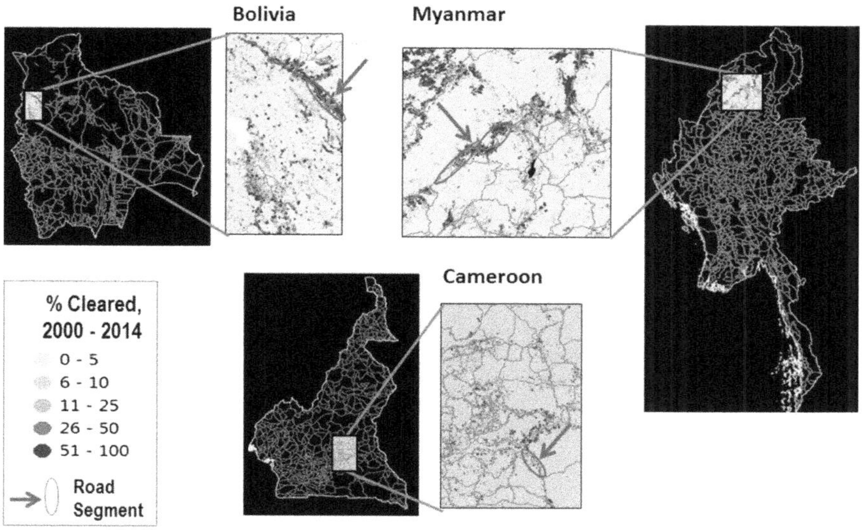


*Figure 8.1* Forest clearing and road networks, 2000–2014. *Source:* digital maps (shape files) provided by Delorme, Inc. (to author).

The basic shape of the clearing/distance relationship illustrated in Figure 8.1 can be captured by an exponential function that we employ for the econometric analyses in this chapter:

$$p = \beta_0 h^{\beta_1} \tag{8.15}$$

where $\beta_1 < 0$

$p$ = Change in percent cleared in a 250 m cell

$h$ = the cell's distance from the road

For econometric work, we translate the function to its linear form in the logarithms of $h$ and $p$.

## 8.4 Estimation of the Forest Clearing Model

The estimation exercise in this chapter draws on the insights of previous research and the theoretical model in Section 8.3 to incorporate five critical determinants of forest clearing in road corridors: distance from the road, transport cost to the nearest market centre, the agricultural opportunity value of the land, terrain slope, and legal protection status. We extend previous work on road transport cost and deforestation by introducing explicit estimation of road quality effects in a network access model. First, we divide all road segments into 500 m increments and use Geographical Information

System (GIS) to determine the network path with the shortest travel distance from each increment midpoint to an urban centre with populations of more than 50,000 in number. Then we separate the distance into the parts travelled on secondary and primary roads.

### 8.4.1 Model Specification

The dependent variable in our estimating Equation (8.16) is a decimal percentage, so we impose the appropriate asymptotic limits [0, 1] by specifying the forest clearing rate as a log-odds ratio.

$$f_i = \beta_0 + \beta_1 \ln d_{ij} + \left[\beta_2 + \beta_3 \gamma_{ij}\right] \ln D_{ij} + [\beta_4 + \beta_5 \ln e_i] \ln s_{ij} \qquad (8.16)$$

$$+\beta_6 \ln p_i + \beta_7 \ln a_i + \varepsilon_i$$

Expected signs: $\beta_1$, $\beta_2$, $\beta_4$, $\beta_6$ <0; $\beta_3$, $\beta_7$>0
where

$$f_i = ln\left[\frac{c_i}{1-c_i}\right]$$

$c_{ij}$ = Cumulative percent cleared in 2014, cell $i$
$d_{ij}$ = Distance of cell $i$ from nearest road segment j
$D_{ij}$ = Shortest network distance from $i$ via segment j to the nearest urban centre
$\gamma$ = Primary Road share of distance from $i$ to the nearest urban centre
$s_i$ = Slope of cell $i$ (measured as within-cell standard deviation of elevation)
$e_i$ = Elevation of cell i
$p_i$ = Legal protection status of cell i
$a_i$ = Agricultural opportunity value of land in cell i
$\varepsilon_{it}$ = Random error term

A priori, we expect the impact on forest clearing to be negative for distance from the nearest road ($\beta_1 < 0$); negative for travel distance to the nearest urban centre ($\beta_2 < 0$), moderated by the share of primary roads travelled ($\beta_3 > 0$); negative for more steeply-sloped terrain ($\beta_4 < 0$), possibly affected by average elevation ($\beta_5 \gtreqless 0$); negative for legal protection status ($\beta_6 < 0$), although this will be affected by country-specific enforcement factors; and positive for the agricultural opportunity value of the land ($\beta_7 > 0$).

### 8.4.2 Estimation Areas

We estimate the model for all cells in World Wildlife Fund's (WWF's) moist tropical forest eco-regions of each country.

#### 8.4.3 Variable Measures

Our data and sources are as follows.

**Hansen pixels cleared:** per 250 m cell, the percent of 30 m Hansen pixels cleared. This incorporates two measures: percent cleared prior to 2001, and annual clearing from 2001 to 2014 (Hansen et al. 2013).
**Distance from road segment:** distance from the centroid of each cell to the nearest road segment, calculated in ArcGIS 10.
**Distance travelled to the nearest urban centre via secondary and primary road segments:** Calculated in ArcGIS 10 from Delorme digital road maps.
**Elevation:** Average elevation for a cell, calculated from the CGIAR-SRTM dataset (3 seconds resolution), and aggregated to 30 seconds resolution by DIVA-GIS (http://www.divagis.org/gdata ).
**Terrain slope:** Standard deviation of pixel-level elevation measures within a cell.
**Legal protection status:** 1 if the cell is in a protected area identified by the World Database on Protected Areas (WDPA); 0 otherwise. The WDPA shape file has been downloaded from http://www.protectedplanet.net/.
**Agricultural opportunity value:** mean value for a cell, calculated from the high-resolution global grid developed by Deveny et al. (2009). Raster resolution: .0025 decimal degrees. The Deveny data have been drawn from two sources: (1) Foregone agricultural rents from Naidoo and Iwamura (2007), who integrate spatial information on crop productivity, livestock density, and prices to produce a global map of the gross economic rents from agricultural lands. (2) Spatially explicit calculation by Kindermann et al. (2006) of income foregone from a one-time timber harvest when timber rents exceed agricultural rents.

#### 8.4.4 Estimation

In this exercise, we have addressed two potentially significant estimation issues. The first is simultaneity between forest clearing and distance to the nearest urban centre. As Damania and Wheeler (2015) and others have noted, road location may be related to the relative profitability of forest clearing. We address this problem via instrumental variables, using geodetic distance from each road increment midpoint to the nearest urban centre as our instrument.

The second potential problem is spatial autocorrelation, which may have significant effects on our regression results. We address this problem with a spatial econometric estimator,[6] using the inverse-distance specification of the spatial weights' matrix.

Tables 8.2 to 8.4 present our estimation results for three sample sizes. The first three columns in the table present estimates for randomly drawn

*Table 8.2* Regression Results: Bolivia. All variables in logs except the dummy variable for protected status Dependent variable: Log odds ratio, cumulative forest cleared %, 2014

| | *Random Sample (10000 obs.)* | | | *20% Random Sample* | | *All Observations* | |
|---|---|---|---|---|---|---|---|
| | *OLS* | *Bootstrap* | *Spatial* | *OLS* | *Bootstrap* | *OLS* | *Bootstrap* |
| | *(1)* | *(2)* | *(3)* | *(4)* | *(5)* | *(6)* | *(7)* |
| **Distance from road** | -0.326 (15.39)** | -0.326 (12.03)** | -0.323 (15.34)** | -0.323 (129.25)** | -0.323 (21.37)** | -0.327 (292.22)** | -0.327 (25.03)** |
| **Distance to nearest Urban centre (DU)** | -0.499 (11.79)** | -0.499 (7.33)** | -0.488 (11.67)** | -0.531 (104.99)** | -0.531 (15.56)** | -0.530 (234.72)** | -0.530 (16.77)** |
| **DUx Primary Road share** | 0.215 (16.88)** | 0.215 (11.78)** | 0.209 (16.60)** | 0.209 (137.29)** | 0.209 (19.56)** | 0.209 (307.60)** | 0.209 (26.71)** |
| **Slope (Std. dev. of elevation)** | -0.797 (7.79)** | -0.797 (5.01)** | -0.772 (7.59)** | -0.812 (66.22)** | -0.812 (11.48)** | -0.828 (150.89)** | -0.828 (12.65)** |
| **Slope x Elevation** | 0.148 (10.54)** | 0.148 (7.04)** | 0.143 (10.26)** | 0.147 (87.73)** | 0.147 (16.25)** | 0.149 (198.87)** | 0.149 (17.63)** |
| **Protected Area** | -0.245 (4.19)** | -0.245 (3.11)** | -0.246 (4.23)** | -0.236 (33.70)** | -0.236 (5.22)** | -0.236 (75.20)** | -0.236 (6.97)** |
| **Agricultural Opportunity value** | 0.356 (14.84)** | 0.356 (10.93)** | 0.354 (14.84)** | 0.367 (126.99)** | 0.367 (20.63)** | 0.364 (282.02)** | 0.364 (24.57)** |
| **Constant** | -1.559 (6.69)** | -1.559 (4.13)** | -1.059 (4.13)** | -1.357 (48.30)** | -1.357 (7.59)** | -1.341 (106.77)** | -1.341 (7.11)** |
| **Observations** | 9998 | 9998 | 9998 | 705260 | 705260 | 3526359 | 3526359 |
| **R-squared** | 0.20 | 0.20 | | 0.19 | 0.19 | 0.19 | 0.19 |

Absolute value of t statistics in parentheses
* significant at 5%; ** significant at 1%

*Table 8.3* Regression Results: Cameroon. All variables in logs except the dummy variable for protected status Dependent variable: Log odds ratio, cumulative forest cleared %, 2014

| | *Random Sample (10000 obs.)* | | | *20% Random Sample* | | *All Observations* | |
|---|---|---|---|---|---|---|---|
| | *IV* | *Bootstrap IV* | *Spatial IV* | *IV* | *Bootstrap IV* | *IV* | *Bootstrap IV* |
| | *(1)* | *(2)* | *(3)* | *(4)* | *(5)* | *(6)* | *(7)* |
| **Distance from road** | -0.097 (11.21)** | -0.097 (6.64)** | -0.094 (11.06)** | -0.094 (85.35)** | -0.094 (13.74)** | -0.093 (188.37)** | -0.093 (13.83)** |
| **Distance to nearest Urban centre (DU)** | -0.374 (27.54)** | -0.374 (20.84)** | -0.345 (25.39)** | -0.370 (223.72)** | -0.370 (30.90)** | -0.372 (501.44)** | -0.372 (42.74)** |
| **DUx Primary Road share** | 0.187 (29.47)** | 0.187 (18.53)** | 0.177 (28.08)** | 0.192 (237.17)** | 0.192 (34.52)** | 0.192 (530.80)** | 0.192 (38.13)** |
| **Slope (Std. dev. of elevation)** | -0.499 (12.19)** | -0.499 (10.37)** | -0.515 (12.78)** | -0.551 (104.31)** | -0.551 (20.61)** | -0.543 (229.91)** | -0.543 (17.86)** |
| **Slope x Elevation** | 0.061 (10.52)** | 0.061 (8.20)** | 0.063 (11.02)** | 0.068 (90.44)** | 0.068 (15.71)** | 0.067 (199.75)** | 0.067 (15.82)** |
| **Protected Area** | -0.363 (12.65)** | -0.363 (8.72)** | -0.366 (12.94)** | -0.325 (89.78)** | -0.325 (16.53)** | -0.327 (201.42)** | -0.327 (16.25)** |
| **Agricultural Opportunity value** | 0.388 (43.30)** | 0.388 (31.24)** | 0.375 (42.08)** | 0.391 (342.24)** | 0.391 (67.15)** | 0.389 (761.91)** | 0.389 (58.52)** |
| **Constant** | 0.003 (0.04) | 0.003 (0.03) | 0.192 (2.74)** | -0.007 (0.82) | -0.007 (0.12) | -0.006 (1.55) | -0.006 (0.13) |
| **Observations** | 10000 | 10000 | 10000 | 645901 | 645901 | 3229507 | 3229507 |
| **R-squared** | 0.41 | 0.41 | | 0.41 | 0.41 | 0.41 | 0.41 |

Absolute value of t statistics in parentheses
* significant at 5%; ** significant at 1%

*Table 8.4* Regression Results: Myanmar. All variables in logs except the dummy variable for protected status Dependent variable: Log odds ratio, cumulative forest cleared %, 2014

| | *Random Sample (10000 obs.)* | | | *20% Random Sample* | | *All Observations* | |
|---|---|---|---|---|---|---|---|
| | *IV* | *Bootstrap IV* | *Spatial IV* | *IV* | *Bootstrap IV* | *IV* | *Bootstrap IV* |
| | *(1)* | *(2)* | *(3)* | *(4)* | *(5)* | *(6)* | *(7)* |
| **Distance from road** | -0.188 (21.82)** | -0.188 (15.53)** | -0.186 (21.67)** | -0.181 (224.06)** | -0.181 (26.62)** | -0.181 (502.01)** | -0.181 (30.26)** |
| **Distance to nearest Urban centre (DU)** | -0.349 (17.84)** | -0.349 (12.41)** | -0.340 (17.50)** | -0.335 (184.49)** | -0.335 (26.95)** | -0.336 (413.39)** | -0.336 (21.88)** |
| **DUx Primary Road share** | 0.063 (10.45)** | 0.063 (7.29)** | 0.060 (10.10)** | 0.060 (105.20)** | 0.060 (13.29)** | 0.060 (238.00)** | 0.060 (13.45)** |
| **Slope (Std. dev. elevation)** | -0.444 (14.99)** | -0.444 (11.85)** | -0.440 (14.97)** | -0.467 (169.14)** | -0.467 (20.26)** | -0.468 (379.01)** | -0.468 (20.54)** |
| **Slope x Elevation** | 0.043 (11.81)** | 0.043 (9.23)** | 0.042 (11.70)** | 0.044 (131.35)** | 0.044 (17.32)** | 0.044 (293.71)** | 0.044 (16.16)** |
| **Protected Area** | -0.775 (24.83)** | -0.775 (20.00)** | -0.761 (24.52)** | -0.780 (266.24)** | -0.780 (34.58)** | -0.782 (596.76)** | -0.782 (34.92)** |
| **Agricultural Opportunity value** | 0.080 (11.50)** | 0.080 (7.27)** | 0.080 (11.55)** | 0.075 (113.94)** | 0.075 (13.67)** | 0.074 (254.01)** | 0.074 (14.96)** |
| **Constant** | 1.335 (12.53)** | 1.335 (8.80)** | 1.431 (13.27)** | 1.319 (133.43)** | 1.319 (19.79)** | 1.324 (299.47)** | 1.324 (16.68)** |
| **Observations** | 10000 | 10000 | 10000 | 1153615 | 1153615 | 5768082 | 5768082 |
| **R-squared** | 0.21 | 0.21 | | 0.20 | 0.20 | 0.21 | 0.21 |

Absolute value of t statistics in parentheses
* significant at 5%; ** significant at 1%

samples of 10,000 cells. These are dispersed across enormous cell populations in very large areas in Bolivia (3.4 million cells), Cameroon (3.3 million), and Myanmar (5.8 million). A priori, we would expect this dispersal to minimize the estimation bias and inconsistency produced by spatial autocorrelation among neighbouring cells.

Columns (1–3) present results for instrumental variables (IV) (1), IV with bootstrapped standard errors (a robustness check, calculated from more-dispersed subsamples of 5,000 observations) (2), and spatial econometric estimation using IV (3). We also include IV and bootstrapped IV estimates (from 20,000-observation subsamples) for much larger randomly drawn samples (20% for each country), and for all cells in each country. We are unable to provide spatial econometric estimates for the 20% and full samples because the calculation of spatial weights matrices is infeasible for such huge observation sets.

In any case, the results in Tables 8.2 to 8.4 are reassuring: For each country, all estimated parameters have the expected signs and very high statistical significance. Within each country, the estimates are quite stable across sample sizes and estimation modes. To facilitate comparison, Table 8.5 presents median parameter estimates.

As previously noted, all parameter estimates for all three countries have the expected signs and significance levels greater than 99%. We highlight results for the distance-related variables.[7] The median elasticity of distance from the road is greatest for Bolivia (–0.326) and least for Cameroon (–0.094). The same pattern holds for distance to the nearest urban centre and its interaction with the share of primary roads travelled. For Bolivia, the median elasticity is –0.530 for travel solely on secondary roads and –0.321 (–0.530 + 0.209) for travel solely on primary roads. Cameroon has lower elasticities for travel solely on secondary roads (–0.372) and primary roads (–0.18), while Myanmar is similar to Cameroon for secondary roads (–0.336) and Bolivia for primary roads (–0.276).

All three countries have negative elasticities for terrain slope, as expected, and the effect of slope diminishes with elevation. Responsiveness is greatest

*Table 8.5* Median parameter estimates

| *Variable* | *Bolivia* | *Cameroon* | *Myanmar* |
|---|---|---|---|
| Distance from road | -0.326 | -0.094 | -0.181 |
| Distance to nearest urban centre (DU) | -0.530 | -0.372 | -0.336 |
| Dux Primary Road share | 0.209 | 0.192 | 0.060 |
| Slope (Std. dev. Of elevation) | -0.812 | -0.543 | -0.467 |
| Slope x Elevation | 0.148 | 0.067 | 0.044 |
| Protected Area | -0.236 | -0.327 | -0.780 |
| Agricultural opportunity value | 0.364 | 0.389 | 0.075 |
| Constant | -1.357 | -0.006 | 1.324 |

for Bolivia and similar for Cameroon and Myanmar. Protected areas have significantly lower forest clearing in all three countries. Myanmar has the largest estimated effect, followed by Cameroon and Bolivia. As expected, forest clearing is higher in areas with higher agricultural opportunity values. The estimated response elasticity is nearly identical for Bolivia and Cameroon and substantially lower for Myanmar.

## 8.5 Implications for Forest Clearing

The estimates reported for each country in Tables 8.2 to 8.4 are quite stable across estimation techniques and sample sizes, yielding very similar model-based predictions. To illustrate the implications of our results, we use the full-sample results in column (7) for a general prediction exercise: We upgrade all secondary road links to primary status, changing the primary road share to 1.0 for all observations, and predict the resulting changes in clearing for all moist tropical forest cells. Table 8.6 provides summary results by moist forest eco-region; we focus on areas with maximum (80–100%) clearing.

For Bolivia, results predict changes of significant size in four moist forest eco-regions. The greatest proportional change occurs in the Southern Andean Yungas in southern Bolivia, where the area that is 80–100% cleared after upgrading is 10,390 hectares i.e., 6.9 times greater than the area in 2014 (1,500 hectares). The greatest absolute change occurs in the Bolivian Yungas, where upgrading increases the area of maximum (80–100%) clearing 2.8-fold, from 19,820 to 55,660 hectares. Significant change also occurs in the Southwest Amazon moist forests (central, western and northern areas), where the maximum cleared area increases from 164,790 hectares to 177,500 hectares.

Cameroon has substantially greater predicted impacts than Bolivia in both absolute and proportional terms. The greatest change by far occurs in the Cameroonian Highlands forests (extending from western to north-central Cameroon), where the 80–100% cleared area expands from 4,170 to 392,000 hectares, i.e., a 94-fold increase. Large changes are visible in the Northwestern Congolian lowland forests (central and southeastern Cameroon), where the maximum cleared area expands from 10,190 to 118,020 hectares – an 11.6-fold increase. Substantial expansion also occurs in the Cross-Sanaga-Bioko coastal forests (western Cameroon – from 24,140 to 68,900 hectares) and the Atlantic Equatorial coastal forests (southwest Cameroon – from 11,650 to 24,090 hectares). Large areas of clearing rate change from upgrading roads in the highest category (15–25%) are visible in southwestern, western, and north-central Cameroon, along with large areas of change in the next category (10–15%) in the centre, south, and southwest.

In Myanmar, estimates indicate that road upgrading will have widely distributed impacts on Myanmar's moist forest eco-regions. The greatest

*Table 8.6* Road Improvement Impact by Moist Forest Eco-region

| | | *Area cleared 80–100% (thousand hectares)* | | | |
|---|---|---|---|---|---|
| *Country* | *Moist Forest Eco-region* | *2014* | *After Upgrading* | *Change* | *Impact Ratio* |
| Bolivia | Southern Andean Yungas | 1.50 | 10.39 | 8.90 | 6.9 |
| | Bolivian Yungas | 19.82 | 55.66 | 35.84 | 2.8 |
| | Madeira-Tapajós moist forests | 30.36 | 33.93 | 3.57 | 1.1 |
| | Southwest Amazon moist forests | 164.79 | 177.50 | 12.71 | 1.1 |
| | Iquitos varzeá | 0.15 | 0.16 | 0.01 | 1.1 |
| | Monte Alegre varzeá | 0.01 | 0.01 | 0.00 | 1.0 |
| Cameroon | Cameroonian Highlands forests | 4.17 | 392.00 | 387.83 | 94.0 |
| | Northwestern Congolian lowland forests | 10.19 | 118.02 | 107.83 | 11.6 |
| | Cross-Sanaga-Bioko coastal forests | 24.14 | 68.90 | 44.76 | 2.9 |
| | Atlantic Equatorial coastal forests | 11.65 | 24.09 | 12.44 | 2.1 |
| | Mount Cameroon and Bioko montane forests | 1.56 | 2.50 | 0.95 | 1.6 |
| Myanmar | Irrawaddy freshwater swamp forests | 1.04 | 2.98 | 1.95 | 2.9 |
| | Irrawaddy moist deciduous forests | 55.13 | 91.78 | 36.65 | 1.7 |
| | Myanmar coastal rainforests | 30.16 | 48.64 | 18.48 | 1.6 |
| | Chin Hills-ArakanYoma montane forests | 15.28 | 23.92 | 8.63 | 1.6 |
| | Northern Indochina subtropical forests | 108.61 | 166.42 | 57.81 | 1.5 |
| | Tenasserim-South Thailand semi-evergreen rainforests | 22.43 | 31.51 | 9.08 | 1.4 |
| | Mizoram-Manipur-Kachin rainforests | 30.85 | 41.40 | 10.55 | 1.3 |
| | Northern Triangle subtropical forests | 26.08 | 34.81 | 8.73 | 1.3 |
| | Kayah-Karen montane rainforests | 38.97 | 49.90 | 10.94 | 1.3 |
| | Lower Gangetic Plains moist deciduous forests | 0.00 | 0.00 | 0.00 | . |

expansion of maximum (80–100%) cleared area occurs in the Northern Indochina subtropical forests (eastern Myanmar), from 108,610 to 166,420 hectares; Irrawaddy moist deciduous forests (central Myanmar), from 55,130 to 91,780 hectares; and Myanmar coastal rain forests (western and southern Myanmar), from 30,160 to 48,640 hectares. Expansions in the range 8,000–11,000 hectares occur in the Chin Hills-Arakan Yoma montane forests (western Myanmar), Tenasserim-South Thailand semi-evergreen rain forests (southern Myanmar), Mizoram-Manipur-Kachin rain forests (western and northern Myanmar), Northern Triangle subtropical forests (northern Myanmar), and Kayah-Karen montane rain forests (east-central Myanmar).

## 8.6 Incorporating Biodiversity

We develop a variety of biodiversity indicators to identify concentrations of diverse species and their vulnerability to encroachment and habitat loss in road corridors.

### *8.6.1 Species Density*

We identify resident animal species in each cell using thousands of digital range maps (shape files) provided by the International Union for the Conservation of Nature (IUCN) (https://www.iucnredlist.org/resources/spatial-data-download) and BirdLife International (http://datazone.birdlife.org/species/requestdis). We measure species density as the species count for each cell.

### *8.6.2 Species Vulnerability*[8]

Species density provides critical information for assessing ecological risks, but at least three other elements are needed:

(1) ***Geographic vulnerability***, which can be proxied by ***endemicity***: the proportion of each species' range that lies within each cell. Species that reside in very few cells may be particularly vulnerable to habitat encroachment. Endemicity treats all species equally at the global level since each species has a total count of one. Total endemicity for each cell – the sum of its species endemicity measures – assigns higher values to cells inhabited by species whose ranges are relatively limited. By implication, forest clearing in higher-value cells may be particularly destructive for the remaining critical habitat.
(2) **Density of endangered and critically endangered species.** Risk assessment is particularly critical for species listed as endangered by the IUCN. We measure endangered species density as the count of endangered and critically endangered species in each cell.

(3) **A measure of *extinction risk*** that adds the insights of the international scientific community. We convert Red List status codes to extinction probabilities using the methodology of Mooers et al. (2008).[9] For species indicator construction, we normalize these probabilities so that a weight of 1.0 is assigned to species in the highest category (Critically Endangered).

Table 8.7 tabulates conversions from Red List codes to normalized species weights, using four probability assignments. Three employ IUCN estimates to derive measures of extinction probability over the next 50, 100, and 500 years. The fourth draws on Isaac et al. (2007), who combines a direct extinction risk measure with a measure of each species' isolation on a phylogenetic tree.[10]

### *8.6.3 Biome Vulnerability*

Measures based on animal species alone provide an incomplete accounting of biodiversity. A more complete measure would incorporate plants and insects, using indices similar to those we have developed for animals. Although no such indices exist at the requisite geographic scale, WWF has provided a first approximation by segmenting the world into 825 terrestrial eco-regions. WWF defines an eco-region as 'a large unit of land or water containing a geographically distinct assemblage of species, natural communities, and environmental conditions.'[11] Accordingly, we adopt the eco-region as a general proxy for distinctive plant and insect species, as well

*Table 8.7* Normalized Species Aggregation Weights[a]

| | | *Normalized extinction probabilities* | | | |
|---|---|---|---|---|---|
| | | | *IUCN: Future years* | | |
| *IUCN Code* | *Status* | *Isaac*[b] | *50* | *100* | *500* |
| CR | Critically Endangered | 1.00000 | 1.00000 | 1.00000 | 1.00000 |
| EN | Endangered | 0.50000 | 0.43299 | 0.66770 | 0.99600 |
| VU | Vulnerable | 0.25000 | 0.05155 | 0.10010 | 0.39000 |
| NT | Near Threatened | 0.12500 | 0.00412 | 0.01000 | 0.02000 |
| LC | Least Concern | 0.06250 | 0.00005 | 0.00010 | 0.00050 |
| | Rounded Weight Ratios | | | | |
| | CR:EN | 2 | 2 | 1 | 1 |
| | CR:VU | 4 | 19 | 10 | 3 |
| | CR:NT | 8 | 243 | 100 | 50 |
| | CR:LC | 16 | 20,000 | 10,000 | 2,000 |

[a] Data source: Mooers et al. (2008).
[b] From calculations by Mooers et al., based on Isaac et al. (2007).

as animal species that are not represented in the range maps provided by IUCN and BirdLife International.

For incorporating WWF eco-regions in this exercise, we identify all moist forest eco-regions in Bolivia, Cameroon, and Myanmar; and compute the percent of total moist forest area in a country accounted for by each eco-region. Then we compute its vulnerability index as the inverse of its area share and assign the appropriate index value to each cell. This accounting assigns high values to cells in smaller eco-regions, where clearing single cells may pose more significant threats to ecosystem integrity.

### 8.6.4 A Composite Biodiversity Indicator

Alternative vulnerability indicators may yield significantly different risk metrics. For a more general assessment, we calculated correlation coefficients for our seven biodiversity indicators for our 250 m cells in each country (see Table 8.8). Two things are immediately apparent: First, pairwise correlations vary enormously: from 1.00 to –0.38 in Bolivia; 0.98 to –0.03 in Cameroon; and 0.99 to –0.39 in Myanmar. Second, the same clusters appear in all three tables: correlations are high among species counts; endemicity and Isaac extinction risk; and endangered species counts and the three IUCN extinction risk indicators. The biome indicator is a distinct outlier in all three tables, with pairwise correlations that vary from positive and small to negative and relatively large.

With such potentially huge differences in metrics, it is important for a vulnerability indicator methodology to accommodate different risk-weighting schemes in a consistent and plausible way. To accommodate diverse concerns, we adopt a conservative strategy for indicator construction. First, we divide all measures of endemicity, biome vulnerability and extinction risk by their maximum values and multiply by 100 to create indexes in the range 0–100. This ensures comparability in measurement. Then, for each 250 m cell, we select the maximum index value as our risk indicator.

In Bolivia, peak indicator values are found in a relatively small appendage area in the east and a roughly triangular area in the northwest. High values also occur in a broad arc from the northernmost area, around to the west, and into the centre-west area of the dominant moist tropical forest area. Beyond these high-value areas, the index declines progressively in gradient bands.

Indicator clustering is pronounced in Cameroon, with areas of peak value in the southwest surrounded by declining value gradients. In Myanmar, the highest indicator values occur in a band from centre to south along the eastern border. West of these areas, values decline in gradient bands. Another band of relatively high values is visible along the country's northern and western boundaries, extending southward into west-central Myanmar.

*Table 8.8* Biodiversity Indicator Correlation Coefficients – Bolivia, Cameroon, and Myanmar

| | *Species count* | *Endangered species count* | *Endemicity* | *Isaac extinction risk* | *IUCN 50-Yr. extinction risk* | *IUCN 100-Yr. extinction risk* | *IUCN 500-Yr. Extinction Risk* |
|---|---|---|---|---|---|---|---|
| **Bolivia** | | | | | | | |
| Endangered Species Count | 0.43 | | | | | | |
| Endemicity | 0.98 | 0.34 | | | | | |
| Isaac Extinction Risk | 0.99 | 0.51 | 0.97 | | | | |
| IUCN 50-Yr. Extinction Risk | 0.47 | 0.98 | 0.40 | 0.56 | | | |
| IUCN 100-Yr. Extinction Risk | 0.51 | 0.98 | 0.44 | 0.60 | 1.00 | | |
| IUCN 500-Yr. Extinction Risk | 0.58 | 0.92 | 0.51 | 0.67 | 0.96 | 0.98 | |
| Biome (Ecoregion) Risk | −0.38 | −0.16 | −0.37 | −0.38 | −0.19 | −0.20 | −0.23 |
| **Cameroon** | | | | | | | |
| Endangered Species Count | 0.42 | | | | | | |
| Endemicity | 0.85 | 0.27 | | | | | |
| Isaac Extinction Risk | 0.98 | 0.58 | 0.82 | | | | |
| IUCN 50-Yr. Extinction Risk | 0.58 | 0.93 | 0.51 | 0.71 | | | |
| IUCN 100-Yr. Extinction Risk | 0.58 | 0.97 | 0.44 | 0.72 | 0.98 | | |
| IUCN 500-Yr. Extinction Risk | 0.67 | 0.91 | 0.47 | 0.80 | 0.92 | 0.97 | |
| Biome (Ecoregion) Risk | 0.09 | −0.01 | 0.07 | 0.08 | −0.03 | −0.01 | 0.02 |
| **Myanmar** | | | | | | | |
| Endangered Species Count | 0.42 | | | | | | |
| Endemicity | 0.97 | 0.41 | | | | | |
| Isaac Extinction Risk | 0.98 | 0.59 | 0.94 | | | | |
| IUCN 50-Yr. Extinction Risk | 0.64 | 0.92 | 0.61 | 0.78 | | | |
| IUCN 100-Yr. Extinction Risk | 0.62 | 0.96 | 0.59 | 0.77 | 0.99 | | |
| IUCN 500-Yr. Extinction Risk | 0.71 | 0.88 | 0.66 | 0.83 | 0.91 | 0.95 | |
| Biome (Ecoregion) Risk | −0.26 | −0.26 | −0.26 | −0.31 | −0.39 | −0.34 | −0.27 |

In summary, the risk indicators have two clear characteristics. First, they are far from uniformly distributed: Northwest Bolivia, southwest Cameroon, and eastern Myanmar account for major shares of total indicator values. Second, our construction of an 'envelope' composite index from the seven sub-indices generates relatively smooth spatial gradient patterns that are evident in all three countries.

## 8.7 Road Upgrading and Ecological Risk

### *8.7.1 Area Calculations*

We calculate expected biodiversity loss for a cell as the product of its biodiversity indicator value and the change in its cleared forest percentage induced by road upgrading. To facilitate comparison, we normalize the results to indices in the range [0–100] for each country and display the results in Figure 8.2. The Bolivian case (Figure 8.2: left panel) is dominated by large areas with high expected losses (index values 60–100) in the west and southwest, along with some road corridor areas across the north and east, along a central axis, and in the southernmost moist forest area. A striking feature of the Bolivian results is the skewed spatial distribution, including large areas where expected losses are relatively low.

The Cameroon results (Figure 8.2: centre panel) provide a striking contrast. As in Bolivia, some areas in the higher expected loss categories (60–100) are visible in the southwest, west, and north. However, the spatial distribution of expected losses is far less skewed than Bolivia's. Cameroon's areas of lowest expected loss generally flank the corridors of primary roads that are not candidates for upgrading. Beyond these corridors lie large areas with intermediate expected losses (40–60).

Myanmar (Figure 8.2: right panel) also exhibits a more even distribution of expected losses than Bolivia's. Large areas in the highest expected loss categories (60–100) are visible in the far north, a band from the north to the east, and scattered areas in the west and south. Flanking these areas are large areas with intermediate expected losses (40–60). Again, areas with the lowest expected losses are in corridors flanking roads that already have primary status.

### *8.7.2 Identifying Critical Road Links*

Since our methodology ties forest clearing impacts to specific road links, we can also use our high-resolution database to grade those links by expected biodiversity losses when upgrading occurs. We compute mean expected losses in corridors extending 9.10 km on either side of the Delorme-identified secondary road links in moist forest areas. We normalize to the range [0–100] for ease of comparison.[12]

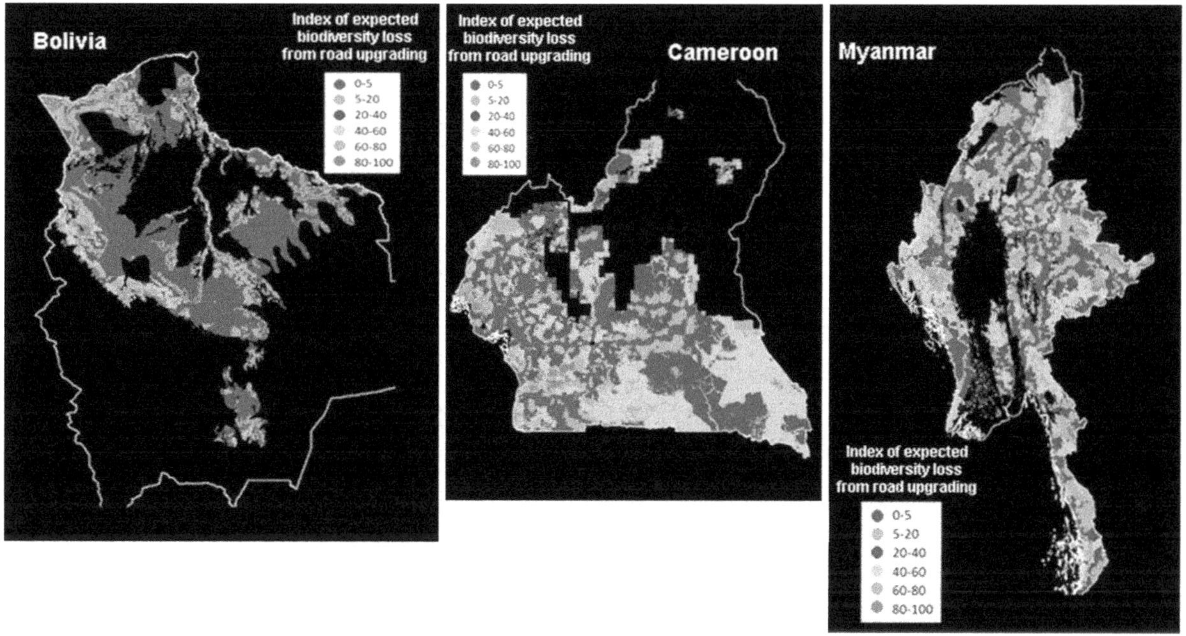


*Figure 8.2* Index of expected biodiversity loss due to road upgrading. *Source:* digital maps (shape files) provided by Delorme, Inc. (to author).

In Bolivia, the largest clusters of critical road links are in the centre-north and far south, with smaller clusters visible in the north, east, and west. Their relatively skewed spatial distribution reflects Bolivia's skewed area distribution of expected losses. In contrast, the distribution of critical corridors in Cameroon reflects its more evenly distributed expected losses from road upgrading. Road clusters in the most critical category are visible in the southwest, west, and north. Critical links in the lower priority categories are more widely scattered. Like Cameroon, Myanmar exhibits a more even distribution of critical road corridor clusters than Bolivia. Large clusters of the most critical corridors are visible in the east, with smaller clusters linked to next-priority corridors in the north, west, and south. Again, clusters in the lower priority categories are widely scattered.

The illustrative applications in this section provide high-resolution spatial measures that can inform environmentally sensitive road upgrading programmes. We use our econometric results and composite ecological vulnerability indicators to measure expected biodiversity losses for moist tropical forest cells, each of which is linked to the nearest urban market by roads at varying quality levels. Our approach identifies areas where road upgrading will produce high expected biodiversity losses, as well as road corridors that are particularly vulnerable. Since road improvement will inevitably accompany rural development, we believe that the identification of ecologically vulnerable areas and road corridors can make two useful contributions to infrastructure planning. First, with limited budgets, it can help steer road upgrading programmes towards corridors where expected biodiversity losses are minimized. Second, it can highlight vulnerable areas where additional conservation measures may be warranted.

## 8.8 Summary and Conclusions

In this chapter, we have developed, estimated, and applied a spatially explicit model that links road upgrading to forest clearing and biodiversity losses in moist tropical forest areas. We have chosen one World Bank IDA country from each major tropical forest region (Latin America (Bolivia), Africa (Cameroon), and Asia (Myanmar)) for illustrative purposes. However, our approach is applicable to every moist tropical forest country because we employ standard global databases:[13] High resolutions forest-clearing information from Hansen et al. (2013); information on biodiversity and protected areas from IUCN and WWF International, digital road maps from Delorme, Inc., digital elevation maps from DIVA-GIS; and information on agricultural opportunity values from Deveny et al. (2009). Using the 30 m Hansen data, we estimate forest clearing rates for all 250 m cells in the moist tropical forests of Bolivia, Cameroon, and Myanmar. For each 250 m cell, we use GIS to measure the distance to the closest point on the nearest road; the distance-minimizing route to the nearest urban market, with explicit measurement of distances travelled on secondary and primary roads; mean elevation; terrain slope (the standard deviation of within-cell elevation measures); the mean agricultural opportunity value of the land; and legal protection status.

We use an appropriately specified econometric model to estimate the effects of these variables on the cumulative percent of forest cleared in 2014. We take explicit account of spatial autocorrelation, as well as simultaneity in the relationship between forest clearing and road location. Our parameter estimates for the three countries are extremely robust, with the expected signs and very high statistical significance in all cases. The estimated elasticities exhibit little variation across alternative samples and estimators for each country, but significant differences across countries.

We focus particularly on the variables that measure distance to the nearest market and its partition into secondary and primary road links. We find that distance response elasticities are substantially lower for primary road links because their higher average vehicle speeds and lower maintenance costs reduce the effect of distance to market.

Econometric measurement of road quality effects enables us to estimate the deforestation impact of programmes that upgrade secondary roads to primary status. To illustrate our methodology, we explore the impact of upgrading all secondary roads to primary status in the moist tropical forest regions of Bolivia, Cameroon, and Myanmar. We find highly non-uniform spatial distributions, with significant impacts in some areas of all three countries and effects that are more evenly distributed in Cameroon and Myanmar than in Bolivia.

With our model-based predictions in hand, we measure biodiversity risk in each 250 m cell using eco-region information from WWF International and thousands of species range maps from IUCN and BirdLife International. We develop seven measures that incorporate biome status, species density, endemicity, and extinction risk. We find weak bivariate correlations for some of these measures, so we develop a composite index for each 250 m cell by selecting the highest of the seven, each normalized to the range [0 100].

We compute an expected loss measure for each cell by multiplying its composite biodiversity index by the predicted increase in forest clearing percent from secondary road upgrading. We map the results to identify priority areas with high expected losses, along with ecologically critical road corridors within those areas. We find highly diverse patterns of expected forest clearing and biodiversity loss that would be difficult to anticipate without this kind of analysis.

Since road upgrading will inevitably accompany rural development programs, we believe that explicit identification of ecologically vulnerable areas and road corridors can provide two valuable types of information. First, with limited budgets, it can help steer road upgrading programmes towards corridors where expected biodiversity losses will be minimized. Second, it can inform the adoption of appropriate protection measures in vulnerable road corridors and neighbouring areas. Since our methodology can be applied to any country case at relatively low cost, we believe that more widespread application could provide useful assistance for environmentally sensitive infrastructure planning.

## Notes

1 The theoretical model in this section was first developed by one of the co-authors (Wheeler) in collaborative work with Richard Damania on road upgrading and forest clearing in the Congo Basin countries (Damania and Wheeler, 2015). Many thanks to Richard for his insights and suggestions.

2 We incorporate potential profits without explicit assumptions about local price dynamics. Local profitability (and forest-clearing responses) will be greater if farmers are price-takers in regional markets. The clearing response to road investment will be smaller in cases where production from newly cleared land is sufficient to reduce farm gate prices. We are indebted to our colleague Carter Brandon for this point.

3 For a complete list of WWF eco-regions, see http://wwf.panda.org/about_our_earth/ecoregions/ecoregion_list/. (accessed on 3 April 2020)

4 We use the 250 m approximation for expositional convenience. Our cell sides are 0.0025 decimal degrees in length. This translates to 278.3 meters on a side, yielding cell areas of 77,450.9 square meters or 7.75 hectares.

5 Our estimate also incorporates the Hansen 30 m estimates of tree cover in 2000.

6 We use the Stata estimator spreg.

7 Given our model specification, each parameter estimate is interpreted as the elasticity of the log-odds ratio for forest clearing with respect to the relevant right-hand variable.

8 Much of the index design work described in this section was first undertaken in collaboration with Richard Damania for the Congo Basin countries. See Damania and Wheeler (2015).

9 The IUCN's current classification categories are Critically Endangered, Endangered, Vulnerable, Near Threatened and Least Concern.

10 A phylogenetic tree is a branching tree diagram that traces the evolutionary descent of different species from a common ancestor. Species in sparse (isolated) branches of a phylogenetic tree are relatively unique, since they share common descent patterns with fewer other species.

11 Complete information about the WWF terrestrial eco-regions is available online at http://wwf.panda.org/about_our_earth/ecoregions/ (accessed on 2 July 2021).

12 This exercise focuses on the impact of generalized secondary road upgrading. It incorporates a network analysis methodology that can also be used to estimate expected losses associated with upgrades from secondary to primary status in individual road corridors. This would entail identifying all road segments linked to the closest urban market via these corridors, calculating the change in distance shares for the relevant secondary and primary road links, and predicting the forest clearing impact in all cells lying closest to the affected road links.

13 The Delorme digital road maps are available for a fee; all other data sources are in the public domain.

## References


Arcand, Jean-Louis, P. Guillaumont, and S. G. Jeanneney. 2008. "Deforestation and the Real Exchange Rate". *Journal of Development Economics* 86 (2): 242–262. doi:10.1016/j.jdeveco.2007.02.004.

Agarwal, Deepak K., A. E. Gelfand, and J. A. Silander. 2002. "Investigating Tropical Deforestation Using Two-Stage Spatially Misaligned Regression Models". *Journal of Agricultural, Biological, and Environmental Statistics* 7 (3): 420–439. doi:10.1198/108571102348.

Barbier, Edward B., and J. C. Burgess. 1996. "Economic Analysis of Deforestation in Mexico". *Environment and Development Economics* 1 (2): 203–239. doi:10.1017/s1355770x00000590.

Buys, P., U. Deichmann, and D. Wheeler. 2010. "Road Network Upgrading and Overland Trade Expansion in Sub-Saharan Africa". *Journal of African Economies* 19 (3): 399–432. doi:10.1093/jae/ejq006.

Cattaneo, A. 2001. "Deforestation in the Brazilian Amazon: Comparing the Impacts of Macroeconomic Shocks, Land Tenure, and Technological Change". *Land Economics* 77 (2): 219–240. doi:10.2307/3147091.

Chowdhury, Rinku Roy. 2006. "Driving Forces of Tropical Deforestation: The Role of Remote Sensing and Spatial Models". *Singapore Journal of Tropical Geography* 27 (1): 82–101. doi:10.1111/j.1467-9493.2006.00241.x.

Cropper, M., C. Griffiths, and M. Mani. 1999. "Roads, Population Pressures, and Deforestation in Thailand, 1976–1989". *Land Economics* 75 (1): 58–73. doi:10.2307/3146993.

Cropper, M., J. Puri, and C. Griffiths. 2001. "Predicting the Location of Deforestation: The Role of Roads and Protected Areas in North Thailand". *Land Economics* 77 (2): 172–186. doi:10.2307/3147088.

Damania, R. and D. Wheeler. 2015. "Road Improvement and Deforestation in the Congo Basin Countries". *World Bank Policy Research Working Paper No. 7274*.Washington DC: World Bank. https://openknowledge.worldbank.org/bitstream/handle/10986/22002/Road0improveme0ongo0Basin0countries.pdf?sequence=1&isAllowed=y (accessed on 26 June 2021).

Dasgupta, S., D. Hammer, R. Kraft, and D. Wheeler. 2014. "Vyāghranomics in Space and Time: Estimating Habitat Threats for Bengal, Indochinese, Malayan and Sumatran Tigers". *Journal of Policy Modeling* 36 (3): 433–453. doi:10.1016/j.jpolmod.2014.01.014.

De Pinto, A., and G. C. Nelson. 2008. "Land Use Change with Spatially Explicit Data: A Dynamic Approach". *Environmental and Resource Economics* 43 (2): 209–229. doi:10.1007/s10640-008-9232-x.

Deininger, Klaus W., and B. Minten. 1999. "Poverty, Policies, and Deforestation: The Case of Mexico". *Economic Development and Cultural Change* 47 (2): 313–344. doi:10.1086/452403.

Deininger, Klaus W., and B. Minten. 2002. "Determinants of Deforestation and the Economics of Protection: An Application to Mexico". *American Journal of Agricultural Economics* 84 (4): 943–960. doi:10.1111/1467-8276.00359.

Deveny, A et al. *Forest Carbon Index: The Geography of Forests in Climate Solutions*. Joint Report by Resources for the Future and Climate Advisers. 2009. https://www.climateadvisers.com/wp-content/uploads/2017/07/2009-12-Forest-Carbon-Index.pdf (accessed on 28 June 2021).

Ewers, R. M., W. F. Laurance, and C. M. Souza. 2008. "Temporal Fluctuations in Amazonian Deforestation Rates". *Environmental Conservation* 35 (04): 303–310. doi:10.1017/s0376892908005122.

Hansen, M. C., P. V. Potapov, R. Moore, M. Hancher, S. A. Turubanova, A. Tyukavina, and D. Thau et al. 2013. "High-Resolution Global Maps of 21St-Century Forest Cover Change". *Science* 342 (6160): 850–853. doi:10.1126/science.1244693.

Igliori, Danilo Camargo. 2006. "Deforestation, Growth and Agglomeration Effects: Evidence from Agriculture in the Brazilian Amazon". Department of Land Economy, University of Cambridge. https://www.econstor.eu/bitstream/10419/118493/1/ERSA2006_719.pdf (accessed on 26 June 2021).

Isaac, Nick J.B., S. T. Turvey, B. Collen, C. Waterman, and J. E.M. Baillie. 2007. "Mammals on the EDGE: Conservation Priorities Based on Threat and Phylogeny". *Plos ONE* 2 (3): e296. doi:10.1371/journal.pone.0000296.

Joint Research Center (JRC). 2003. *European Commission Global Land Cover 2000 Project*, 2003. http://bioval.jrc.ec.europa.eu/products/glc2000/glc2000.php (accessed on 26 June 2021).

Kaimowitz, D., P. Mendez, A. Puntodewo, and J. Vanclay, 2002. "Spatial Regression Analysis of Deforestation in Santa Cruz, Bolivia". In *Land Use and Deforestation in the Amazon*, edited by C.H. Wood and R. Porro, 41–65, University Press of Florida. https://espace.library.uq.edu.au/view/UQ:8009/R075_upf_pp.pdf (accessed on 26 June 2021).

Kindermann, Georg E, M. Obersteiner, E. Rametsteiner, and I. McCallum. 2006. "Predicting the Deforestation-Trend under Different Carbon-Prices". *Carbon Balance and Management* 1 (15): 1–17. doi:10.1186/1750-0680-1-15.

Laurance, William F., M. Goosem, and Susan G.W. Laurance. 2009. "Impacts of Roads and Linear Clearings on Tropical Forests". *Trends in Ecology & Evolution* 24 (12): 659–669. doi:10.1016/j.tree.2009.06.009.

Li, Man, A. De Pinto, J. M. Ulimwengu, L. You, and R. D. Robertson. 2014. "Impacts of Road Expansion on Deforestation and Biological Carbon Loss in the Democratic Republic Of Congo". *Environmental and Resource Economics* 60 (3): 433–469. doi:10.1007/s10640-014-9775-y.

Mooers, A., D. P. Faith, and W. P. Maddison. 2008. "Converting Endangered Species Categories to Probabilities of Extinction for Phylogenetic Conservation Prioritization". *Plos ONE* 3 (11): e3700. doi:10.1371/journal.pone.0003700.

Naidoo, R., and T. Iwamura. 2007. "Global-Scale Mapping of Economic Benefits From Agricultural Lands: Implications For Conservation Priorities". *Biological Conservation* 140 (1–2): 40–49. doi:10.1016/j.biocon.2007.07.025.

Nelson, Andrew and Kenneth M. Chomitz. 2009. *Protected Area Effectiveness in Reducing Tropical Deforestation: A Global Analysis of the Impact of Protection Status*. Evaluation Brief 7, Independent Evaluation Group, World Bank, October. ISBN-13: 978-1-60244-123-1. https://ieg.worldbankgroup.org/sites/default/files/Data/reports/protected_areas_eb.pdf (accessed on 26 June 2021).

Pfaff, Alexander. 1997. "What Drives Deforestation in the Brazilian Amazon? Evidence from Satellite and Socioeconomic Data". *Policy Research Working Paper No. 1772*, World Bank. doi: 10.1596/1813-9450-1772.

Reymondin, Louis, Karolina Argote, Andy Jarvis, Carolina Navarrete. Alejandro Coca, Denny Grossman, Alberto Villalba, and Paul Suding. 2013. *Road*

*Impact Assessment Using Remote Sensing Methodology for Monitoring Land-Use Change in Latin America: Results of Five Case Studies.* Inter-American Development Bank Environmental Safeguards Unit, Technical Note No. IDB - TN - 561. https://publications.iadb.org/publications/english/document/Road-Impact-Assessment-Using-Remote-Sensing-Methodology-for-Monitoring-Land-Use-Change-in-Latin-America-Results-of-Five-Case-Studies.pdf (accessed on 26 June 2021).

Rudel, T., L. Schneider, M. Uriarte, B. L. Turner II, R. DeFries, D. Lawrence, J. Geoghegan, S. Hecht, A. Ickowitz, E. F. Lambin, T. Birkenholtz, S. Baptista, and R. Grau. 2009. "Agricultural intensification and changes in cultivated areas, 1970–2005". *Proceedings of the National Academy of Science*106 (49): 20675–20680. doi:10.1073/pnas.0812540106.

San, Nu Nu, H. Löfgren, and S. Robinson. 2000. "Structural Adjustment, Agriculture, and Deforestation in the Sumatera Regional Economy". TMD Discussion Paper No. 52, International Food Policy Research Institute. https://www.pep-net.org/fileadmin/medias/pdf/recommended_readings/TDP_52_san.pdf (accessed on 26 June 2021).

Vance, C., and J. Geoghegan. 2002. "Temporal and Spatial Modelling of Tropical Deforestation: A Survival Analysis Linking Satellite and Household Survey Data". *Agricultural Economics* 27 (3): 317–332. doi:10.1111/j.1574-0862.2002.tb00123.x.

Wheeler, David, Daniel Hammer, Robin Kraft, Susmita Dasgupta, and Brian Blankespoor. 2011. "Economic Dynamics and Forest Clearing: A Spatial Econometric Analysis for Indonesia". Center for Global Development Working Paper No. 280. http://www.cgdev.org/content/publications/detail/1425820 (accessed on 28 June 2021).

Zikri, Muhammad. 2009. "An Econometric Model for Deforestation in Indonesia". *Working Paper in Economics and Development Studies, No. 200903.* Center for Economics and Development Studies, Department of Economics, Padjadjaran University. https://core.ac.uk/download/pdf/9306319.pdf (accessed on 26 June 2021).

# Part III

# Climate Change and Development

Chapter 9

# Regional Climate Vulnerabilities in South Asia

## A Development Perspective

*Anil Markandya, Muthukumara Mani, Vaideeswaran Sankaran, and Prema Sai Narasimhan*

### Introduction

The South Asia Region (SAR) is recognized as being highly vulnerable to climate change. Increasing temperatures and changes in seasonal rainfall patterns are already having effects on agriculture across the SAR. Low-lying areas of Bangladesh and the Maldives are increasingly vulnerable to flooding and cyclones. The Climate Risk Index by German Watch has placed the two SAR countries – Pakistan and Bangladesh – as among the top ten globally in terms of being affected by extreme events in the decade 1999–2018 and has Nepal and India ninth and seventeenth, respectively in that ranking.[1] The Climate Change Vulnerability Index constructed by Maple croft[2] for 2017 showed the SAR countries as lying between medium to extreme risk (Bangladesh, Pakistan, Nepal, and sections of South India).

The prospects for the near future from the changes in climate that are unavoidable are quite alarming. South Asia is already a hotspot for natural disasters, accounting for around 40% of globally recorded disaster events. Climate change will increase their frequency and intensity.[3] The combination of climatic changes could lead to about 62 million people in the region being pushed below the extreme poverty line by 2030.[4] If climate change continues unabated, it is only a matter of time before the region's hard-won development gains are diminished. Eight hundred million South Asians – or half the region's population – are at risk of seeing their standards of living and incomes declining from rising temperatures, more erratic rainfall, reduced crop yields, and increased water scarcity. By 2030, demand for water in the largest South Asian economies will be double the availability of supplies,[5] and with increased flooding will push more people away from their homes to seek safer places.[6]

In this chapter, we examine the different pathways through which climate change makes the region highly vulnerable and what can be expected in the coming decades. These outcomes, of course, are not predetermined. They depend on the measures taken globally to mitigate climate change through a reduction in emissions of greenhouse gases as well as on actions

DOI: 10.4324/9781003253884-13

taken in the region to reduce the vulnerability through actions to adapt to the changes in climate that will occur. The effects of climate change beyond 2030 depend very much on what emissions pathway the world follows (see below).

In addition to impacting the livelihoods of millions in the region and posing a threat to their health and security, climate change could also influence broader development by reducing the economic growth of the region and creating social conflict. We consider what can be expected in this regard and what measures can be taken to reduce these negative influences of climate change on the development prospects of the region.

## 9.1 Regional Climate Impacts

Climate impacts can be divided broadly into temperature, precipitation, frequency, and intensity of extreme events and the rise of the sea level. We discuss each one below:

### *9.1.1 Temperature*

With regard to temperature, increases have been observed, albeit unevenly throughout many parts of the SAR in recent decades. Western Afghanistan and southwestern Pakistan have experienced the largest increases, with annual average temperatures rising by 1.0°C–3.0°C from 1950 to 2010. Southeastern India, western Sri Lanka, northern Pakistan, and eastern Nepal have all also experienced increases of 1.0°C–1.5°C over the same time frame.

Temperature projections depend very much on what kind of path the world will take in terms of Green House Gas (GHG) emissions and global warming. Scenarios representing atmospheric emissions of GHGs and their associated atmospheric concentrations are referred to as Representative Concentration Pathways (RCPs), and the higher the RCP, the more severe are climate change impacts.[7] Two common scenarios considered are (a) a "climate-sensitive" scenario, denoted by RCP 4.5, which represents a future in which some collective action is taken to limit GHG emissions, with global annual average temperatures increasing by 2.4°C by 2100; and (b) a "carbon-intensive" scenario, denoted by RCP 8.5, which is closer to a scenario in which no actions are taken to reduce emissions, and global annual average temperatures increase by 4.3°C by 2100. The Paris Agreement is closer to accepting RCP 4.5 and would limit global temperature increases on average to 2°C in this century. In that case, South Asia is expected to reach 2°C in the northwestern parts of the region by 2050 and 1°C–2°C in the remaining regions. While these impacts would be significant, they are much less than what would be experienced under RCP 8.5.

### 9.1.2 Precipitation and Water

Changes in average precipitation are more difficult to detect because of large year-to-year and inter-decadal variability but also have significant impacts. Consequently, there are contradictory scientific findings on how precipitation is changing based on the analysis of station records.

For the rest of this century, the projections are uncertain in terms of total rainfall for temperatures of up to 2°C, with significant local variations and prospects of shortages of water in some regions. Groundwater resources, which are mainly recharged by precipitation and surface water, are also expected to be impacted by climate change. There will also be issues due to the impacts of climate change on the glaciers that store much of the region's fresh water. Projections of climate change for the region suggest that rising temperatures will continue to impact snow and glacier dynamics with impacts that are severe in some watersheds and will also affect the water resource balance for all countries. Sustainable management of the glaciers may help moderate river flows in the region's major rivers by providing a regular source of fresh water in hot, dry years/seasons and storing water during colder, wetter years/seasons. Well before a global annual average warming of 2°C is reached, a rapid increase in the frequency of low snow years is projected, with a consequent shift towards higher winter and spring runoff.

### 9.1.3 Extreme Events

The large-scale changes in temperature, precipitation, and other meteorological variables that models project as a result of climate change will affect all extreme events related to these variables (droughts, floods, heat waves, and cold spells).[8] It is almost certain that heat waves will become more frequent and intense in the future in most regions of the world, including the SAR. Most models indicate that the number of days with extreme temperatures on the subcontinent will be relatively less frequent if global temperature increases can be kept to 2°C than if they go up to 4°C. Such events, which have been extremely rare in the past, will increase substantially and cover about 20% of the surface area of the Indian subcontinent. The increase in the frequency of these events would occur in the near term and level off by mid-century.[9] Overall, droughts are likely to become more common – and it is likely that in many locations where droughts already are an issue, the situation will worsen. Droughts are expected to pose an increasing risk in parts of the region, particularly Pakistan while increasing wetness is projected for southern India.

### 9.1.4 Sea Level Rise and Coastal Flood Risks

With the coastlines being located close to the equator, projections of local sea level rise show a greater increase compared to higher latitudes. Sea level rise is projected to be approximately 100 to 115 cm by the 2090s in a 4°C world, and 60 to 80 cm in a 2°C world, by the end of the 21st century relative to 1986–2005, with the highest values (up to 10 cm more) expected for the Maldives. This is generally around 5–10% higher than the global mean, and a 50 cm sea level rise would likely occur by 2060.[10] This global rise combined with local mechanisms – including changes in water currents and local geological dynamics – will increase land loss from erosion, water salinization, and flood risks from storm surges in most coastal areas. Coastal flood risks are already large, as illustrated by the disastrous consequences of Tropical Cyclone "Sidr" in Bangladesh in 2007, and they will only increase over time.

With higher temperatures, atmospheric circulations are modified, influencing winds and storms globally. For tropical storms, the best estimate today is that their overall number may decrease, even as the most intense storms may become more frequent. In addition, tropical cyclones may start affecting new coastal areas that are likely to be less prepared and more vulnerable. For extra-tropical storms, there is little agreement on how they will evolve, although models suggest that their intensity will increase, and their mean trajectory will shift towards higher latitudes.

## 9.2 Effects of the Projected Impacts on People and the Economy

These significant physical impacts of climate change will, in turn, have an effect on livelihoods and the economy. We consider these under the following categories:

a. Effects of water availability and temperature increase on agriculture, including extreme events such as droughts.
b. Damages from floods in river basins and along the coastline due to sea level rise and storm surges.
c. Health effects of heat waves and human productivity implications.
d. Migration within the countries and within the SAR.
e. Impacts of floods and extreme heat on cities.

### *9.2.1 Water Supply and Its Effects on Agriculture*

Projections show that climate change aggravates the increasing pressure on water resources due to high rates of population growth and associated demand in South Asia. While some watersheds may see an increase in total runoff, others could see a decrease and, importantly, the changes will be unevenly distributed across seasons. For the Indus, the mean flow is projected to increase by the 2080s for warming levels of around 2°C by about 65%, with low flow increasing by 30% and the high flow increasing by

78%. For the Ganges-Brahmaputra system, the mean flow increased by only 4%, whereas the low flow decreased by 13% and the high flow by 5%. Given these large changes in seasonal amplification of river flows and rainfall amounts even for 2°C warming, major investments in water storage capacity will be needed in order to utilize the potential benefits of increased seasonal runoff for improved water availability throughout the year. Not only infrastructure for flood protection will have to be built, but water basins also that cross international borders will need to be given special consideration. These include those that cross borders between Afghanistan and Pakistan; Pakistan and India; Nepal and India; and India and Bangladesh. Actions tailored specially to these regions are discussed later in the chapter. Another distinction needs to be made between the highlands, including the Himalayas, the plains, and the coastal areas in terms of planning a response.

Climate change is projected to have a significant and often adverse impact on agricultural production, the development of the sector, and the economic benefits derived from it. The effects of rainfall deficits, extreme rainfall events, and flooding are projected to be important factors, although their impacts will vary. In combination with heat stress, further limitations on groundwater resources and salinization resulting from sea level rise and higher temperatures, agricultural production is negatively affected in most of the SAR (with some small exceptions in high-altitude places). The resulting decline in agricultural revenues and increases in food prices were analyzed in the Shockwaves study[11] for their impacts on the poor in the countries of the region. They found that while agricultural revenues generally have a small positive effect on reducing people in extreme poverty across the SAR (higher prices compensate for the decline in yields), the increase in prices for urban consumers has a larger negative effect, increasing the numbers in extreme poverty by around five million (but with large uncertainty ranges). The same applies when looking at the incomes of the bottom 40% of the population.

In addition to its effects on poverty, these agricultural changes are also expected to impact human health. Estimates of the health effects focus on undernutrition due to higher food prices and, in turn, their effects on stunting (low height for age). The World Health Organization (WHO) model predicts 20,700 additional deaths by 2030 in the SAR, albeit an uncertainty range that is very wide: there could be 39,000 fewer deaths or as many as 80,000. In terms of stunting, it predicts 2 million more children will be stunted (1.2 to 2.9) in 2030 and 2.7 million (2.4 to 3.1) by 2050.[12]

### 9.2.2 *Infrastructure Damages due to River Floods, Sea Level Rise, and Storm Surges*

Precipitation is the major cause of flooding, and the risks from flooding have grown, mainly due to population and economic growth in coastal regions and low-lying areas. In the year 2000, approximately 38 million people were exposed to floods in the SAR; almost 45 million were exposed in 2010, accounting for approximately 65% of the global population exposed to floods.[13] Deltaic regions, in particular, are vulnerable to more severe flooding, loss of wetlands, and a loss of infrastructure and livelihoods as a consequence of sea level rise and climate-induced extreme events.

Recent work shows that the proportion of the population prone to river flooding increases rapidly with higher levels of warming. Globally about twice as many people are predicted to be flood prone in 2100 in a 4°C world compared to a 2°C scenario[14]. Arnell and Gosling (2013) find that increases in flooding risk are particularly large over South Asia by the 2050s, both in percentage and absolute terms. Reinforcing this are recent projections of the consequence of snow reductions in the Himalayan region: increasing frequency of extremely low snow years causes extremely high northern hemisphere winter and spring runoff increasing flood risks.[15]

Coastal cities of Dhaka, Karachi, Kolkata, and Mumbai – urban areas that are home to more than 80 million people face a substantial risk of flood-related damage over the next century. The entire country of Maldives is already coping with sea level rise and storm risks and planning for significant increases.

Arnell and Gosling (2013) estimate the effects of these disasters on extreme poverty and on the incomes of the bottom 40% of the population by income in the region for different climate change scenarios. Based on plausible modelling, the study assumed that the fraction of the population that will be affected annually by a flood or a drought increased by 20% in the optimistic scenario and by 40% in the pessimistic scenario and that the fraction of the population affected annually by a storm surge, or a cyclone increases by 10% in the optimistic scenario and by 50% in the pessimistic scenario by 2030. The results show that about five million more people could go into extreme poverty by that date and the bottom 40% lose about 1% of their income as a result.[16]

### *9.2.3 Health Effects of Heat Waves and Productivity Effects of Higher Temperatures*

Extreme temperature events such as the 2015 heat wave that killed more than 3,500 people continue to threaten the region, causing health and productivity related impacts. Central India is the most vulnerable to heat. Given the strong projections for more very high-temperature days, people are expected to suffer the effects of such events in large numbers, despite better warnings and preventive measures (Azhar et al. 2017). The WHO model estimates deaths from such events to be about 9,200 (7,300 to 10,600) by 2030.

In addition, higher temperatures will result in a loss of productivity for those who must work outdoors or who do not have climate controls inside their working premises. Recent evidence suggested that each degree in warming could reduce labour productivity by 1 to 3%, at least for people working outdoor or without air conditioning.[17] Losses due to higher temperatures were estimated in 2010 to have been around US$69 billion and to go up to US$563 billion[18], equivalent to 4.8% of the SAR's 2017 GDP.

The impacts of the significant losses in health and productivity will be felt more in the poorer sections of the population. The South Asia application of Shockwaves study estimates that as many as 17 million more people could go into extreme poverty as a result of these factors, with the greater share arising from health impacts. The bottom 40% could lose anything from 1% to 4% of their incomes. It is important to note, however, that the uncertainty bounds on these estimates are large.

### *9.2.4 Local Air Pollution and Its Effects on Health*

Serious health effects associated with the combustion of fossil fuels are a major issue. The region is at the epicentre of the threat to public health from air pollution, which contributed to around 11% of all deaths and approximately 40 million disability-adjusted life years (DALYs). Nearly 95% of South Asians live in areas where ambient (outdoor) fine particulate matter concentrations (small dust or soot particles in the air) exceed the World Health Organization's Air Quality Guideline of 10 $\mu g/m^3$. Of the top 20 cities in the world with the poorest air quality in 2016, 17 are in the SAR (Health Effects Institute 2019).

Apart from the health consequences, air pollution also has economic costs through reduced productivity and increased expenditures on medical care. A World Bank and IHME study[19] quantified the economic cost of forgone labour productivity and the broader measure of welfare losses discussed above in South Asia. The forgone economic output of the region attributable to public health impacts of ambient air pollution exposure in 2013 was put at US$31 billion, which is about 0.4% of the regional gross domestic product (GDP).[20] The broader measure of welfare losses in South Asia due to public health impacts of ambient air pollution were US$256 billion, i.e., more than 3.1% of GDP.[21]

### *9.2.5 Migration within the Region and to Other Parts of the World*

Migration is increasingly a concern in the SAR. As living conditions deteriorate, families will initially seek to adapt where they live, but if that proves impossible, they will move. They will migrate from less viable areas with lower water availability and crop productivity and from areas affected by rising sea levels and storm surges. The poorest and most climate-vulnerable areas will be the hardest hit. These trends, alongside the emergence of 'hot-spots' of climate in and out-migration, will have major implications for climate-sensitive sectors and for the adequacy of infrastructure and social support systems. A World Bank report 'Groundswell' assessed the implications of climate change in terms of additional migration across different parts of the world, including South Asia.[22] Although international flows are significant, projections were that internal migration is the main form of movement in the SAR.

The number of climate migrants is projected to increase from 1.7 to 6.1 million people (0.1 to 0.3% of the population) in 2020 to 16.9 to 35.7 million (0.7 to 1.6% of the population) by 2050 across scenarios. These projections are largest in the pessimistic reference scenario (35.7 million), lower under the more inclusive development scenario (21.2 million) and lowest under the more climate-friendly scenario (16.9 million). The lower numbers suggest positive effects of better development policies and lower global emissions but are still significant, nevertheless. The driving factors for the migration are natural disasters, such as glacial lake outburst floods, storm surges, droughts, cyclones, and heavy precipitation; late onset or failed monsoons; and other climate hazards. These numbers, although large, should be seen relative to the overall level of non-climate migration in the region. Other internal migrants are expected to grow from 33.8 million in 2020 to 119.9 million by 2050 across scenario averages.

Migration is projected into the Gangetic Plain and in western Bangladesh initially, spreading out to many of India's regions in the south as well as in west Bangladesh. There is also projected to be significant out-migration from coastal zones, but the figures have wide ranges, including possible in-migration under some models (World Bank 2018, Groundswell report).

### 9.2.6 *Impacts of Floods and Extreme Heat on Cities*

The effects of climate-related disasters are often exacerbated in cities due to interactions with urban infrastructure systems, growing urban populations, cultures, and economic activities. Cultural, demographic, and economic characteristics of urban residents, city governments, built environment, ecosystem services, and human-induced stresses, such as over-exploitation of resources and environmental degradation, define the vulnerability of cities to climate-related disasters. More frequent climate and extreme weather events are being experienced in some urban areas, and the frequency and severity of these events are projected to increase in the coming decades.[23]

Coastal cities are particularly exposed to cascading risks resulting from a combination of climatic changes, including increased temperature, increased river flooding, rising sea levels, and increasingly intense tropical cyclones and their consequences.[24] For example, in the case of Mumbai, it is projected that by the 2080s and with a warming of 3°C–3.5°C above pre-industrial levels, there is a doubling of the likelihood of an extreme event like the 2005 floods (and a return period reduced to around 1 in 90 years).

In addition to coastal flooding and storms, cities are also expected to be affected by severe heat events. Inland cities, in particular, suffer from urban heat island effects and higher temperatures.[25] For instance, the number of high-temperature days in India has increased over the past 50 years, especially since the 1990s, in highly-populated cities like Mumbai, Delhi, Chennai, and Jaipur.[26] One study shows extremely high temperatures and heat index values in Delhi, Dhaka, and Faisalabad.[27] It also finds that people living in informal neighbourhoods in the cities are consistently exposed to more heat than people in richer neighbourhoods.

## 9.3 National Climate Vulnerabilities and Priority Actions

While there are several cross-cutting vulnerabilities across the region, there are more specific vulnerabilities in each country. From the country reviews conducted by the authors, as well as consultations carried out with key stakeholders in the respective countries, the assessment manifests locally expressed concerns.

In Bangladesh, coastal flooding and extreme events have a significant impact on infrastructure as well as agriculture and livelihoods. In India, the greatest impacts of climate change are on agriculture and coastal cities. There is also great concern about growing water scarcity and critical levels of local air pollution in the country.

In Pakistan, agricultural output will be affected, annual river flows are projected to decline, and coastal livelihoods are vulnerable to sea level rise, floods, and storms. In the case of Bhutan, with its fragile mountain ecosystem, concerns are greatest in relation to the way in which climate change will alter water availability and cause natural disasters such as landslides.

Sri Lanka faces the greatest climate vulnerabilities in agriculture and fisheries, and in coastal regions, with the impacts particularly stronger in zones where extreme events impact most. In Nepal, late onset or diminished monsoons pose a major risk to crops everywhere, and insufficient water availability is also a concern for hydropower generation. In Afghanistan, key concerns arise with respect to effects on agriculture, hydropower, and clean water. Finally, the low-lying islands in the Maldives are highly vulnerable to beach erosion from sea level rise, causing significant loss to land and coastal infrastructure and losses to its important tourism industry.

## 9.4 Actions Needed to Adapt to the Climate Impacts

The wide range of negative effects of climate change must be countered through a programme of country-specific national and subnational actions. Governments in all eight countries in the region are actively involved in this through a range of strategy and planning documents. In this review, we look at areas where the proposed measures need further strengthening and how this might be achieved. This can be said to constitute a regional gap analysis.

### 9.4.1 Institutional Setting

Although climate change is a common challenge facing the region, there are no regional organizational initiatives to facilitate climate action. The governments within the regional setting are not effectively collaborating to bring together policy reform, institutional reform, and investments to counter climate change implications in a collective way. The South Asian Association for Regional Cooperation (SAARC) had established an Inter-Governmental Expert Group on Climate Change. In 2010, SAARC Heads of State adopted the Thimphu Statement on Climate Change which is a clear indication of their commitment and determination to enhance cooperation among the Member States. This Statement outlined several initiatives to be implemented both at the national and regional level to address the adverse effects of climate change. However, these initiatives have not been implemented as intended.

Political commitment to tackle climate change is strong, but not enough resources have been committed to making it operational. Most national governments resolve and commit to addressing climate change in various forums such as the Conference of Parties on a regular basis. They have accepted the Nationally Determined Commitments (NDCs) and have national or subnational action plans. Further, as an organizational set-up, councils or committees at the highest level are established, e.g., the Government of Nepal's Climate Change Council. However, in terms of making operational their commitment, the SAR country governments are unable to do so because of other development issues that require urgent, immediate action.

As the national coordinating climate change units are based in the environmental ministries, they lack implementation orientation. Mainstreaming of the climate agenda in sector ministries is still falling short. Respective environmental ministries are the nodal agencies in the administrative structure of the national governments for the planning, promotion, coordination, and overseeing the implementation of environmental (including climate change) and forestry policies and programmes. However, these ministries tend to have a strong scientific and regulatory orientation as those are their primary functions. Therefore, these ministries tend not to have the required leverage to drive implementation in the other sector departments or ministries. Mainstreaming of climate change in the sector ministries is the only way forward but is still in its nascent stage in the SAR.

Governments, donors, the private sector, and civil society organizations are working in their respective silos in terms of implementing climate actions. In their effort to drive the Nationally Determined Contributions (NDC)[28] and National Adaptation Plan (NAP)[29] implementation, governments are initiating different activities in the various sectors. Donors – both multilateral and bilateral – are driving activities to meet their respective country commitments. The private sector is pursuing activities that make business sense, i.e., wherein returns-on-investments are justified. And civil society organizations are engaged in climate-related activities that are in line with their constituency, whether it is nature conservation or agriculture. All of these are consistent with NDC and NAP but are not necessarily derived from them as priorities. While all these activities are good contributions, synergies are not explored and, therefore, the effectiveness of coordinated action is not realized. Although much of the power to deal with the climate-related challenges has been devolved to the subnational governments, they do not have the capacity for effective action.

Further, knowledge on climate change is yet to reach the lowest level of the government in order to facilitate grass-root level action. For instance, in Nepal, in the context of federalization, the local governance knowledge and capacity need to be strengthened. Barring a few exceptions wherein donor agencies or civil society organizations are engaged with the local community, the subject of climate change is confined to national-level governments. In the case of India alone, there is a lot of planning at the state level. However, there is not much at the district or village level. Further, the traditional public finance management systems are not geared for climate change responsiveness.

### 9.4.2 Climate Data, Analytics, and Knowledge

Further work is required in downscaling of General Circulation Models (GCM)[30] and Regional Climate Models (RCM)[31] to predict climate change impacts at the national and subnational level. This is a clear gap that needs to be progressively addressed as new technologies, methods, and computing power become available to downscale predictions and make them relevant at the grassroots level. The outputs of the predictions should be gainfully used in water resource planning and agriculture planning. At best, only 3-day and 7-day predictions are being given to the end-user sectors. This needs to be substantively improved for effective decision-making.

Climate predictions do not reach the end-user. Rainfall predictions need to be improved from 1-day or 3-day to 1-week predictions in order to improve decision-making at the farm level. For instance, in certain subnational areas (Karnataka) in India, these predictions are effectively communicated to the farmers for suitable decision-making. This enables the farmer in improving productivity and overall agricultural production. Such data sharing is presently not practised widely in the SAR.

### 9.4.3 Sectoral Issues

The water resources sector is underprepared. Climate impacts and associated vulnerabilities include erratic rainfall, increases in water flow due to glacier melts within and between countries, and extreme events such as floods. Water allocation across the various end-users will have to be dynamic and flexible. Adoption of water allocation models to improve water supply planning across various sectors, improvements in water use efficiency in the major demand sectors, and the use of water markets with appropriate water pricing are to be mainstreamed. Such systematic approaches are yet to be developed. The capacity to plan for shortfalls and excesses in the rainfall has not yet been built. The variations in water availability have implications for the hydropower sector as well. Energy planning has not yet accounted for the vagaries of water availability. Overall, climate-resilient water resources management is recognized to be required but is at a nascent stage operationally.

Though climate-smart agriculture has been initiated, much more needs to be done. Many of the SAR countries have introduced development projects that promote climate-smart agriculture. There needs to be both a broadening – in terms of its replication across the region – and a deepening – in terms of holistically addressing choice of crop, seeds, soil-water management, and irrigation approaches – of climate-smart agriculture practices in order to build greater resilience in this sector. Further, the agriculture sector needs to consider the loss of productivity in the context of heat stress, given the predictions of higher temperatures during the summer months in the SAR.

Disaster management does not integrate climate vulnerabilities. Conventionally, disaster management is human-centric and does not consider climate-induced impacts on ecosystems as a whole. Natural capital has a role in human-centric disaster management, but it needs to be protected as well. The aspects of nature's role and its resilience are not yet adequately integrated. While the disaster management sector aims to move beyond relief and recovery to disaster risk reduction and preparedness, there is a need to integrate climate vulnerabilities with a particular focus on their implications on natural capital.

Coastal assets and livelihoods are not adequately prepared for increased intensity and frequency of cyclones and sea level rise. Coastal agriculture, coastal fisheries, aquaculture, and other livelihoods are going to be adversely affected. For instance, the threat of sea level rise in the low-lying areas, e.g., the Kuttanad area in Kerala, India, is likely to change the cultivation patterns along the coast due to saltwater intrusion in their agricultural fields. Their climate preparedness is not commensurate with what is required.

### 9.4.4 Climate Finance and Investments

There is a major shortfall between funds required and funds available to address climate change. In all the countries, the stated requirement of funds is far greater than what has been made available. Clearly, there is a major shortfall in terms of international fund flows, governments' own budget provisions and private sector funding. Even though the stated requirement of funds is not in any level of detail, the shortfall is not debatable. With the limited availability of funds, there is a limited chance for all the investments to have significant coverage and be able to sustain beyond the investment period. There are some examples of investments that have had a demonstrative impact, e.g., climate-resilient seeds used in agriculture, with a potential for dissemination across the agriculture economy.

The capacity to raise climate finance needs to be improved. Across the region, it was recognized that the financial support made available under the United Nations Framework Convention on Climate Change (UNFCCC) to developing countries involved procedures that were complex. Some governments have established Climate Finance Unit within the Ministries of Finance, e.g., in Afghanistan, to coordinate international finance available. These are still in an early stage, and significant strengthening of capacity is required.

There is an absence of coordination among donor agencies. While there are efforts underway in different countries, e.g., in Nepal, to better coordinate among donor agencies, a lot more can be done in order to improve the effectiveness of the technical and financial support that the governments are receiving to deal with climate change.

Understanding of economics and financial implications is weak. The delayed monsoons affect the agricultural economy. Climate-induced disasters cause damage to large infrastructures such as roads and urban and coastal assets. Damage and reconstruction have financial repercussions. The understanding that better preparedness through implementing climate adaptation and climate proofing will benefit the economy is not well-appreciated. Largely, the prevailing approach is an ex-post one. There is a need to enable a better understanding of the economics of climate adaptation and resilience (Adams et al. 2013).

Methodology for loss and damage due to climate change has not been established. The UNFCCC has defined loss and damage to include harm resulting from climate-induced extreme events such as cyclones and flash floods and the gradual changes such as the sea level rise and shifts in monsoon patterns. Establishing liability and compensation for loss and damage has been a need for all vulnerable and developing countries, including those in the SAR. There has been little or no progress even in establishing the methodology for the same.

## 9.5 Conclusion: Perspectives for Long-Term Growth and Development

The effects of climate on development have been the subject of considerable literature over a number of years. There are broadly three schools of thought on the impact of geography and climate on human development: (i) climate determines development; (ii) climate is important; and (iii) climate used to be important but is no longer (Toi 2009). The view of environmental determinism is seen more as a historical factor and less important today, but the view that climate is important for development, although not the dominant factor, has a strong following (Sachs 2003). The main pathways scholars see for the climate to influence development is through poor health and infrastructure that is vulnerable to climate extremes. The third view focuses on the role of institutions to address the climate challenges (Acemoglu et al. (2001, 2002); Easterly and Levine (2003) and Rodrik et al. (2004)). They argue that climate did influence institutions in the past in a way that slowed development, especially in colonized countries, but now climate and geography have little power to explain the current distribution of income across the nations of the world once the effects of education, the rule of law, the quality of governance have been accounted for.

It is difficult to maintain the position that climate (or at least climate change) has no influence on development prospects at the present time. The increased frequency of extreme events and the impact they have on growth is well documented. So are the loss of agricultural productivity and the health effects of climate. All these are present in South Asia, as this chapter shows. Surely the important task is to understand how climate change is influencing development through these effects and what actions are needed to mitigate the effects, in part through reducing the level of climate change through a global path of decarbonization, and in part by addressing proactively the challenges that are arising in different sectors of the economy. In this review, we have noted the particular climate-related issues arising in South Asia. They are by no means minor, and they demand concerted action to prevent them from arresting the development of the region.

## Notes

1 German Watch 2019
2 Maple croft 2017
3 Hirji et al. 2017
4 World Bank 2015 and 2016
5 Ibid.
6 Mani et al. 2018
7 Ibid.
8 See Havlík et al. 2015, Hallegatte et al. 2016 and World Bank 2013.
9 Ibid.
10 Ibid.
11 Ibid.
12 WHO 2014
13 Ibid.
14 Arnell et al. 2013
15 Arnell and Gosling, 2013
16 The 5 million figures are, of course, dominated by the effects in India.

17 Hallegatte et al. 2016, Ibid. More detailed estimates for different occupations are given in DARA (2012).
18 DARA (2012), Ibid. It has made estimates for all countries for 2030.
19 The World Bank and IHME, 2016
20 Another US$43 billion is attributable to Household Air Pollution. (Figures are expressed in 2011 PPP adjusted US dollars.)
21 Another US$396 billion attributable to Household Air Pollution. (Figures are expressed in 2011 PPP adjusted US dollars.) The total is more than four and a half times larger than welfare losses in 1990.
22 World Bank, 2018.
23 *Rosenzweig et al. 2018.*
24 World Bank, 2013.
25 Ibid.
26 Jaswal et al. 2015.
27 Jacobs et al. 2019.
28 Nationally determined contributions (NDCs) are at the heart of the Paris Agreement and the achievement of these long-term goals. NDCs embody efforts by each country to reduce national emissions and adapt to the impacts of climate change. The Paris Agreement (Article 4, paragraph 2) requires each Party to prepare, communicate and maintain successive nationally determined contributions (NDCs) that it intends to achieve. Parties shall pursue domestic mitigation measures with the aim of achieving the objectives of such contributions.
29 The National Adaptation Plan (NAP) process is a country-driven process where national governments analyze current and future climate risks and deliberate with stakeholders how the risks can be addressed. The process provides a basis for countries to identify and prioritize medium-and long-term adaptation options and implement them through respective strategies. Established in 2010 by the United Nations Framework Convention on Climate Change (UNFCCC) as part of the Cancún Adaptation Framework, the NAP process complements the existing short-term national adaptation programmes of action (NAPAs) by providing a systematic approach to plan for adaptation at the national level.
30 General circulation models (GCMs) are mathematical models capable of representing physical processes of the atmosphere and ocean to simulate the response of global climate to the increasing greenhouse gas emission (IPCC 2013; Eckstein et al. 2019).
31 A regional climate model (RCM) is a numerical climate prediction model forced by specified lateral and ocean conditions from a general circulation model (GCM) or observation-based dataset (reanalysis) that simulates atmospheric and land surface processes while accounting for high-resolution topographical data, land-sea contrasts, surface characteristics, and other components of the Earth system.

## References

Acemoglu, D., S. Johnson, and J. A. Robinson. 2001. "The Colonial Origins of Comparative Development: An Empirical Investigation". *American Economic Review* 91 (5): 1369–1401. doi:10.1257/aer.91.5.1369.

Acemoglu, D., S. Johnson, and J. A. Robinson. 2002. "Reversal of Fortune: Geography and Institutions in the Making of the Modern World Income Distribution". *The Quarterly Journal of Economics* 117 (4): 1231–1294. doi:10.1162/003355302320935025.

Adams, S., Baarsch, F., Bondeau, A., Coumou, D., Donner, R., Frieler, K., Hare, B., Menon, A., Perette, M., Piontek, F. and Rehfeld, K.2013. *Turn Down the Heat: Climate Extremes, Regional Impacts, and the Case for Resilience*. The World Bank. ISBN (electronic): 978-1-4648-0056-6. https://openknowledge.worldbank.org/bitstream/handle/10986/14000/9781464800559s.pdf?sequence=6&isAllowed=y (accessed on 27 June 2021).

Arnell, Nigel W., and S. N. Gosling. 2013. "The Impacts of Climate Change on River Flow Regimes at the Global Scale". *Journal of Hydrology* 486: 351–364. doi:10.1016/j.jhydrol.2013.02.010.

Arnell, N. W., J. A. Lowe, S. Brown, S. N. Gosling, P. Gottschalk, J. Hinkel, and B. Lloyd-Hughes et al. 2013. "A Global Assessment of the Effects of Climate Policy on the Impacts of Climate Change". *Nature Climate Change* 3 (5): 512–519. doi:10.1038/nclimate1793.

Azhar, G., S. Saha, P. Ganguly, D. Mavalankar, and J. Madrigano. 2017. "Heat Wave Vulnerability Mapping for India". *International Journal of Environmental Research and Public Health* 14 (4): 357. doi:10.3390/ijerph14040357.

DARA. 2012. *Climate Vulnerability Monitor: A Guide to the Cold Calculus of a Hot Planet*. ISBN:978-84-616-0567-5. https://daraint.org/wp-content/uploads/2012/10/CVM2-Low.pdf (accessed on 27 June 2021).

Easterly, William, and Ross Levine. 2003. "Tropics, Germs, And Crops: How Endowments Influence Economic Development". *Journal of Monetary Economics* 50 (1): 3–39. doi:10.1016/s0304-3932(02)00200-3.

Eckstein, D., Künzel, V., Schäfer, L. and Winges, M. 2019. *Global Climate Risk Index 2020*. German Watch. ISBN:978-3-943704-77-8. https://germanwatch.org/sites/germanwatch.org/files/20-2-01e%20Global%20Climate%20Risk%20Index%202020_10.pdf (accessed on 27 June 2021).

Hallegatte, S., Bangalore, M., Bonzanigo, L., Fay, M., Kane, T., Narloch, U., Rozenberg, J., Treguer, D. and Vogt-Schilb, A. 2016. *Shock Waves: Managing the Impacts of Climate Change on Poverty*. The World Bank. ISBN: 978-1-4648-0673-5. https://openknowledge.worldbank.org/bitstream/handle/10986/22787/9781464806735.pdf (accessed on 27 June 2021).

Havlík, Petr, Valin, Hugo, Gusti, Mykola, Schmid, Erwin, Leclère, David, Forsell, Nicklas, Herrero, Mario, Khabarov, Nikolay, Mosnier, Aline, Cantele, Matthew, Obersteiner, Michael. 2015. "Climate Change Impacts and Mitigation in the Developing World: An Integrated Assessment of the Agriculture and Forestry Sectors". *Policy Research Working Paper; No. 7477*. Washington, DC: World Bank © World Bank. https://openknowledge.worldbank.org/handle/10986/23441 (accessed on 7 July 2021).

Health Effects Institute. 2019. *State of Global Air*. Boston. https://www.stateofglobalair.org/sites/default/files/soga_2019_report.pdf (accessed on 27 June 2021).

Hirji, R., Nicol, A. and Davis, R. 2017. *South Asia Climate Change Risks in Water Management: Climate Risks and Solutions-Adaptation Frameworks for Water Resources Planning, Development, and Management in South Asia*. World Bank. https://openknowledge.worldbank.org/bitstream/handle/10986/29685/124894-WP-P153431-PUBLIC-Climate-Change-and-WRM-Summary-Report-FINAL-web-version.pdf?sequence=1&isAllowed=y (accessed on 27 June 2021).

IPCC. 2013. *Climate Change 2013: The Physical Science Basis. Contribution of Working Group I to the Fifth Assessment Report of the Intergovernmental Panel on Climate Change*. Stocker, T.F., D. Qin, G.-K. Plattner, M. Tignor, S.K. Allen, J. Boschung, A. Nauels, Y. Xia, V. Bex and P.M. Midgley (eds.). Cambridge, United Kingdom and New York, NY, USA: Cambridge University Press, 1535 pp. doi:10.1017/CBO9781107415324.

Jacobs, C., T. Singh, G. Gorti, U. Iftikhar, S. Saeed, A. Syed, F. Abbas, B. Ahmad, S. Bhadwal, and C. Siderius. 2019. "Patterns of Outdoor Exposure to Heat in Three South Asian Cities". *Science of the Total Environment* 674: 264–278. doi:10.1016/j.scitotenv.2019.04.087.

Jaswal, A. K., P. C. S. Rao, and V. Singh. 2015. "Climatology and Trends of Summer High Temperature Days in India during 1969–2013". *Journal of Earth System Science* 124 (1): 1–15. doi:10.1007/s12040-014-0535-8.

Mani, M., S. Bandyopadhyay, S. Chonabayashi, A. Markandya, and T. Mosier, 2018. *South Asia's Hotspots: The Impact of Temperature and Precipitation Changes on Living Standards*. The World Bank. ISBN (paper): 978-1-4648-1155-5. https://openknowledge.worldbank.org/bitstream/handle/10986/28723/9781464811555.pdf?sequence=5&isAllowed=y (accessed on 2 April 2021).

Maple Croft. *Climate Change Vulnerability Index 2017*. https://reliefweb.int/sites/reliefweb.int/files/resources/verisk%20index.pdf (accessed on 21 October 2021).

Rodrik, D., A. Subramanian, and F. Trebbi. 2004. "Institutions Rule: The Primacy of Institutions over Geography and Integration in Economic Development". *Journal of Economic Growth* 9 (2): 131–165. doi:10.1023/b:joeg.0000031425.72248.85.

Rosenzweig, C., W. Solecki, P. Romero-Lankao, S. Mehrotra, S. Dhakal, and S. Ali Ibrahim. 2018. *Climate Change and Cities: Second Assessment Report of the Urban Climate Change Research Network*. Cambridge University Press. https://doi.org/10.1017/9781316563878.007 (accessed on 27 June 2021).

Sachs, J. D. 2003. "Institutions Don't Rule: Direct Effects of Geography on per Capita Income". *NBER Working Paper 9490*, National Bureau of Economic Research. http://www.nber.org/papers/w9490 (accessed on 7 January 2021).

Tol, Richard S. J. 2009. "The Economic Effects of Climate Change". *Journal Of Economic Perspectives* 23 (2): 29–51. doi:10.1257/jep.23.2.29.

WHO, 2014. *Quantitative Risk Assessment of the Effects of Climate Change on Selected Causes of Death, 2030s and 2050s*. World Health Organization. ISBN: 978 92 4 150769 1. https://apps.who.int/iris/handle/10665/134014 (accessed on 8 February 2021).

World Bank. 2013. *The World Bank Annual Report 2013*. Washington, DC, USA. https://openknowledge.worldbank.org/handle/10986/16091 (accessed on 7 August 2022)

World Bank. 2015. "Climate Change Impacts and Mitigation in the Developing World: An Integrated Assessment of the Agriculture and Forestry Sectors". *Policy Research Working Paper 7477*. Washington, DC: World Bank. https://openknowledge.worldbank.org/handle/10986/23441 (accessed on 28 June 2021).

World Bank. 2016. *World Bank Group Climate Change Action Plan*. Washington, DC: World Bank Group. http://pubdocs.worldbank.org/en/677331460056382875/WBG-Climate-Change-Action-Plan-public-version.pdf (accessed on 10 March 2021).

World Bank. 2018. *Groundswell: Preparing for Internal Climate Migration*. Washington, DC: https://www.worldbank.org/en/news/infographic/2018/03/19/groundswell---preparing-for-internal-climate-migration (accessed on 27 May 2021).

The World Bank and IHME. 2016. *The Cost of Air Pollution: Strengthening the Economic Case for Action*. Washington, DC: World Bank Group. http://documents1.worldbank.org/curated/en/781521473177013155/pdf/108141-REVISED-Cost-of-PollutionWebCORRECTEDfile.pdf (accessed on 8 October 2021).

Chapter 10

# Climate-Smart Agriculture in Developing Economies

## An Analysis of Strategies and Policies

*Achiransu Acharyya*

### Introduction

The primary income source for an estimated 70% of the world's poor who live in rural areas is agriculture (World Bank 2016). Globally, around 1.3 billion smallholders and landless workers work in the agricultural sector (World Bank 2016). However, in the coming years, the output from the agricultural sector is becoming increasingly uncertain. Climate variability and climate change will have a negative impact on food security and the agricultural livelihoods of the poorest farmers and forest-dependent people. Along with degradation of land, rise in food and energy prices, and fall in investment support in agriculture, the change in climate will lead to an increase in poverty and food insecurity for the poorest smallholder farmers (Smit et al. 1996; Acharyya 2014). Moreover, the impacts of global climate change are unequally distributed as women and men farmers living within the most fragile environments, like conflict-prone areas, drylands, mountain areas, and coastal zones, will be more prone to shocks and stresses.

Most of the poor smallholder farmers are situated in the South and Southeast Asia as also in Sub-Saharan (SSA) Africa. In these regions, agricultural production will need to increase substantially to feed the growing and urbanizing populations, particularly in Sub-Saharan Africa and South Asia. Estimates of the rise in food production required for this vary between 25 and 70%, counting on the assumptions made about efficiency and consumption pattern changes (Alexandratos and Bruinsma 2012; Hunter et al. 2017). Higher production of food is necessary for the situation of a changing climate and frequency of increased climate variability (Porter et al. 2014). However, along with higher food output, reductions in the carbon cost of farming and its contribution to greenhouse emission and improvement in the nutritional outcomes are also necessary (Tubiello et al. 2008).

Under the above circumstances, the question arises, how well are smallholder farmers in lower-income countries adapting to the various challenges they face due to climate change? One response to these recognized

DOI: 10.4324/9781003253884-14

needs has been the development of approaches such as climate-smart agriculture (CSA). It is a practical idea that can be used by farmers for reorientation and transformation of agricultural development under the existence of climate change (Lipper et al. 2014; Acharyya and Ghosh 2017). Climate-smart agriculture (CSA) or climate-smart farming (CSF), as defined and presented by Food and Agricultural Organization (FAO 2013), tries to integrate the various dimensions of sustainable development by jointly focusing on both the problems of food security as well as climate challenges. These magnitudes of sustainable development are based essentially on the three pillars of economics, community, and the environment. The primary objective is to cooperatively accomplish sustainability in agriculture along with increasing production and income using the three mentioned pillars (FAO 2013). Its goal is to realize sustainable agricultural development for food security.

This chapter tries to assess the readiness of smallholder farmers in developing countries to accept climate-smart farming practices in terms of the role of government and institutions. Section 10.2 discusses in detail the impact of climate change on agriculture and small farmers in the regions of South Asia, Southeast Asia, and Sub-Saharan Africa. The importance of climate-smart farming for sustainable livelihood in agriculture is discussed in Section 10.3. Section 10.4 does a reality check on the initiatives taken by the government and other organizations for the adaptation of climate-smart agriculture by farmers in developing countries. Section 10.5 is the concluding section.

## 10.1 Impact of Climate Change on Agriculture in developing countries

In South Asia, it is anticipated that the annual average maximum temperature may rise by 1.4 to 1.8°C in 2030 and 2.1 to 2.6°C in 2050, and thus, heat-stressed expanse in the area could rise by 12% in 2030 and 21% in 2050 (Tesfaye et al. 2017). An estimation of the potential food output from the Indo-Gangetic Plains (IGP) shows that due to heat stress, nearly half the main food basket of the South Asian region may become unsuitable for wheat production by 2050 (Ortiz et al. 2008). Even somewhat modest warming of 1.5 to 2°C in South Asia can acutely impact the stability and availability of water resources due to rising monsoon variability and glacial meltwater, thereby portending future agricultural productions (Vinke et al. 2017).

With its negative influence on agricultural production and natural resources, global climate change will bring more significant variation in crop production, food supplies, and market prices and can intensify incidents of poverty and food insecurity in South Asian countries, which may adversely affect the livelihood of many people within the region (Schmidhuber and Tubiello 2007; Bandara and Cai 2014; Wang et al. 2017; Acharyya 2021).

Estimations of the impact of climate change show that food price changes between 2000 and 2050 would be 2.5 times higher for major food crops (e.g., wheat, rice, maize, and soybean) and 1.5 times for livestock products (i.e. pork, lamb, beef, and poultry) (Nelson et al. 2009). Therefore, in the situation of the inadequacy of adaptation measures to climate change, according to Ahmed and Suphachalasai (2014), South Asia could suffer an equivalent of 1.8% loss of its annual gross domestic product (GDP) by 2050 and a loss of 8.8% by 2100. The average total economic losses are projected to be 8.7% for India, 6.6% for Bhutan, 9.4% for Bangladesh, 2.6% for the Maldives, 6.5% for Sri Lanka, and 9.9% for Nepal. Since agriculture provides livelihood to over 70% of the people, employs almost 60% of the labour force, and contributes 22% of the regional gross domestic product (GDP) in South Asia (Wang et al. 2017), these losses in GDP will have severe ramifications on people and communities in the region relying heavily on agriculture (Ahmed and Suphachalasai 2014). Therefore, an improved understanding of the impacts of global climate change in agriculture and accordingly the adaptation practices to deal with these impacts are essential to reinforce the sustainability of agriculture and to orient the policies that reduce poor farmers' vulnerability to global climate change in South Asia.

The IPCC 4th Assessment Report (IPCC 2007) states that Southeast Asia is predicted to be seriously suffering from the adverse impacts of global climate change. Since most people in the region rely heavily on agriculture and natural resources for primary income, climate change has been and will continue to be a critical factor affecting productivity in the region. In the last five years, there has been a rise in the frequency of floods, drought periods, and many significant devastating cyclones. Moreover, water, soil, and land resources are continuing to decline. In Thailand, Vietnam, Indonesia, and the Philippines, the mean annual temperatures are estimated to increase by 4.8°C by 2100.

Consequently, the average water level during the same period will rise by 70 cm (ADB 2009). In Southeast Asia, annual rainfall fluctuations are foreseen to continue till 2040 (Cruz et al. 2007) and a rise in the occurrence of severe weather, including precipitation events and heat waves. A surge in tropical cyclone intensities by 10–20% is anticipated, and temperatures are projected to rise by about 0.7–0.9°C (Cruz et al. 2007). Sea levels have risen by 1–3 mm/year in the last few decades, marginally higher than the global average (ADB 2009).

In Southeast Asia, rice is the major crop. Therefore, it is worrying that a significant portion of the rice-growing areas of the region is becoming vulnerable due to the consequences of global climate change (Masutomi et al. 2009). Countries in the region, in fact, are showing a gradual and relative stagnation in output levels caused by significant production barriers, especially for rice (ADB 2009). Changes in average temperature and temperature fluctuations greatly influence not only the expansion duration but also the expansion pattern and, therefore, the productivity of rice crops. A decrease of 10% in rice yield has been found to be related to every one-degree Celsius increase in temperature (ADB 2009). The yield of dry-season rice crops within the Philippines decreased by as much as 15% for every one-degree Celsius increase within the seasonal mean temperature (Peng et al. 2004). Such temperature extremes and temperature variations and heightening global climate change effects may cause a significant fall in the production of global rice (Furuya and Koyama 2005; Li and Wassmann 2011), leading to an adverse impact on agricultural production and consequently on the socio-economic conditions of the poor farmers.

Projected estimations reveal that there could also be an additional fall of 3.8% in rice production in Southeast Asia under the impact of climate change this century, mainly due to water scarcity and increased temperatures (Murdiyarso 2000). Under the circumstances, by 2100, Philippines, Indonesia, Thailand, and Vietnam are projected to experience a possible decline of about 50% in their rice yield, assuming the present status quo (ADB 2009), and this fall would range from 34% in Indonesia to 75% in the Philippines.

Climate change is also emerging as a significant challenge to agriculture development in Sub-Saharan Africa. The progressively erratic and unpredictable nature of weather systems on the continent has placed a further burden on food security and rural livelihoods. The lengthened drought in Ethiopia and the extensive destruction of houses and farms in the recent record flooding in Burkina Faso show the extent of the threat posed by Africa's changing climate. The Intergovernmental Panel on Climate Change (IPCC 2007) report provides an extensive assessment of the expected effects of climate change on agriculture in the African region. It estimates that the African region will be the foremost region susceptible to climate change globally, thanks to the multiple stresses of poor infrastructure, poverty, and governance. Temperatures are likely to increase by between 1.5 and 4°C in this century. Future estimations on yield reduction show a fall of up to 50%, and consequently, crop revenue is forecast to fall as much as 90% by 2100 (Boko et al. 2007; Acharyya 2021).

The agriculture sector is also likely to experience periods of prolonged droughts and floods during El Nino events. Agriculture losses of between 2 and 7% of GDP are expected by 2100 in parts of the Sahara, 2 to 4% and 0.4 to 1.3% in Western and Central Africa and Northern and Southern Africa, respectively. Arid and semi-arid land could expand coverage by 60–80M ha. Fisheries will be particularly affected due to changes in sea temperatures that could decrease trends in productivity by 50 to 60%. Agricultural productivity in Africa will be further undermined by a reduction in fertile agricultural land available and an expansion in the coverage of low potential land (Boko et al. 2007).

Compared with 24% of undernourished people inhabiting the region presently, estimated forecasts show that Sub-Saharan Africa will outmatch Asia as one of the most food insecure regions with the inhabiting of 40 to

50% of undernourished people globally by 2080 (World Bank 2008). Levels of viable arable land for production are predicted to decline by 2080, with 9 to 20% of arable land becoming much less suitable for agriculture. In response to variations in temperature and precipitation, Africa is predicted to ascertain a rise in crop pests and diseases additionally to altered soil fertility. Moreover, increasing unemployment and falling incomes are expected to hit agriculture zones together with worsening health.

Under the above circumstances, climate-smart farming (CSF) or climate-smart agriculture (CSA) offers an opportunity for the developing countries to identify research, develop, and scale-up technologies and practices that respond to the changing climate and meet increasing food demands. CSA is now looked upon as a pathway for the development of scientifically oriented policy, backed by investment conditions to obtain food security under climate change in a sustainable manner. The significance, concurrence, and expansive ambit of the impact of change in climate on agricultural arrangement make an imperative requirement for comprehensive integration of these impacts into the future agricultural planning of the country backed by programmes and investments.

In the next section, we look at the various features of climate-smart farming that makes it an acceptable proposition for many farmers in developing countries to adapt to climate change through climate-smart farming practices.

## 10.2 Key Features of Climate-Smart Farming

Climate-smart farming or climate-smart agriculture (CSA) is an integrative approach to address the interlinked challenges of food security, climate change impact, and ecological sustainability (Lipper and Zilberman et al. 2018; Steenwerth et al. 2014; Acharyya and Ghosh 2017; Acharyya 2021). To accomplish CSA, the three objectives are defined thus: (i) sustainably increasing agricultural productivity to support an equitable increase in farm incomes, food security and development; (ii) adapting and building the resilience of agricultural and food security systems to climate change; (iii) and reducing greenhouse gas emissions from agriculture (FAO 2013) as shown in Figure 10.1.

A variety of institutional, technological, and policy choices has been suggested to help agriculture become climate smart, including agricultural diversification, weather insurance, stress-tolerant crop varieties, spatial weather forecasts, community management of soil and water, as also strategies related to carbon management (Vermeulen et al. 2012; Lipper et al. 2014; Long et al. 2016; Thornton et al. 2017; Shirsath et al. 2017; Khatri-Chhetri et al. 2017). These strategies have economic impacts and varying costs. Moreover, the effectiveness of these strategies depends on the agro-ecological condition of the neighbourhood, and their adoption is

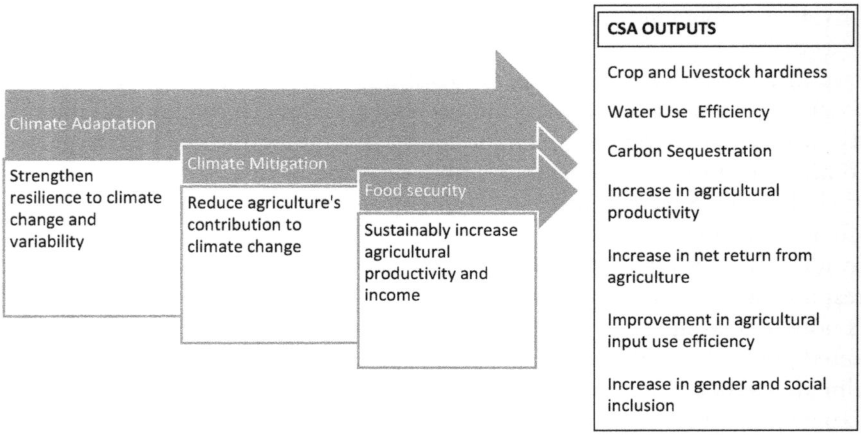


*Figure 10.1* Integrative Approach of Climate-Smart Agriculture. *Source:* Author's illustration.

very much motivated by the socio-economic characteristics of the agrarian society of that particular area (Khatri-Chhetri et al. 2017; Sapkota et al. 2017). Hence, the application of CSA necessitates proper investment decisions in both on-farm capital and broader agricultural outreach programmes. Furthermore, climate-smart investment can have a good range of scales starting from the local field to the national level. It is improbable that investment in any single process will provide optimal benefits but rather an integrated portfolio of interventions is necessary to best support adaptation to global climate change in agriculture across a range of scales. This spatial complexity is compounded by the long-time frames associated with climate change, requiring further consideration of when as well as where to prioritize investment in any set of intervention options. In some situations, CSA may produce triple-win outcomes: increased productivity in combination with reduced impacts to climate risks and shocks and mitigation of climate change through reduced greenhouse gas (GHG) emissions.

Usually, however, the application of CSA will involve focusing on tradeoffs between the three pillars and measuring the costs and benefits of several options supported by stakeholders' objectives. Furthermore, CSA is context specific, and although some interventions could also be climate smart in some places, there are not many interventions that are applicable to all or any situations, altogether ecosystems, and in all sets of various institutional arrangements and political realities.

But CSA is not a group of practices or technologies; it's rather an approach for integrating multiple interventions across a variety of food systems, landscapes, value chains, and government regulations or policies (Lipper et al.

2014). The array of CSA strategies is vast, from water and soil management to carbon finance and incentive systems for the use of low-carbon agriculture (FAO 2013). Its entry points range from technologies and practices to the elaboration of global climate change models and scenarios, information technologies, insurance schemes, and processes to strengthen the institutional and political enabling environment, particularly for marginalized groups. For the smallholder farmer, the range of options would depend on the context-specificity underlining the value of the act of priority setting in resource-constrained scenarios.

Under the circumstances, the role of the government becomes crucial in the promotion of climate-smart agricultural practices. While determining the breadth and means of pursuing options for improving welfare outcomes, the government must consider constraints in the form of biophysical relationships and institutional, behavioural, and political constraints. The biophysical relationships consist of several elements. The foundation or beginning is the production function, which links the economic outputs to ecological inputs and weather. One of the fundamental challenges in framing agricultural policies is considering the heterogeneous impact on agricultural productivity of global climate change.

Furthermore, modelling the assembly function must consider both continuous and discrete variables. A step in such a direction would allow research and technology adoption as a reaction to global climate change (Mendelsohn and Dinar 1999; Antle and Capalbo 2010; Arslan et al. 2015). Understanding the stochastic nature of the assembly function, particularly concerning weather realizations, will also be important in designing programmes like insurance and inventory to deal with the challenges of climate change.

The externality function is the second biophysical element that expresses the correlation between economic actions and the different externalities generated by them (Zilberman 2014). In the context of CSA, the greenhouse gas emissions are the most, but not sole, externality considered. Several agricultural practices and related investments also generate both positive and negative local externalities. Overuse of inorganic fertilizer generates greenhouse gas emissions and may also pollute local water sources (Norse 2012). At the farm and ecosystem levels, investment in soil and water conservation structures can lead to positive spillover benefits to the productivity of neighbouring farmland (McCarthy et al. 2011).

Also, adopting and using any new technology is generally seen to be risky by the poor farmer who faces risk and uncertainty about its performance (Foster and Rosenzweig 2010). Moreover, along with risk preference, the diffusion of technology adoption as an adaptation to global climate change will also depend on and will be a function of the heterogeneity of farmers' access to capital, the existing institutions that will promote or impede adoption and the underlying agro-ecological conditions (Zilberman et al. 2012).

In developing countries, political constraints also constitute a significant impediment to new technology adoption and innovations promoted by institutions. It is well known that innovations of new technologies and their adoption result from economic choices that take place through policies and incentives (Hayami and Ruttan 1971).

In developing economies, government policy is influenced not only by economic conditions but also by environmental and political considerations (Buchananand Tollison 1984; Rausser et al. 2011). These suggest that individual government policy choice problems are derived from their own economic constraints so that the decision to implement policies that favour certain technologies over others will be a function of this political calculus. For example, if political decision favours high economic growth, then the technologies promoted as a consequence may have a direct conflict both with resilience and low emission growth goals.

In addition to economic considerations, additional political constraints will bound the range of feasible policy and legal actions to deal with global climate change. Some policy solutions to global climate change might not be politically feasible, and realistic policy design must consider the feasibility of solutions within various local and international contexts.

For example, it is politically much easier and perhaps beneficial to the political regime, and it also makes sense to legislate policies that improve human well-being and social welfare no matter what happens to global climate change. A 'no-regret' constraint may bind the set of policies that might be valuable under certain future conditions to people who also address pressing problems such as those of food security or sustainability of land usage, thereby satisfying both the environmental and distributional purposes.

The institutional constraints include input, labour markets, and output as also property rights and security of tenure, information dissemination systems like agricultural extension and meteorology, insurance and credit markets, social safety net programmes, and environmental regulations. Along with these, institutional constraints also include the international trading system and local import and export transactions, and foreign direct investment regulations.

The institutional environment has a considerable effect on the farmers' capability and incentives to invest in CSA-based practices and adapt to changing climate conditions.

In developing economies, many a time, thin value supply chains restrict farmers' ability to get the necessary inputs in a timely manner and sell their output at a profit. Integrated supply chains can necessarily lower the swings in the market value of outputs in response to extreme weather events, thereby lowering the vulnerability of rural households to poor crop output and consequently high food prices (Reardon and Timmer 2007). Thin or absent credit markets, often combined with very limited insurance mechanisms, dampen incentives to form any sort of investment on farm, and limits the alternatives available to risk-averse farmers to adapt. Furthermore, if the property rights systems are not clearly defined, it may lead to insecurity of land tenure and thereby limit incentives to invest in land (Holden et al. 2009).

The ability to adapt to global climate change will also suffer from the knowledge dissemination system and farmers' ability to access weather forecasts and longer-term climate predictions and include that information into adaptation and coping strategies. Furthermore, investments and coordinating changing practices at scales higher than the household level would be necessary for improving the resilience of the agricultural system. The ability to coordinate investments in tree planting or checking dams across many small communities or to invest in larger-scale infrastructure to improve the resilience of a watershed will depend on, among other things, most importantly, land use regulations, local property rights, and powers of eminent domain, as also environmental regulations. The ability to coordinate actions across communities will also depend on the collective role of institutions and local-level governance structures (Meinzen-Dick et al. 2004; Pender et al. 2006). It is the capacity to relax institutional constraints that will play a crucial role in lowering household vulnerability and raising system resilience among the household farmers.

Reducing household vulnerability and increasing system resilience are often accomplished by expanding and promoting ex-ante risk management strategies and ex-post coping strategies. At the household level, ex-ante risk management strategies include adopting sustainable land management (SLM) techniques; irrigation; drought, heat, and flood-resistant crop varieties and livestock breeds; and diversifying land and labour activities. Actions that can be embarked upon to augment the capacity of farm households to handle the extreme climate shocks when they occur include access to social safety net programmes, access to attractive and effective insurance instruments, and access to information and infrastructure to re-allocate labour to lower vulnerable areas.

The government can also think of providing various incentives to the farmers to change their behaviour patterns to more climate-adaptive farming. Such potential actions may include direct subsidies for adopting certain investments, payment for environmental and ecosystem services programmes, and practices such as SLM practices and water conservation in irrigation practices, as well as providing subsidies for eco-friendly inputs or participation in various climate-related insurance schemes. Under the situation of an uncertain climatic future, the government can also initiate policies to raise the adaptive capacity of the farmers by promoting and pursuing the least-cost strategies of adaptation, where migration due to weather is also included.

Adaptive capacity may be a function of obtainable risk management and risk coping mechanisms and includes broader measures to enhance decision-making under uncertainty. Uncertainty increases the worth of fixing place sophisticated monitoring and evaluation systems and continual learning

(IPCC 2012). Greater adaptive capacity is related to expanding the range of options to manage climate extremes and potentially changed climate patterns and increasing the power to exercise those options when needed.

For instance, many researchers find that it's precisely wealthier farmers who are more ready to diversify their income sources, reconfirming long-standing findings in most Sub-Saharan African countries (Davis et al. 2014; Arslan et al. 2015). Hence, policies such as allocation of off-farm labour in reaction to a weather shock imply not only that labour opportunities are being created somewhere within the country but also that farmers are informed about the location of those opportunities and are able to either get or afford transportation facilities to go to the particular workplace and also have acquired sufficient knowledge and skills to be hired in that place.

Adaptive capacity and resilience are more or less complementary traits. Better adaptive capacity can raise a system's capacity to adjust to swings in climatic and biophysical conditions. But when the pressures outpace some benchmark or threshold, adaptive capacity can also prepare systems to transform completely, make people adapt to the structural transformation and through the change in adaptation enable the farmer households to survive in the new adaptive scenario and perhaps even enjoy a better livelihood.

Similarly, greater adaptive capacity can enable farm households to scale back vulnerability. Still, at some point, the most straightforward option could also be for a minimum of some household family members to depart from the agricultural sector or diversify their livelihood to best adapt to changing climate conditions. At the system level, adaptive capacity also will be required to deal with potential mass migration from areas not suitable for agricultural production

The above discussion on adaptive capacity and adaptation captures a serious potential trade-off between pursuing strategies that enable farmers to enhance their well-being in the face of global climate change in the ensuing agricultural system versus approaches that allow for the system itself to change in reaction to climate change (Adger et al. 2014). Insurance and safety net payments are classic samples of policies that enable people to withstand extreme events more competently within the present system.

Availability of irrigation, improved and more well-established security of tenure, and investments in flood control infrastructure have similar impacts. In certain circumstances, particularly changes in weather patterns that make current production systems impossible or unprofitable, the government and other institutions will have to determine whether to continue pursuing increasing or additional strategies or whether to accept and accommodate migration or advocate a structural change in the system of production.

Lastly, in pursuance of low carbon emissions and economic growth, the government can assess opportunities and strategies. Specific processes, such as sustainable investment in land and CSA practices, can generate lower emissions and greater food security (Lipper et al. 2014). However, in most developing countries, the current incentives are too few to promote the widespread adoption of such practices. Economic growth strategies based on low carbon emissions pose higher trade-offs with both immediate and long-term food security objectives and necessitates international financing, especially given that most of the developed countries have contributed very little to cumulative greenhouse gas (GHG) emissions. Where there are opportunities for external and suitable financing for CSA, adaptive capacity will need to be created to promote a switch to low carbon emissions agricultural growth strategies (WBCSD 2015).

The question arises, given the seriousness of the situation with respect to agriculture, how much are the poor farmers in the developing economies of South Asia and sub-Saharan Africa adapting to climate-smart agriculture? In the next section, we attempt a reality check on the issue.

## 10.3 Adaptation to Climate-Smart Farming in Developing Economies: A Reality Check

Based on the above discussion, it is essential to understand how smallholder farmers in lower-income countries adapt to the many challenges they face due to climate change. Research in CSA has led to a few agricultural policy changes in different countries over the last decades. A contemporary inquiry of case studies across the tropics shows that only 16% of households have been actively intensifying their production in the previous 10 to 15 years (Thornton et al. 2018). There are many constraints facing smallholders regarding the adoption of agricultural technology, so how are interventions to be taken to the scale needed if food and nutrition security is to be achieved?

In the above context, we look at how different developing economies are adapting to climate-smart farming under climate change. We concentrate on those countries where the farmers are poor and in large numbers, where the farm size is small and where most of the farmers cannot adapt to CSA individually due to lack of investment. Either they must form groups, such as cooperatives and make a joint effort, or they need external help from the government. We first look at the countries of South and Southeast Asia and then the countries of Sub-Saharan Africa to understand the reality of adaptation to climate-smart farming by the farmers.

### *10.3.1 Climate-Smart Farming in South and Southeast Asia*

More than 75% of the rural poor in the Asian continent live in South Asia and depend on rainfall for their agricultural output and livestock and forestry for their livelihoods (World Social Report 2020). Projections for climate impact on agriculture in South Asia are quite alarming, particularly when weighed alongside the adaptive capacity with an estimated population increase of 2.3 billion in this century and a considerable fall in agricultural productivity.

Since there will be large spatial variations in impacts across the different countries of the region, it is imperative to look at the climate change impacts at the country-specific level. Cline (2007) projected that, by 2080, the agricultural output might fall by 22% in Bangladesh without the benefits of carbon fertilization and by 10% if the country can reap the benefits of carbon fertilization by promoting significantly greater facilities of irrigation. It may be added that irrigation requirements have a significant correlation with temperature, and for every 1°C rise in temperature, irrigation requirements go up by 10% (Cline 2007). The situation in Sri Lanka is only slightly better, with an 8% decline even with carbon fertilization. As a result of the loss of floodplains and destruction of habitat, the fisheries sector could face the most detrimental effect.

In India, due to its size, different regions could experience differentiated effects. The four climate-sensitive zones are the Himalayan region, Northeast, Western Ghats, and the coastal areas. The warming might be more pronounced within the northern parts of India. The extreme variation in minimum and maximum temperatures are likely to increase under changing climatic conditions, and a few places could get more rain while some places will remain dry. Apart from Punjab and Rajasthan in the Northwest and Tamil Nadu in the South, which show a slight decrease in rainfall, on average, one can expect a 20% rise in summer monsoon rainfall across most of the states of the region. Although in some states, the number of rainy days could come down (e.g., in Madhya Pradesh), the intensity is expected to rise in most parts of the country (e.g., in the Northeast). In India, gross per capita water availability could decline from 1,820 $m^3$/year in 2001 to as low as 1,140 $m^3$/year in 2050 (Gupta and Deshpande 2004).

Agriculture is not only highly vulnerable to the impacts of climate change but is also a major source of GHG emissions globally. In 2014, the South Asian countries together accounted for almost 8% of the global agricultural GHG emissions (FAO 2017). The two-way relationship between global climate change and agriculture is thus clearly established. It involves a technique that simultaneously addresses the difficulty of the vulnerability of the world and the fall of GHG emissions from the sector.

Lowering the vulnerability involves various adaptation measures, such as increasing the resilience of the sector to climatic stresses and shocks by strengthening the existing infrastructure and improving the adaptive capacity of the farmers. Reduction in GHG emissions would involve mitigation strategies that would decrease the amount of process and energy-based emissions and involve introducing agro-ecological systems that promote carbon sequestration. Incidentally, the nature of the relationship that exists between climate change and agriculture is also true for the policies and institutions that focus on development and affect GHG emissions.

There is a growing emphasis on CSA in South Asia, as can be seen from the fact that the Asian Development Bank (ADB) has given an assurance to increase its annual climate financing for the region two-fold to US$6 billion by 2020, of which US$2 billion has been allocated for adaptation, including through CSA (ADB 2015). In South Asia (Table 10.1), countries that have piloted and scaled-up CSA include India, Bangladesh, Nepal, and Sri Lanka. The National Mission for Sustainable Agriculture (NMSA) is one of the eight key missions outlined under the National Action Plan by India on global climate change. The mission aims to bolster agricultural productivity, especially in the rain-fed areas of the country, through integrated farming, resource conservation, water use efficiency, and soil health management. The National Innovations on Climate Resilient Agriculture (NICRA) programme assists in the nationwide exercise through piloting

*Table 10.1* CSA Policies and Strategies in South Asia

| *Organizations and Countries* | *Initiatives for CSA* |
|---|---|
| Asian Development Bank | Committed to double annual climate financing to US$ 6 billion for Asia-Pacific by 2020, US$ 2 billion will be for adaptation including through CSA. |
| Bangladesh Climate Change and Strategy Action Plan (BCCSAP) Bangladesh | Adopted in Five Year Plans |
| National Solar Mission of India | Targets renewable energy generation of 175 gigawatts by 2022. Also supports the replacement of fossil fuel-based water pumps for agricultural use to solar pumps. |
| National Innovations on Climate Resilient Agriculture, India | Aims to enhance resilience of Indian agriculture to climate change and climate vulnerability through strategic research and technology demonstration. |
| National Mission for Sustainable Agriculture, India | Supports climate change adaptation and mitigation research, pilot, and model projects, to develop climate-smart management practices and integrated farming system models suitable to specific agro-climatic conditions. |
| Climate-Smart Villages(CSVs) in India and Nepal | CSVs are being scaled-up in over 2,000 villages in the Indian states of Haryana, Madhya Pradesh, and Maharashtra. The Government of Nepal has started to pilot and scale out the CSVs approach in different agro-ecological zones from 2016. |
| Renewable Energy Promotion Policy in Nepal | Aims to provide support for water pumping systems in irrigation managed by individuals, a community, or a private company. |
| GoSL – Ministry of Environment 2011, Sri Lanka | Broad policy statements under the thematic areas of vulnerability, adaptation, mitigation, sustainable consumption and production, and knowledge management form part of the National Climate Change Adaptation Strategy |

and research and has established over 150 Climate Resilient Villages across the country (Rao et al. 2016).

The Agriculture Development Strategy of Nepal plans to offer a range of CSA-based technologies through its extension services. A national work plan for scaling up Alternate wetting and drying, a CSA practice, has been produced in Bangladesh. The country will also get a World Bank loan of US$ 214 million for the promotion of agricultural technology programme, involving one million farmers. Bangladesh Climate Change Strategy and Action Plan (BCCSAP) provide a comprehensive strategy for actions, including the formulation of programmes and projects (Ministry of Environment and Forests, Government of Bangladesh 2009). In addition, Bangladesh has incorporated the BCCSAP into its Seventh Five Year Plan (2016–2020). They have developed a National Plan for Disaster Management and a plan to implement the policy directives and basic principles of the SAARC Comprehensive Framework on Disaster Management (SAARC 2006).

The concept of Climate-Smart Villages (CSVs) – adaptation of CSA technologies in such villages, CSA practices and services promoted in collaboration with the local community and organizations is increasing in India. The Indian states of Maharashtra, Haryana, and Madhya Pradesh plan to promote CSVs in over 2000 villages. The Government in Nepal has focused on implementing the CSV idea as part of a national endeavour to adapt to climate change.

Being an island country, Sri Lanka falls into a special category because it faces increased threats due to increased water levels. In Sri Lanka, the constitution promulgates for the preservation and protection of the environment. The National Climate Change Adaptation Strategy for Sri Lanka (2011–2016) has adopted the broad policy statements under the CSA areas of vulnerability, adaptation, mitigation, sustainable consumption and production, as also effective CSA knowledge management (GoSL-Ministry of Environment 2010). Important areas associated with agriculture, livestock, and fisheries are directly addressed under the themes of adaptation and mitigation. In Sri Lanka, all waters, including surface water and groundwater, are treated as being owned by the state and are managed by the government in cooperation with the people. Also, an extensive disaster management plan is in place. The various measures taken by South Asian countries to promote CSA are shown in Table 10.1.

Due to its long coastlines, high population concentration, and intensive economic activity in the coastal belts, Southeast Asia (SEA) is one of the most vulnerable areas to global climate change. Its population is poor and heavily relies on primary natural resources such as agriculture, forestry, and fishery. Climate hazards like rising temperature, erratic rainfall patterns, and extreme climatic events (such as strong typhoons and severe droughts) cause adverse effects and impacts on ecosystems, livelihoods, and many other aspects of human societies in the region. For the poor farmers, climate change jeopardizes agricultural output and food security and ecological balance and hinders sustainable development.

Under the circumstances, the most vulnerable countries of SEA must respond through measures that will reduce the adverse effects and impacts of climate change (adaptation) by significantly reducing greenhouse gas emissions (mitigation).

Maize, rice, and cassava are the main staple crops in SEA. Sustainable production of these major crops is adversely suffering from climate hazards leading to reduced yields and productivity. Plans and actions to adjust with and to adapt to climate change are critical to enhancing the resilience of crop production systems to the uncertainties of weather and the adverse effects of a changing climate.

Many CSA practices are now used in the crop output process in SEA, starting from practices that are indigenous in nature and farmland-tested crop management measures to knowledge-based solutions, and these have given good results for the enhancement of climate resilience (Wassmann et al. 2011). While the suitability of these practices is location and situation specific, they may be modified or adjusted to be applicable in other areas with similar conditions. To achieve the wide use of CSA practices (scaling-up), it is important to understand the technical issues and investigate the operational and institutional limitations. Documented CSA practices and recently developed and tested climate adaptation measures form the Association of Southeast Asian Nations (ASEAN) knowledge base, from which cost-efficient and practical strategies to market climate resilience in rice and other crops throughout SEA are often used.

The lead role of advocating regional guidelines for promoting CSA was taken by ASEAN Ministers of Agriculture and Forestry (AMAF) from 2015 onwards. Such policies give a permissive framework for materializing CSA within the region, and these are supported by native and national efforts. Countries including Cambodia, Myanmar, the Philippines, and Vietnam, have adopted national CSA-related policies and programmes (Antle and Crissman 1990). The shared vulnerability to the consequences of global climate change of the many Southeast Asian countries encourages cross-country and inter-regional collaboration and knowledge exchange. ASEAN Climate Resilience Network facilitates knowledge exchange and regional cooperation efforts on CSA. Recently, the Southeast Asian Regional Centre for Graduate Study and Research in Agriculture (SEARCA) has also created a structured programme for the partners on CSA. Table 10.2 shows CSA policies and strategies adopted by Southeast Asian countries.

*Table 10.2* CSA Policies and Strategies in Southeast Asia

| *Organizations and Countries* | *Initiatives for CSA* |
|---|---|
| ASEAN Regional Guidelines for Promoting CSA Practices | Provides voluntary guidelines for countries in Southeast Asia for scaling-up of CSA practices. |
| ASEAN Climate Resilience Network | A platform for regional exchange, particularly for sharing information, experiences, and expertise on CSA. |
| SEARCA Climate Change Adaptation and Mitigation Programme for Agriculture and Natural Resource (SEARCA's CChAM) Umbrella programme | SEARCA's *Climate Change Adaptation and Mitigation (CChAM) Framework* is envisioned to contribute to the twin goals of food security and poverty reduction through ensuring climate change resilience in the agricultural production and sustainable natural resources management in Southeast Asia. |
| Cambodia's Climate Change Priorities Action Plan for Agriculture, Forestry and Fisheries 2014–2018 | Promoting and scaling up CSA is part of the priority actions identified in the plan. The plan is currently being implemented with support from multisectoral partners and donors. |
| Myanmar Climate-Smart Agriculture Strategy | Focuses on technical, policy and investment conditions to achieve sustainable agricultural development for food security and nutrition through climate resilient and sustainable agriculture. |
| Vietnam 20-20-20 programme. Reduction of GHG emissions in agriculture and rural areas by 2020 | Issued in 2012, the programme aims to reduce total GHG emissions from agriculture and rural development sector by 20% by 2020, while growing the sector's productivity and reducing poverty through the application of CSA. |

### 10.3.2 Climate-Smart Farming in Sub-Saharan Africa

Agriculture is the mainstay of economic livelihood for several Sub-Saharan African countries. It employs about 60% of the region's labour force and accounts for 25% or more of gross domestic product (Africa Renewal, United Nations 2014). This notwithstanding, in recent times, agricultural productivity within the region has declined, and food insecurity and hunger remain a serious concern. Evidence suggests that smallholder farmers, hunters, and fishers in Africa are the toughest hit by the results of weather variability and global climate change (Dercon and Christiaensen 2011). Hence it is extremely important to create resilience and adapt to the changing climate in a way that ensures that a growing population is fed sustainably without further depleting natural resources. There are significant efforts underway to develop, deploy, and proportion CSA practices and technologies as an efficient response to the global climate change challenges faced by the agriculture sector.

The broad acceptance of CSA practices in Sub-Saharan Africa is slow. This is mainly due to the fact that the majority of the smallholder poor farmers do not have the necessary capital for such technical innovations and sustainable methods. Hence governments of the countries in these regions need to invest in agricultural research and development. They also need to invest in infrastructure development and institutional support to get the benefits from CSA and achieve adaptation and mitigation to climate change and ensure food security for their people.

Several drives have been taken in the promotion and scaling-up of CSA in the African region, recognizing that agriculture is vital for the African economy and the conditions of climate change must be taken into account for agricultural development. The various measures taken by African countries to promote CSA are shown in Table 10.3.

As shown in Table 10.3, several CSA initiatives are closely linked with continent-wide initiatives in sub-Saharan Africa. The New Partnership for Africa's Development (NEPAD) agency is leading the implementation of the African Union-NEPAD Agriculture global climate change programme, which aims to possess 25 million farm households practising CSA by 2025 (GACSA 2016). A crucial drive taken by the Continent helping in this effort is the Africa CSA Alliance, a partnership between NEPAD Agency and five international Non-Governmental Organizations (NGOs) and linking closely with previous continental initiatives to transform agriculture in Africa, such as the Comprehensive Africa Agriculture Development Programme (CAADP). The aim of the Alliance is to accomplish enabling a minimum of six million farm households with CSA practices, thereby contributing to NEPAD's 2025 goal of reaching 25 million farm households (GACSA 2016). Launched at COP 21 in Paris, the Africa Climate Business Plan (ACBP) attempts to scale back Africa's adaptation gap by deploying technical expertise, mobilizing financing, and promoting the appointment of stakeholders towards climate action. With respect to the adoption of CSA practices, the ACBP has resolved to help 25 million African farmers who are farming on three million hectares of farmland and, in the future, improve CSA policy implementation capacity in at least 20 countries by 2026 (World Bank 2015).

Recently, a substitute CSA programme, known as VUNA (meaning 'harvest'),[1] has been initiated in East and Southern Africa. The objective of the DFID-funded[2] programme is to transform agricultural systems in East and Southern Africa to be suitable for the changing climate. The smallholder farmers are helped by VUNA to adapt to climate change. VUNA also helps in the accomplishment of regional and national priorities to remodel agriculture in the face of climate change, which aligns with the CAADP pillars.

The three Regional Economic Communities, Common Market for Eastern and Southern Africa (COMESA), East African Community (EAC),

*Table 10.3* CSA Policies and Strategies in Africa

| *Organizations and Countries* | *Initiatives for CSA* |
|---|---|
| AU-NEPAD Agriculture Climate Change Programme | Aims to have 25 million farm households practicing CSA by 2025. |
| Africa Climate Business Plan (ACBP) | Supports the adoption of CSA practices by 25 million African farmers, on 3 million hectares of farmland and improve CSA policy implementation capacity in at least 20 countries. |
| Africa CSA Alliance | Supports the scaling-up of CSA practices to at least 6 million farming households. |
| VUNA | £23 million DFID-funded programme that supports smallholder farmers to adapt to climate change. Initial focus on Malawi, Mozambique, Tanzania, Zambia, and Zimbabwe. |
| Adaptation of African Agriculture Initiative | Aims to mobilize US$ 30 billion for adaptation in the agriculture sector in Africa. Focal areas include management of soils, agricultural water, and climate risks. |
| African Development Bank Feed Africa strategy | Focuses on providing funds to support climate-smart agricultural practices. |
| Climate Resilient Green Economy (CRGE) Strategy, Ethiopia | Through this strategy, Ethiopia aims to achieve carbon-neutral middle-income status before 2025. The strategy aims to improve crop and livestock production. |
| Uganda Climate-Smart Agriculture Programme(2015–2025) | The vision for this programme is climate-resilient and low-carbon agricultural and food systems contributing to increased food security, wealth creation and sustainable economic growth in line with the National Vision 2040. |
| Agriculture Climate Resilience Plan (ACRP) 2014–2019, Tanzania | The ACRP addresses increasing economic, social and climatic impacts accelerated by climate change, and invoke CSA as a central approach to increasing yield and mitigating economic shocks at the smallholder farm level. |
| Country Climate-Smart Agriculture Framework Programmes (CSA-FP) | Identifies strategic priorities for agricultural development and growth in a changing climate and aligned with the AU/NEPAD Comprehensive Agriculture Development Programme (CAADP) and national strategies and policies. |

and Southern Africa Development Community (SADC), collaborate on a project that is supporting investments in national CSA programmes adoption of conservation agriculture, and focusing on the linkages between agriculture, land use and forestry and attempting at Reduced Emissions from Deforestation and Degradation (REDD). The goal is improvement in livelihood and food security benefits of at least 1.2 million smallholder farmers.

Uganda, Kenya, Tanzania, Botswana, and Namibia have built CSA Framework Programmes (CSAFPs) at the national level, a joint initiative supported by CCAFS, the World Agroforestry Centre (ICRAF), the International Centre for Tropical Agriculture (CIAT), COMESA, and NEPAD. The CSAFP's goal is to help countries integrate their National Agricultural Investment Plans (NAIPs) and agricultural sector programmes with the national global climate change action plans and strategies to ensure a common and holistic approach. In addition, Kenya and Tanzania are also working to develop national CSA strategies. In Ethiopia, climate change has been internalized into different national policies, strategies, and programmes. In particular, the Climate Resilient Green Economy (CRGE) initiative, which is supported by the Green Economy Strategy (GES) and the Climate Resilience Strategy (CRS), focuses on improving crop and livestock production practices for higher income of farmers and promotion of food security, while reducing emissions.

The CSA practices and initiatives that have been implemented, most often, have exhibited great promise for boosting Africa's agricultural productivity in a sustainable way. In areas where there is effective uptake, the agricultural sector has become more adaptive and resilient to climate variability, and farmers are protected against changes in weather patterns, pests, and diseases (Neate 2013). By fostering the sustainable management of natural resources, enhancing ecosystem services, and building climate resilience, CSA offers unique opportunities to tackle adaptation, mitigation, and food security objectives. Given the pivotal role of agriculture in reducing hunger, poverty, and food insecurity within the region, Sub-Saharan African countries will promote CSA practices and technologies in the coming days.

## 10.4 Conclusion

In this chapter, an attempt has been made to lay out a conceptual framework to underpin the CSA concept rooted in agricultural development. Initially, the chapter commenced by calling attention to the most important characteristics of climate change that requires a transition in attention to new research and for innovations in technologies, government programmes, policies, and institutions. These changes include increased frequency and intensity of climate extreme events, with potentially disastrous impacts on already vulnerable smallholder's dependent on rain-fed agriculture; permanent changes in weather patterns making certain areas unsuitable for agricultural production under existing conditions, and the need to reduce emissions from the agricultural sector while ensuring growth in the sector. These changes strongly highlight the necessity to consider the heterogeneity of impacts and know the implications of decision-making under uncertainty.

They also point to the increased value of an expanded set of technological and institutional options to affect both heterogeneity and uncertainty, particularly the increased value of flexibility broadly understood.

Adaptation to global climate change may take several forms: innovation and adoption of latest technologies, adoption of existing technologies, temporary or permanent migration, changes in agricultural activities and trade patterns, and expanded range of engaging and feasible insurance products. Adaptation in most cases also will include addressing institutional failures and constraints like reducing tenure insecurity, increasing access to relevant information, and improving the power to coordinate actions across a watershed or ecosystem. Some strategies of adaptation will mean a system-level discrete transition accomplished through broad-based structural change. While the answer cannot provide the precise changes in technologies or institutions that might end in the simplest outcomes, it can help to define the characteristics or principles associated with upgraded technologies or exceedingly efficient institutional mechanisms and structures.

Various policies, actions, investments, and partnerships are initiated to put the idea of CSA into application at the worldwide, regional, and national levels. Many of those efforts are in the early stages, and their impacts cannot yet be fully quantified; however, some general lessons are often drawn to ensure the success of those efforts.

The experiences from sub-Saharan Africa and South and Southeast Asia show that regional cooperation and knowledge exchange between countries is one of the primary keys to success. The aim to promote regional cooperation, especially through South-South cooperation, should be aimed further.

Also, CSA actions are context-specific and vary depending on regional, national, and local priorities. For example, South Asia's critical areas of emphasis include the scaling-up of Climate-Smart Villages (CSVs) and renewable energy. In contrast, in Sub-Saharan Africa, there is a greater emphasis on increasing the resilience of smallholder farmers.

Hence, effective prioritization and targeting are necessary to realize CSA policies and strategies successfully. The realization of these initiatives will be determined by the sustainability of investment and financing.

Although several major commitments are made by international financial institutions, the private sector, development agencies, and national governments, many of the efforts are funded for brief periods only (perhaps two to five years). A long-term view is needed to allow farmers to grasp concepts fully, as well as to realize the benefits of these interventions. It is worth mentioning here that while the role of the private sector in efforts to promote CSA is noticeable at the global scale, their role is limited when it comes to operations at the national and regional levels where most initiatives are either led by the respective governments or various international organizations.

Thus, there is a necessity for more engagement of the private sector at the national and regional levels, including reaching out to the many small and medium enterprises in the developing economies. The success of CSA, while very progressive, should be done with utmost monitoring and evaluation using some metric scale so that the initiatives taken can be integrated into operational efforts.

## Notes

1 For details see https://tcsaa.or.tz/project/vuna/ (accessed on 2 October 2021).

2 The Department for International Development (DFID) was the government department of the United Kingdom responsible for administering foreign aid. The goal of the department was 'to promote sustainable development and eliminate world poverty'. DFID was a ministerial department from May 1997 to September 2020. The Department for International Development has closed. It has been replaced by the Foreign, Commonwealth & Development Office (FCDO).

## References

Acharyya A. 2014. "Groundwater, Climate Change and Sustainable Well Being of the Poor: Policy Options for South Asia, China and Africa". *Procedia: Social and Behavioral Sciences* 157: 226–235. doi: 10.1016/j.sbspro.2014.11.025.

Acharyya, A. 2021. "Integrating Climate Change Adaptation and Vulnerability Reduction for Sustainable Development in South Asia and Africa". In *Economic Effects of Natural Disasters: Theoretical Foundations, Methods, and Tools*, edited By Taha Chaiechi, pp. 547–557. London: Academic Press, Elsevier. doi:10.1016/B978-0-12-817465-4.00032-7.

Acharyya, A., and M. Ghosh. 2017. "Climate Change Smart Farming Practices: A Review". In *Smart Farming: Problems and Prospects*, edited by Kamal R. Gupta and V.B Angadi, 135–155. Mumbai: Gaurang Publishing Globalize Private Limited. ISBN: 978-81-933546-3-6.

ADB (Asian Development Bank). 2009. *The Economics of Climate Change in Southeast Asia: A Regional Review*. Manila: Asian Development Bank. https://www.adb.org/sites/default/files/publication/29657/economics-climate-change-se-asia.pdf (accessed on 18 February 2020).

ADB (Asian Development Bank). 2015. *ADB to Double Annual Climate Financing to $6 Billion for Asia- Pacific by 2020*. Manila: Asian Development Bank. https://www.adb.org/news/adb-double-annual-climate-financing-6-billionasia-pacific-2020 (accessed on 16 February 2021).

Adger, W.N., J.M. Pulhin, J. Barnett, G.D. Dabelko, G.K. Hovelsrud, M. Levy, Ú. Oswald Spring, and C.H. Vogel. 2014. "Human Security". In *Climate Change 2014: Impacts, Adaptation, and Vulnerability. Part A: Global and Sectoral Aspects. Contribution of Working Group II to the Fifth Assessment Report of the Intergovernmental Panel on Climate Change*, edited by Field, C.B., V.R. Barros, D.J. Dokken, K.J. Mach, M.D. Mastrandrea, T.E. Bilir, M. Chatterjee, K.L. Ebi, Y.O. Estrada, R.C. Genova, B. Girma, E.S. Kissel, A.N. Levy, S. MacCracken, P.R. Mastrandrea, and L.L. White, 755–791. Cambridge, UK and New York: Cambridge University Press. https://www.ipcc.ch/site/assets/uploads/2018/02/WGIIAR5-Chap12_FINAL.pdf (accessed on 27 June 2021).

Africa Renewal. 2014. *Special Edition on Agriculture*. https://www.un.org/africarenewal/sites/www.un.org.africarenewal/files/Africa_Renewal_Special_Edition_2014_en.pdf (accessed on 17 August 2021).

Ahmed, M., and S. Suphachalasai. 2014. *Assessing the Costs of Climate Change and Adaptation in South Asia*. Manila: Asian Development Bank. http://hdl.handle.net/11540/46.(accessed on 19 August 2021).

Alexandratos, N., and J. Bruinsma. 2012. "World Agriculture Towards 2030/2050: The 2012 Revision". *ESA Working Paper No. 12-03 June 2012*, Agricultural Development Economics Division, Food and Agriculture Organization of the United Nations. http://www.fao.org/3/ap106e/ap106e.pdf(accessed on 17 August 2021).

Antle, J.M., and S.M. Capalbo. 2010. "Adaptation of Agricultural and Food Systems to Climate Change: An Economic and Policy Perspective". *Applied Economic Perspectives and Policy* 32 (3): 386–416. doi:10.1093/aepp/ppq015.

Antle, J.M., and C.C. Crissman. 1990. "Risk, Efficiency, and the Adoption of Modern Crop Varieties: Evidence from the Philippines". *Economic Development and Cultural Change* 38 (3): 517–537. doi:10.1086/451813.

Arslan, A., N. McCarthy, L. Lipper, S. Asfaw, A. Cattaneo, and M. Kokwe. 2015. "Climate Smart Agriculture? Assessing the Adaptation Implications in Zambia". *Journal of Agricultural Economics* 66 (3): 753–780. doi:10.1111/1477-9552.12107.

Bandara, J.S., and Y. Cai. 2014. "The Impact of Climate Change on Food Crop Productivity, Food Prices and Food Security in South Asia". *Economic Analysis and Policy* 44 (4): 451–465. doi:10.1016/j.eap.2014.09.005.

Boko, M., I Niang, A. Nyong, C.A. Githeko, M. Medany, B. Osman-Elasha, R. Tabo, and P Yanda, 2007. "Climate Change 2007: Impacts, Adaptation and Vulnerability". *Contribution of Working Group II to the Fourth Assessment Report of the Intergovernmental Panel on Climate Change*, 433–467. Cambridge UK: Cambridge University Press. https://archive.ipcc.ch/publications_and_data/ar4/wg2/en/ch9.html (accessed on 16 August 2020).

Buchanan, J.M., and R.D. Tollison. 1984. *The Theory of Public Choice—II*. University of Michigan Press. https://www.press.umich.edu/7229/theory_of_public_choice_ii (accessed on 19 August 2021).

Cline, W.R. 2007. "Global Warming and Agriculture: Impact Estimates by Country". Washington, DC: Centre for Global Development and Peterson Institute for International Economics. https://www.cgdev.org/publication/9780881324037-global-warming-and-agriculture-impact-estimates-country (accessed on 17 August 2020).

Cruz, R.V., H. Harasawa, M. Lal, S. Wu, Y. Anokhin, B. Punsalmaa, Y. Honda, M. Jafari, C. Li, and N. HuuNinh. 2007. *Asia. Climate Change 2007: Impacts, Adaptation and Vulnerability. Contribution of Working Group II to the Fourth Assessment Report of the Intergovernmental Panel on Climate Change*. Edited by M.L. Parry, O.F. Canziani, J.P. Palutikof, P.J. van derLinden, and C.E. Hanson, 469–506. Cambridge, UK: Cambridge University Press. https://archive.ipcc.ch/publications_and_data/ar4/wg2/en/ch10.html (accessed on 11 January 2020).

Davis, B., S. Di Giuseppe, and A. Zezza. 2014. "Income Diversification Patterns in Rural Sub-Saharan Africa: Reassessing the Evidence". *World Bank Policy Research Working Paper No. 7108*. Available at SSRN. http://ssrn.com/abstract=2524162 (accessed on 8 July 2021).

Dercon, S., and L. Christiaensen. 2011. "Consumption Risk, Technology Adoption and Poverty Traps: Evidence from Ethiopia". *Journal of Development Economics* 96 (2): 159–173. doi:10.1016/j.jdeveco.2010.08.003.

FAO. 2013. *Climate-Smart Agriculture Sourcebook Executive Summary*. Rome: Food and Agriculture Organization of the United Nations. https://ccafs.cgiar.org /resources/publications/climate-smart-agriculture-sourcebook (accessed on 28 February 2021).

FAO. 2017. *The Future of Food and Agriculture – Trends and Challenges*. Rome: Food and Agriculture Organization of the United Nations. http://www.fao.org/3 /i6583e/i6583e.pdf (accessed on 15 August 2021).

Foster, A.D., and M.R. Rosenzweig. 2010. "Microeconomics of Technology Adoption". *Annual Review of Economics* 2 (1): 395–424. doi: 10.1146/annurev. economics.102308.124433.

Furuya, J., and O. Koyama. 2005. "Impacts Of Climatic Change on World Agricultural Product Markets: Estimation of Macro Yield Functions". *Japan Agricultural Research Quarterly: JARQ* 39 (2): 121–134. doi:10.6090/ jarq.39.121.

GACSA. 2016. *Regional CSA Alliances and Platforms: Information Sheet: The Africa CSA Alliance (ACSAA) and the NEPAD-iNGO Alliance on CSA. Global Alliance for Climate-Smart Agriculture*. Rome, Italy: Food and Agricultural Organization. http://www.fao.org/fileadmin/user_upload/gacsa/docs/Final_report_of_the_CSA _Alliances_Platforms_and_Networks_meeting_June_17_GACSA_Annual_Forum .pdf(accessed on 29 March 2021).

GoSL – Ministry of Environment. 2010. *Sri Lanka's Second National Communication on Climate Change. Climate Change Secretariat*. Colombo: Government of Sri Lanka. https://unfccc.int/resource/docs/natc/lkanc2.pdf (accessed on 28 July 2021).

GoSL – Ministry of Environment. 2011. *National Climate Change Adaptation Strategy for Sri Lanka 2011–16*. Colombo: Government of Sri Lanka. https:// www.climatechange.lk/adaptation/Files/Strategy_BookletFinal_for_Print_Low _res(1).pdf(accessed on 28 July 2021).

Gupta, S.K., and R.D. Deshpande. 2004. "Water for India in 2050: First-order Assessment of Available Options". *Current Science* 86 (9): 1216–1224. https:// www.jstor.org/stable/i24104106 (accessed on 29 July 2021).

Hayami, Y., and V.W. Ruttan. 1971. *Agricultural Development: An International Perspective*. Baltimore, MD/London: The Johns Hopkins Press. https:// digitalrepository.unm.edu/cgi/viewcontent.cgi?article=3351&context=nrj (accessed on 24 July 2021).

Holden, SteinT., K. Deininger, and H. Ghebru. 2009. "Impacts of Low-Cost Land Certification on Investment and Productivity". *American Journal of Agricultural Economics* 91 (2): 359–373. doi:10.1111/j.1467-8276.2008.01241.x.

Hunter, Mitchell C., R.G. Smith, M.E. Schipanski, L.W. Atwood, and D.A. Mortensen. 2017. "Agriculture in 2050: Recalibrating Targets for Sustainable Intensification". *Bioscience* 67 (4): 386–391. doi:10.1093/biosci/bix010.

IPCC. 2007. *Climate Change 2007: Synthesis Report. Contribution of Working Groups I, II and III to the Fourth Assessment Report of the Intergovernmental Panel on Climate Change*, edited by Core Writing Team, Pachauri, R.K and Reisinger, A., 104 pp. Geneva, Switzerland: IPCC. https://www.ipcc.ch/report/ ar4/syr/ (accessed on 14 May 2020).

IPCC. 2012. *Managing the Risks of Extreme Events and Disasters to Advance Climate Change Adaptation. A Special Report of Working Groups I and II of the Intergovernmental Panel on Climate Change.* Edited by Field, C.B., V. Barros, T.F. Stocker, D. Qin, D.J. Dokken, K.L. Ebi, M.D. Mastrandrea, K.J. Mach, G.-K. Plattner, S.K. Allen, M. Tignor, and P.M. Midgley, 582 pp. Cambridge, UK, and New York: Cambridge University Press. https://www.ipcc.ch/site/assets/uploads/2018/03/SREX_Full_Report-1.pdf (accessed on 15 May 2020).

Khatri-Chhetri, Arun, P.K. Aggarwal, P.K. Joshi, and S. Vyas. 2017. "Farmers' Prioritization of Climate-Smart Agriculture (CSA) Technologies". *Agricultural Systems* 151: 184–191. doi:10.1016/j.agsy.2016.10.005.

Li, T., and R. Wassmann. 2011. *Modeling Approaches for Assessing Adaptation Strategies in Rice Germplasm Development to Cope with Climate Change* (available at:http://www.fao.org/fileadmin/templates/agphome/documents/IRRI_website/Irri_workshop/LP_16.pdf).(accessed on 28 July 2021).

Lipper, L., and D. Zilberman. 2018. "A Short History of the Evolution of the Climate SmartAgriculture Approach and its Links to Climate Change and Sustainable Agriculture Debates". In: *Climate Smart Agriculture: Building Resilience to Climate Change*, edited by Lipper, L., N. McCarthy, D. Zilberman, S. Asfaw and G. Branca: 13–30. Rome: Springer International Publishing, Food and Agricultural Organization. https://link.springer.com/book/10.1007%2F978-3-319-61194-5(accessed on 8 July 2021).

Lipper, L., Thornton, P., and Campbell, B. et al. 2014 "Climate-smart Agriculture for Food Security". *Nature Climate Change* 4: 1068–1072. doi:10.1038/nclimate2437.

Long, T.B., V. Blok, and I. Coninx. 2016. "Barriers to the Adoption and Diffusion of Technological Innovations for Climate-Smart Agriculture in Europe: Evidence from the Netherlands, France, Switzerland and Italy". *Journal of Cleaner Production* 112: 9–21. doi:10.1016/j.jclepro.2015.06.044.

Masutomi, Y., K. Takahashi, H. Harasawa, and Y. Matsuoka. 2009. "Impact Assessment of Climate Change on Rice Production in Asia in Comprehensive Consideration of Process/Parameter Uncertainty in General Circulation Models". *Agriculture, Ecosystems & Environment* 131 (3–4): 281–291. doi:10.1016/j.agee.2009.02.004.

McCarthy, N., L. Lipper, and G. Branca. 2011. *Climate Smart Agriculture: Smallholder Adoption and Implications for Climate Change Adaptation and Mitigation.* MICCA Working paper, No. 4. Rome: Food and Agriculture Organization of the United Nations. http://www.fao.org/3/i2575e/i2575e00.pdf (accessed on 30 November 2020).

Mendelsohn, R., and A. Dinar. 1999. "Climate Change, Agriculture, And Developing Countries: Does Adaptation Matter?" *The World Bank Research Observer* 14 (2): 277–293. doi:10.1093/wbro/14.2.277.

Meinzen-Dick, R., M. DiGregorio, and N. McCarthy. 2004. "Methods for Studying Collective Action in Rural Development". *Agricultural Systems* 82 (3): 197–214. doi:10.1016/j.agsy.2004.07.006.

MoEF. 2009. *Bangladesh Climate Strategy and Action Plan 2009.* Dhaka, Bangladesh: Ministry of Environment and Forests, Government of the People's Republic of Bangladesh. https://www.iucn.org/downloads/bangladesh_climate_change_strategy_and_action_plan_2009.pdf (accessed on 17 August 2021).

Murdiyarso, D. 2000. "Adaptation to Climatic Variability and Change: Asian Perspectives on Agriculture and Food Security". *Environmental Monitoring Assessment* 61: 123–131. doi:10.1023/A:1006326404156.

Neate P.J. 2013. *Climate-Smart Agriculture Success Stories: From Farming Communities Around the World*, 1–42. CCAFS (Research Program on Climate Change, Agriculture and Food Security) & CTA (Technical Centre for Agricultural and Rural Cooperation). https://hdl.handle.net/10568/34042 (accessed on 14 May 2020).

Nelson, G.C., M.W. Rosegrant, J. Koo, R. Robertson, T.Sulser, T. Zhu, C. Ringler, S. Msangi, A. Palazzo, M. Batka, M. Magalhaes, R. Valmonte-Santos, M. Ewing, and D. Lee. 2009. *Climate Change: Impact on Agriculture and Costs of Adaptation*. Washington, DC: International Food Policy Research Institute. https://www.ifpri.org/publication/climate-change-impact-agriculture-and-costs-adaptation (accessed on 2 May 2020).

Norse, D. 2012. "Low Carbon Agriculture: Objectives and Policy Pathways". *Environmental Development* 1 (1): 25–39. doi:10.1016/j.envdev.2011.12.004.

Ortiz, R., K.D. Sayre, B. Govaerts, R. Gupta, G.V. Subbarao, T. Ban, D. Hodson, J.M. Dixon, J.Iván Ortiz-Monasterio, and M. Reynolds. 2008. "Climate Change: Can Wheat Beat the Heat?" *Agriculture, Ecosystems & Environment* 126 (1–2): 46–58. doi:10.1016/j.agee.2008.01.019.

Pender, J., F. Place, and S. Ehui, eds. 2006. "Strategies for Sustainable Land Management in the East African Highlands". IFPRI: Washington, DC. https://www.ifpri.org/publication/strategies-sustainable-land-management-east-african-highlands (accessed on 13 November 2018).

Peng, S., J. Huang, J.E. Sheehy, R.C. Laza, R.M. Visperas, X. Zhong, G.S. Centeno, G.S. Khush, and K.G. Cassman. 2004. "Rice Yields Decline with Higher Night Temperature from Global Warming". *Proceedings of the National Academy of Sciences* 101 (27): 9971–9975. doi:10.1073/pnas.0403720101.

Porter, J.R., L. Xie, A.J. Challinor, K. Cochrane, S.M. Howden, M.M. Iqbal, D.B. Lobell, and M.I. Travasso. 2014. "Food security and food production systems." In *Climate Change 2014: Impacts, Adaptation, and Vulnerability. Part A: Global and Sectoral Aspects. Contribution of Working Group II to the Fifth Assessment Report of the Intergovernmental Panel on Climate Change*, pp. 485–533. Cambridge, United Kingdom and New York, NY, USA: Cambridge University Press. https://www.ipcc.ch/site/assets/uploads/2018/02/WGIIAR5-Chap7_FINAL.pdf (accessed on 27 August 2021).

Rao, S.Ch., K.A. Gopinath, J.V.N.S. Prasad, P. Kumar, and A.K. Singh. 2016. "Climate Resilient Villages for Sustainable Food Security in Tropical India: Concept, Process, Technologies, Institutions, and Impacts". *Advances in Agronomy* 140: 101–214. doi:10.1016/bs.agron.2016.06.003.

Rausser, G.C., J. Swinnen, and P. Zusman. 2011. *Political Power and Economic Policy: Theory, Analysis, and Empirical Applications*. Cambridge, UK and New York: Cambridge University Press. https://openknowledge.worldbank.org/bitstream/handle/10986/15575/wps6433.txt?sequence=2&isAllowed=y (accessed on 27 August 2021).

Reardon, T., and C.P. Timmer. 2007. "Transformation of Markets for Agricultural Output in Developing Countries since 1950: How Has Thinking Changed?" *Handbook of Agricultural Economics* 3: 2807–2855. http://www.sciencedirect

.com/science/article/B7P5B ... 28531f619106238c1010 (accessed on 27 August 2021).

SAARC Disaster Management Centre. 2006. SAARC Comprehensive Framework on Disaster Management. http://saarc-sdmc.org/sites/default/files/framework.pdf (accessed on 15 August 2021).

Sapkota, T.B., J.P. Aryal, A. Khatri-Chhetri, P.B. Shirsath, P. Arumugam, and C.M. Stirling. 2017. "Identifying High-Yield Low-Emission Pathways forthe Cereal Production in South Asia". *Mitigation and Adaptation Strategies for Global Change* 23 (4): 621–641. doi:10.1007/s11027-017-9752-1.

Schmidhuber, J., and F.N. Tubiello, 2007. "Global Food Security Under Climate Change". *Proceedings of the National Academy of Sciences* 104: 19703–19708. https://www.semanticscholar.org/paper/Global-food-security-under-climate-change Schmidhuber-Tubiello/75f6ded070b6a5c540c61ffafa58028ef77686f8 (accessed on 15 August 2021).

Shirsath, Paresh B., P.K. Aggarwal, P.K. Thornton, and A. Dunnett. 2017. "Prioritizing Climate-Smart Agricultural Land Use Options At A Regional Scale". *Agricultural Systems* 151: 174–183. doi:10.1016/j.agsy.2016.09.018.

Smit, B., D. McNabb, and J. Smithers. 1996. "Agricultural Adaptation to Climate Variation". *Climate Change* 33: 7–29. doi:10.1007/BF00140511.

Steenwerth, K.L., A.K. Hodson, A.J. Bloom, M.R. Carter, A. Cattaneo, C.J. Chartres, J.L. Hatfield, K. Henry, J.W. Hopmans, W.R. Horwath, B.M. Jenkins, E. Kebreab, R. Leemans, L. Lipper, M.N. Lubell, S. Msangi, R. Prabhu, M.P. Reynolds, S.S. Solis, W.L. Sischo, M. Springborn,P. Tittonell, S.M. Wheeler, S.J. Vermeulen,E.K. Wollenberg, L.S. Jarvis, and L.E. Jackson. 2014. "Climate-smart Agriculture Global Research Agenda: Scientific Basis for Action". *Agriculture and Food Security* 3: 11. doi:10.1186/2048-7010-3-11.

Tesfaye, K., P.H. Zaidi, S. Gbegbelegbe, C. Boeber, D.B. Rahut, F. Getaneh, K. Seetharam, O. Erenstein, and C. Stirling. 2017. "Climate Change Impacts and Potential Benefits of Heat-Tolerant Maize in South Asia". *Theoretical and Applied Climatology* 130 (3–4): 959–970. doi:10.1007/s00704-016-1931-6.

Thornton, P., K. Aggarwal, and D. Parsons. 2017. "Prioritizing Climate Smart Agricultural Interventions at Different Scales". *Agricultural Systems* 151: 149–252. doi:10.1016/j.agsy.2016.12.007.

Thornton, P.K., P. Kristjanson, W. Forch, C. Barahona, L. Cramer, and S. Pradhan. 2018. "Is Agricultural Adaptation to Global Change in Lower-Income Countries on Track to Meet the Future Food Production Challenge" *Global Environmental Change* 52: 37–48. doi:10.1016/j.gloenvcha.2018.06.003.

Tubiello, F., J. Schmidhuber M. Howden, PG. Neofotis, S. Park, E. Fernandes, and D. Thapa. 2008. *Climate Change Response Strategies for Agriculture: Challenges and Opportunities for the 21st Century*. World Bank. http://www.indiaenvironmentportal.org.in/files/dp42Combined_web.pdf (accessed on 23 August 2021).

Vermeulen, S.J., P.K. Aggarwal, A. Ainslie,C.Angelone, B.M. Campbell, A.J. Challinor, J.W. Hansen, J.S.I. Ingram, A. Jarvis, P. Kristjanson, C. Lau, G.C. Nelson, P.K. Thornton, and E. Wollenberg. 2012. "Options for Support to Agriculture and Food Security Under Climate Change". *Environmental Science and Policy* 15 (1): 136–144. doi:10.1016/j.envsci.2011.09.003.

Vinke, K., M.A. Martin, S. Adams, F. Baarsch, A. Bondeau, D. Coumou, R.V. Donner, A. Menon, M. Perrette, K. Rehfeld, A. Robinson, M. Rocha, M. Schaeffer,

S. Schwan, O. Serdeczny, and A. Svirejeva Hopkins. 2017. "Climatic Risks and Impacts in South Asia: Extremes of Water Scarcity and Excess". *Regional Environmental Change* 17: 1569–1583. doi:10.1007/s10113-015-0924-9f.

Wang, S.W., W.K. Lee, and Y. Son. 2017. "An Assessment of Climate Change Impacts and Adaptation in South Asian agriculture". *International Journal of Climate Change Strategies and Management* 9 (4): 517–534. doi:10/1108/IJCCSM-05-2016-0069.

Wassmann, R., S.B. Jagadish, K. Peng, Y. Hosen, and B.O. Sander. 2011. *Rice Production and Global Climate Change: Scope for Adaptation and Mitigation Activities.* Rome: FAO. http://www.fao.org/fileadmin/templates/agphome/documents/IRRI_website/Irri_workshop/LP_16.pdf) (accessed on 20 July 2021).

WBCSD. 2015. *Low Carbon Technology Partnerships initiative – Climate Smart Agriculture – Action Plan Report.* Geneva: World Business Council for Sustainable Development. https://climateinitiativesplatform.org/index.php/LCTPI_Low_Carbon_Technology_Partnership_initiative_(Main) (accessed on 19 July 2021).

World Bank. 2008. *Agriculture and Poverty Reduction, World Development Report 2008.* Washington, DC: World Bank. https://openknowledge.worldbank.org/handle/10986/5990 (accessed on 18 July 2021).

World Bank. 2015. *Accelerating Climate-Resilient and Low-carbon Development: Progress Report on the Implementation of the Africa Climate Business Plan.* World Bank. Washington, DC. https://openknowledge.worldbank.org/handle/10986/30932 (accessed on 15 July 2021).

World Bank. 2016. *World Data Bank- Agriculture Indicators.* Washington, DC: World Bank. https://data.worldbank.org/indicator (accessed on 28 July 2021).

World Social Report. 2020. *Inequality in a Rapidly Changing World.* Department of Economic and Social Affairs, United Nations. https://www.un.org/development/desa/dspd/wp-content/uploads/sites/22/2020/02/World-Social-Report2020-FullReport.pdf (accessed on 23 August 2021).

Zilberman, D. 2014. "The Economics of Sustainable Development". *American Journal of Agricultural Economics* 96 (2): 385–396. doi:10.1093/ajae/aat075.

Zilberman, D., Z. Jinhua, and A. Heiman. 2012. "Adoption Versus Adaptation, with Emphasis on Climate Change". *Annual Review of Resource Economics* 4 (1): 27–53. doi:10.1146/annurev-resource-083110-115954.

Chapter 11

# Pandemic, Climate Change, and Sustainable Development

*Jyoti K. Parikh*

## Introduction

If, during the last year, someone showed us videos of cities after cities with empty streets, with very few souls moving with masks, closed offices, industries, schools, colleges etc., for extended periods, we would have dismissed it as a poor science fiction movie. At the same time, if someone forecasted that by April 2020, air pollution in Delhi (Kumariand Toshniwal, 2020), Karachi, Beijing (Chen et al., 2020), and for that matter in most cities of the world would vanish, rivers will be cleaner (Lokhandwala et al., 2020), birds will be back, and carbon dioxide emissions will go down (Kumar et al., 2020), it would have also been dismissed as a romantic pipe dream. That both of these can happen only a few months later would have been unthinkable.

A positive outcome of the COVID-19 pandemic is that countries and the world are now ready to listen more to global concerns and be much more prepared to make amends to their thinking process. Climate change now seems like an old problem about which we know a lot. We are ready to listen and accept new ideas and have already adapted many new ways of life because we understand now how fragile and vulnerable our societies are. We have accepted that reducing unnecessary consumption is not so difficult (Aruga et al., 2020; Beyer et al., 2021) because we have experienced it first-hand. But now, the other side of it is de-growth, zero growth, and slowing down of economies (Sharma et al., 2020). It was something several groups such as Gandhians, environmentalists, ecologists, and others were advocating – some for a long time, at least in terms of materialism so that all sections of society progress together and some in the recent past, especially in the affluent societies. On the other hand, we have realized how important it is to ensure equity for a sustainable future.

However, such drastic mitigation, which came at a great cost of human miseries (Sengupta et al., 2020; Choudhari, 2020), especially the poor, is not acceptable, and no one is rejoicing. So, while emerging from this, what lessons shall we keep and what spirals should we get out of? What do

DOI: 10.4324/9781003253884-15

we understand about the long-term prospects of our societies in terms of resources, economic growth, and employment?

## 11.1 Objectives

The havoc created by the successive waves of the pandemic is documented daily. Even before the pandemic, the growth dynamics was leading us towards energy efficiency and renewable energy (IEA, 2020a). Moreover, due to the already partial digital transition earlier, it was possible to ride through many economic activities ranging from deliveries of essentials to working from home. Let us examine in what ways the pandemic has advanced the cause of reducing climate change and in what way it has reversed the trend. First of all, quite a few changes were already occurring for one or even two decades gradually and started to manifest in our societal behaviour. However, lockdowns due to COVID-19 showed the actual magnitude, especially what is possible in the near future and what already became a reality much earlier and what is yet to come. In particular, we take stock of what was already happening in our societies.

A. Climate positive changes: Here, we include technology substitution and increased efficiency and technology transformation through smartphones that led to the acceptance of online working, shopping, learning, conferencing, communicating. These pre-existing trends reduce Green House Gas emissions and are accelerated after the pandemic.
B. Climate negative changes: Increased waste generation, reduced public transport, and increased air transport can also increase emissions and waste. These also accelerated due to the pandemic.

Let us examine each of the above.

## 11.2 Climate Mitigation

Two very important measures for climate mitigation are renewable energy substitution for fossil fuels and energy efficiency. There are still almost 940 million without electricity (Hannah Ritchie, 2019) and 2.8 billion without clean cooking fuels (IEA, 2020b). Their needs must be met, increasing $CO_2$ emissions substantially but for the saving grace of technology change and substitution. Now that overall global population growth is declining (United Nations Population Division, 2017), it is possible to reach all with basic needs and services.

### 11.2.1 Technology Substitution

*Example of Coal-Based Power Supply Substituted by Renewable Energy*

People need electricity but are indifferent to how it is produced, i.e., whether it is from coal, solar, hydro, or renewable, as long as it is there when the power is switched on.

An illustrative diagram for the coal supply chain is shown in Figure 11.1. It consists of activities such as coal mining, coal transportation, coal processing (pulverization or coal beneficiation, or coal washing to remove dust and ash), and finally, power generation that requires boilers with 1500-degree centigrade steam and turbines. The latter involves a 60% loss of energy, considering the efficiency of 40%. In the developed countries, the efficiency is high, but in India, it is about 30% for the old and lesser for the older plants (Central Electricity Authority, 2020). Moreover, coal supply indirectly requires steel, cement, land, and labour for installation and running on a daily basis, as shown in Figure.11.2. Steel and cement have their own supply chains similar to the coal supply chain for power-based coal generation.

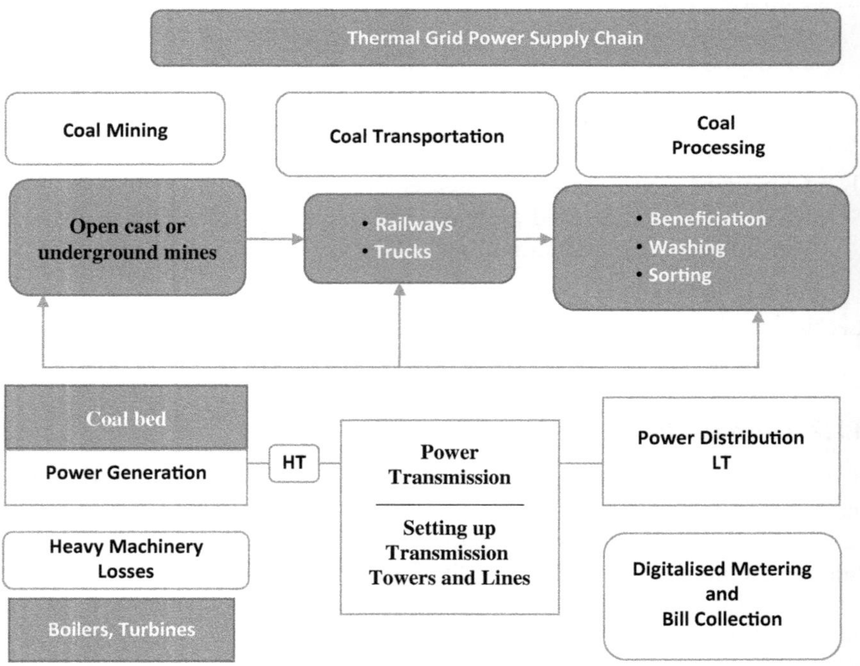


*Figure 11.1* The coal-based power supply chain. *Source:* Author's illustration.

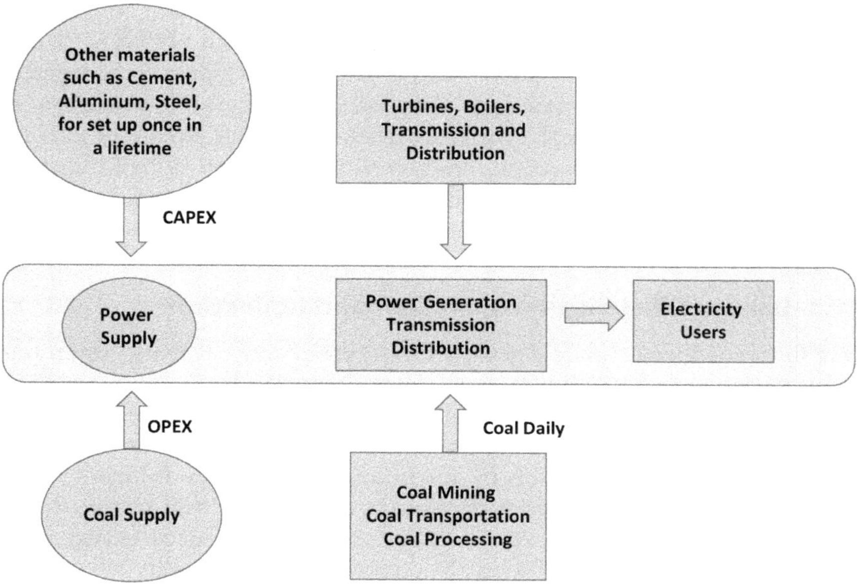


*Figure 11.2* Power supply from coal – value chains for generation and delivery. *Source:* Author's illustration.

When one Gigawatt (GW) of coal generation is replaced by renewable energy on a daily basis, say solar or wind, the entire coal supply chain is replaced by the renewable chain with one major difference. It is done only once in 25 years. That is, what goes on day after day for 25 years in the coal-based generation is done by solar panel or wind installation using the sun or the wind, respectively. But the catch is that it does only when the sun or wind is there. So, we need at least three times as much capacity, as the solar energy of that strength is available for eight hours maximum so that the excess can go into the storage system to store electricity for the hour's sun or wind, when it is not there.

Moreover, solar energy requires different materials for one-time construction. Their construction materials have to be mined but not in such large quantities because they are required once in the lifetime of the solar panels, say two decades. Storage batteries may have a life of five years as of now. They are not required to run the generating plant as the coal plant.

Thus, we see that considerable dematerialization takes place in electricity production on the supply side. This will have repercussions on the transportation sector as coal is a major bulk commodity for railways and trucks, mining and industries sectors, and naturally will affect GDP and employment.

Naturally, long-term and overall employment in the power sector would fall. Although, during the growth phase, it may appear that jobs in the Renewable Energy (REN) sectors have increased currently (IRENA, 2019). They are for once-in-25 years jobs for constructing the plants or its replacement jobs and often part-time jobs. Yet, during the renewable transition on a large scale, they may seem a lot and even a continuous stream of jobs till the transition is done. Moreover, these are skilled and semi-skilled and clean jobs, often located near where people live. On the other hand, coal mine jobs are not clean jobs and are for unskilled or semi-skilled persons.

## 11.3 Energy Efficiency through Demand Reduction

Due to the pandemic, people got used to online shopping, work, entertainment, socializing, all of which would have required transport by cars or even by trains or planes. Large business from events and conferences also triggered tourism and consumption of food and drinks by the travellers. These got reduced considerably by communicating through webinars which are getting higher worldwide participation beyond the local people in the conventional events. Thus, very rapidly, consumers reduced energy consumption without compromising their comfort or the quality of services they need.

Even before the pandemic, consumers had switched to energy-efficient appliances and lifestyles. For example, Light Emitting Diode (LED) bulbs require 80% less energy than their earlier incandescent bulbs. Other appliances such as air conditioners, refrigerators, and washing machines are more efficient by a factor of 2 to 5 compared to 15 years ago. Industry and manufacturing processes such as steel, textiles, and cement have also become far more efficient. Thus, the electricity needed is less than before, and growth rates have declined. The rapid demand for power and growth one sees during earlier five-year plans has drastically slowed down already during this decade (CEA, 2020). Such a scenario still exists despite the number of households with access to electricity rising, from 55.8% in 2001 and 67.2% in 2011 (Census of India, 2011) to more than 90% in 2019. Thus, now the trend of energy efficiency that existed before got strengthened by the behavioural change brought by the pandemic. Some of the earlier trends may not be fully restored, and the recent behavioural changes may remain so, even beyond the pandemic, due to their success.

## 11.4 Transformative Technologies: Mobile and Internet

While the supply-side changes are often due to technological progress on the production side, the demand side refers to changes in consumption patterns. Major disruptions are taking place there as well. The most significant impact has been made by information technology (IT) that has

*Table 11.1* List of Gadgets Replaced by Smartphones

| *Almost replaced* | *Partially replaced* |
|---|---|
| Camera | eBook reader |
| Video recorder/handycam | Pen drive |
| Radio | Wristwatch |
| Portable music player/mp3 player | Television |
| Calculator | Set top box |
| Voice recorder | Remote |
| GPS | Landline phone |
| Flashlight | Pager |
| Scanner | Speakers |
| Compass | Desktop/laptop |
| Portable gaming device | |
| Barcode scanner | |
| Portable video player / mp4 player | |
| Clock | |
| Alarm clock | |

brought efficiency *while reducing materials, labour, and pollution*. Take, for example, mobile phones and the internet. Table 11.1 shows how many appliances manufactured earlier are replaced partially by cellphones; some are almost entirely replaced, barring niche users with hobbies, certain habits, and tastes. Most appliances pertain to communication, information, entertainment, and social needs. It shows that certain appliances, particularly cameras, video recorders, music players, and document scanners, are replaced as they are obsolete or seldom needed by some users for specific purposes. Thus, a considerable number of appliances are replaced with ease. The number of mobiles per 100 population currently at 137.47% in urban and 59.14% in rural India has access to mobile phones. (There are 1,515,971,713 active mobile phone numbers in India as of October 2020; 638.43 million in urban, 525.54 million in rural; as on 31 July 2020; Telecom Statistics, Government of India).

However, the access to these gadgets is not uniform, and the disparity can lead to magnified inequities socially.

## 11.5 Disruptions in Service Industries

It has also dematerialized the service sector, reducing materials and, therefore, $CO_2$ emissions, unfortunately also employment. On the one hand, it has connected us globally, even during the pandemic, but on the other, it has isolated us by enabling us to carry on without stepping out of our homes or from our own localized world, avoiding transportation again, and thereby finishing many lines of businesses. During the pandemic, life was far less difficult for us because, over the last 20 years, the reach of the internet

*Table 11.2* Data on IT across India

| *Percentage of population with data access* | *Percentage* |
|---|---|
| Percentage of households with computers | 15.2% |
| Total Internet subscribers in India | 637 million |
| Internet subscribers per 100 inhabitants | 48.48 |

Source: Telecom Statistics India, 2019; Nielsen & IAMAI, 2019.

and mobile technologies had expanded substantially – cellphones covering almost 90% of households in India and the internet in 22.64% of households. More data is shown in Table 11.2 above.

## 11.6 Waste Generation and Private Transportation

While the electric power sector, which accounts for more than 65% of $CO_2$ emissions (Shakti Foundation, 2021), may lean towards reducing Green House Gases (GHGs), the increase in waste generation due to much heightened personal hygiene concerns (Kulkarni et al., 2020) will increase not only due to discarding of masks and individual protecting equipment apparels but also due to increase in one-time use of food and drink-related objects such as cups, dishes, cutlery, and containers. That concern is likely to overstay beyond the pandemic.

The second challenge is that reluctance to use public transport will remain, which will be a significant blow to GHG savings from transportation (Shakti Foundation, 2018). Indian Railways closed its services for nine months and started limited services in November 2020. People were going by bus or private transport. In Delhi, the metro and other public transport remained closed for six months. The situations in other cities, especially metros, are similar. Intercity transport was started through air travel, which is likely to be a preferred mode as it reduces the period of contact significantly.

## 11.7 Equal Access to Digital Connectivity for Sustainable Development

The pandemic showed us how important it is to ensure digital connectivity for all in order to be a functional society. This could address the critical aspects of human well-being such as health, education, and essential supply services such as food and medicines. Those who could shop online during the pandemic could ensure basic needs. Children who could log onto the internet studied, and the remaining missed an entire year's education. Those who had one smartphone for the family for making a living or if the family had two or more school-going children would miss the entire year's education. Professionals who did business and academics held webinars. The privileged ones continued to be in touch with friends and felt secure by remaining in contact with close relatives, whether in the neighbourhood or abroad, without emotional deprivation and worries.

On the other hand, those who did not have suffered the most losses of livelihoods, education, health treatments, and loneliness and worried about their families. The pandemic showed the vast difference between the digital haves and have nots. It is clear that we need to move towards comprehensive digital connectivity for equal access to all opportunities for each citizen of the country. This needs to be the goal beyond the pandemic, even when our lives become normal someday. Why?

The digital infrastructure is from the beginning largely with the private sector. Therefore, on the supply side, the government's push and budgets are needed mainly for expediting decisions about spectrum allocation, ensuring standardization, quality control, etc. However, the demand side needs to be pushed for the connectivity of the masses by making it affordable and ensuring that every household and person has it.

The Government of India is well aware of the importance and has launched various services on the Digital India platform for e-education, e-health, e-payment, etc. Though these initiatives can potentially lead to people's empowerment, they are supply-side initiatives. Without equitable access to digital connectivity at the household level, these platforms can be used only by the privileged. However, over the last two decades of efforts, the availability of mobiles per 100 persons in 2020 reached 137.4% in urban and 59.14% in the rural population. The internet users were nearly 50%, but desktop and laptop users were only 15%. These include the devices used for business purposes available only at work and not available always to non-working spouses and school-going children at home (Digital in India 2019 – Round 2 Report. Nielsen and Internet and Mobile Association of India – IAMAI).

There was a massive jump in the IT budget allocation in 2020–2021: it was 59,000 crores compared to 14,000 crores in the earlier two years. Perhaps this was harder to spend in this year of pandemic. If budgeted two years earlier, dropped calls, poor network, travelling kilometres on the bike to get network, etc., could have been avoided.

So, there is a need for a stimulus package to strengthen the supply side by encouraging investment in the digital infrastructure and speedy allocation process for 5G infrastructure. Although India is the second-largest market for smart devices, it needs to be '*átmanirbhar*' (self-reliant) to make them affordable. Perhaps a scheme like that of LED bulbs could be launched so that the prices fall on bulk demand; consumers pay part of it, and the states and the Government of India can finance the investment for upscaling the bulk orders. The WTO rules may permit giving preference to domestic manufacturers in public procurement.

This effort could be integrated with new education policy and health initiatives, including responses to Covid such as treatment and now vaccines. A monitoring mechanism is needed to ensure that the budgeted amount is not only spent but has reached the intended goals and fulfilled the objectives.

You cannot go wrong with a stimulus in the form of digital connectivity that leads to enhanced productivity and increased efficiency for all businesses, a cleaner environment from less unnecessary travels, as well as ensures social justice with better education, health, and future for all generations. Let the digital push be the cornerstone of India's future strategy. It could change the destiny of millions.

## 11.8 Conclusion

The pandemic has shown us that switching off human activities can quickly alter and restore the environment. What is needed is that human activities need to be less and less damaging yet cost-effective. While one year is too short a time to affect climate trends directly, one can say that the pandemic has put us on a different path than before, accelerating some earlier trends positively and some negatively. Behavioural changes now seem feasible options more than before. Second, the problem would be to address the equity issues and ensure sustainable development goals where we have slipped quite a bit during the pandemic (Srivastava et al., 2020). In sum, the pandemic has changed the course of our development path towards more digitization and renewable energy, both of which are climate-friendly and can benefit society, provided we ensure the poor section is not digitally deprived.

While the technologies are improving in terms of resource efficiency and productivity, increased consumption and population are at the heart of environmental degradation. We need to ensure the human well-being of the vast sections of the marginalized society while also reducing the waste produced by the higher echelons.

The environmental challenge is our own making and can be addressed, but the question is of timing, how quickly and how strongly we can act. Economic growth for only a few may worsen inequality. The widening gaps may be difficult to bridge in a shrinking space for economic growth, with so many job sectors either being defunct or shunned with additional people. It is also high time to think of Universal Basic Income to ensure minimum standards for all and income transfers to ensure human development across the country.

Waste reduction and transport sectors are more challenging after the pandemic is over; the balance between the damaging and helping impact on the pandemic and climate change would be the challenge.

Economic growth and poverty reduction are the main priorities for developing country policymakers. Yet, climate change mitigation can offer these countries the opportunity to revisit development strategies from a new perspective. Climate change considerations place renewed urgency on some options, such as energy efficiency, renewable energy, and sustainable land-use policies. They argue for a better understanding of the connections to other environmental problems. They also argue for improving the integration of environment and development issues and other issues, such as income distribution. Despite limited attention from policymakers, climate change policies could have significant ancillary benefits for the local environment. The reverse is also true, as synergies exist between transport, energy, forestry and environmental sustainability policies and climate change objectives (e.g., mitigation and adaptation). In order to maximize the potential for synergy, increased institutional capacity and awareness-building measures will also be needed.

## References

Aruga, K., Md. M. Islam, and A. Jannat. 2020. "Effects Of COVID-19 On Indian Energy Consumption". *Sustainability* 12 (14): 5616. doi:10.3390/su12145616.

Beyer, Robert C.M., S. Franco-Bedoya, and V.Galdo. 2021. "Examining the Economic Impact of COVID-19 In India Through Daily Electricity Consumption and Night-time Light Intensity". *World Development* 140: 105287. doi: 10.1016/j.worlddev.2020.105287.

Census of India. 2011. *Source of Lighting*. Office of the Registrar General & Census Commissioner India. Ministry of Home Affairs. Government of India. http://www.censusindia.gov.in/2011census/hlo/Data_sheet/India/Source_Lighting.pdf (accessed on 10 June 2021).

CEA, Central Electricity Authority. 2020. New Delhi. https://cea.nic.in/wp-content/uploads/pdm/2020/12/growth_2020.pdf (accessed on 10 June 2021).

Chen, K., Meng W., Conghong H., P. L Kinney, and P. T.Anastas. 2020. "Air Pollution Reduction and Mortality Benefit During The COVID-19 Outbreak in China". *The Lancet Planetary Health* 4 (6): e210–e212. doi:10.1016/s2542-5196(20)30107-8.

Choudhari, R. 2020. "COVID 19 Pandemic: Mental Health Challenges of Internal Migrant Workers of India". *Asian Journal of Psychiatry* 54: 102254. doi: 10.1016/j.ajp.2020.102254.

Digital in India. 2019. *Round 2 Report*. Nielsen and Internet and Mobile Association of India – IAMAI.https://cms.iamai.in/Content/ResearchPapers/2286f4d7-424f-4bde-be88-6415fe5021d5.pdf (accessed on 19 June 2021).

Hannah Ritchie. 2019. "Access to Energy". *OurWorldInData.org*. https://ourworldindata.org/energy-access (accessed on 18 June 2021).

IEA. 2020a. *World Energy Outlook 2020*. Paris: IEA. https://www.iea.org/reports/world-energy-outlook-2020 (accessed on 18 June 2021).

IEA. 2020b. *SDG7: Data and Projections. Access to Affordable, Reliable, Sustainable, and Modern Energy for All*. Flagship Report. October 2020. International Energy Agency. https://www.iea.org/reports/sdg7-data-and-projections/access-to-clean-cooking (accessed on 18 June 2021).

IRENA. 2019. *Renewable Energy and Jobs. Annual Review 2019*. International Renewable Energy Agency. https://www.irena.org//media/Files/IRENA/Agency/Publication/2019/Jun/IRENA_RE_Jobs_2019-report.pdf (accessed on 18 June 2021).

Kulkarni, B. N., and V. Anantharama. 2020. "Repercussions of COVID-19 Pandemic on Municipal Solid Waste Management: Challenges and Opportunities". *Science Of the Total Environment* 743: 140693. doi: 10.1016/j.scitotenv.2020.140693.

Kumari, P., and D. Toshniwal. 2020. "Impact of Lockdown Measures During COVID-19 On Air Quality: A Case Study of India". *International Journal of Environmental Health Research* 32(3): 1–8. doi:10.1080/09603123.2020.1778646.

Kumar, P., S. Hama, H. Omidvarborna, A. Sharma, J. Sahani, K.V. Abhijith, S. E. Debele, J. C. Zavala-Reyes, Y. Barwise, and A. Tiwari. 2020. "Temporary Reduction in Fine Particulate Matter Due to "Anthropogenic Emissions Switch-Off" During COVID-19 Lockdown in Indian Cities". *Sustainable Cities and Society* 62: 102382. doi: 10.1016/j.scs.2020.102382.

Lokhandwala, Snehal, and Pratibha Gautam. 2020. "Indirect Impact of COVID-19 on Environment: A Brief Study in Indian Context". *Environmental Research* 188: 109807. doi: 10.1016/j.envres.2020.109807.

Sengupta, S., and M. K. Jha. 2020. "Social Policy, COVID-19 and Impoverished Migrants: Challenges and Prospects in Locked Down India". *The International Journal of Community and Social Development* 2 (2): 152–172. doi:10.1177/2516602620933715.

Shakti Foundation. 2018. *GHG Emissions from India's Electricity Sector. Policy Note*. https://shaktifoundation.in/wp-content/uploads/2018/06/GHG-Emissions-from-Electricity-Sector.pdf (accessed on 18 June 2021).

Shakti Foundation. (2021). *Transmission Reform Agenda and Action Plan*. https://shaktifoundation.in/wp-content/uploads/2021/10/Transmission-reform-agenda-and-action-plan.pdf (accessed on 18 June 2021).

Sharma, G. D., G. Talan, and M. Jain. (2020). "Policy Response to The Economic Challenge from COVID –19 In India: A Qualitative Enquiry". *Journal Of Public Affairs*.e2206 doi:10.1002/pa.2206.

Srivastava,A., R. K. Sharma, and A. Suresh. (2020). Impact of Covid-19 on Sustainable Development Goals. *International Journal of Advanced Science and Technology*, 29(9s), 4968–4972. http://sersc.org/journals/index.php/IJAST/article/view/17764 (accessed on 18 June 2021).

Telecom Statistics India. 2019. *Economics Research Unit. Department of Telecommunications. Ministry of Communications. Government of India*. https://dot.gov.in/sites/default/files/Telecom%20Statistics%20India-2019.pdf?download=1 (accessed on 10 June 2021).

Telecom Subscription Data, Telecom Regulatory Authority of India. n.d. (as on 31st July 2020) https://www.trai.gov.in/sites/default/files/PR_No.84of2020.pdf (accessed on 18 June 2021).

United Nations Population Division. 2017. *World Population Prospects*. New York. https://population.un.org/wpp/Download/Archive/Standard/ (accessed on 10 June 2021).

# Part IV

# Economics of Environmental Policy

Chapter 12

# Environmental Policy in India

## Retrospect and Recent Developments

*Kanchan Chopra*

### Introduction

I am indeed glad to be a part of this volume in honour of Professor Rabindra N. Bhattacharya, one of the pioneers in environmental economics research and teaching in India. As a tribute to his early initiatives in the field, I thought it best to focus on a review of environmental policy in India and the role environmental and ecological economics concepts and frameworks have played in shaping policies in the last few decades in India. Some recent developments causing concern are also examined.

The Indian agenda on the environment stands at crossroads today. Two kinds of influences are driving this agenda, albeit they operate at different scales and move at different speeds. The first influence is the consequence of an awareness and understanding of the impending environmental crises of various kinds, at least among some sections of society. There is ample recognition of the urgent need to regulate some aspects of economic activity in the interest of conservation and to build institutions and social norms to assist such regulation. Judicial intervention and slowly evolving legal codes (pushed ahead often by grassroots movements and precipitated by conflicts and their documentation) also illustrate an intention of taking note of and introducing regulation of environment-damaging economic activity. In the background, the evolving natural and social sciences (with different disciplines converging in their pursuit of a policy paradigm for this challenging problem confronting our times) play a role, albeit a supporting one.

The second element in the system, moving at a much faster pace, demands more rapid economic growth in the shorter run. This set of actors is driven by unconstrained market forces, irresponsible industrialization, and urbanization. As it happens, the dominant political economy discourse often stresses development, employment, and more jobs, often at the cost of longer-run sustainability. This discourse urges that projects need to be cleared fast. Bureaucratic governance procedures are not accepted as readily as they were in the past, and there is, therefore, cause for concern that this accent on

DOI: 10.4324/9781003253884-17

speed may be at the cost of the environment. Some of these changes were documented as early as 2016 by an editorial in the *Economic & Political Weekly* (EPW).[1] It seems that in several cases, compromises are being made to ensure fast implementation of projects, overruling earlier advice on caution. Such compromises could happen in the context of a range of issues such as the implementation of the Forest Rights Act, a moratorium on the industry in heavily polluted areas or wetlands regulation acts.

Which way will the balance tilt? Will a judicial mix of development and environmental protection, speed, and caution, be possible? One cannot help being pessimistic about the likelihood, in particular as one looks at the recent policy signals, such as the Draft Environmental Impact Assessment, 2020.

In such a divisive policy environment, it is useful to recall some of the reasons why the issues relating to the environment are critical for planet earth and its human and non-human inhabitants. Section 12.1 provides a perspective by pointing out towards early warnings on the impending issues found in the literature. Section 12.2 then evaluates the role played in policy formulation by the further evolution of knowledge. Sections 12.3 and 12.4 examine the evolution of policy in India, in particular the ominous portents from some recent developments. The last two sections (12.5 and 12.6) conclude with a few pointers for the future.

## 12.1 Early Warnings

Boulding, in a seminal paper published in 1966,[2] made a few points that deserve reiteration in today's fractured policy context. Interestingly, these points also encapsulate the directions towards which research has tried to move policy since then. Boulding emphasized the difference between ways in which economies could be organized in terms of a striking metaphor of the difference between 'the cowboy economy' and 'the spaceship economy'. In the former, there always exist new frontiers to explore, new resources to exploit and so on. Note his words,

> the cowboy being symbolic of the illimitable plains and also associated with reckless, exploitative, romantic, and violent behaviour, which is characteristic of open societies. ... The economy of the future might similarly be called the 'spaceman' economy, in which the earth has become a single spaceship, without unlimited reservoirs of anything, either for the extraction or for pollution.

In the 'spaceman economy', the earth is likened to a spaceship where stocks of resources are fixed. *So, one functions always with an eye on the stock.* In such an economy, consumption and production are desirable but only within limits. Note, further, the following, another early warning, from the same paper:

> The essential measure of the success of the economy is not production and consumption at all, but the *nature, extent, quality, and complexity of the total capital stock,* including in this the state of the human bodies and minds which form a part of the system. In the spaceman economy, what we are primarily concerned with is stock maintenance, and any technological change which results in the maintenance of a given total stock with a lessened throughput is clearly a gain. This idea that both production and consumption are (at times) bad things rather than good things is very strange to economists, who have been obsessed with the income-flow concepts to the exclusion, almost, of capital-stock concepts.

This early warning went unheeded, and the world moved relentlessly towards higher and higher levels of production and consumption, ignoring, in particular, the natural capital stock. The political context in India too has privileged growth and globalization, more so since 1991. The din of 'development' and globalization has grown. Large corporates have expanded, the extractive nature of the industry has taken its toll on minerals and resources, and lifestyles of the rich have reached hitherto unheard-of levels of opulence. The not so privileged try to follow suit, treating these as their role models. They do not succeed most of the time. But the unbridled opulence of the rich and the super-rich results in a high degree of inequality and is resource intensive.

Urbanization, an integral part of the above process, has brought with it its own set of environmental disasters and problems. Air and water pollution and poorly designed cities are found all over the country. This has resulted in a new set of challenges and opportunities in the form of overcrowding, seasonal waterlogging and falling groundwater tables, and diminishing green covers and biodiversity. As a consequence, both social and environmental sustainability has been threatened. A slew of environmental issues faces us today, biodiversity loss, water, air pollution, increasing frequency of extreme events, and climate change being the main ones among them. In this chapter, we shall examine whether or not environmental policy evolved to meet these challenges. Was available knowledge used to create the political will necessary for evolution?

## 12.2 Arresting the Recklessness: Evolution of Understanding to Aid Action

Can the reckless pursuit of growth at the cost of ecological sustainability be attributed to the absence of an understanding of the issues? As it is often said, a good policy comes from good theory.

Further, are ideas, sometimes welded into theory and translated into policy, significant in shaping policy? While the practical world of political economy may not think so, we have it on the authority of John Maynard Keynes that they do. Note the following:

> The ideas of economists and political philosophers, both when they are right and when they are wrong, are more powerful than is commonly understood. Indeed, the world is ruled by little else. Practical men, who believe themselves to be quite exempt from any intellectual influences, are usually slaves of some *defunct* economist. Madmen in authority are usually distilling their frenzy from some academic scribbler *of a few years back*. I am sure that the power of vested interests is vastly exaggerated compared with the gradual encroachment of ideas[3]

Note, however, that he said, 'defunct economist' and 'academic scribbler of a few years back'. So, according to him, we expect the policy to follow theory but with a lapse of time. Hence the question arises, 'What was the natural and social science capital anchor available to policymakers in environmental policy, and how has it evolved over the years?'

This stock of knowledge can be thought of as a mix of 'concepts, frameworks and models'. While the details of the models are the stuff of academia, we will, in this chapter, focus on the concepts and frameworks that have emerged from the last few decades of deliberations on environment and ecology.

The oldest and most lasting among ideas that define environmental impacts of human activity is that of "'externalities'. Following closely is 'cost-benefit analysis', both private and the social variety. Governments have designed pollution taxes based on these principles, even as they have been critiqued by other environmental-related disciplines. Ecologists consider such exercises to yield answers which give 'permission to pollute'. Sociologists focus on inequalities in access to wealth and power of different stakeholders. Both seem to favour well-implemented laws to protect both people and spaces that are vulnerable. From these sciences came the concepts of 'irreversibility, resilience, and vulnerability'. Of late, these have entered the policy arena as well, at least in some developed countries.

But concepts need to be held together by frameworks in order to result in a consistent policy. What is the relevant framework? Each of the sciences referred to above has at its core different models of human behaviour and the human-nature interface. Economics is built primarily on a concern for the individual human, ecology on the supremacy of all things natural and sociology on communities and justice.

Frameworks, if they are to help in going beyond concepts, need to set up a scheme of thinking that provides space for these diverse philosophical foundations and focuses the sight of the policymaker on all aspects of the problems involved. We argue here that such frameworks have a greater and more lasting impact on decision-making and policy, in particular, on environmental issues. They provide space for alternative modes of viewing them.

The Millennium Ecosystem Assessment (MA) provided an overarching framework that sought to bring together the understanding from different disciplines into a single conceptual framework. The MA constituted a paradigm shift in framing the issues, bringing nature in not as a receptacle for pollutants or a resource but as a series of ecosystems with their contributions to human well-being. Understandings of the nature of the human impact on the environment were made more precise, sometimes starker. The conceptual framework of the Millennium Ecosystem Assessment provided multiple pathways for the links between human well-being and ecosystems to be viewed. These pathways left the scope for different disciplinary perspectives to be accommodated. In sum, the best available knowledge was brought together in the belief that it would have a bearing on decision-making. Further, in this framework, information and feedback from stakeholders are at the centre of the decision-making cycle, which conceptualized the process of policymaking.[4]

In recent years, the framework for conceptualization provided by the MA has led to several other developments. See, for instance, the understanding concerning planetary boundaries.[5] That there exist limits within which our economic activity can expand and enlarge itself has been reiterated time and again by natural scientists, most recently in two widely quoted papers indicating 'a safe operating space for humanity'[6] that international and sometimes intergovernmental initiatives have also followed. Examples include The Economics of Ecosystem Services and Biodiversity (TEEB) and the Intergovernmental Science-Policy Platform for Biodiversity and Ecosystem Services (IPBES) (Ferrier et al. 2016). It carries forward and improves on the MA's framework. The TEEB has also carried forward this strain of work. These developments should help keep the focus on biodiversity and ecosystem services alive and aid in continued documentation of the state of knowledge on these issues for the benefit of policymakers.[7]

## 12.3 Arresting the Recklessness: Parallel Developments in India

Interestingly, parallel to the above progress from academia, or even preceding it, the decade of the 1980s witnessed the rise of a forward-looking approach with regard to the environment within the government in India. A full-fledged Ministry was set up, and an unconventional agenda on land and water management had started to unfold from within the government. Dialogue with other stakeholders was the order of the day. A number of policy initiatives in the 1980s and 1990s proceeded simultaneously to bring environmental governance (Kashwan 2013) and its vocabulary into the domain of law.

The late 1980s saw new initiatives in forest and watershed development policy and guidelines. In several different hues, Joint Forest Management was adopted in the early years of this decade. Parallelly, the watershed was recognized as an ecological unit for analysis and action by the Watershed Guidelines of 1992 (due to the Hanumantha Rao Committee report). These guidelines even mandated the setting up of an institutional structure with people's participation at the core, prior to the release of any government funds for the development of watersheds. It seemed that there was a willingness within the government to accept new modes of thinking. The 1990s saw the beginning of some change. As commented upon by Hanumantha Rao,

> the single most important factor accounting for the positive impact of the watershed development under the government-sponsored programme ... is community participation and decentralization of programme administration made possible under the new guidelines. This has come about on account of political and bureaucratic commitment to the new strategy.[8]

With regard to international issues such as climate change too, India was in a relatively comfortable position in the early 1990s. Gupta and Mandal (2015) stated,

> India started the UNFCCC negotiations in the early nineties from a position of strength. It had attended the Stockholm Conference at the highest level; it had passed several laws to protect the environment, it had some internationally renowned climate scientists, it had strong green activists who had ensured that the 1992 Rio Earth Summit included the right to development as one of the pillars of the new world.

However, consequent on developments in the discourse within the country, India put equality of per capita emissions at the centre of the concern for climate justice, arguing that the global commons needed to be shared equally. This remained the cornerstone of the Indian position for a long time. At that time, very little attention was paid to the impact of climate change on India. The science seemed ambivalent about the likely effects, and it was agreed that "the challenge of development was far more significant than the threat of climate change" (Reddy 1993).[9]

As a culmination of these admittedly piecemeal efforts, in 2006, the Government of India produced a document called 'National Environment Policy'. Whereas sector-specific policies had existed, and numerous acts purported to lay down rules to protect the environment,[10] this was the first time that a policy for "the environment" was being put in place. The National Environment Policy 2006 was the outcome of extensive consultations with experts in different disciplines, central ministries, members of parliament, state governments, industry associations, academic and research institutions, civil society, NGOs, and the public.

Going through this document, one is encouraged to think that thinking within government would, in the future, be guided by accepted principles in the disciplines of ecology and economics. Some state-of-the-art theoretical concepts, e.g., the themes of resilience and vulnerability, are mentioned in it. See, for instance, the following,

> The poor are also more vulnerable to loss of resilience in ecosystems. Large reductions in resilience may mean that the ecosystems on which livelihoods are based break down, causing distress. The loss of the environmental resource base can result in certain groups of people being made destitute, even if overall, the economy shows strong growth.

Further, as a part of the principles underlying the policy, two are mentioned: (a) the precautionary approach to deal with areas where knowledge may not be enough or uncertainty high and (b) the existence of 'entities with incomparable value'.

The 'polluter pays' principle, a cornerstone of environmental economics, also finds a mention. To ensure that the 'polluter pays' principle could be implemented, the principle of legal liability is also accepted with the suggestion that civil liability is added along with existing criminal liability (which has not worked as per the policy) in cases of environmental pollution. It is stated, 'Civil liability for environmental damage would deter environmentally harmful actions and compensate the victims of environmental damage'. Further, 'conceptually, the principle of legal liability may be viewed as an embodiment in the legal doctrine of the "polluter pays" approach, itself deriving from the principle of economic efficiency'.

A two-pronged approach seemed to underlie the policy: that of using economic principles up to a point and falling back on caution where the incomparable value or uncertain knowledge existed. The statement took into account the current state of knowledge. Also, as a part of strategies and actions to follow up on the policy, a revisit of the regulatory regimes prevalent in relation to the environment was suggested.

Later, initiatives were taken to bring the national statistical and planning systems in line with developments in green accounting. These took the form of expert group reports. The Green Accounting Committee Report (2013) was one such effort that attempted to introduce alternative wealth-based concepts of welfare into the national statistical system.[11] Another was the Planning Commission Report (2014) on low carbon growth. Alternative scenarios were studied to provide the nature of trade-offs if a 'green growth' path was to be followed.

A few Acts enacted in the same period were also forward-looking, e.g. The Forest Rights Act (2006) provided for community forest rights and promised to undo historical injustices. The FRA (2006) sought to push the process towards a better articulation of objectives and criteria. It requires the state to define criteria for Critical Wildlife Habitat and further demonstrate that the coexistence of local communities with wildlife was not possible before moving towards a rehabilitation process. This was different from the Wildlife Protection Act (1972), which gives the state the power to declare an area as a national park or wildlife sanctuary and then evict people out of it.[12] Similarly, the multidimensional recommendations of the Tiger Task Force in 2005 created a ray of hope. It is important to note that all these initiatives took place at a time when a larger narrative of 'growth' that privileged development projects of all kinds pervaded the economy.

In retrospect, as we scan the last two decades, some elements favouring a more participative and environment-friendly development process have been put in place, at least partially. The Right to Information Act, the National Rural Employment Guarantee Act and movements towards Panchayat's control of natural resources are in place. The NREGA mandates that natural resource-based projects be given priority.

There is indeed a kind of lagged acceptance of some ideas from scientific research with a lag of 10 or 12 years, by which time thinking has moved forward, and policy still falls short.

Further, feedback learning from policy implementation is itself the moving force behind the progress of some aspects of social science. All this happens in a somewhat piecemeal fashion with a very little analytical framework to define it. A co-evolution between the development of both the natural and the social sciences and the design of policy from a systems' perspective seems a far cry at the present moment.

All the same, this to-and-fro movement has taught us a great deal about the inter-linkages of sectors such as forests, mining, and water. Discerning analysts of the media have also noted the steady increase in space newspapers are giving to issues of the environment.

## 12.4 The Environmental Impact Assessment: The Practical Aspect of Implementing Policy

Assessing the environmental impact of a development project comprises the practical counterfoil to the framework set up by overarching policies and Acts. Environmental impact assessments (EIA) are essentially the process of evaluating the environmental effects of a project *prior to decision-making*. In India, EIAs have the statutory backing of the Environmental Protection Act (1986). However, till 1994, conducting an EIA was an administrative decision. In 1994, an EIA notification was promulgated by the Ministry of Environment and Forests, making EIA mandatory for setting up new projects (under Schedule A) and for expansion and modernization of activities.

Further, in 2006, the Ministry notified a new EIA legislation making it mandatory for mining, thermal power plant, river valley and infrastructure projects as well as for several small electroplating and foundry units to get environmental clearance. The onus for ensuring the same was divided between the central and state governments. In addition, several steps in conducting an EIA were also outlined. Notably, these included a public hearing with the project affected persons.

The EIA process and its implementation have been the target of extended criticism from civil society because of the shoddy character of many assessments conducted. This may have been due partly to political expediency and partly to the absence of requisite knowledge and expertise.

Be that as it may, the last five years or so have seen a steady movement towards haste in implementing projects. Even while this was being taken note of and commented on, the Draft EIA 2020 has directed attention towards itself.

## 12.5 Recent Developments: Going Back Two Steps: The Draft EIA 2020

The EIA (2020) notification was placed by the Ministry of Environment, Forest, and Climate Change (MoEFCC) for public comments in June 2020. The expectation was that it would fill the lacunae in the existing process while at the same time improving administrative implementation. Contrary to expectation, it fundamentally changes the EIA process. It does this in several ways, some of which are explained below.

(a) By reclassifying industries and excluding major industries from the EIA process

The EIA's scope has shrunk vastly with this notification, in direct contradiction to its mandate of safeguarding the environment. It reclassifies 40 types of industries under a category that makes them exempt from needing prior environmental clearance. The construction industry is one such beneficiary, as the new draft requires that only the largest industries be fully scrutinized while the others escape appraisal. The move is alarming since the construction industry is one of the most polluting industries. In urban areas, it is one of the main contributors to increased air pollution levels. Various linear infrastructure projects like highways, multimodal corridors, etc., have been reclassified and thus are exempted from a full appraisal and public hearing. Such projects often involve fragile ecosystems like forests, wetlands, grasslands, floodplains, and deserts. Constructions here would likely cause irreversible damage to wildlife habitat and ecosystem functioning.

(b) By legitimizing post-facto environmental clearance

The EIA 2020 draft notification directly contradicts the basic precautionary principle of environmental governance, enshrined in the policy statement of 2006. It legitimizes *post-facto* clearance, *so a project would be able to run even without environment clearance.* Such *post-facto* clearances for infrastructural expansions are known to cause irreversible damage to the ecology in regions that have high biodiversity value. The idea that environmental degradation can be compensated monetarily is not applicable in all contexts. The damage to the quality of water, soil, air, ecosystems, and wildlife, and indeed, human health is often irreversible.[13]

(c) By subverting the public hearing process

The EIA 2020 draft notification exempts various types of projects from having to conduct public hearings before beginning construction. Additionally, even up to 50% of expansions in industrial capacity are exempted from the public hearing. Exempting projects from public hearing strips citizens – often vulnerable communities – from having any voice in decisions that will directly impact their health and well-being and affect their livelihood.[14]

The importance of public consultations has been repeatedly highlighted by the Honorable Supreme Court, as in the case of Lafarge *Umami Mining Private Limited v. Union of India.* Removing public consultations takes away from local communities their democratic right and the only opportunity to voice their concerns on projects and other developments that directly impact their lives.

(d) By preventing citizens from taking cognizance of violations

The power to officially report environmental violations in projects under the EIA 2020 draft notification rests only with the project developers and government authorities, leaving no scope for directly affected communities to report violations.

Note, however, that the ambivalence in government policy orientation continues too. A Government of India report by the Ministry of Earth Sciences released in June 2020, titled 'Assessment of Climate Change over the Indian Region' warns:

> the rapid changes in India's climate [projected by climate models] will place increasing stress on the country's natural ecosystems, agricultural output, and freshwater resources, while also causing escalating damage to infrastructure. These portend serious consequences for the country's biodiversity, food, water and energy security, and public health.
>
> (Raghavan K. et al. 2020)

So, while one Ministry of Earth Sciences is drawing attention to the serious consequences of climate change for the economy, the MoEFCC is occupied with drafting EIA notifications that will ensure rapid and callous approval of projects. Could the irony be more dramatic?

## 12.6 Conclusion: Whither Policy, Any Directions?

The to and fro in environmental policy implicit in the vacillation discussed above is indeed a consequence of the interaction between different sets of stakeholders: those with a strong interest in 'more income today' and the approach of 'after me, the deluge' and those that depend on local resources for livelihoods, sometimes called the 'ecosystem people'. In between these two is the silent majority, with some degree of awareness and knowledge, a gradually increasing and vocal group.

The present state of affairs can also be viewed as the outcome of an interaction between well-known dilemmas.[15] The first has to do with a preference for the present over the future. Economists have long struggled with the why and wherefore of it. It impacts environmental issues critically. Time scales of ecological events are, at times, in terms of centuries, whereas economists think at best in terms of two or three decades and politicians in terms of a maximum of five years. How do we resolve issues relating to a unified complex socio-ecological system in such a situation?[16]

The second has to do with the treatment of agents situated unequally with respect to wealth, power, or knowledge. The more equal a society is with respect to each of these attributes, the better is likely to be the implementation of adaptive learning cycles and deliberative processes in practice. The existence of poly-centric centres of decision-making with competing relationships can only flourish inequitable situations. Else we go back to the patron-client relationship of a top-down decision-making process. Some would even say that the nature of the state militates against any such purposeful deliberation. Kaswhan (2013) argues that the greening of a Machiavellian state is only possible if environmentalists in developing countries are able to create a constituency that brings together 'the environmentalism of the poor' and 'the findings of the scholarship on the commons' and requires governments to act. He maintains that independently these stakeholders are not able to ensure 'the Machiavellian state to act'. Be that as it may, a political voice for the environment is definitely the need of the hour.[17]

The third dilemma concerns the nature of governance, partly following from and overlapping with the first two. With a preference for present growth and with unequal entities coming together as decision-makers, the governance of laws will leave much to be desired. With the best legislation on the environment, and the most adaptive learning processes in place, the state of the environment would continue to deteriorate. It is a question of ensuring that laws put in place are followed. As Jairam Ramesh puts it,

> When closure notices are served to distilleries or paper mills illegally discharging wastes into India's most holy Ganga River, it is not a question of 'environment versus development' but again one of whether standards mandated by law are to be enforced effectively or not.[18]

In looking for solutions to these dilemmas, we need new and reformed institutions for facilitating a change in human behaviour, to increase local appreciation of shared global concerns, and to correct collective action failures that cause global-scale problems. However, this change in behaviour assumes acceptance of common norms, both nationally and internationally. Such norms are more likely to emerge with decreases in inequalities in the distribution of income and power and more interactions across the globe which facilitate the emergence of international institutions.[19]

This brings us back, full circle, to the issue of distributional justice and shared norms. In conclusion, it is true that shared values with regard to the linkages between economy, society, and nature need to inform policymaking at both macro and project levels. It is these that we need to move towards as we simultaneously strengthen the institutional, informational, and databases that enable us to do so.

## Notes

1 See Economic and Political Weekly EPW Editorial (2016).
2 See Boulding, K. E, (1966). This paper was first presented at the Sixth Resources for the Future Forum on Environmental Quality in a Growing Economy in Washington, D.C. on March 8, 1966.
3 See Keynes, John Maynard (1936) for the details.
4 See Chapter 8 of Millennium Ecosystem Assessment (2003) for details.
5 See Steffen, W. et al. (2015) for planetary boundaries and Millennium Ecosystem Assessment (2003) for the conceptual framework referred to.
6 See Rockstrom et al. (2009) and Steffen et al. (2015).
7 For more details on the knowledge-policy interlinkages, see Chapter 5 of Chopra (2017).
8 See Hanumanth Rao (2000) It is a different matter how these worked out in practice (*in reference as Rao 2000*). Several writers have commented on it. Note in particular Baviskar (2008).
9 For a succinct exposition of the Indian position see S. Lele (2011) in Dubash edited volume.
10 A number of reviews exist. See among others Sankar (1998) and Sankar (2001).
11 See Government of India (2013) and (2014). No follow-up on either seems to have taken place.
12 See the discussion in Lele (2017).
13 A recent example of the dire consequences of *post-facto* regulation is the gas leak at the LG Polymers factory in Visakhapatnam on 7 May 2020, which killed 12 people, and left several hundred ill, and ailing. This unit was operating without an Environmental Clearance (EC) and was due to be considered for grant of a *post-facto* EC (Sumit Bhattacharjee, 6 June 2020) (*in reference as Bhattacharjee Sumit*).

14 A recent example of this was seen in Baghjan, Assam, where a gas-rig operated by Oil India Ltd (OIL) leaked uncontrollably for 12 days before catching fire. The continuous leak of toxic gases like methane, propane and propylene combined with oil and condensate has severely affected agricultural fields of local communities, while also displacing them to temporary refugee camps. OIL has escaped conducting public hearings before expanding for drilling in this landscape and was given an EC regardless (Simantik Dowerah 12 June 2020) (*in reference as Dowerah Simantik*).
15 For a discussion of these dilemmas, see also Chapter 6 of Chopra (2017).
16 Some progress has been made by recent work on determining 'safe planetary boundaries' for human activities but areas of concern remain.
17 For conclusions on such lines, see Chapter 4 of Chopra (2017) on environmental justice movements in India.
18 While also arguing for pragmatic laws, he gives several other examples as well. See J. Ramesh (2015) (*in reference as Ramesh, J. 2015*).
19 For a similar conclusion see Walker et al. (2009).

## References


Baviskar, A. 2008. "The dream machine the model development project and the making of the state". In *Growth, Equity, Environment and Population: Economic and Sociological Perspectives*, edited by K. Chopra and C. H. H. Rao, 287–307. New Delhi: Sage Publications.

Bhattacharjee, Sumit. 2020. "Visakhapatnam gas leak | How negligence and violations led to a deadly disaster". *The Hindu*. June 06. https://www.thehindu.com/news/cities/Visakhapatnam/visakhapatnam-gas-leak-how-negligence-and-violations-led-to-a-deadly-disaster/article31761949.ece (accessed on 11 June 2021).

Boulding, Kenneth E.1966, "The Economics of the Coming Spaceship Earth" In H. Jarrett (ed.). *Environmental Quality in a Growing Economy*, 3–14. Baltimore: Resources for the Future/Johns Hopkins University Press.

Chopra, Kanchan. 2017. *Development and Environmental Policy: The Last few Decades*. New York: Springer.

Dowerah, Simantik. 2020. "Baghjan fire: Oil India's failure to stand by local community after blaze, protect ecology ruins its image in Assam". *Firstpost*. June 12, 2020. https://www.firstpost.com/india/baghjan-fire-oil-indias-failure-to-stand-by-local-community-after-blaze-protect-ecology-ruins-its-image-in-assam-8464251.html (accessed on 11 June 2021).

Editorial. 2016. "Choosing Speed over Diligence". *Economic and Political Weekly* 51 (23): 9. https://www.epw.in/journal/2016/23/editorials/choosing-speed-over-diligence.html (accessed on 19 June 2021).

Ferrier, Simon et al. 2016. *The Methodological Assessment Report on Scenarios and Models for Biodiversity and ecosystem Services*. Kuala Lumpur: Summary for Policy Makers, IPBES. https://ipbes.net/sites/default/files/downloads/pdf/2016.methodological_assessment_report_scenarios_models.pdf (accessed on 18 June 2021).

Government of India, Central Statistical Office. 2013. *Report of the Expert Group on Green National Accounting*. https://www.cbd.int/financial/hlp/doc/literature/Green_National_Accouts_in_India_1may13.pdf (accessed on 19 June 2021).

Government of India, Planning Commission. 2014. *Final Report of the Expert Group on Low Carbon Strategies for India*. https://indiaclimatedialogue.net/2014/06/04/low-carbon-strategies-inclusive-growth-final-report-expert-group/ (accessed on 19 June 2021).

Government of India, Union Ministry of Environment and Forests. 2005. *Joining the dots (The report ofthe tiger task force): New Delhi*. https://ntca.gov.in/assets/uploads/Reports/Joining_the_dot.pdf (accessed on 19 June 2021).

Government of India, Union Ministry of Environment and Forests. 2006. *National Environmental Policy*. https://www.india.gov.in/national-environment-policy-2006 (accessed on 10 May 2021).

Government of India, Union Ministry of Environment, Forests and Climate Change. 2020. *Environmental Impact Assessment Notification*. http://parivesh.nic.in/writereaddata/Draft_EIA_2020.pdf (accessed on 18 April 2021).

Gupta, J and T. Mandal. 2015. *Hot Air, Climate Negotiations and India*, India Climate Dialogue. Under Creative Commons. Attribution-Non-Commercial-No-Derivs 2.0 England and Wales Licence. https://indiaclimatedialogue.net/2015/12/01/hot-air-climate-negotiations-and-india-2/ (accessed on 17 June 2021).

Kashwan, Prakash. 2013. "Greening A Machiavellian State? Insights For International Environmental Governance". *Journal of Political Sciences & Public Affairs* 1 (2). doi:10.4172/2332-0761.1000e106.

Keynes, John Maynard, 1936. *The General Theory of Employment, Interest and Money*. London: Macmillan.

Lele, S. 2011. "Climate Change and the Indian Environment Movement". In *Handbook of Climate Change and India: Development, Politics and Governance*, edited by Navroz K. Dubash, 208–217. London: Routledge, Taylor and Francis.

Lele, S. 2017. "Forest Governance: From co-option and conflict to Multilayered Governance?" *Economic and Political Weekly* 52(25–26). 24th June 2017: 55–58. https://www.epw.in/journal/2017/25-26/forest-rights-act/forest-governance.html (accessed on 19 June 2021).

Millennium Ecosystem Assessment. 2003. *Ecosystems and Human Well-being, A Framework for Assessment*. Washington, DC: Island Press. https://pdf.wri.org/ecosystems_human_wellbeing.pdf (accessed on 15 June 2021).

Raghavan, K. et al. 2020. *Assessment of Climate Change over the Indian region: A Report of the Ministry of Earth Sciences*. MoES, Government of India. https://reliefweb.int/sites/reliefweb.int/files/resources/Assessment%20of%20climate%20change%20over%20the%20Indian%20region%20%20A%20report%20of%20the%20Ministry%20of%20Earth%20Sciences%20%28MoES%29%2C%20Government%20of%20India.pdf (accessed on 19 June 2021).

Ramesh, J. 2015.*Green Signals: Ecology, Growth and Democracy in India*. New Delhi: Oxford University Press.

Rao, C. H. 2000. "Watershed Development in India: Recent Experiences and Emerging Issues". *Economic and Political Weekly* 35 (45), 4th Novembor, 2000: 3943–47. https://www.epw.in/journal/2000/45/special-articles/watershed-development-india.html (accessed on 14 June 2021).

Reddy, Jeevananda S., 1993. *Agroclimatic Agrometeorological Techniques*. Jeevan Charitable Trust.

Rockström, J., W. Steffen, K. Noone, Å. Persson, F. Stuart Chapin, E. F. Lambin, and T. M. Lenton et al. 2009. “A Safe Operating Space for Humanity”. *Nature* 461 (7263): 472–475. doi:10.1038/461472a.

Sankar, U. 1998. “Laws and Institutions relating to environmental protection in India”. MSE Occasional Paper No. 2. https://www.mse.ac.in/wp-content/uploads/2016/09/op_sankar.pdf (accessed on 25 January 2021).

Sankar, U. 2001. “Environmental Policy”. In *Environmental Economics*, edited by U Sankar. 398–447. Oxford University Press, New Delhi.

Steffen, W., K. Richardson, J. Rockström, S. E. Cornell, I. Fetzer, E. M. Bennett, and R. Biggs et al. 2015. “Planetary Boundaries: Guiding Human Development on a Changing Planet”. *Science* 347 (6223). doi:10.1126/science.1259855.

Walker, B., S. Barrett, S. Polasky, V. Galaz, C. Folke, G. Engström, and F. Ackerman et al. 2009. “Looming Global-Scale Failures and Missing Institutions”. *Science* 325 (5946): 1345–1346. doi:10.1126/science.1175325.

Chapter 13

# Household Waste Management and the Role of Gender in Nepal

*Mani Nepal, Marina Cauchy, Apsara Karki Nepal, and Chanda Gurung Goodrich*

## Introduction

Cities in South Asia are growing rapidly and, in most cases, without planning. Although urban growth brings economic opportunities to the city residents when managed properly, it creates all sorts of challenges when it is unplanned. It also reduces the permeable areas of the city as poor people tend to migrate to the cities and live in the slums, which are mostly built on low-lying floodplains or over swamps (McGranahan, Balk, & Anderson, 2007), making high-intensity rainfall problematic as the run-offs may overwhelm city infrastructure (Douglas et al., 2008). The problem gets aggravated when solid waste is dumped in open spaces, and the drainage system results in flooding and waterlogging (Pervin et al., 2019). When the run-offs run over unplanned and unmanaged waste dumpsites, leachate ends up in the soil, polluting the groundwater. Since most cities in developing countries use groundwater for household use, groundwater pollution creates a public health problem. Improperly disposed plastic waste not only blocks the city drainage systems but also ends up in water bodies such as rivers and lakes and ultimately affecting the marine ecosystem (Ferronato & Torretta, 2019). Therefore, managing the unplanned urban growth and municipal solid waste will be some of the key challenges local authorities will face in the coming years (Cohen 2006; Hoornweg and Bhada-Tata 2012).

In Nepal, urbanization is increasing at an alarming rate, putting enormous pressure on municipal services, particularly for managing the growing amount of waste generated (World Bank 2018). Before 2015, Nepal had less than 20% urban population. In 2015, Nepal adopted a new constitution, which has changed the political and administrative structure of the country. As a result of this change, the urban population suddenly jumped to 67% overnight. This change is due to the new administrative structure. Several villages have been clubbed together as new municipalities despite the fact that these new municipalities do not have the basic infrastructures (roads, hospitals, and safe drinking water). In the coming years, the headquarters of these municipalities are expected to have improved physical infrastructure

DOI: 10.4324/9781003253884-18

and basic facilities, encouraging the rural population to migrate to these newly improved cities. Due to the lack of proper infrastructure, most of the wastes produced in municipalities across Nepal are not being managed properly, creating environmental and health threats, especially in the slum and squatter areas, where the residents are less likely to afford better services and are often neglected by city officials.

In the coming years, these urban clusters are expected to have a better provision of basic services that incentivize rural to urban migration. This fact is found in most cities in Nepal, especially those around the main highways, reaching an annual urbanization rate of 3–4% (Bakrania, 2015) for the fastest-growing ones. This puts a lot of pressure on public services as it increases the amount of waste the cities have to deal with. Thus, waste management is one of the major challenges of unplanned urbanization. At the moment, municipal solid waste is not managed properly as a small fraction of the waste generated in the urban areas has been collected by waste collectors. The rest of the waste is burnt, dumped in open space, or used as fertilizer after composting. Scattered waste generally ends up in the drainage system that blocks the flow during excessive rainfall, resulting in water logging and urban flooding (Pervin et al., 2019).

For managing solid waste (MSW) properly, the segregation of different types of waste at the source is the first and the foremost important element. Without segregation at the source, the three key principles of MSW management – reduce, reuse, and recycle (3Rs) – could not be implemented properly. A study using data from Nepal's municipalities suggests that recycling plastic waste at a reasonable rate (67% recovery rate) could finance plastic-related waste management costs in Nepal (Bharadwaj, Rai, & Nepal, 2020). In addition to the 3Rs, properly disposing of the remaining waste is equally important, without which cities may face water logging issues when improperly disposed waste blocks the drainage canals (Pervin et al., 2019). Providing information on how to manage household waste better and installing waste bins in the streets help in increasing the cleanliness of the neighbourhood (Nepal et al. 2021). Housing price appreciates significantly in clean neighbourhoods in comparison to unclean neighbourhoods of the city (Nepal, Rai, Khadayat, & Somanathan, 2020). Therefore, 3Rs should now be 4Rs (reduce, reuse, recycle, and proper disposal), where the final R is taken for granted in general, but this is one of the equally important elements of MSW management. In Bharatpur, the majority of the city residents feel that the waste pick-up service has not been managed properly, and they are willing to pay 10–28% extra fee on top of the regular fee that they have been paying if the service gets improved (Rai, Nepal, Khadayat, & Bhardwaj, 2019).

Segregating household waste at the source means the involvement of household members in waste management, which sounds like a trivial issue but requires awareness of why segregation at the source is needed and how to do it properly. Studies suggest that sharing knowledge and experiences improves environmental values among citizens (Oskamp et al., 1991), while peer influence increases the probability of segregation at source and composting (Park, Lamons, & Roberts, 2002) and increases the reuse of discarded materials (Ekere, Mugisha, & Drake, 2009). Incorporating awareness programmes in school education would help entrench this kind of behaviour (Licy et al. 2013). Once environmentally friendly behaviour is established, such as recycling, it continues and being part of an environmental organization strengthens commitment to supporting the improvement of environmental quality (Torgler, García-Valiñas, & Macintyre, 2008).

This chapter focuses on the role of gender in the at-source segregation of household waste and recycling behaviour. There is a lack of understanding of the gender dynamics involved in at-source segregation, composting of biodegradable waste and recycling of useful materials. Therefore, using relatively large size of gender-disaggregated household survey data from one of the metropolitan cities in Nepal (Bharatpur), we try to better understand how gender roles and relations influence waste management at household level by examining the role of gender on at-source segregation, composting of biodegradable waste, and recycling of useful materials. We find that households where women take charge of managing household waste segregate waste at-source more often and tend to compost more in comparison to households where men are in charge of managing the household waste. However, there is no difference in recycling (selling to the collectors) of paper and plastic materials based on who manages the household waste. Still, more often than men, women tend to either give the paper/plastic waste to the collectors (for free) or throw it outside, suggesting that it is important to understand who is to be targeted to make a change in properly managing solid waste.

## 13.1 Inter-Linkages between Gender and Household Waste Management

Waste generation and management depend on social and cultural factors. Each society deals with these issues in different ways because demographic characteristics and socio-cultural norms and practices vary among places, societies, and communities (Vineeshiya and Mahees 2019). Gender relations are not equal and vary throughout the world in daily life as well as at work. These asymmetrical relations are based on traditional and stereotypical dimensions of the sexual division of labour upon which notions of gender are constructed. Therefore, one has to start to underline the importance and need to analyze environmental issues on the basis of gender. Conventional gender roles assign women the reproductive roles, i.e., work and activities related to domestic and care work such as childbearing and caring, care activities within the household that support family well-being such as cooking, cleaning, fetching water, washing, and attending to sick and elderly; while men are assigned the productive role, i.e., work related to activities that produce goods and services for consumption or trade (Moser 1989: Muhammad and Manu 2013).

Such gender division of roles has prompted suggestions that women tend to be more concerned about the environment (Davidson et al. 1996) and that they have a stronger sense of civic responsibility and willingness to improve the living conditions of the households, making them more active in social changes and thus an important channel of communication (Bulle, 1999), and that women are more altruist than men (Dietz, Kalof, & Stern, 2002).

Other studies have found that women are more likely to express their concern about the environment while men are more likely to influence other's behaviours (Dunlap, 1983); women are significantly more concerned than men about the local issue but not regarding global issues (Blocker & Eckberg, 1989) but less likely to take action (Blocker & Eckberg, 1997). On the contrary, Teal & Loomis (2000) found no significant impact of gender on willingness to pay for environmental programmes.

Various studies have shown the linkages between gender and waste management. Gender issues are present in waste management, from day-to-day handling activities at household levels to decision-making processes at the highest levels (Muchangos and Vaughter, 2019). Four main thematic areas have been identified in waste and gender by scholars and practitioners working in these areas. These are the gendered definition of waste, the gendered division of responsibilities for waste; community-based initiatives; and policy and practice (Tiwari 2001, Muller and Schienberg 1998, Scheinberg et al. 1999). Each of these is explained briefly below.

### Gendered definition of waste

Women's and men's individual decisions and choices are shaped by a combination of the roles and expectations assigned to them by the socio-cultural and gender structure and norms. This extends to the field of waste, and hence, 'waste is not a (gender) neutral concept' (Muchangos and Vaughter, 2019:4). Although waste is defined as something that does not have any value or is of use, individuals may differ in identifying and defining what is of value or useful for whatever reason. Thus, men and women will define something as waste depending on their role. For example, at the household level, something that is of no use or value for men may be of use for women as compost or animal feed, and similarly, something that is scrap to women could be of use to men as some machinery part.

*Gendered division of responsibilities for waste:* The division of responsibilities in waste management roles is also influenced by gender. The gender division of roles places all the work and activities related to cleaning and waste handling in the household and at times in the community on women, as this is part of their reproductive role and that too without pay. Waste management at the household level falls under women's role as part of their domestic work and thus places them in the position of waste collection, reuse, and sell at the household level (GWA and WASTE 2010, Scheinberg et al. 1999, Wilson et al. 2015). Gender plays a significant role in waste management outside the household level too. For instance, due to women, particularly women from poorer households, lower income-generating opportunities in developing countries for various reasons, including lack of skill, education, training, capital, women form the predominant group to survive by recovering materials from waste (Dias and Fernandez 2013, Muchangos and Vaughter 2019, Furedy 1990, Nguyen et al. 2003, Ocean Conservancy 2019, Scheinberg et al. 1999). However, at the higher levels of waste management – processing, planning, and decision-making – outside of the household, it is the men who are the main actors (GWA and WASTE 2010, Samson2003, Tiwari 2001, Woroniuk and Schalkwyk 1998).

Diving deeper into looking at different meanings and streams of waste, the link with gender in terms of power relations become evident as gender inequalities in access and control over resources come into play. For example, given the gender structures prevalent in most communities, women have less access and control over resources; therefore, when waste materials become valuable and income resources, then women often have limited access to these (GWA and WASTE 2010, Scheinberg et al. 1999, Woroniuk and Schalkwyk 1998). This is true not just at the community (or higher) level of waste management but also household level because although often household is looked like an indivisible unit, in reality, women and men within the household have differential access and control of resources (Kabeer, 1994). These clearly demonstrate that gender structure and dynamics are intricately linked to waste management.

***Community-based initiatives:*** Women's role and responsibility for cleanliness extends to the community level, and thus, they are actively involved in taking and depositing the household waste at the community collection and dump sites, often also keeping the community area clean, but all these are voluntary unpaid work (Samson 2003, Fredericks 2008). As soon as these waste collections and dumping work become monetized, there is usually a shift, with men taking over this work and women being pushed away (Muller and Schienberg 1998, Scheinberg et al. 1999, Wilson and Velis 2015). It is also often found that women who work in waste activities as paid workers are assigned to the lowest rung, underpaid, and work in dangerous social and human conditions; hence they are considered low-class citizens (GWA and WASTE 2010, Muller and Schienberg 1998, Samson 2003).

Gender also influences the micro waste enterprises in terms of access to finance and waste material(s). Given the inequality in access to resources, women have less access to financial resources to set up such enterprises.

Furthermore, there is also the association of certain materials for setting up such micro-enterprises to either men or women; for instance, plastic and textiles wastes are associated with women, while metal and construction wastes that are regarded as 'resource-intensive and physically demanding' are associated with micro-enterprises of men (Muchangos and Vaughter, 2019:5).

***Policy and practice:*** The gender structure and division of labour and roles places the women's role in the domestic and private sphere while the men's role is in the public sphere. As an extension of this and women's subordinate position in society is the curtailment of women's decision-making rights. Consequently, women are often restricted from accessing public positions, their political participation is curtailed, and their views and needs are often not considered. Despite women's high involvement in waste management activities at the household, and sometimes at the community level, they are absent in the higher decision-making and policy levels resulting in limited, if not none, integration of gender issues and women's roles in the programmes, plans, and policies. All these processes and levels are male-dominated (GWA and WASTE 2010, Muller and Schienberg 1998, Woroniuk and Schalkwyk 1998) and are reflected in the absence of consideration of gender perspectives and gender needs of women in waste management policy, information and education practice (Muchangos and Vaughter 2019, Schultz and Stiess 2009, Tiwari 2001, Wilson et al. 2015).

This chapter tries to explore behavioural differences between men and women in waste management habits and practices. It also attempts to examine if and to what extent gender affects waste management practices. Previous studies have tackled these questions in different places of the world with similar answers. A study (Bennagen, Nepomuceno, & Covar 2002) found that women tend to have a higher probability of segregating waste in comparison to men in Manila, and so did Beall (1997) in Bangladesh and Pakistan. A major reason for this is that in developing countries, following the gender norms and practices, the husband goes to work while the wife stays at home and is responsible for the unpaid care work (Addaati L et al. 2018), of which waste segregation is a part. Taking the premise that environmental behaviours are shaped by socio-cultural and political factors, this study, focusing on Nepal, explores this further.

## 13.2 Material and Method

### 13.2.1 Study Area and Waste Management System

This study is based on a household survey from Bharatpur Metropolitan City (BMC), one of the six metropolitan cities in Nepal, with a population size of around 300,000. This city is located in south-central Nepal, which is the fourth biggest city in the country. Out of 29 wards (smaller administrative units of the Metro), this study covers 14 wards as these wards are relatively more urban, comprising the core city area and its surroundings.

A few years back, the Asian Development Bank conducted a survey across the municipalities of Nepal in order to understand the volume of waste generated in Nepal's urban centres (ADB 2013). During that time, Bharatpur generated 32.5 tons of household waste and around 7 tons of commercial waste daily. Of this, 80% was organic, but only 25% of the waste was collected for disposal. After restructuring the city in 2017, Bharatpur Metro is spending approximately 2% of its total budget (NPR 80 million or US$0.7 million out of NPR 4.15 billion total city budget) on municipal waste management and related issues. This municipal budget is complemented by user fees collected from the households and businesses for disposing of solid waste generated by the households and the businesses.

Two private companies are providing door-to-door waste collection services in the city under a public-private partnership, where households who subscribe to the service pay NPR 30–100 (30 cents to US$1) and businesses pay NPR 200–4,000 (US$2–40), depending on the frequency of the waste collection service per month and volume of waste generated by the business entity. Currently, the subscription to the service is voluntary, and around 70% of city residents are subscribing to the waste collection service (Rai et al., 2019). Since the service fee is nominal and does not cover the full cost of waste management, the city provides a lump-sum subsidy to the private companies to cover their waste management cost.

Those households who do not subscribe to the service either compost biodegradable waste, feed the animals, burn, or dump in open space or drains, clog the drainage system (Pervin et al., 2019) and pollute both surface and groundwater with public health consequences. The collected waste is dumped on the riverbank in the absence of a sanitary landfill. The city encourages its inhabitants to compost organic waste by providing a 50% subsidy on a composter and door-to-door collection of plastic waste from some areas. However, due to heavy subsidies on the composter, the supply of composters is limited each year.

A major problem reported is that the pick-up service is irregular, and the frequency of the collection varies across neighbourhoods, making the pick-up time uncertain (Rai et al., 2019). As a result, households put their waste outside their houses to be picked up by the waste collector, but rag pickers often search through the waste piles hoping to get reusable and recyclable material, thus leading to scattering the plastic wastes in the streets, open spaces, and drainage canals, increasing the risk of waterlogging (Pervin et al., 2019). The study suggests that housing price in such unclean neighbourhoods is 25% less in Bharatpur as compared to cleaner neighbourhoods (Nepal et al., 2020), suggesting ample benefits for keeping the neighbourhoods clean.

Plastic waste is one of the key components of municipal solid waste, and some municipalities are implementing a ban on the use of single-use plastic bags. The success of such a ban on the use of single-use plastic bags has mixed results in Nepal, which mainly depends on the enforcement of the ban with sufficient fines for the violators (Bharadwaj, Baland, & Nepal, 2020). Therefore, putting extra tariffs on importing the raw materials to make single-use plastic materials (bags and bottles) may help encourage recycling plastic waste since the additional tariff makes the virgin plastic raw material expensive (Bharadwaj, Rai, et al., 2020).

### *13.2.2 Methodology*

One of the key outcome variables ($y$) is whether the households segregate household waste as the source, which is a binary variable, where $y = 1$ means that the household segregates household solid waste, and $y = 0$ means that they do not segregate it. Using different sets of control variables, we try to understand what influences the source waste segregation decision and the role gender plays in this decision. The logistic regression model provides internal consistency as it constrains the probability between 0 and 1, whereas linear probability models (LPM) do not assure this. However, in practice, the coefficients estimated from the LPM approximate the marginal effects from logistic regressions. Therefore, we use both LPM and logistic regression for our analysis.

In the study area, some households segregate paper and plastic waste from degradable waste while others do not. Therefore, we have collected information on the segregation of waste as a whole, the segregation of plastic and paper waste for selling, and the segregation of degradable waste for composting. For paper/plastic waste disposal methods, two options are identified: (1) sell to the vendors, or (2) give to waste collector, including burning or throwing it elsewhere. As households could use different options to manage paper/plastic waste (part of their waste could be sold and the other part given to the waste collector or thrown out/burnt) and these decisions are not independent of each other, the error terms are likely to be correlated. To address this issue, we use seemingly unrelated regressions (SUR). To analyze the degradable waste management decision, a simple logit or linear probability regression is enough as the households' responses are divided into two categories: managed at home (in composter or pit) or not.

Differentiating home management from other methods is an issue of interest as managing municipal solid waste at home is beneficial for two reasons: (a) it would reduce the waste collection burden and lower the waste management costs for the municipality and (b) household could compost the organic waste that could be used as fertilizer and sell reusable and recyclable items once they segregate the waste at source for extra income. In addition, these activities are beneficial to the local environment.

## 13.3 Data and Variables

### 13.3.1 Data Collection

For the research, primary data were collected from the Bharatpur Metro. The research team organized several consultation meetings, including focus group discussions with the relevant stakeholders (city officials, private companies that manage, collect, and dispose of municipal solid waste, and service seekers). These stakeholder consultations helped identify the main issues that the city faces while managing municipal solid waste. With this information, the research team was able to develop a context-specific questionnaire for the household survey.

Out of 29 wards (smaller administrative units), we collected data from 14 wards, which mainly form the core city area and the surroundings. Five women enumerators, who were trained for the survey, interviewed households during the September–October period of 2017. To ensure consistency, a field supervisor was also present whenever support was needed. Each enumerator interviewed about 210 households, with a total of 1,050 households in the sample. These 1,050 households were selected using a stratified random sampling technique, where the study area was first stratified into 14 segments (by ward). Within each ward, there were several smaller communities called Tole Lane Organizations (TLOs), with approximately 100 households on average in each TLO. In the study area, there were around 350 TLOs. We first randomly selected 150 TLOs using the proportional to population sampling method from 14 wards, and within each TLO, we randomly selected 7 households for the survey. The response rate was 100% since none of the households sampled for the survey declined to participate in the survey. If the household head was not available in the first visit, the enumerator visited the household a second time. Electronic devices were used for collecting the data, which helped the field supervisor with real-time monitoring of the survey for quality control.

### 13.3.2 Descriptive Statistics

Table 13.1 provides the basic statistics of the data used for the analysis. The total sample is divided into two groups based on who manages the household waste: men and women. The first part of the table shows the descriptive statistics of the outcome variables, while the second part shows the control variables used for the analysis. Out of the total sample, 62% of the respondents and 82% of the household waste managers were women. The decision to segregate household waste depends on perceived costs and benefits. However, rather than monetary costs, we use households' characteristics to understand the waste segregation decision.

*Table 13.1* Variables and Descriptive Statistics

| | *Variable description* | *Women* | *Men* | *Difference (t-stat)* |
|---|---|---|---|---|
| Outcome variables | | | | |
| Waste segregation | = 1 if the hh segregates waste | 0.87 | 0.65 | −5.903 *** |
| Waste Disposal Method | | | | |
| Home | = 1 if waste managed at home | 0.73 | 0.43 | 7.81 *** |
| Waste collector | = 1 if waste is given to waste collector | 0.86 | 0.88 | −0.68 |
| Other2 | =1 if waste is managed by another method | 0.90 | 0.93 | −1.26 |
| Paper and plastic management | | | | |
| Sold | = 1 if this waste is sold | 0.24 | 0.09 | 5.97*** |
| Other3 | = 1 if waste is given to waste collector or other | 0.86 | 0.63 | 6.17*** |
| Degradable waste management | | | | |
| Home4 | = 1 if waste managed at home | 0.72 | 0.37 | 8.966*** |
| Other5 | = 1 if it is not managed at home | 0.28 | 0.63 | −8.966*** |
| Control Variables | | | | |
| Age of the disposer | Age of the disposer (in years) | 40.72 | 44.82 | 3.621*** |
| Age of the hh head | Age of the hh head (in years) | 42.63 | 44.59 | 1.694* |
| Education | | | | |
| Education in years | highest education attained by respondent (in years) | 8.3 | 10.66 | 6.934*** |
| Low education | 5 years or less | 0.29 | 0.14 | 5.308*** |
| Med-Low Edu | between 5 and 9 years | 0.19 | 0.11 | 3.14*** |
| Med-High Edu | between 10 and 11 years | 0.25 | 0.26 | −0.337 |
| High Edu | 12 years or more | 0.27 | 0.48 | −5.482*** |
| Log monthly Expenditure | hh's monthly expenditure (in thsd NPR) | 3.15 | 3.3 | 6.934*** |
| Rented | = 1 if hh have rented room/ flat | 0.24 | 0.13 | −3.697*** |
| Family size | family size of the respondent | 5.01 | 4.97 | −0.217 |
| Degradable waste | percentage of degradable waste per week | 0.77 | 0.72 | −3.092*** |
| Ethnicity (% of total) | | | | |
| Brahman/Kshetry | = 1 if ethnicity is brahman/ kshetry | 0.63 | 0.73 | 2.597*** |
| Hill Dalit | if ethnicity is hill dalit | 0.04 | 0.04 | −0.122 |
| Hill Indigenous | = 1 if ethnicity is hill indigenous | 0.3 | 0.21 | −2.635*** |
| Tarai Indigenous | = 1 if ethnicity is tarai indigenous | 0.02 | 0.01 | −1.127 |
| Other | = 1 if ethnicity another one | 0.01 | 0.01 | −0.073 |

Source and note: Household Survey 2017; *** $p < 0.01$, ** $p < 0.05$, * $p < 0.1$

In the analysis, we control for both the waste disposer's age and the respondent's age (who is also the household head) since they are likely to be two different individuals and may have an impact on the decision to segregate the waste at home. One can think that an older household head has more experience and maybe more likely to reuse items than a younger one, and this will affect waste segregation decisions at the household level. Moreover, the age of the disposer is also likely to influence segregation decisions for similar reasons. We measured education in two different ways – years of schooling and education categories (illiterate, low, low-medium, medium, high school, and above). This was done because the effect of the schooling may not be linear. Increasing education by one year at a low level of education is likely to be different from the increase of one year at a higher level. Plus, with those categories, one can see the differential impact of education by gender: women have lower levels of education in the sample (48% of male and 27% of female in the sample has higher educational level). Other control variables are demographic characteristics and ethnicity of the households (Table 13.1).

## 13.4 Results

We discuss the key results in this section. We divide the results and discussion into three parts: (i) waste segregation at source: whether the household segregates waste at source, (ii) paper and plastic waste management: how paper and plastic waste is dealt with and (iii) degradable waste management: if degradable waste is composted at home or managed differently. In Table 13.2, results are displayed in three different segments where standard errors are clustered at the TLO level, and ward level fixed effects are used to account for heterogeneity across the wards that are not accounted for in the data or other unobservable. Such heterogeneity includes party affiliation of elected ward Chairs, their style of management, and other institutional differences across the wards. Such a fixed-effects model could minimize the omitted variable bias for a causal interpretation of the results.

### *13.4.1 Waste Segregation at Source*

The first segment of Table 13.2 shows marginal effects from logit regression from three different models where the outcome variable is whether the household segregates the waste generated at home and if there is any difference based on the gender of the waste manager at home. The first model is the basic model, where we control for household demographics and the education of the respondents. In the second model, we control for additional variables, including ethnicity, household consumption, and total waste generated. In the third model, we measured education in terms of

*Table 13.2* Gender and Household Waste management

| | *Waste segregation decision* | | | *Paper and plastic* | | *Degradable waste* |
|---|---|---|---|---|---|---|
| | *(1)* | *(2)* | *(3)* | *Sold* | *Other* | *At home* |
| Women disposure | 0.075** (0.037) | 0.090*** (0.035) | 0.088** (0.035) | 0.037 (0.028) | 0.123** (0.035)* | 0.119*** (0.038) |
| Women respondent | 0.073** (0.029) | 0.069** (0.029) | 0.062** (0.03) | −0.016 (0.023) | 0.069** (0.028) | 0.050* (0.029) |
| Disposer's age | 0.000(0.001) | 0.001 (0.001) | 0.001 (0.001) | 0.001 (0.001) | 0.000 (0.001) | 0.000 (0.002) |
| Respondent's age | 0.003** (0.002) | 0.003* (0.002) | 0.002(0.002) | −0.001(0.001) | 0.003**(0.001) | 0.002(0.002) |
| Resp's edu (yrs) | 0.081*** (0.025) | 0.071*** (0.027) | | 0.000 (0.002) | 0.005* (0.003) | 0.005 (0.004) |
| Log monthly exp | | 0.004 (0.017) | 0.006 (0.018) | 0.030* (0.016) | −0.008 (0.020) | 0.014 (0.027) |
| Hill dalit | | −0.089 (0.057) | −0.092 (0.056) | −0.116 *** (0.045) | −0.104* (0.055) | −0.081* (0.045) |
| Hill indigenous | | −0.035* (0.020) | −0.035* (0.029) | 0.01 (0.020) | −0.043* (0.024) | −0.027 (0.027) |
| Tarai indigenous | | −0.107*** (0.041) | −0.111** (0.043) | 0.021 (0.063) | −0.081 (0.077) | −0.129* (0.077) |
| Other ethnicity | | −0.052 (0.066) | −0.048 (0.068) | 0.072 (0.088) | −0.176 (0.107) | −0.102 (0.075) |
| Family Size | | −0.001 (0.005) | −0.002 (0.005) | 0.005 (0.004) | 0.001 (0.005) | 0.004 (0.005) |
| Rented home | | −0.031 (0.022) | −0.029 (0.022) | −0.035 (0.021) | 0.000 (0.026) | −0.025 (0.021) |
| HH total waste | | 0.009*** (0.003) | 0.009*** (0.003) | | | |
| Constant | | −2.780*** (0.707) | −3.002*** (0.820) | −1.933** (0.773) | −0.099 (0.085) | 0.281*** (0.104) |
| Observations | 1,050 | 1,050 | 1,050 | 1,050 | 1,050 | 1,050 |
| Log pseudo-likelihood | −347.52 | −336.33 | −337.78 | | | −387.74 |
| Pseudo *R*-squared | 0.27 | 0.29 | 0.3 | | | 0.42 |
| *R*-Squared | | | | 0.57 | 0.28 | |
| Breusch-Pagan Stat | | | | 22.22*** | | |

Notes: Instead of years of schooling, levels of education (low, medium, medium-high, and high) are controlled for in Model 3, but coefficients are insignificant and not reported in the table to save space. In each regression, we control for ward-level fixed effects; clustered standard errors at the TLO level are reported in parentheses; *** $p < 0.01$, ** $p < 0.05$, * $p < 0.1$.

categories (low, low-medium, medium, high with illiteracy as the base) as the effect of education may be non-linear.

Results suggest that when women are managing the household waste, it increases the probability of segregating the waste by around nine percentage points compared to the situation where men are managing the household waste (with an average segregation rate of 65% when men manage the household waste). This means that women tend to segregate household waste more than men by approximately nine percentage points. This result is robust to alternative specifications and significant at the 5% level.

The coefficients for the respondent age are positive and significant in all three models, suggesting that experience matters for segregating household waste. The respondent education seems to matter as well when used as years of schooling, but the level of education does not make much difference in segregating household waste.

Renting and family size seems to have no significant effect on the likelihood of segregating waste. This is interesting because one could expect those renting the house would segregate less as they probably care less about the place they rent and also because they are less likely to have animals to feed organic waste. Finally, the amount of total waste has a positive and significant effect on the probability of segregation at the source, meaning that as the total amount of waste increases, the likelihood of segregating waste at the source increases. Possibly, a larger volume of waste may indicate a better chance of earning some additional income from recycling and also the economies of scale for composting the degradable waste after segregation.

### *13.4.2 Paper and Plastic Waste Disposal*

The survey collects two methods of managing paper and plastic waste: (a) selling to the vendors (after segregation) or (b) other (keeping all waste together and sending it with the waste collectors or managing differently that includes burning and throwing out). Since these two decisions are interdependent, we use seemingly unrelated regression (SUR). The Breusch-Pagan test[1] is significant in suggesting the interdependent error process of these two models, requiring joint estimation. Our interest here is to see if the waste is segregated at home and recycled to the extent possible and if gender has a role in this, which not only helps to recycle paper and plastic waste but also lowers the waste management costs of the municipality as a household may also compost the degradable waste once segregated.

Our results (Table 13.2, second block) indicate that gender of the waste manager does not have much influence on selling (recycling) paper/plastic waste, meaning that men and women do not tend to have different behaviour regarding selling recovered paper and plastic from the waste stream. They may both sell when there is such an opportunity.

For 'other' methods (it includes – given to waste collector for free, burning, throwing elsewhere), the coefficient of women waste manager seems to be significant, suggesting that women waste managers tend to give paper/plastic waste to waste collector more often for free or manage it with alternative methods (throwing, burning, etc.). When women dispose of waste, the probability of using 'other method' increases by 12.3 percentage points in comparison to men managing the paper/plastic waste, keeping the other variables into account, suggesting that some targeted interventions on the awareness-related activities may help the household waste manager for properly disposing of household waste.

### 13.4.3 Degradable Waste

How the households manage the degradable waste is the final outcome variable, which is measured as binary (= 1 if degradable waste is managed at home (put in a pit/composter or fed to animals, 0 otherwise)). Since it is a binary outcome variable, we use logit regression. The last column of Table 13.2 reports the marginal effects. When women are the managers of household waste, the probability of composting or feeding to animals increases by 12 percentage points as compared to the men counterparts. When the respondent is a woman (household head), the probability of managing degradable waste at home increases by five percentage points, keeping other controls into account.

## 13.5 Discussion and Conclusion

In this chapter, we examine whether gender matters in household waste management decisions. Given the gender division of roles and responsibilities in Nepali culture, over 80% of the household waste managers are women, and they tend to segregate household waste more often than their male counterparts (7.5 to 9 percentage points more than men) and also tend to compost the degradable waste more often (12.3 percentage points higher) at home, but women more often tend to either give the paper/plastic waste to the collector for free or throw away instead of selling; and importantly education does not seem to have any influence on this. The socialization process as per gender structure is clearly the dominant factor in shaping the behavioural patterns of waste management at the household level.

Based on the gender division of labour, women are primarily responsible for all domestic work related to cleaning, food preparation, family health, maintenance of the home, and homestead, while men have the responsibility of the provider and income earning. With these basic primary responsibilities, women and men may view, manage, and prioritize domestic waste and its disposal differently (Muller and Schienberg, 1997). The gender construct shapes the way men and women value and revalue waste materials for different purposes, such as domestic use, other uses, saving on expenditure or for income, and so have different definitions of what is waste or garbage. Thus, as mentioned above, there is a gendered definition of waste, garbage, and resources (Muller and Schienberg 1997, Muller 2015, Poswa 2004), which reflects in the way they manage and dispose of waste.

The gender inequalities in access to and control over resources are also a critical dimension. Often women do not have equal access, right, or allocation of family finances, particularly where the woman does not earn an income herself. Consequently, this affects the choices women have on waste disposal methods. Time, another precious resource, also comes into play as women have multiple roles. Women are primarily involved in reproductive work, but at the same time, they are also involved in productive work and community work. Thus, given women's heavy workloads, they often have less available time, leading to men and women assigning different values to time spent on waste disposal.

We witness all these clearly in the findings described above, given in the following:

1. The gendered notion of women being the ones to take care of the health and hygiene of the household ingrains in women their responsibility of segregating and managing the household waste.
2. As a means of saving expenditure, women tend to manage degradable waste at home.
3. Women's gender roles also extend to caring for animals and managing home gardens; therefore, more women compost and use the waste to feed animals.
4. Women's way of valuing or revaluing waste as well as the value given to time spent on waste disposal differs from men leading to the finding that women waste managers are more likely to either throw or give the paper/plastic waste to the waste collectors (or throw/burn).

Overall, our study revealed that the gender of the household waste manager has differential impacts on waste disposal and degradable waste management approach, where women waste managers more often tend to segregate household waste and compost the degradable waste as compared to the situation where men are the managers of the household waste. Thus, gender roles, norms, and practices significantly shape the different behaviours of men and women when it comes to managing household waste. The finding that education, renting a house, or the size of the family does not play a significant factor in practice shows how deeply the socialization of gender roles and norms is entrenched in society. These factors are subsumed under gender roles and relations.

Given the gender structure and practices, women and men have different roles and priorities in the households and communities, which can be in contradiction to or in competition with each other, and this extends to waste management too. Therefore, it is crucial to recognize gender roles and relationships to efficiently plan and implement waste management.

These findings are important since segregating waste at home, recycling recyclable papers/plastics wastes, and composting degradable waste at home not only help in reducing the volume of the waste that goes to the landfill and extend the life of the landfill sites but also generates compost fertilizers to the households and also some cash income if they sell paper/plastic waste. South Asians also prefer to see waste to energy programmes from segregated organic waste (Haque et al. 2019). Such behavioural change for at-source segregation of waste and managing it properly not only helps generate resources for sustainable financing of the municipal solid waste management (Bharadwaj, Rai, et al., 2020) but also leads to appreciating housing property value in cleaner neighbourhoods (Nepal et al., 2020).

Since men and women tend to manage household waste differently, it is necessary to reach out to the right group of people to raise awareness for better management of household waste. For example, focusing on women may be a good option for policies to be effective since the majority of the household waste managers are women (over 80% in our sample) who are more likely to segregate and compost degradable waste.

Since women play a major role in the consumption and generation of waste at the household level, it is important to value their role and recognize them as a key to bringing about changes in their waste disposal and management habits by 'creating campaigns and information that are geared towards them' for effective behaviour changes. As primary caregivers, they can also be relied upon to share such awareness with the members of their family and children in particular (Ocean Conservancy, 2019:54). At the same time, the critical point is that such information and campaign should not be based on gender stereotypes, and directed only at women, and ignores the importance of changing men's behavioural patterns and attitudes towards waste management activities (GWA and WASTE 2010, Schultz and Stiess 2009). There need to be targeted messages for both men and women as well as for the different age groups.

Our results suggest that if the municipality intends to reduce the volume of the municipal solid waste at source, it would be better to provide training to women waste managers since they make up around 80% of the total waste managers in the sample and will have more effect in comparison to providing such training to men. Two kinds of policies are needed; (i) awareness-raising policies and (ii) economic incentives, where one cannot go without the other. Indeed, people need to be aware of the benefits of segregation but also need economic incentives to make sure they segregate the waste at the source. For example, pricing municipal waste collecting services differently based on whether households segregate waste and charging a lower monthly fee to those who segregate would be a good starting point for encouraging households for at-source segregation. Lack of awareness and incentives will lead to improper management of municipal solid waste, such as littering, even though waste bins are available. Not practising the 4Rs[2] leads to several problems such as not segregating household waste at home, not participating in cleanup activities, and not being cooperative in finding a solution for waste management. These problems can amplify, and the city can face more important challenges such as the clogging of drains, especially during the rainy season leading to waterlogging (Pervin et al., 2019). Waterlogging pollutes the surrounding environment and can become a major public health problem during rainy seasons when city residents use groundwater (using hand pumps) for drinking. Thus, changing city residents' behaviour is the key to solving the city's waste management problem since nothing can be done if the city residents are not aware of the drawbacks that their actions are causing. Understanding gender role in household waste management helps cities design appropriate intervention programmes.

## Acknowledgement

The authors would like to acknowledge the funding support from the International Development Research Center (IDRC), Ottawa, Canada (Grant #08283-001) under the Cities and Climate Change Research (2017-2020). The International Center for Integrated Mountain Development (ICIMOD), where three of the authors are affiliated, acknowledges with gratitude the support of the Governments of Afghanistan, Australia, Austria, Bangladesh, Bhutan, China, India, Myanmar, Nepal, Norway, Pakistan, Sweden, and Switzerland. The authors would like to acknowledge excellent research support from Rajesh K Rai, Madan S Khadayat, Clean Up Nepal, and coordination support from Birat Ghimire during the fieldwork and consultation process. However, the analysis, views as well as interpretations of the results presented in this research are those of the authors and should not be attributed to their affiliated organizations, their supporters or the funding agency.

## Notes

1 The Breusch–Pagan (BP) test is one of the most common tests for heteroskedasticity. It begins by allowing the heteroskedasticity process to be a function of one or more of the independent variables, and it is usually applied by assuming that heteroskedasticity may be a linear function of all the independent variables in the model.
2 **R**educe, **R**euse, **R**ecycle, and p**R**oper disposal (4Rs).

## References

Addaati, L. et al. 2018. *Care Work and Care Jobs for the Future of Decent Work*. Geneva: ILO. https://www.ilo.org/wcmsp5/groups/public/---dgreports/---dcomm/---publ/documents/publication/wcms_633135.pdf (accessed on 15 August 2020).

Asian Development Bank. 2013. *Solid Waste Management in Nepal: Current Status and Policy Recommendations*. Manila, Philippines: Asian Development Bank. https://www.adb.org/sites/default/files/publication/30366/solid-waste-management-nepal.pdf (accessed on 18 February 2021).

Bakrania, S. 2015. *Urbanisation and Urban Growth in Nepal (GSDRC Helpdesk Research Report 1294)*. Birmingham, UK: GSDRC, University of Birmingham. http://www.gsdrc.org/wp-content/uploads/2015/11/HDQ1294.pdf (accessed on 19 August 2020).

Beall, J. 1997. "Thoughts on Poverty from a South Asian Rubbish Dump: Gender, Inequality and Household Waste." *IDS Bulletin*, 28(3), 73–90. https://core.ac.uk/download/pdf/286044643.pdf (accessed on 18 June 2020).

Bennagen, M. E., G. Nepomuceno, and R. Covar. 2002. *Solid Waste Segregation and Recycling in Metro Manila: Household Attitudes and Behavior*. Quezon City: Resource, Environment and Economic Centre for Studies (REECS) https://www.nswai.org/docs/Solid%20Waste%20Segregation%20and%20Recycling%20in%20Metro%20Manila.pdf (accessed on 19 August 2020).

Bharadwaj, B., J. M. Baland, and M. Nepal. 2020a. "What Makes a Ban on Plastic Bags Effective? The Case of Nepal." *Environment and Development Economics* 25(2): 95–114. doi:10.1017/S1355770X19000329.

Bharadwaj, B., R. K. Rai, and M. Nepal. 2020b. "Sustainable Financing for Municipal Solid Waste Management in Nepal." *Plos One* 15(8), e0231933. doi:10.1371/journal.pone.0231933.

Blocker, T. J., and D. L. Eckberg. 1989. "Environmental Issues as Women's Issues: General Concerns and Local Hazards." *Social Science Quarterly* 70(3): 586–593. http://www.worldcat.org/title/environmental-issues-as-womens-issues-general-concerns-and-local-hazards/oclc/669247860 (accessed on 1 January 2020).

Blocker, T. J., and D. L. Eckberg. 1997. "Gender and Environmentalism: Results from the 1993 General Social Survey." *Social Science Quarterly* 74(1):841–858. https://psycnet.apa.org/record/1997-38825-002 (accessed on 15 January 2020).

Bulle, S. 1999. *Issues and Results of Community Participation in Urban Environment: Comparative Analysis of Nine Projects on Waste Management (UWEP Working Document 11)*. Gouda: ENDA/WASTE. https://www.ircwash.org/sites/default/files/Bulle-1999-Issues.pdf (accessed on 16 August 2020).

Cohen, B. 2006. "Urbanization in Developing Countries: Current Trends, Future Projections, and Key Challenges for Sustainability." *Technology in Society* 28 (1–2): 63–80. doi:10.1016/j.techsoc.2005.10.005.

Davidson, Debra J., and W. R. Freudenburg. 1996. "Gender and Environmental Risk Concerns." *Environment and Behavior* 28 (3): 302–339. doi:10.1177/0013916596283003.

Dias, S., and L. Fernandez .2013. "Waste Pickers – A Gendered Perspective." In *Powerful Synergies: Gender Equality, Economic Development and Environmental Sustainability*, United Nations Development Programme. http://wiego.org/publications/wastepickers-gendered-perspective (accessed on 18 May 2020).

Dietz, T., L. Kalof, and P. C. Stern. 2002. "Gender, Values, and Environmentalism." *Social Science Quarterly* 83 (1): 353–364. doi:10.1111/1540-6237.00088.

Douglas, I., K. Alam, M. Maghenda, Y. Mcdonnell, L. Mclean, and J. Campbell. 2008. "Unjust Waters: Climate Change, Flooding and the

Urban Poor in Africa." *Environment and Urbanization* 20 (1): 187–205. doi:10.1177/0956247808089156.

Dunlap, R. E. 1983. "Male-Female Differences in Concern for Environmental Quality." *International Journal of Women's Studies*, 6(4): 291–301. https://psycnet.apa.org/record/1984-30243-001 (accessed on 16 August 2020).

Ekere, W., J. Mugisha, and L. Drake. 2009. "Factors Influencing Waste Separation and Utilization Among Households in the Lake Victoria Crescent, Uganda." *Waste Management* 29(12): 3047–3051. doi:10.1016/j.wasman.2009.08.001.

Ferronato, N., and V. Torretta. 2019. "Waste Mismanagement in Developing Countries: A Review of Global Issues." *International Journal of Environmental Research and Public Health* 16 (6): 1060. doi:10.3390/ijerph16061060.

Fredericks, R. 2008. "Gender and the Politics of Trash in Dakar: Participation, Labor and the "Undisciplined" Woman." In *Thinking Gender Papers; UCLA Cent. Study Women*. Los Angeles, CA. http://www.gdrc.info/docs/waste/011.pdf (accessed on 16 August 2020).

Furedy, C. 1990. "Women and Solid Wastes in Poor Communities." In Infrastructure for Low-Income Communities: Proceedings of the 16th WEDC International Conference, edited by Smith, M. D. Hyderabad, India, 27–31 August 1990, 51–54. https://repository.lboro.ac.uk/ndownloader/files/17230724/1 (accessed on 17 August 2020).

GWA, and WASTE. 2010. "No capacity to waste." In *Training Module Gender and Waste*. Dieren, The Netherlands: GWA. http://genderandwater.org/en/gwa-products/capacity-building/no-capacity-to-waste/at_download/file (accessed on 16 August 2020).

Haque, A. K., H. D. Lohano, P. Mukhopadhyay, M. Nepal, F. Shafeeqa, and S. P. Vidanage. 2019. "NDC Pledges of South Asia: Are the Stakeholders Onboard?" *Climatic Change* 155 (2): 237–244. doi:10.1007/s10584-019-02417-6.

Hoornweg, D., and P. Bhada-Tata. 2012. "What a Waste: A Global Review of Solid Waste Management." *Urban Development Series; Knowledge Papers no. 15*. Washington, DC: World Bank. © World Bank. License: CC BY 3.0 IGO. https://openknowledge.worldbank.org/handle/10986/17388 (accessed on 18 June 2020).

Kabeer N. 1994. *Reversed Realities: Gender Hierarchies in Development Thought*. London: Verso Publishers.

Licy, C. D., R. Vivek, K. Saritha, T. K. Anies, and C. T. Josphina. 2013. "Awareness, Attitude and Practice of School Students Towards household Waste Management." *Journal of Environment*, 2(6):147–150. https://eprints.manipal.edu/139087/ (accessed on 16 June 2020).

McGranahan, G., D. Balk, and B. Anderson. 2007. "The Rising Risks of Climate Change: Urban Population Distribution and Characteristics in Low Elevation Coastal Zones." *Environment and Urbanization* 19: 17–37. doi:10.1177/0956247807076960.

Moser, C. 1989. "Gender Planning in the Third World: Meeting Practical and Strategic Gender Needs." *World Development* 17(11): 1799–1825. doi:10.1016/0305-750X(89)90201.

Muchangos, dos Letícia, and P. Vaughter. 2019. "Gender Mainstreaming in Waste Education Programs: A Conceptual Framework." *Urban Science* 3 (1): 29. doi:10.3390/urbansci3010029.

Muhammad, M. N., and H. I. Manu. 2013. "Gender Roles in Informal Solid Waste Management in Cities of Northern Nigeria: A Case Study of Kaduna Metropolis." *Academic Research International. Part-I: Natural and Applied Sciences* 4 (5): 142–153. SAVAP International. http://www.savap.org.pk/journals/ARInt./Vol.4(5)/2013(4.5–16).pdf (accessed on 16 June 2020).

Muller, M. 2015. "Gender, Social Inequality and Waste Management." *World Bank, Draft Planning Guide for MSWM (Solid Waste Management)*. online document. https://www.wiego.org/sites/default/files/resources/files/Dias-Ogando-gender-and-waste-toolkit-book-three.pdf (accessed on 15 August 2020).

Muller, M. S., and A. Schienberg. 1997."Gender and Urban Waste Management." Paper presented at the Gender, Technology and Development Conference, organized by TOOL/ TOOLCONSULT, Amsterdam. https://www.gdrc.org/uem/waste/swm-gender.html (accessed on 16 August 2020).

Muller, M. S., and A. Scheinberg. 1998. Gender and Waste Electronic Discussion Group, 9–31 May 1998. Gouda, The Netherlands: WASTE. http://www.gdrc.info/docs/waste/004.pdf (accessed on 15 April 2020).

Nepal, M., R. K. Rai, M. S. Khadayat, and E. Somanathan. 2020. "Value of Cleaner Neighborhoods: Application of Hedonic Price Model in Low Income Context." *World Development* 131: 104965. doi:10.1016/j.worlddev.2020.104965.

Nepal, M., B. Bhardwaj, A. K. Nepal, M. S. Khadayat, I. A. Pervin, R. K. Rai, and E. Somanathan, 2021. "Making Urban Waste Management and Drainage Sustainable in Nepal" In *Climate Change and Community Resilience: Insights from South Asia*, pp. 325–338. New York: Springer.

Nguyen, H., C. G. Chalin, T. M. Lam, and V. W. Maclaren.2003. "Health and Social Needs of Waste Pickers in Vietnam." Research paper. *Canadian International Development Agency (CIDA) WASTE-ECON Programme South East Asia*. http://sites.utoronto.ca/waste-econ/GenderBook.pdf (accessed on 30 April 2020).

Ocean Conservancy. 2019. *The Role of Gender in Waste Management. GA Circular*. Singapore: GA Circular. www.gacircular.com https://oceanconservancy.org/wp-content/uploads/2019/06/The-Role-of-Gender-in-Waste-Management.pdf (accessed on 19 April 2020).

Oskamp, S., M. J. Harrington, T. C. Edwards, D. L. Sherwood, S. M. Okuda, and D. C. Swanson. 1991. "Factors Influencing Household Recycling Behavior." *Environment and Behavior* 23 (4): 494–519. doi:10.1177/0013916591234005.

Park, W. M., K. S. Lamons, and R. K. Roberts. 2002. "Factors Associated with Backyard Composting Behavior at The Household Level." *Agricultural and Resource Economics Review* 31 (2): 147–156. doi:10.1017/s1068280500003968.

Pervin, I. A., S. M. M. Rahman, M. Nepal, A. Kalam E. Haque, H. Karim, and G. Dhakal. 2019. "Adapting to Urban Flooding: A Case of Two Cities in South Asia." *Water Policy* 22 (S1): 162–188. doi:10.2166/wp.2019.174.

Poswa, T. T. 2004. "The Importance of Gender in Waste Management Planning: A Challenge for Solid Waste Managers." In Proceedings: 8th World Congress on Environmental Health, 22–27 February 2004. Durban, South Africa. https://www.academia.edu/6889691/Importance_of_Gender_in_Waste_Management-_A_Challenge_for_Solid_Waste_Managers (accessed on 15 April 2020).

Rai, R. K., M. Nepal, M. S. Khadayat, and B. Bhardwaj. 2019. "Improving Municipal Solid Waste Collection Services in Developing Countries: A Case of Bharatpur Metropolitan City, Nepal." *Sustainability* 11 (11): 3010. doi:10.3390/su11113010.

Samson, M. 2003. *Dumping on Women: Gender and Privatisation of Waste Management*. Union Gauteng, South Africa: Municipal Services Project (MSP) and the South African Municipal Workers. https://www.municipalservicesproject.org/sites/municipalservicesproject.org/files/publications/Samson-2003-Dumping_on_Women_Gender_privatisation_waste_management.pdf (accessed on 9 January 2020).

Scheinberg, A., M. Muller, and E. L. Tasheva. 1999. Gender and Waste: Integrating Gender into Community Waste Management: Project Management Insights and Tips from an e-mail Conference, 9–13 May 1998. Urban Waste Expertise Programme (UWEP) and the Netherlands Development Assistance (NEDA), working document 12. https://www.ircwash.org/sites/default/files/Scheinberg-1999-Gender.doc (accessed on 26 April 2020).

Schultz, I., and I. Stiess. 2009. *Gender Aspects of Sustainable Consumption Strategies and Instruments*. EUPOPP Work Package 1, Deliverable 1.1. *Öko-Institut*. http://www.isoe-publikationen.de/uploads/media/eupopp-gender-isoe-2009.pdf (accessed on 29 April 2020).

Teal, G. A., and J. B. Loomis. 2000. "Effects of Gender and Parental Status on the Economic Valuation of Increasing Wetlands, Reducing Wildlife Contamination and Increasing Salmon Populations." *Society & Natural* Resources 13(1), 1–14. doi:10.1080/089419200279207.

Tiwari, N. 2001. *Gender Roles in Environmental Household Waste Management: A Case Study inPalmerston North, New Zealand*. Palmerston North, New Zealand: Ph.D. Thesis, Massey University. https://mro.massey.ac.nz/handle/10179/7193 (accessed on 16 April 2020).

Torgler, B., M. García-Valiñas, and A. Macintyre. 2008. "Justifiability of Littering: An Empirical Investigation." (Working Paper no. 2008-8). Basil, Switzerland: Center for Research in Economics, Management, and the Arts. http://www.crema-research.ch/papers/2008-08.pdf ( accessed on 18 October 2020).

Vineeshiya, M. N., and M. T. M. Mahees. 2019. "Environmental Attitudes and Discourse of Community Participation in Solid Waste Management." *International Educational Applied Research Journal (IEARJ)* 03(08), E-ISSN: 2456-6713. https://www.academia.edu/42886219/ENVIRONMENTAL_ATTITUDES_AND_DISCOURSES_OF_COMMUNITY_PARTICIPATION_IN_SWM_SRI_LANKA (accessed on 20 October 2020).

Wilson, D. C., L. Rodic, P. Modak, R. Soos, A. Carpintero, K. Velis, and O. Simonett. 2015. *Global Waste Management Outlook*. Nairobi, Kenya: United Nations Environment Programme (UNEP). https://www.uncclearn.org/wp content/uploads/library/unep23092015.pdf (accessed on 18 October 2020).

Wilson, D. C. and C. A. Velis 2015. "Waste Management – Still a Global Challenge in the 21st Century: An Evidence-Based Call for Action." *Waste Management & Research* 33(12): 1049–1051. doi:10.1177/0734242X15616055

World Bank. 2018. *What a Waste 2.0 Introduction*. https://openknowledge.worldbank.org/handle/10986/30317 (accessed on 24 August 2020).

Woroniuk, B., and J. Schalkwyk. 1998. *Waste Disposal & Equality between Women and Men*. Stockholm, Sweden: Swedish International Development Cooperation Agency (SIDA). https://www.oecd.org/dac/gender-development/1849277.pdf (accessed on 24 August 2020).

Chapter 14

# Fabricated Electric Fencing

## A Promising Strategy for Reducing Crop Damages from Wildlife in Bhutan

*Jamyang Choda, Heman Das Lohano, and Priya Shyamsundar*

### Introduction

Natural ecosystems offer numerous benefits, including clean water, air and food, climate regulation, disease management, spiritual fulfilment, and aesthetic enjoyment (Springer 2009; MEA 2005), making conserving the earth's biodiversity vital for human survival and well-being (Marchal et al. 2011). A large literature identifies the value of the many goods and services freely provided by nature to different beneficiaries (Sunderlin et al. 2005, Angelsen et al. 2014). Forests are also important for meeting the Sustainable Development Goals, particularly Goal One, which seeks to reduce poverty (Miller et al. 2020: Cheng et al. 2017: Razafindratsima 2020). Over 1.6 billion people live within 5 km of forests (Newton et al. 2020), many of whom live in poverty (Miller et al. 2020). Some 40% of the extremely rural poor are estimated to live in forest and savannah areas (FAO and UNEP 2020). Thus, in key geographies, forests and trees are critical to meeting the 2030 agenda for sustainable development (Wolff 2018, 2021: Miller et al. 2020).

Forests and trees contribute to poverty reduction in multiple ways (Miller and Hajjar 2020; Cheng *et al.* 2017). Many households depend on forests and trees for subsistence goods and services, and people can increase their asset base by using timber and non-timber products for commerce (Vedeld et al. 2004 2007; Angelsen et al. 2014: Shyamsundar et al. 2020). Forests also act as a safety net, helping smooth consumption during lean periods (Pattanayak and Sills 2001; Wunder et al. 2014). In addition, forest ecosystem services, such as heat reduction, pollination, and flood regulation services, contribute to health and livelihood activities (Campbell et al. 2018; Wolff et al. 2018; Das and Vincent 2009; MEA 2005). Thus, it is important that sustainable forest management and poverty reduction be undertaken as linked efforts in forested landscapes.

While there are many benefits from forest conservation, forests also generate negative externalities that can be particularly costly to forest-proximate communities. The costs of conservation stem from multiple sources,

DOI: 10.4324/9781003253884-19

including displacement of people from areas that are protected, limitations on access and use of natural resources, land-grabbing and encroachment, forest fires, crop and livestock predation by wild animals, pest infestation, and zoonotic disease (Jagger et al. 2020; Brockington and Wilkie 2015; Springer 2009). Notably, the distribution of costs and benefits of forest conservation can vary. Often, the benefits from conserving biodiversity and the earth's ecosystems accrue globally, while the costs of protection can be borne by local communities (IUCN 2005). If forest-related external costs are ignored and remain unaddressed, long-term efforts to safeguard ecosystem services can be weakened (MEA 2005).

Human-wildlife conflicts, important since the evolution of human history, prevail wherever there is an overlap between human needs and wildlife requirements (Goldstein et al. 2006:IUCN 2005: UNDP 2013)), with increasing human population density and reductions in wildlife habitats contributing to growth in conflicts (Linkie et al. 2007: Nyhus 2016). Conflicts in Asia and Africa typically arise because farmers lose a significant proportion of their crops to elephants (Naughton-Treves, Lisa. 2008: Lamarque et al. 2009: Madhusudan and Sankaran 2010: Rangarajan et al. 2010). A large body of evidence from across South Asia documents the benefits and costs associated with forest conservation to local communities (Sharma *et al.* 2020; Shyamsundar and Ghate 2014; Shyamsundar et al. 2018), especially as they pertain to human-wildlife conflicts (Anand and Radhakrishna 2017; Neupane et al. 2017). Recent research from Nepal, for instance, attributes some 25% of crop production losses to elephant raids in the Terai region (Neupane *et al.* 2017). In Bhutan, a study of 274 households living around the Jigme Singye Wangchuck National Park, one of its largest national parks, points to all households bearing crop damages, mainly from wild pigs (*Sus scrofa*) (Wang et al. 2006 and Wang and Macdonald 2006). Some 20% of farmers reported a loss of domestic animals to wild predators, resulting in annual financial losses of 17% of per capita income on average (Wang and Macdonald 2006).

People use numerous strategies, both lethal and non-lethal, to prevent and reduce the impact of wildlife-related conflict (Conover 2002: Kaczensky et al. 2004). Economic measures include crop or livestock insurance and compensation schemes (Ogra, Monica V. 2008: Ogra, M., and R. Badola 2008: Karanth et al. 2012: Johnson et al. 2018: Palden 2019). Common mitigation measures include expensive government-assisted infrastructure and small, low-cost measures undertaken by individual households (Nyhus 2016). While electric fencing needs significant investments in both establishment and maintenance, several studies point to their effectiveness (Chettri et al. 2013; Wildlife Conservation Division 2013). If properly erected, these fences are durable and protect against multiple species and have been a successful strategy in India, Kenya, Namibia, and many other nations (O'Connell-Rodwell et al. 2000:

Kolowski and Holekamp 2006: Kioko et al. 2008: Kalam et al. 2018). In Namibia, for instance, electric fencing has contributed to large-scale reductions in human-elephant conflicts (Hoare 2001). Despite high costs, electric fencing is cost-effective in reducing elephant attacks, which has, in turn, allowed the farmers to harvest increased yields (Kioko *et al.* 2008, O'Connell-Rodwell *et al.* 2000).

While it is not possible to fully eradicate wildlife impacts from human-used landscapes, humans and wildlife can coexist with favourable government policies and societal support (Nyhus,2016). In this context, our study aims to evaluate the viability of a low-cost strategy deployed to prevent wildlife-related damages in Bhutan, a highly forested country with significant human-wildlife interactions.

## 14.1 Human-Wildlife Conflict in Bhutan

With a 0.7 million population, Bhutan is a small landlocked country in the Eastern Himalayas. Some 60% of Bhutan's population depend on agriculture (NSB 2014, Dendup and Tshering 2018). Bhutan has more than 70% forested area, and over half of its total area is protected (World Bank 2020). Bhutan has been very successful in its conservation efforts and derives significant extended benefits from ecosystem services (WWF 2016).

Bhutan is internationally recognized for its conservation and environmental efforts (WWF 2016). The protection of nature and the environment is central to the Royal Government of Bhutan's goals to promote Gross National Happiness Commission (GNHC 2000). Due to its strong conservation policies, Bhutan today remains the only carbon-neutral country in the world (National Environment Commission 2019). However, this success comes with costs. Human-wildlife conflict is a serious issue, with farmers losing substantial amounts of crops and livestock to wildlife annually (MoAF 2008; Sangay and Vernes 2008: Wang 2004).

Based on agricultural statistics from the Ministry of Agriculture and Forest, it is observed that the incidence of human-wildlife conflict in Bhutan is increasing. Figure 14.1 shows that the average loss of crops to wild animals has gradually increased from 6,144 metric tonnes (MT) in 2013 to 8251 MT in 2017.

There are regional variations in wildlife damage. Average crop losses to wild animals were highest in the southern region (2,297.8 MT), followed by the eastern region (2,029 MT). The western region experienced the least loss with 1,280.7 MT in the same time period (Fig.14. 2 A). Figure 14.2 B shows the average loss of crops in metric tonnes from 2013 to 2017. Maize is the most damaged crop (4,216.9 MT), followed by paddy (1,692.1 MT) and potato (1,123.7MT). We note that the main cereal crops grown by Bhutanese farmers are paddy, maize, wheat, buckwheat, and millet (DOA, Department of Agriculture – 2013, 2014, 2015, 2016, 2017).

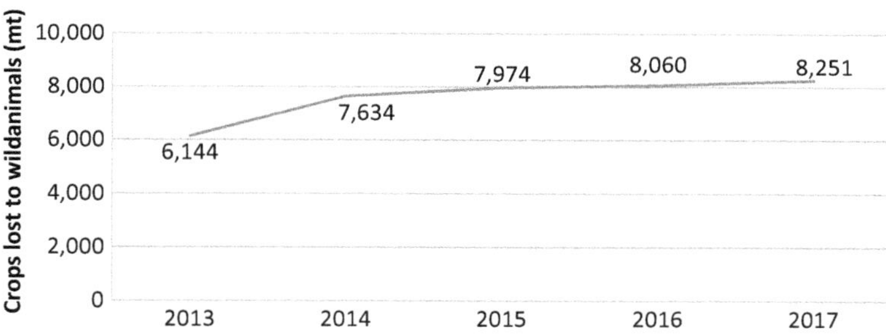


*Figure 14.1* Average crop lost to wild animals in Metric Tonnes (MT) from 2013 to 2017. Note: Crops include maize, paddy, potato, buckwheat, millet, barely, wheat, and vegetables. *Source:* Agriculture Statistics, Ministry of Agriculture and Forest, RGOB, 2013–2017.

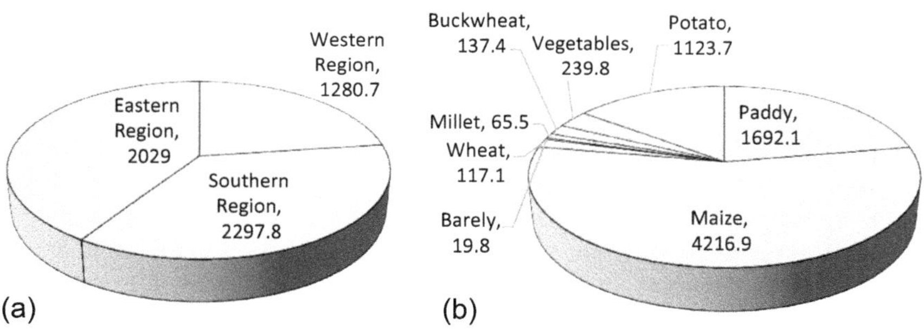


*Figure 14.2* Average loss of crops (MT) to wild animals from 2013 to 2017 by crop type (A) and region (B). *Source:* Agriculture Statistics, Ministry of Agriculture and Forest, RGOB, 2013–2017.

Farmers in Bhutan spend a significant number of days and nights guarding their crops against wild animals. Figure 14.3 shows that farmers in the eastern region spend the highest number of days (54) and nights (70) guarding their crops, followed by the western region with 70 nights and 42 days. There is a slight difference in the number of cropping months between crops; however, the average number of cropping months in Bhutan is around seven months. For example, maize and paddy are grown in March and harvested in October; on the other hand, potato is planted in February and harvested in July/September (Katwal et al. 2009 and Ghimiray et al. 2013). Considering the average duration of cropping months in Bhutan, Bhutanese farmers spend more than half of their cropping season guarding their crops against wild animals.

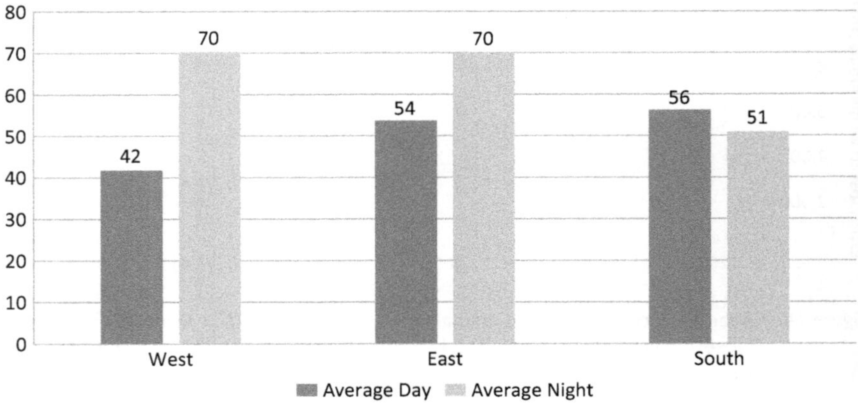


*Figure 14.3* Average number of days and nights spent on guarding crops against wildlife by region (2014–2017). *Source:* Agriculture Statistics, Ministry of Agriculture and Forest, RGOB, 2014–2017.

Recognizing the seriousness of the human-wildlife conflict, the government, communities, and households have initiated different efforts to protect wildlife. One policy response has been in the form of compensation schemes. A first attempt was made in 2011 by the Nature Conservation Division, Ministry of Agriculture (Ministry of Agriculture and Forest, Royal Government of Bhutan 2020) to create a human-wildlife endowment fund. This fund, set up to pay compensation to communities for wildlife damages to crops and domestic animals, was piloted in Bjena, Nubi, and Dangchu in West, Langchenphu, Tsamang, and Chimung in the east, Dhur, Nubi, and Nabji-Korphu in central areas, and Sibsoo and Lhamozingkha in the south (Wildlife Conservation Division 2013). However, this community-based mechanism largely failed because of a lack of community contribution and some mismanagement (Wildlife Conservation Division 2013; Kuensel 2019). The current government is now seeking to launch an alternate financial scheme. It plans to raise US$35 million in order to create a fund that would payout Nu. 16 million (~ US$ 213,000)[1] annually through a crop and livestock insurance scheme (Kuensel 2019).

The government of Bhutan has also invested in and installed electric fences in many areas to protect crops (Dema 2015). A regional agriculture research centre in eastern Bhutan developed its own low-cost fabricated electric fencing system, which has been piloted in different places east of Bhutan. This system is claimed to be very effective in crop protection against wildlife (Chettri et al. 2013: Zangmo 2013). This fence was installed at a very low cost of about 8,870 Nu. per kilometre, uses local inputs such as a fabricated energizer, fence wire, iron nails, high-density polyethylene (HDPE) pipe and wooden poles (Bumdeling Wildlife Sanctuary 2018: Wildlife Conservation Division (WCD) 2010).

In contrast, the most commonly introduced electric fences in Bhutan cost approximately 259,402 Nu. per kilometre (Wildlife Conservation Division 2013). At first sight, the locally fabricated electric fence seems to be the best option economically. This study evaluates the costs and benefits of FEF to ascertain its economic viability.

## 14.2 Study Area and Data

Our study area is a small administrative area, Bartsham *Gewog*, in eastern Bhutan. Bhutan is administered by 20 districts, with each district divided further into Gewogs. Bartsham *Gewog* (in Trashigang District), with a population of 465 households (3,465 people), is made up of five smaller administrative units or *Chiwogs*. Among the five Agriculture Research and Development Centres, Wengkhar (one of the four major agriculture research centres in Bhutan, and it is located in the eastern region) installed locally Fabricated Electric Fencing in Muktangkhar *Chiwog*. FEF in this *Chiwog* covers around 40 households and 187 acres of land. This is one of 41 *Chiwogs* where locally fabricated electric fencing was piloted by the government between 2006 and 2014 (Penjor et al. 2014).

To understand the impacts of FEFs, we undertook a survey of farm households and collected plot-specific information from farmers in Muktangkhar and four neighbouring *Chiwogs*. The sampling frame for identifying households for the survey was drawn from the list of households obtained from the Bartsham *Gewog* Office. Bartsham *Gewog* had 465 officially registered households, of which 120 were empty. This can be largely ascribed to people having migrated to other places, especially urban centres. We first undertook a census of Mugtangkhar *Chiwog* and identified 30 households for our survey after excluding empty households. In addition, we randomly selected 20 households from each of the other four *Chiwogs* using Excel's random number generator. Thus, we sampled and surveyed 110 households (32% of a total of 345 households, excluding empty households) in the *Gewog* (Table 14.1). This study is based on the primary data collected from household surveys in May 2014.

The household survey collected information on demographic characteristics, landholdings, and plot-level information such as cultivated or fallow, reason for leaving fallow, distance of the plot from the nearest forest, types of crops grown, area of the plot, ever experience crop damage by wild animal in last one year or not, types of protective measures used, cost of putting up different mitigation measures, expected output, actual output harvested, crop damage by wildlife and others. A series of key interviews and focus group discussions (FGD) also informed the study.

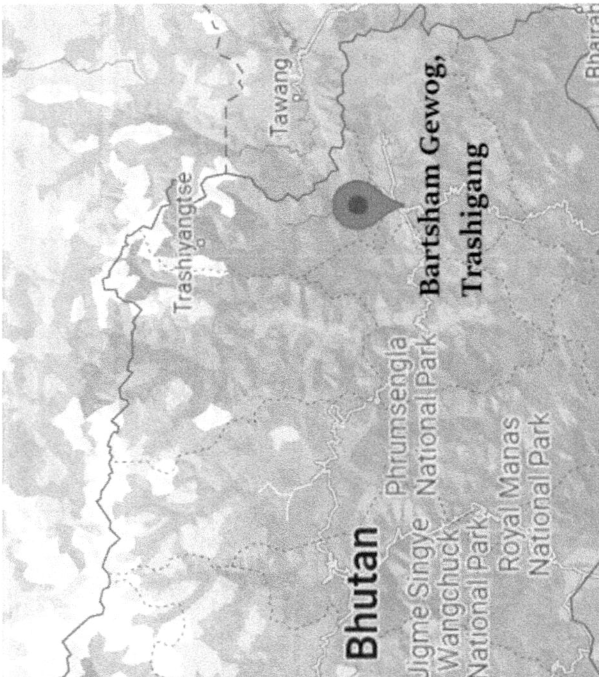


*Figure 14.4* Map of the study area, Bartsham Gewog, Trashigang. *Source:* Geopolitical map of Bhutan (available in Google maps).

*Table 14.1* Sampled Households and Plots for Bartsham Gewog

| *Sl.no* | *Name of the chiwogs* | *No. of households registered* | *No. of empty households* | *Actual no. of households* | *No. of households sampled and surveyed* | *No. of plots* |
|---|---|---|---|---|---|---|
| 1 | Trashang | 109 | 21 | 88 | 20 | 87 |
| 2 | Nangkhar | 136 | 42 | 94 | 20 | 114 |
| 3 | Kumung | 108 | 29 | 79 | 20 | 86 |
| 4 | Dzongthung | 67 | 13 | 54 | 20 | 128 |
| 5 | Muktangkhar (Locally Fabricated Electric Fencing area) | 45 | 15 | 30 | 30 | 119 |
| Total | | 465 | 120 | 345 | 110 | 534 |

Note: In total, 465 households are officially registered under the Bartsham subdistrict, among which 120 were empty because of migration.

## 14.3 Methods

To assess the economic returns to locally fabricated electric fencing (FEF), we estimate the costs and benefits of crop production at the farm level, considering the probability of crop damages from wildlife with and without fencing. We first examine the effect of FEF on the probability of crop damage by wildlife by estimating an econometric model using plot-level data from the household survey. Next, using plot-level data from farms without FEF, we estimate the average damages in Nu. per acre on the plots that were damaged by wild animals. The annual benefit of having FEF per acre is calculated by multiplying average crop damage per acre on damaged plots and reduction in the probability of crop damage by wild animals under FEF. The annual benefit of FEF is also calculated for 15 km FEF by multiplying the annual benefit per acre (Nu.) and area under cultivation. The benefit from the scrap value of the FEF is also considered at the end of the life span of the fence. Finally, a cost-benefit analysis is conducted using the total benefits and total costs associated with 15 km FEF installed in the study area.

### *14.3.1 Econometric Model to Estimate the Probability of Crop Damages*

Damage to crops results from a variety of factors that go beyond the specific type of mitigation. Through discussions with local farmers, we identified six factors that might influence crop damage by wild animals at the plot level. These factors include types of crops grown, types of protective measures used, type of land, the distance of the plot from the nearest forest and total area under cultivation. Five major crops are grown in the region, maize, potato, paddy, groundnut, and chilli, and were considered for the analysis. Protective measures against wildlife predation used in the region include fabricated electric fence (FEF) and other measures such as a private lethal electric fence, guarding wood, bamboo, and stone fences. The distance of the plot from the nearest forest is important as it identifies how far wildlife has to travel to get to crops. This is measured in terms of metres, and the total area sown is measured in acres.

To examine the determinants of the crop damage incidence by wild animals, we estimate the following probit model.

$$Prob[Y = 1|X] = F(X\beta), \tag{14.1}$$

where $Y = 1$ if the crops on the farm plot were damaged by wild animals in 2013, otherwise 0. $X$ denotes the explanatory variables which may be associated with the crop damage incidence. The explanatory variable FEF = 1 if the plot is under the mitigation by FEF; otherwise, 0. Explanatory variable types of crops grown include maize, potato, paddy, and groundnut, which are dummy variables, while reference dummy variable crop is chilli. The other explanatory variables include the type of land (1 if dry land and 0 if wetland), the distance of the plot from the nearest forest in metres, and total area sown in acres. Equation (14.1) is estimated by a probit model using the maximum likelihood estimation method. Marginal effects are computed at the mean values of the explanatory variables.

### *14.3.2 Cost-Benefit Analysis*

For the cost-benefit analysis, we calculated the benefit–cost ratio (BCR) and net present value (NPV) of using FEFs with the following equations:

$$NPV = \sum_{t=1}^{T} \frac{(B_t\_C_t)}{(1+r)^t} \tag{14.2}$$

$$BCR = \frac{\sum_{i=1}^{r} \frac{B_t}{(1+r)^t}}{\sum_{i=1}^{r} \frac{C_t}{(1+r)^t}} \tag{14.3}$$

where $r$ is the discount rate, $t$ is the year, $B_t$ is the benefits from FEF, $C_t$ is the cost of FEF in time t, and $T$ is the lifespan of FEF.

Benefits from FEF in each year ($B_t$) are the decrease in crop damages, computed as:

$$B_t = -\Delta Probf \times \overline{CLNF} \tag{14.4}$$

where $\Delta Probf$ is the marginal effect of FEF at the average values of other explanatory variables, computed after estimating the probit model given in Equation (14.1) as follows:

$$\Delta Probf = Prob[Y = 1|FEF = 1] - Prob[Y = 1|FEF = 0] \tag{14.5}$$

$\overline{CLNF}$ is equal to the average crop losses on damaged plots that are without FEF (Nu. per acre) times 49 acres, which are protected by 15 km fence.

In the study, the size of FEF is 15 km around the farmland, so we conducted a cost-benefit analysis for the entire 15 km FEF. We assume the lifespan of fabricated electric fencing to be ten years. To discount future benefits and costs, we used a discount rate of 13%, based on the lending rate of Bhutan Development Bank Limited (BDBL), the sole financial institution for providing microfinance to agriculture and rural development in the country. However, our sensitivity analysis considers different discount rates (10 % and 16%).

The installation cost of FEF per km is obtained from an impact study on locally fabricated electric fencing (Chettri et al. 2013). The maintenance cost was estimated by interviewing the community leader responsible for monitoring and maintenance of the FEF. The maintenance cost includes labour charge and replacement of fabricating energizer, wires, nails, insulant pipes, and poles.

## 14.4 Results and Discussion

### *14.4.1 Human-Wildlife Conflicts in Bartsham Gewog*

The seriousness of the human-wildlife conflict in Bhutan and particularly in the Bartsham subdistrict is clear from the household survey. In the study area, the average landholding size per household is 3.3 acres, of which the average cultivated land is 1.63 acres per household (Table 14.2). More than 50% (1.7 acres per household) of agricultural plots are left fallow without any cultivation (Figure 14.5A). The major reason for leaving lands fallow, as identified by 74% of households, is due to wildlife-related problems (Figure 14.5B).

While wildlife causes damage to crops, domestic animals, and property in Bhutan, we focus mainly on crop damages in this study. The main crops grown in the Bartsham are maize, potato, paddy, groundnut, and chilli. Plots without FEF are reported to have lost crop worth of Nu. 10,862 per acre to wild animals, while plots with FEF are reported to have lost crop worth of Nu. 9,076 per acre per year (Table 14.3).

*Table 14.2* Descriptive Statistics of Household-level Characteristics

| *Variables* | *Mean* |
|---|---|
| Household Size (No.) | 2.9 |
| Age of Household members (No. of years) | 36.6 |
| Age of the Household Heads (HH) (No. of years) | 56 |
| Illiterate (proportion) | 0.72 |
| Farming as a primary occupation of household head (proportion) | 0.92 |
| Total farmland area per household (Acres) | 3.3 |
| Cultivated land per household (Acres) | 1.63(49.5%) |
| Fallow land per household (Acres) | 1.76 (50.5%) |
| Wetland in Acres (proportion) | 0.28 |

Note: Other Occupations includes *Gomchen* (lay priest) and shopkeepers; Wetland are irrigated terrace paddy fields, considered wetlands in Bhutan.

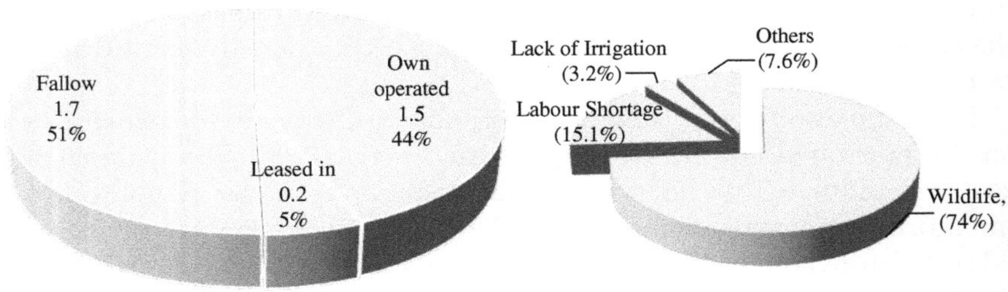


*Figure 14.5* Land usage status acre per household in Bartsham Gewog (A) and reasons for leaving the land fallow (B) (N=251). *Source:* Author's Field survey.

*Table 14.3* Descriptive Statistics of Plot-Level Characteristics

| | *Plots with FEF (mean)* | *Plots without FEF (mean)* |
|---|---|---|
| Plots damaged by wildlife (1 if damaged, 0 otherwise, so mean represents proportion) | 0.34 | 0.67 |
| ***Damaged Plots*** | | |
| Crop losses in Nu. per acre | 9,076 (9,790) | 10,862 (12,616) |
| ***All Plots (overall)*** | | |
| Distance from the nearest forest (in 100 metres) | 0.63 (1.2) | 1.95 (3.3) |
| Area under cultivation (Acres) | 0.65 (0.59) | 0.62 (0.61) |
| Times of damage by wildlife (No.) | 6.8 (10) | 6.2 (7) |
| Maize (dummy) proportion | 0.33 | 0.67 |
| Potato (dummy) proportion | 0.09 | 0.91 |
| Paddy (dummy) proportion | 0.21 | 0.79 |
| Groundnut (dummy) proportion | 0.95 | 0.05 |
| Chilli (dummy) proportion | 0.20 | 0.80 |
| Total area sown per plot (Acres) | 0.60 (0 .51) | 0.50 (0.67) |
| **No. of observations** | **75** | **208** |

### *14.4.2 Factors Explaining the Crop Damages by Wildlife in Bartsham*

After running the probit model, we estimated the marginal effects of the probit model (Table 14.4), which suggest that agricultural plots with FEF are 42% less likely to experience crop damage compared to those plots without FEF. These results indicate that the use of FEF is associated with a decrease in the likelihood of crop damages. Table 14.4 depicts that there is no significant difference in terms of damage among five different crops, namely maize, potato, paddy, groundnut, and chilli. The type of land and size of the area cultivated also do not influence damages. Distance of plot from the nearest forest also determines the crop damage, with damage reducing significantly as distance increases.

### *14.4.3 Cost of Installing Fabricated Electric Fencing*

The initial investment cost for installing FEF was estimated to be Nu. 8,870 per kilometre (Table 14.5). This includes initial costs of supplies and labour.

Maintenance costs, based on the labour charge for monthly clearing of grass underneath (undertaken by every household), replacement of wires, poles, pipe, nails, and the fabricating energizer (every alternate year), were estimated at Nu. 2,600 per km, Nu. 4,045 per km for the years 2, 4, 6, 8, 10 and Nu. 4,300 per km for the years 3, 5, 7, 9. The small difference in the annual maintenance costs in odd and even years is accounted for by the replacement costs of the fabricated energizer every alternate year (Table 14.6).

### *14.4.4 Cost-Benefit Analysis*

Finally, we undertook a cost-benefit analysis to examine the benefits of FEF. As noted, the total installation investment, which includes the price of

*Table 14.4* Probit Regression of Factors Influencing Crop Damage by Wild Animals

| | *Marginal effect* | *St. error* |
|---|---|---|
| Dependent variable Y = 1 if crops were damaged by Wild Animals | | |
| Fabricated Electric Fence (Dummy[1]) (0/1) | −.4219923 | (.08007) *** |
| Maize (0/1) | .1764755 | (.10183) * |
| Potato (0/1) | −.0043202 | (.0835) |
| Paddy | .0992049 | (.11937) |
| Groundnut | .0808236 | (.12329) |
| Dryland (Dummy[2]) | −.0292053 | (.13389) |
| Distance of plot from the forest (in 100 metres) | −.0278417 | (.01054) *** |
| Total Area Sown (Acres) | .1127222 | (.07012) * |
| No. of observations | 283 | |
| Pseudo $R^2$ | 0.1033 | |
| LR $Chi^2$ (8) | 39.59 | |
| Prob > $Chi^2$ | 0.0000 | |

Note: ***$p < 0.01$, ** $p < 0.05$, *$p < 0$. The reference category is plots without fabricated electric fence.

*Table 14.5* Installation Cost of Fabricated Electric Fencing for One Kilometre

| *Item* | *Rate (Nu)* | *Quantity* | *Unit* | *Amount (Nu)* |
|---|---|---|---|---|
| Fabricated Energizer | 1,700 | 1 | No. | 1,700 |
| Fence wire (GI SWG 16) | 90 | 25 | Kg | 2,250 |
| HDPE pipe for pole insulation (32 mm diameter) | 32 | 30 | Meter | 960 |
| Iron nail 3" | 80 | 8 | Kg | 640 |
| Wooden poles | 10 | 33 | No | 320 |
| Labour cost of installation | 100 | 30 | Person-days | 3,000 |
| **Total cost/km** | | | | **8,870** |

Source: *Penjor T, (2010), Progress on electric fencing RDC Wengkhar*

*Table 14.6* Cost–Benefit Analysis for Fabricated Electric Fence (FEF)

| *Costs and benefits* | *Analysis for fence of 15 km* |
|---|---|
| **Investment cost (15 km fence)** | |
| Investment cost of Fabricated Electric Fence (FEF) at Year 0 (Nu) | 133,050 |
| **Maintenance cost per annum** | |
| Year 1 | 39,000 |
| Years 2, 4, 6, 8, 10 | 60,675 |
| Years 3, 5, 7, 9 | 64,500 |
| **Benefits per annum** | |
| Probability of crop damage by wildlife reduced due to Fabricated Electric Fence (FEF) | 0.42 |
| Crop losses under damaged plots without FEF (Nu. per acre) | 10,862 |
| Annual benefit of FEF per acre (Nu. per acre) (= 0.42 × 1,0862) | 4562 |
| Annual benefit of FEF for 49 acres (Nu.) (Years 1–10) | 22,3540 |
| Scrap value fence at Year 10 | 16,875 |
| **Cost–benefit analysis (CBA)** | |
| Discount rate | 13% |
| Present value of costs (Nu.) | 450,732 |
| Present value of benefits (Nu.) | 1,217,953 |
| Benefit–cost ratio | 2.7 |
| **Sensitivity analysis** | |
| **Discount rate** | 10% |
| Present value of costs (Nu.) | 495,001 |
| Present value of benefits (Nu.) | 1,380,062 |
| Net present Value of Electric Fencing (Nu.) to protect 49 acres | 885,061 |
| Benefit-cost ratio | 2.8 |
| **Discount rate** | 16% |
| Present value of costs (Nu.) | 414,251 |
| Present value of benefits (Nu.) | 1,084,244 |
| Benefit–cost ratio | 2.6 |

Note: Our survey data in 2014 show that 15 km Fabricated Electric Fence covers 49 acres of cultivated land in Muktangkhar Chiwog. The fence provides additional protection as it also covers fallow land and other uses of land.

wires, poles, nails, and labour, is approximately Nu. 8,870 per kilometre. Maintenance costs per km/year amount to Nu. 2,600 in year 1, Nu. 4,045 per year during even years and Nu. 4,300 per year during odd years.

The annual financial benefit of the intervention is estimated to be Nu. 223,540 for the whole 15 km fence and Nu.14,903 per kilometre. Our survey data indicate that 15 km fabricated electric fence covers 49 acres of cultivated land in Muktangkhar Chiwog. Thus, our analyses of costs and benefits for 15 km of fencing estimate the economic returns to 49 protected acres of land.

Considering a life span of FEF of 10 years and a discount rate of 13%, the net present value of low-cost fencing over a ten-year period is estimated to be Nu. 1,217,953 for a 15 km fence or Nu. 81,197 per kilometre (see Table 14.6). This amounts to a benefit-cost ratio of 2.7. The benefit-cost analysis suggests that the investment in the FEF is highly viable on economic grounds.

## 14.5 Discussion and Conclusion

Crops lost to wild animals are a prominent issue in Bhutan and farmers lose a substantial amount of revenue due to wildlife annually, in addition to damage from natural disasters (MoAF Statistics, 2013–2017). Our micro-study in Bartsham *Gewog* forces this broader understanding and shows that farmers bear significant crop losses as a result of wildlife predation. Additionally, a large proportion of agricultural land is left fallow, and the main reason identified by households is wildlife damage. Losing crops to wild animals and leaving lands fallow contributes to rural poverty in Bhutan. This phenomenon is also responsible for driving people from rural areas to cities in search of better economic opportunities.

Bhutan's government has initiated various mitigation measures to tackle human-wildlife conflict. For example, the Ministry of Agriculture has installed hundreds of kilometres of electric and solar fencing and also offers economic compensation for wildlife damages. In some areas, the government has installed more affordable locally fabricated electric fencing, which costs less than a third of the costs of regular electric fencing. Many villages remain without any intervention, posing a huge challenge to the government because of its own limited ability to finance mitigation measures and provide technical support.

Our study suggests that locally fabricated electric fencing is a cost-effective and economically viable option to reduce wildlife predation. Results indicate that the probability of crop damage reduces by 42% in plots with FEF, saving the average farmer Nu. 10,862 per acre, resulting in a total saving of approximately Nu. 223,540 annually from 15 km of fencing over its ten-year lifespan. The benefit-cost ratio is estimated as 2.7, which shows that FEF is an economically viable investment that can be scaled up.

Human-wildlife conflicts can have serious ecological and economic consequences. These include long-term extinction of species because of retaliatory wildlife killing and changes in the functioning of ecosystems, as well as serious losses to human life, crops, livestock, and property (Nyhus 2016; Dickman 2010). Human costs also emerge from managing crop predation, including physical and mental health effects from stress and labour associated with protecting crops and livestock (Orga 2008; Chowdhury *et al.* 2008; Dixon *et al.* 2009). Bhutan has made huge investments in conserving its environment. It would only be appropriate to strengthen these investments through additional measures such as fabricated electric fencing that can cost-effectively provide some protection to rural communities that bear the costs of wildlife predation.

## References

Anand, S. and S. Radhakrishna. 2017. "Investigating Trends in Human-Wildlife Conflict: Is Conflict Escalation Real or Imagined?" *Journal of Asia-Pacific Biodiversity* 10 (2): 154–161. doi:10.1016/j.japb.2017.02.003.

Angelsen, A., P. Jagger, R. Babigumira, B. Belcher, N. J. Hogarth, S. Bauch, J. Börner, C. Smith-Hall, and S. Wunder. 2014. "Environmental Income and Rural Livelihoods: A Global-Comparative Analysis". *World Development* 64: S12–S28. doi:10.1016/j.worlddev.2014.03.006.

Brockington, Daniel, and David Wilkie. 2015. "Protected Areas and Poverty". *Philosophical Transactions of The Royal Society B: Biological Sciences* 370 (1681): 1–6. doi:10.1098/rstb.2014.0271

Bumdeling Wildlife Sanctuary. 2018. "Socio-economic Status of Residents inside Bumdeling Wildlife Sanctuary". In *Field Assessment Reports: Studies Performed to Explore and Document Facts for Wildlife Conservation, Bumdeling Wildlife Sanctuary*. Bhutan: Trashiyangtse. http://www.bhutantrustfund.bt/wp-content/uploads/2019/04/Wildlife-Conservation-Field-Studies-Conducted-by-Bumdeling-Wildlife-Sanctuary.pdf (accessed on 19 April 2020).

Campbell, A. J., L. G. Carvalheiro, M. M. Maués, R. Jaffé, T. C. Giannini, M. A. B. Freitas, B. W. T. Coelho, and C. Menezes. 2018. "Anthropogenic Disturbance of Tropical Forests Threatens Pollination Services to Açaí Palm in The Amazon River Delta". *Journal of Applied Ecology* 55 (4): 1725–1736. doi:10.1111/1365-2664.13220.

Cheng, S. H., S. Ahlroth, S. Onder, P. Shyamsundar, R. Garside, P. Kristjanson, M. C. McKinnon, and D. C. Miller. 2017. "What Is the Evidence for The Contribution of Forests to Poverty Alleviation? A Systematic Map Protocol". *Environmental Evidence* 6 (10): 1–11. doi:10.1186/s13750-017-0088-9.

Chettri, P. B., T. Penjor, C. Nima, and D. Yangzom. 2013. "Impact Assessment on Selected Socio-economic Indicators of Farming Communities after Fencing Their Agriculture Farms Using Locally Fabricated Electrical Fence in Eastern Bhutan". *Journal of Renewable Natural Resources* 9 (1): 129–140. https://www.bja.gov.bt/wp-content/uploads/2019/06/RNR-Journal-of-Bhutan-2013.pdf (accessed on 13 June 2020).

Chowdhury, A. N., R. Mondal, A. Brahma, and M. K. Biswas. 2008. "Eco-Psychiatry and Environmental Conservation: Study from Sundarban Delta, India". *Environmental Health Insights* 2: 61–76. doi:10.4137/ehi.s935.

Conover, R. M. 2002. *Resolving Human-wildlife Conflicts. The Science of Wildlife Damage Management.* Florida: Lewis Publishers. https://www.routledge.com/Resolving-Human-Wildlife-Conflicts-The-Science-of-Wildlife-Damage-Management/Conover-Conover/p/book/9781566705387 (accessed on 16 March 2020).

Das, S., and J. R. Vincent. 2009. "Mangroves Protected Villages and Reduced Death Toll During Indian Super Cyclone". *Proceedings of the National Academy of Sciences* 106(18): 7357–7360. https://www.pnas.org/content/pnas/106/18/7357.full.pdf (accessed on 14 June 2020).

Dema, Y. n.d. "Three Gifts per Gewog". *Kuensel*, February 3, 2015. https://kuenselonline.com/three-gifts-per-gewog (accessed on 3 January 2021).

Dendup, N., and K. Tshering. 2018. "Demand for Piped Drinking Water and a Formal Sewer System in Bhutan". *Environmental Economics and Policy Studies* 20 (3): 681–703. doi:10.1007/s10018-018-0211-3.

Department of Agriculture. 2013. "Agriculture Statistics, 2013". Thimphu: Ministry of Agriculture and Forest, Royal Government of Bhutan. https://www.doa.gov.bt/wp-content/uploads/2021/03/Agriculture-Statistics-2013.pdf (accessed on 5 February 2021).

Department of Agriculture. 2014. "Agriculture Statistics, 2014". Thimphu: Ministry of Agriculture and Forest, Royal Government of Bhutan. https://www.doa.gov.bt/wp-content/uploads/2020/06/Agriculture-Statistics-2014.pdf (accessed on 5 February 2021).

Department of Agriculture. 2015. "Agriculture Statistics, 2015". Thimphu: Ministry of Agriculture and Forest, Royal Government of Bhutan. https://www.doa.gov.bt/wp-content/uploads/2020/05/Agriculture-statistics-2015.pdf (accessed on 6 February 2021).

Department of Agriculture. 2016. "Agriculture Statistics, 2016". Thimphu: Ministry of Agriculture and Forest, Royal Government of Bhutan. https://www.doa.gov.bt/wp-content/uploads/2020/05/Agriculture-Statistics-2016.pdf (accessed on 5 February 2021).

Department of Agriculture. 2017. "Agriculture Statistics, 2017". Thimphu: Ministry of Agriculture and Forest, Royal Government of Bhutan. https://www.nsb.gov.bt/agriculture-statistics-reports/ (accessed on 6 February 2021).

Dickman, A. J. 2010. "Complexities of Conflict: The Importance of Considering Social Factors for Effectively Resolving Human-Wildlife Conflict". *Animal Conservation* 13 (5): 458–466. doi:10.1111/j.1469-1795.2010.00368.x.

Dixon, Alan B., A. Hailu, T. Semu, and L. Taffa. 2009. "Local Responses to Marginalisation: Human—Wildlife Conflict in Ethiopia's Wetlands". *Geography* 94 (1): 38–47. doi:10.1080/00167487.2009.12094250.

FAO, and UNEP. 2020. *The state of the world 's forests 2020: Forests, Biodiversity and People.* Rome: FAO. ISBN: 978-92-5-132419-6. http://www.fao.org/3/ca8642en/ca8642en.pdf (accessed on 16 February 2020).

Ghimiray, Mahesh, S. Pandhey, and Ma Lourdes Velasco. 2013. *Tracking of Improved Varieties in South Asia. Bhutan Report on Rice. Estimating Adoption Rate of Modern Rice Varieties in Bhutan.* Thimphu: RNRRC, Department of

Agriculture, Ministry of Agriculture and Forests, Royal Government of Bhutan. http://rcbajo.gov.bt/wp-content/uploads/2016/03/Rice-Adoption-Report.pdf (accessed on 6 February 2020).

Goldstein, I., S. Paisley, R. Wallace, J. P. Jorgenson, F. Cuesta, and A. Castellanos. 2006. "Andean Bear–Livestock Conflicts: A Review". *Ursus* 17 (1): 8–15. doi:10.2192/1537-6176(2006)17[8: abcar]2.0.co;2.

GNHC (Gross National Happiness Commission). 2000. "*Bhutan National Human Development Report 2000: Gross National Happiness and Human Development: Searching for Common Ground*". The Planning Commission Secretariat Royal Government of Bhutan. https://www.gnhc.gov.bt/en/wp-content/uploads/2017/05/nhdr2000.pdf (accessed on 21 June 2020).

Hoare, R. E. 2001. *A Decision Support System for Managing Human-Elephant Conflict Situations in Africa*. Nairobi, Kenya: IUCN African Elephant Specialist Group Report, 110pp. https://www.iucn.org/sites/dev/files/import/downloads/hecdssen.pdf (accessed on 18 May 2020).

IUCN. 2005. *Benefits Beyond Boundaries. Proceedings of the Vth IUCN World Parks Congress*. Gland, Switzerland and Cambridge: IUCN. The UK. ix + 306.ISBN- 2-8317-0829-X. https://portals.iucn.org/library/sites/library/files/documents/2005-007.pdf (accessed on 17 June 2020).

Jagger, P. A., Cheek, J. Z, Miller, D. C., Ryan, C., Razafindratsima, O. H., Shyamsundar, P, and Sills, E. O. 2020. "Key Concepts for Understanding Forest Poverty Dynamics". In Miller et al. (ed) *Forests, Trees and the Eradication of Poverty: Potential and Limitations. A Global Assessment Report*. Vienna: IUFRO World Series 39:240. http://catalogue.unccd.int/1590_forests_trees_poverty_ws39.pdf (accessed on 21 June 2020).

Johnson, McKenzie F., K. K. Karanth, and E. Weinthal. 2018. "Compensation as a Policy for Mitigating Human-Wildlife Conflict around Four Protected Areas in Rajasthan, India". *Conservation and Society* 16 (3): 305–319. doi:10.4103/cs.cs_17_1.

Kaczensky, P., M. Blazic, and H. Gossow. 2004 "Public Attitudes Towards Brown Bears (Ursus arctos) in Slovenia". *Biological Conservation* 118(5): 661–674. doi:10.1016/j.biocon.2003.10.015.

Kalam, Tamanna, Hiten Kumar Baishya, and David Smith. 2018. "Lethal Fence Electrocution: A Major Threat to Asian Elephants In Assam, India". *Tropical Conservation Science* 11: 194008291881728. doi:10.1177/1940082918817283.

Karanth, Krithi K., A. M. Gopalaswamy, R. DeFries, and N. Ballal. 2012. "Assessing Patterns of Human-Wildlife Conflicts and Compensation Around a Central Indian Protected Area". *PloS One* 7(12): e50433. doi:10.1371/journal.pone.0050433

Katwal, T. B., L. Dorji, and N. Wangdi. 2009. "Quality Maize Seed Production through Community Based Seed Production Approach: An Extension Manual". *RNR RC WengkharMongar, Council for RNR Research of Bhutan*. Ministry of Agriculture and Forest. http://rcbajo.gov.bt/wp-content/uploads/2016/03/Maize-CBSP-manual.pdf (accessed on 18 May 2020).

Kioko, J., P. Muruthi, P. Omondi, and P. I. Chiyo. 2008. "The Performance of Electric Fences as Elephant Barriers in Amboseli, Kenya". *South African Journal of Wildlife Research* 38 (1): 52–58. doi:10.3957/0379-4369-38.1.52.

Kolowski, J. M., and K. E. Holekamp. 2006. “Spatial, Temporal, and Physical Characteristics of Livestock Depredations by Large Carnivores along a Kenyan Reserve Border”. *Biological Conservation* 128 (4): 529–541. doi:10.1016/j.biocon.2005.10.021.

Lamarque, François, J. Anderson, R. Fergusson, M. Lagrange, Y. Osei-Owusu, and L. Bakker. 2009. *Human-Wildlife Conflict in Africa: Causes, Consequences and Management Strategies*. Food and Agriculture Organization of the United Nations (FAO). http://www.fao.org/3/i1048e/i1048e00.htm (accessed on 14 March 2020).

Linkie, M., Y. Dinata, A. Nofrianto, and N. Leader-Williams. 2007. “Patterns and Perceptions of Wildlife Crop Raiding in and Around Kerinci Seblat National Park, Sumatra”. *Animal Conservation* 10 (1): 127–135. doi:10.1111/j.1469-1795.2006.00083.x.

Madhusudan, M. D., and P. Sankaran. 2010. “Seeing the Elephant in the Room: Human-Elephant Conflict and the ETF Report”. *Economic and Political Weekly* XIV (49): 29–31. https://file.ejatlas.org/docs/3913/Elephant_Task_Force.pdf (accessed on 16 March 2020).

Marchal, V., R. Dellink, D. Van Vuuren, C. Clapp, J. Chateau, B. Magné, and J. Van Vliet. 2011. “OECD Environmental Outlook to 2050”. *Organization for Economic Co-operation and Development* 8: 397–413.https://www.oecd.org/env/cc/49082173.pdf (accessed on 19 June 2020).

MEA, Millennium Ecosystem Assessment. 2005. *Ecosystems and Human Well-being: Current State and Trends, volume 1*. Washington, DC: Millennium Ecosystem Assessment, Global Assessment Reports. https://www.millenniumassessment.org/documents/document.766.aspx.pdf (accessed on 16 March 2020).

Miller, Daniel C., and R. Hajjar. 2020. “Forests as Pathways to Prosperity: Empirical Insights and Conceptual Advances”. *World Development* 125: 104647. doi:10.1016/j.worlddev.2019.104647.

Miller, Daniel C., S. Mansourian, and C. Wildburger (eds.). 2020. *Forests, Trees and the Eradication of Poverty: Potential and Limitations. A Global Assessment Report*. Vienna: IUFRO World Series 39:240. http://catalogue.unccd.int/1590_forests_trees_poverty_ws39.pdf (accessed on 18 March 2020).

Ministry of Agriculture and Forest, Bhutan. 2008. *Bhutan National Human-Wildlife Conflicts Management Strategy*. Nature Conservation Division, Department of Forests. ISBN 99936-666-3-7. https://www.bt.undp.org/content/dam/bhutan/docs/Energy_environment/Env-publications/2008-HWC%20Mgt%20Strategy.pdf (accessed on 16 March 2020).

Ministry of Agriculture and Forest, Royal Government of Bhutan. December 2020. *Bhutan's Proposed National Forest Reference Emission Level and National Forest Reference Level Submission for Technical Assessment to UNFCCC*. Department of Forests & Park Services. https://redd.unfccc.int/files/final_bhutan_frel_frl_20201207_for_webposting.pdf (accessed on 24 June 2020).

National Environment Commission (NEC). 2019. “National Environment Commission Strategy, 2020”. *Royal Government of Bhutan, Thimphu* http://www.nec.gov.bt/publications/policy-and-strategy (accessed on 19 May 2020).

National Statistical Bureau (NSB). 2014. “Key Indicators” Thimphu: National Statistics Bureau, Royal Government of Bhutan. https://www.nsb.gov.bt/publications/national-account-report/ (accessed on 13 February 2020).

Naughton-Treves, Lisa. 2008. "Predicting Patterns of Crop Damage by Wildlife around Kibale National Park, Uganda". *Conservation Biology* 12 (1): 156–168. doi:10.1111/j.1523-1739.1998.96346. x.

Neupane, D., Ronald L. Johnson, and Thomas S. Risch. 2017. "How Do Land-Use Practices Affect Human—Elephant Conflict in Nepal?" *Wildlife Biology* 2017 (4): wlb.00313. doi:10.2981/wlb.00313.

Newton, P., A. T. Kinzer, D. C. Miller, J. A. Oldekop, and A. Agrawal. 2020. "The Number and Spatial Distribution of Forest-proximate People Globally". *One Earth* 3(3): 363–370. doi:10.1016/j.oneear.2020.08.016.

Nyhus, Philip J. 2016. "Human–Wildlife Conflict and Coexistence". *Annual Review of Environment and Resources* 41 (1): 143–171. doi:10.1146/annurev-environ-110615-085634.

O'Connell-Rodwell, Caitlin E, T. Rodwell, M. Rice, and L. A Hart. 2000. "Living With the Modern Conservation Paradigm: Can Agricultural Communities Co-Exist With Elephants? A Five-Year Case Study in East Caprivi, Namibia". *Biological Conservation* 93 (3): 381–391. doi:10.1016/s0006-3207(99)00108-1.

Ogra, Monica V. 2008. "Human–Wildlife Conflict and Gender in Protected Area Borderlands: A Case Study of Costs, Perceptions, and Vulnerabilities from Uttarakhand (Uttaranchal), India". *Geoforum* 39 (3): 1408–1422. doi: 10.1016/j.geoforum.2007.12.004.

Ogra, M., and R. Badola. 2008. "Compensating Human–Wildlife Conflict in Protected Area Communities: Ground-Level Perspectives from Uttarakhand, India". *Human Ecology* 36 (5): 717–729. doi:10.1007/s10745-008-9189-y.

Palden, T. 2019. "HWC Endowment Fund Targets USD 35 Million" *Kuensel*, May 8, 2019. https://kuenselonline.com/hwc-endowment-fund-targets-usd-35m/ (accessed on 3 Janaury 2021).

Pattanayak, Subhrendu K., and Erin O. Sills. 2001. "Do Tropical Forests Provide Natural Insurance? The Microeconomics of Non-timber Forest Product Collection in the Brazilian Amazon". *Land Economics* 77(4): 595–612. doi:10.2307/3146943

Penjor,T., L. Dorji, C. Nima, D. Yangzom, P.B. Chhetri, T. Norbu, and L. Dorji, 2014. "Electric Fencing (FEF) System: A New Approach to Mitigate Human Wildlife Conflict in Bhutan". *Human-Wildlife Conflict in the Mountains of SAARC Region: Compilation of Successful Management Strategies and Practices*. Thimphu, Bhutan: SAARC Forestry Centre Office. http://sfc.org.bt/images/Success%20Stories%20in%20Human%20Wildlife%20%20Conflict%20Resolution.pdf (accessed on 4 February 2021).

http://www.gnhc.gov.bt/en/wp-content/uploads/2017/05/Bhutan2020_1.pdf (accessed on 3 Janaury 2021).

Rangarajan, M., A. Desai, R. Sukumar, P. S. Easa, V. Menon, S. Vincent, S. Ganguly et al. 2010. *Gajah. Securing the Future for Elephants in India. The Report of the Elephant Task Force.* New Delhi: Ministry of Environment and Forests. https://epub.ub.uni-muenchen.de/56285/1/Gajah.pdf (accessed on 18 January 2021).

Razafindratsima, Onja H., J. Kamoto, E. Sills, D. N. Mutta, C. Song, T. Sunderland, G. Kabwe et al. 2020. *Forest-Poverty Dynamics: Current State of Knowledge. Forests, Trees and the Eradication of Poverty: Potential and Limitations A Global Assessment Report*. International Union of Forest Research Organizations

(IUFRO). https://www.cifor.org/knowledge/publication/7827 (accessed on 12 March 2021).

Sangay, T., and K. Vernes. 2008. "Human–wildlife Conflict in the Kingdom of Bhutan: Patterns of Livestock Predation by Large Mammalian Carnivores". *Biological Conservation* 141(5): 1272–1282. doi:10.1016/j.biocon.2008.02.027.

Sharma, Bishnu P, B. S Karky, M. Nepal, S. K Pattanayak, E. O Sills, and P. Shyamsundar. 2020. "Making Incremental Progress: Impacts of A REDD+ Pilot Initiative in Nepal". *Environmental Research Letters* 15 (10): 105004. doi:10.1088/1748-9326/aba924.

Shyamsundar, P., and R. Ghate. 2014. "Rights, Rewards, and Resources: Lessons from Community Forestry in South Asia". *Review of Environmental Economics and Policy* 8(1): 80–102. doi:10.1093/reep/ret022.

Shyamsundar, P., S. Das, and M. Nepal. 2018. "Forest Dependence and Poverty in the Himalayas—Differences between India and Nepal". In *Ecology, Economy and Society*, edited by Dayal et al., 205–223. Singapore: Springer.

Shyamsundar, P., S. Ahlroth, P. Kristjanson, and S. Onder. 2020. "Supporting Pathways to Prosperity in Forest Landscapes: A PRIME Framework". *World Development* 125: 104622. doi:10.1016/j.worlddev.2019.104622.

Springer, J. 2009. "Addressing the Social Impacts of Conservation: Lessons from Experience and Future Directions". *Conservation and Society* 7 (1): 26–29. doi:10.4103/0972-4923.54794.

Sunderlin, W. D., A. Angelsen, B. Belcher, P. Burgers, R. Nasi, L. Santoso, and S. Wunder. 2005. "Livelihoods, Forests, and Conservation in Developing Countries: An Overview". *World Development* 33 (9): 1383–1402. doi: 10.1016/j.worlddev.2004.10.004.

UNDP. 2013. *Human Wildlife Conflict Management*. ISBN 99936-666-3-7. Kuensel Corporation Limited, Thimphu, Bhutan with financial assistance from Bhutan Trust Fund, WWF Bhutan and UNDP. www.undp.org.bt/Human-Wildlife-Conflict-Management-Project.html (accessed on 5 July 2020).

Vedeld, P., A. Angelsen, E. Sjaastad, and G. Kobugabe Berg. 2004. *Counting on the Environment: Forest Incomes and the Rural Poor*. No. 30026. The World Bank. https://documents.worldbank.org/curated/en/825651468778804896/pdf/300260PAPER0Counting0on0ENV0EDP0198.pdf (accessed on 13 April 2021).

Vedeld, P., A. Angelsen, J. Bojö, E. Sjaastad, and G. K. Berg. 2007. "Forest Environmental Incomes and the Rural Poor". *Forest Policy and Economics* 9(7): 869–879. doi:10.1016/j.forpol.2006.05.008.

Wang, S. W. 2004. *The Impacts of Wildlife Damage and Conservation Policies on Farmer Attitudes in Jigme Singye Wangchuck National Park, Bhutan*. Ithaca: Cornell University.

Wang, S. W., and D. W. Macdonald. 2006. "Livestock Predation by Carnivores in Jigme Singye Wangchuck National Park, Bhutan". *Biological Conservation* 129 (4): 558–565. doi:10.1016/j.biocon.2005.11.024.

Wang, S. W., P. D. Curtis, and J. P. Lassoie. 2006. "Farmer Perceptions of Crop Damage by Wildlife in Jigme Singye Wangchuck National Park, Bhutan". *Wildlife Society Bulletin* 34 (2): 359–365. doi:10.2193/0091-7648(2006)34[359:fpocdb]2.0.co;2.

Wildlife Conservation Division (WCD). 2010. *Analysis of the Contributions of Protected Areas to the Social and Development of Bhutan; Case Study of Bumdeling*

*Wildlife Sanctuary*. Thimphu: MoAF, RGOB. http://www.bhutantrustfund.bt/wp-content/uploads/2019/04/Wildlife-Conservation-Field-Studies-Conducted-by-Bumdeling-Wildlife-Sanctuary.pdf (accessed on 13 April 2021).

Wildlife Conservation Division (WCD). 2013. *Assessment on Impact on Human-Wildlife Conflict Management Intervention to the Local Communities*. Thimphu, Bhutan: Wildlife Conservation Division, Department of Forest, Ministry of Agriculture. https://info.undp.org/docs/pdc/Documents/BTN/HWC%20Assessment%20Report_2013.pdf (accessed on 10 September 2020).

Wolff, N. H., Y. J. Masuda, E. Meijaard, J. A. Wells, and Edward T. Game. 2018. "Impacts of Tropical Deforestation on Local Temperature and Human Well-being Perceptions". *Global Environmental Change* 52: 181–189. doi:10.1016/j.gloenvcha.2018.07.004

Wolff, N. H., L. R. V. Zeppetello, L. A. Parsons, I. Aggraeni, D. S. Battisti, K. L. Ebi, E. T. Game, T. Kroeger, Y. J. Masuda, and J. T. Spector. 2021. "The Effect of Deforestation and Climate Change on All-cause Mortality and Unsafe Work Conditions due to Heat Exposure in Berau, Indonesia: A Modelling Study". *Lancet Planet Health* 5: e882–92.-. doi: 10.1016/S2542-5196(21)00279-5.

World Bank Group. 2020. "Bhutan Systematic Country Diagnostic: Taking Bhutan's Development Success to the Next Level". Washington, DC: World Bank. https://openknowledge.worldbank.org/handle/10986/33286 (accessed on 26 July 2020).

Wunder, S., J. Börner, G. Shively, and M. Wyman. 2014. "Safety Nets, Gap Filling and Forests: A Global-Comparative Perspective". *World Development* 64(1): S29–S42. doi:10.1016/j.worlddev.2014.03.005.

WWF Bhutan. 2016. *What We Do. WWF Bhutan*. World Wildlife Fund Bhutan. http://www.wwfbhutan.org.bt/_what_we_do/. (accessed on 16 July 2020).

Zangmo, T. 2013. "Use of Innovative Electric Fences in the East Show a Sweeping Drop of Human Wildlife Conflict". *The Bhutanese*. January 2013. https://thebhutanese.bt/use-of-innovative-electric-fences-in-the-east-show-a-sweeping-drop-of-human-wild-life-conflict/ (accessed on 9 June 2020).

Chapter 15

# Revisiting the Regional Environmental Economics Networks

## Some Lessons and Reflections

*Bhim Adhikari and Lowine Hill*

### Introduction

Emerging economies and developing countries rely heavily on their environmental resources and associated services for economic prosperity and societal well-being. With countries facing increasing environmental and climate-related risks, there is increasing realization that they must integrate sound and locally relevant economic governance into current environmental discussions. Since their biggest priority is sustainability, it is primordial to understand how changes in the environment may compromise the ability to meet economic growth and poverty reduction goals (MA 2005: Carpenter et al. 2009: Mukhopadhyay et al. 2014). Addressing the gaps in knowledge and capacity is fundamental to addressing multiple challenges related to environmental degradation and climate change. It is critical to identify the economics of changes in ecosystems services (Miler et al. 2008: Mäler et al. 2008) through locally generated knowledge and find ways to translate this knowledge into economic terms to build strategies for achieving sustainability (Dasgupta et al. 2000).

Numerous countries in Asia, Africa, Latin America, and the Caribbean are facing a number of social and environmental challenges that have emerged from the post-colonial period and have spanned until today. While these challenges are not at all compounded in the Global South, the threats of global environmental change have highlighted the social and ecological discrepancies within and between the various regions. Over the past few centuries, these regions have seen a population explosion as well as an increased industrial productive capacity, productivity, and income per capita. However, in recent years, income disparities and widespread environmental degradation have come to light, along with important cultural, political, and social changes, in part due to globalization. Colonization and later globalization, through the introduction of new forms of trade and an increase in the demand for cash crops, metals, and other natural resources, among others, have contributed to a disruption in existing social and support structures (Mercer et al. 2007). As a result, globalization and market

DOI: 10.4324/9781003253884-20

pressures are quickly eroding the capacity of developing countries to effectively cope with current and future environmental challenges. Globalization has reshaped exposure and vulnerability patterns: both risks and losses could ripple and be transmitted through value and supply chains, meaning that even economies not directly exposed to these environmental and climate-related challenges can be at risk (Lavell and Maskrey 2014).

Current development policies and management practices, especially regarding trade-offs and possible synergies across multiple social and ecological aspects, rarely include a thorough economic analysis or take into consideration evidence leading to both improved social and ecological outcomes, even if this evidence exists. Traditional development practices coupled with rapid urbanization and industrialization have put a strong emphasis on wealth generation at the cost of natural resources. These practices struggle to incorporate negative externalities resulting in increased pressure on the environment, from global to local scale (Turner and Pearce 1990: Richards and Davies 1999: Davies and Richards 1999: Baland and Platteau 1996: Delgado-Serrano et al. 2016).

Although many developing countries in the Global South are trying to develop appropriate policies for the environment and climate-related problems, these efforts are constrained by the lack of understanding of the critical role of economics in the appraisal and design of policy interventions at the local level. For example, economic appraisals of institutional and non-technical options are much harder to assess as opposed to technical infrastructural options. Further, developing countries have a high need for better water and energy infrastructure, but given the uncertainty on the exact nature of climate impacts, getting these right decisions is hard and requires advanced decision-making techniques. In addition, the economics of the environment and natural resources are still not well understood. As a result, there are very few locally available studies on economic analysis of 'soft' measures – for instance, that bring forward policymaking and nature-based solutions.

Addressing these challenges are also laden with a number of obstacles: the perception that the solutions available are costly: concerns about cost-sharing among stakeholders: the weak enforcement capability of regulatory agencies: and lack of suitable and relevant mechanisms for financing environmental protection in the long term, beyond the project life cycle. However, the economic analysis of these environmental options can play a critical role in overcoming these barriers (Pearce and Turner 1990: Barbier 2005) and understanding the relationship between economic growth and environmental quality (Arrow et al. 1996).

Asia's size and rapid economic growth give global importance to its environmental problems – it is often assumed that the battle for sustainable development will be won or lost in Asia. The accelerated economic development with China and India leading the way came with numerous and well-known issues: air and water pollution, invasive species, coastal degradation, resource overharvesting (especially fisheries), and the increase in the financial cost of disasters. Causal factors (e.g., the transforming political economy and modes of production, population growth, and external economic and resource pressures) have been poorly understood, particularly since the retention of specialists that are not from the continent and for whom being intimately familiar with the social and ecological realities of the region are difficult. The need to enable researchers to study the policy-relevant economics of environmental and natural resource problems, and to apply concepts, is therefore clear, especially considering emerging complex challenges – these 'wicked problems' that remain priorities.

For instance, in Southeast Asia, transboundary pollution from forest fire hazes in Indonesia, and parts of Malaysia and Thailand, the conservation of terrestrial and marine biodiversity: climate change: and joint water management are at the forefront of sustainability discussion. Similarly, lack of clearly defined property rights, deforestation, biomass burning, housing rents and sanitation infrastructure, and genetically modified cash crops are some of the key environmental and economic issues in South Asia.

In Africa, long-term economic growth increasingly reflects the multidimensional, complex, and interrelated social, demographic, and environmental challenges necessary to foster social transformation. Improved policies to stimulate growth has shown signs of economic progress in sub-Saharan Africa (SSA). However, in most instances, economic development practices have accentuated underlying social issues through perpetuated injustice, concentrated power and further environmental degradation (Newell 2005: Kaijser and Kronsell 2014: Milman and Arsano 2014: Thomalla et al. 2018). In fact, in a large portion of SSA, agriculture, forestry, fisheries, livestock, and natural resource-based activities are central to livelihoods. The economic and social situation in SSA remains fragile and vulnerable to domestic and external shocks, particularly in the light of the compounding impacts of globalization and climate change. In fact, the net economic costs of climate change in the region could be 1.5–3% of GDP each year by 2030 (PACJA 2009).

While people live in some of the world's largest cities in Latin America, contending with pollution and overcrowding, many in Latin America and the Caribbean still depend on activities related to oil, gas, minerals, forests, lands, and fisheries. Natural resources are abundant but are not used efficiently and are degraded. Over the last 50 years, most of the rural population has lost or has experienced a decrease in control over the use and conservation of land, water, medicinal plants, and other genetic/biological resources. The expansion of biofuel crops (e.g., sugar cane, oil palm, soybean, etc.) diminishes food production and security. Poverty levels also persist despite economic growth, demonstrating, for example, that relationships between mining companies and communities are poor. Improving understanding of the issues and how to better manage them will certainly contribute to the region's economic and social development.

The interdisciplinary nature of climate change and environmental degradation, or even, some would argue transdisciplinary (Jahn et al. 2012) – involving disciplines such as social sciences, natural sciences, and engineering as well as the input of non-academic participants from civil society to the private sector – have made the connection between the production, dissemination, and use of economic knowledge in decision-making and action for sustainability quite complex and challenging (Mukhopadhyay et al. 2014 and Muñoz-Erickson and Cutts 2016). In fact, while environmental economics – a discipline that helps understand how valuable the goods and services provided by the environment are to people (see Glover 2010 or Hussen 2004 for more details) – has existed as a discipline for more than 50 years, its value has only been recognized globally only since the 1992 Earth Summit in Rio de Janeiro (Glover 2010). This is at the same date that capacity building – 'the enhancement of the skills of people and the capacity of institutions in resources management through education and training' (Cicin-Sain et al. 1998) – has been declared a key in planning for sustainable development.

Solving development problems in a changing climate is a transdisciplinary task with environmental economists playing a key role in estimating the monetary value of such environmental benefits as improved health so that they can be weighed against costs: compare the cost and effectiveness of alternative policies: assess the impact of environmental action (or inaction) on the poor and show how environmental policies can be financed. The discipline has mostly been used in western/developed countries, but substantial efforts have been made to build and improve the capacity to manage their natural resources and make the economic case for more sustainable development (Glover 2010).

One commonality in all these regions is the important dependence of local economies on natural resources and similar environmental challenges. However, market and policy failures have driven the need to rethink and improve their effectiveness in dealing with environmental problems (Glover 2010). As stated by Glover (2010),

> Environmental economics gives developing countries a unique tool to make development sustainable and to leapfrog over many of the mistakes that industrialized nations have made. They can do so by investing upfront in green technology to avoid clean-up costs later: setting up regulatory regimes that encourage innovation and efficiency and giving businesses incentives to use environmental resources in a sustainable way.

The strong case for capacity building for environmental sustainability was made in countries in the Global South to analyze environmental issues from an economic standpoint (Glover 2010) and knowledge-action networks (KAN) are a response to this need. They are networks where the knowledge flow goes beyond the flow of information in the form of facts, data, etc. but take the form of an exchange of content, normative and political dimensions, and social practices associated with the knowledge by multiple formal and informal actors (Muñoz-Erickson and Cutts 2016). In short, KAN connects the knowledge chain of production, diffusion, and use and helps to study the differential geographic impact of global environmental change (Mukhopadhyay et al. 2014). Based on this premise, four regional environmental economics (EE) networks – the Economy and Environment Program for Southeast Asia (EEPSEA), the South Asian Network for Development and Environmental Economics (SANDEE), the Latin America and the Caribbean Environmental Economics Program (LACEEP), and the Centre for Environmental Economics and Policy in Africa (CEEPA) in Southeast Asia, South Asia, Latin America, and the Caribbean and Africa respectively – have been supported by Canada's International Development Research Centre (IDRC) and other like-minded organizations on the basis that economic development and environmental sustainability are integrally linked. In this context, regional environmental economics (EE) networks have emerged as knowledge-action networks that connect producers and consumers of knowledge (NRC 2007).

Regional EE networks have been tasked to provide efficient means to achieve the goals of sustainability through concrete collaborative arrangements. These networks aim to strengthen the capacity of local researchers in the economic analysis of environmental problems. Each one of these networks is locally grounded, respond to local issues and challenges, and guide local policymakers in assessing the cost of ecosystems services or disservices. Following a similar organizational model (see Figure 15.2), the networks provide research support, basic, and advanced training in topics related to EE, facilitate policy dialogue and information dissemination, and help with regional networking. The capacity-building model of these networks is based on an individual-centre approach that emphasizes personalized support to promising young researchers. It offers small doses of support, applied at the right times, and tailored to individual researchers' needs (Glover 2010), which itself respond to local reality and environmental need. The networks created an environment that fosters peer learning and has been recognized to be a cost-effective way to enhance research capability. Ultimately, by fostering local leadership and capacities, members and graduates of the networks are well-positioned to provide arguments for potential policy interventions and pathways towards culturally sound sustainable economic development, following the objectives given as early as Agenda 21.[1]

This chapter is organized in four parts and focuses on analyzing the effectiveness of the capacity-building model used by these four networks in creating locally relevant EE knowledge and their capacity for fostering knowledge dissemination and intake by policymakers for change. Most of the information presented in this chapter has been gathered both from IDRC's internal reporting processes and from the numerous evaluations of these four networks conducted over the years. First, we introduce the theoretical framework used for this analysis. In the following section, we will discuss the network's achievements in terms of the quality of research outputs, capacity development and policy/outreach influence. Finally, we present the major lessons learned, conclusions, and implications for future large-scale capacity-building projects.

## 15.1 Theoretical Framework

The environmental problems facing the world are numerous and well known. They persist, in part, because their underlying causes are frequently misdiagnosed. Misdiagnosis leads to solutions that are ineffective, excessively costly, or both, which, in turn, leads to policy fatigue. An alternative approach to sound environmental management is needed — one that identifies and influences the underlying incentives that affect environmental behaviour.

Concerns about the relevance and sustainability of environmental economics research in developing countries have prompted donor organizations to focus their attention on capacity-building efforts – whose and what capacity needs strengthening and at what levels – for individuals, organizations, and communities (see Marjanovic et al. 2012 and Paul 1995). Several analytical frameworks have been developed notably by the United Kingdom's Department for International Development (DFID), a long-term partner of IDRC, and the European Centre for Development Policy Management (ECDPM) to promote capacity building in development contexts. In this framework, capacity building includes the capabilities of the group, organization, or network, the ability of the group or organization to learn and adapt, and the performance of the organization in delivering good research and having an impact on policies and practice (DFID 2010). This framework applies to both institutions and organizations and encompasses local realities, mentorship, and external expertise, and group development (DFID 2010).

While both frameworks have provided a strong basis for the analysis of the value of networks in fostering a collaborative environment to address sustainability issues, we argue that these characteristics are not sufficient to foster the creation of new knowledge in order to collaboratively address the complex 'wicked problems' related to sustainable development and global environmental change. Parks et al. (2001) have proposed four networks characteristics that foster community learning: (i) Establish formal learning networks which go across sites and a geographical level, i.e., involve cross-pollination between specific projects; (ii) Develop simple methods for developing and operating such learning networks; (iii) Increase cross-project communication and learning opportunities; and (iv) Increase support to those who are doing the learning.

Based on these characteristics, we posit that capacity development and institutional rules have to be grounded within the wider local context and provide locally relevant knowledge, ideally by local researchers. While an external intervention could be necessary to start the process (in terms of financial and human resources), ultimately, only local stakeholders can support the initiative in the long term. Putting the local context at the forefront reinforces the narrative of capacity building and knowledge co-creation as a cultural process. Second, we argue that the framework has to be explicit regarding the place of mentorship and peer exchange but also on formal learning opportunities in the learning process. Third, professional networks are often not self-sustaining. Providing financial capabilities to peers and fellows (here in the form of small grants) are keys to further ensuring the commitment and relevance of the networks. Finally, collaboration is explicit, encouraged, and nurtured. Not only among peers but a specific vertical and horizontal collaboration that will, in turn, enhance the holistic nature of the knowledge created and shared. The resulting framework is presented in Figure 15.1.

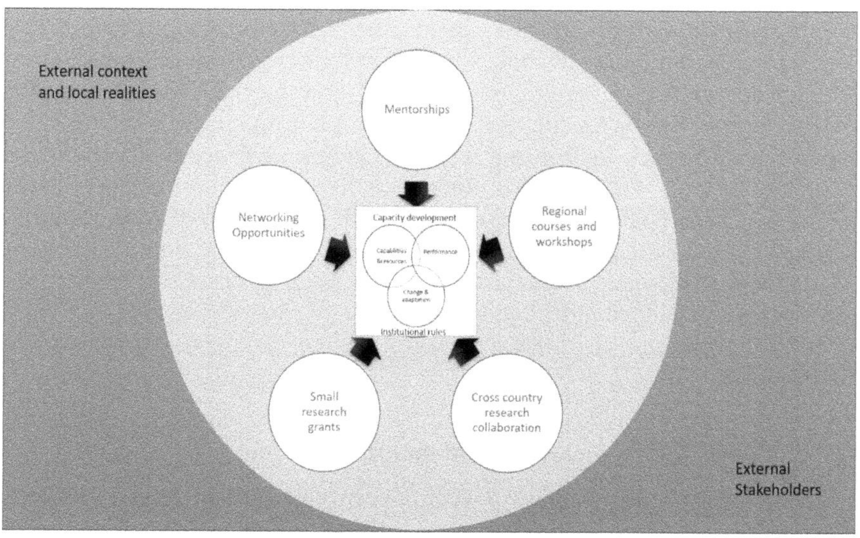


*Figure 15.1* Conceptual framework for networked capacity building. *Source:* Author's illustration

All the aforementioned four networks were created following the overarching principles presented in this framework. In practice, all the networks contribute to the capacity development of their operating region. They do so by (1) building the field of environmental economics (EE) and its research capacity; (2) promoting the relevance of EE in regional and local level decision-making through effective collaboration with relevant stakeholders; (3) investing in efforts that increase the visibility of the participating researchers and their outputs; and (4) safeguards the sustainability of capacity building in EE research by supporting local EE organizations and networks with increased networking opportunities and mentorship for members. Below we explain the different components of the frameworks and how they have been applied in the networks.

### *15.1.1 Regional Courses and Workshops*

One of the first aspects of this capacity-building framework is about regional courses and workshops. Offering courses that build on local researchers' existing knowledge and skills for the conduct of EE research is among the networks' strategies aiming at increasing the number of EE researchers in their respective regions. Because EE as a discipline was not accessible for local researchers, the networks created a vast array of courses to address this gap. Various formats were used in order to cater to busy professionals' concentrated training designed specifically for their needs. Short courses lasting from a day to a month were offered twice-yearly during research workshops. The courses cover a variety of topics relevant to environmental economics, including basic concepts, research methods, environmental science for economists, emerging issues, and communication skills. Examples of courses such as Introductory Course in Environmental and Resource Economics, Research & Proposal Writing, Computable General Equilibrium (CGE) Modeling, Advanced Econometrics, Household modelling, Survey Methods, Climate Change, Climate Science & Policy, Program Evaluation, Paying for Environmental Services, and Policy Tools for Climate Change.

Connecting all these people and activities were twice-yearly 'practitioners' workshops'. Their purpose was to share experience in applying environmental economics methods so that researchers can carry out research of international calibre.

### *15.1.2 Cross-Country Research Collaboration*

A second aspect of the capacity development framework is related to fostering collaboration among peers. Since each network spanned multiple countries, cross-country collaboration enabled researchers, policymakers, and natural resource managers in their respective regions to interact and learn from each other's experiences. The networks created an environment where various stakeholders were able to participate in networks' cutting-edge and innovative research and provided opportunities to work with other leading people in the field of EE that share the same regional realities. However, in some instances, effective transboundary academic collaboration has been extremely difficult due to geopolitical tensions among neighbouring researchers.

### *15.1.3 Small Research Grants*

Small research grants emerged as a central mechanism for the development of local capacities in the field. The majorities of these research grants are about CA$ 10,000–30,000 and are allocated for periods of 12 to 36 months. They were used to encourage researchers to develop projects where they could apply their learning and skills to local environmental policy issues. The grants were allocated in the following manner: the network would organize in-country EE training courses taught by local senior experts or alumni. The course would include components on research design and proposal writing. Participants are then invited to submit research proposals for small-scale projects that fit the budget and time allocated and that are country specific. Recipients are advised by the senior economists and, in some cases, the director, who also organize small in-country workshops for the projects. Some recipients are also invited to biannual workshops. The output of each project is a 20- to 40-page report for the network's working paper series, with an accompanying policy brief targeting local policymakers.

### *15.1.4 Networking Opportunities*

To complement cross-country collaboration, networking opportunities are an important part of the networks. They help foster intellectual dialogue and exchange across their respective regions. For example, the South Asian Network for Development and Environmental Economics (SANDEE) evaluation confirmed the impact of networking opportunities on fellow carders through established relationships with both national and international organizations, which they would not have otherwise been able to reach. The researchers from all these networks frequently expressed that the network secretariats and resource persons were very helpful for making these connections and guiding them in their careers. The desire for this kind of hands-on mentoring and guidance is one of the main things students seek from the best PhD programmes in the world, and the network researchers in the region are receiving this now without studying abroad. In many cases, the informal relationships network researchers form at the research workshops, and specialized training courses would lead to collaborative, cross-country research projects and more joint consulting and policy work.

### 15.1.5 Mentorship

At the beginning of the networks, the main resource persons were originally Northern-based researchers. They were responsible for advising research projects and teaching some of the regional environmental economics and advanced courses. However, as the number of trainees grew, they were gradually replaced by local alumni mentors (Glover 2010). The mentorship system is an important multifaceted tool as it enables grantees to receive a wide range of support over the life of their research projects and the opportunity to take part in several training courses. In addition, it is an important networking tool as grantees can benefit from the network of mentors.

### 15.1.6 Responding to External Context and Local Realities as Well as External Stakeholders

The emphasis on developing locally relevant knowledge, implementing locally designed and managed projects, and supporting local ownership has created an environment where networks can steadfastly respond to the needs of local governments and stakeholders and regional demands. While the networks were created following a similar model, they have evolved to adapt to the local realities, creating highly specialized environmental economists drafting context-specific policy recommendations and conducting locally relevant research. Researchers were particularly encouraged to collaborate with other regional networks but also other donor organizations responding rapidly to local and regional realities by shifting resources to countries in need through a shift in the cross-country allocation of projects, including not only the general environmental economics courses but also specialized courses.

## 15.2 Case Studies

The four regional networks share similar endeavours: they all aim to strengthen local capacities in the economic analysis of environmental problems so that researchers can provide sound advice to key stakeholders. Each network is a flexible and semi-virtual organization dedicated to enhancing research and teaching capacity among aspiring Environmental Economics scholars. They offer research awards and training opportunities, organize workshops, and provide advice, access to literature, publication outlets, and opportunities for comparative research across member countries. The networks draw on advice from a Steering Committee of local and international experts and policymakers.

Each network began with slightly different practices and retained some unique features related to its local context. But over time, a model has evolved that is similar for each network, with analogous operational modalities (Figure 15.2). The approach that has emerged emphasizes personalized support to promising young researchers. This is an alternative to the 'big push' institution-building programmes of the 1970s and 1980s in fields such as agricultural economics, which posted full-time advisors overseas for several years at a time and financed full PhD fellowships. The approach was based on the premise that small doses of support, applied at the right times and tailored to individual researchers' needs, can be a cost-effective way to enhance its research capability. This individual-centred approach is particularly useful in environmental economics, where researchers often need to gather information through specialized in-person survey techniques.

In each network, a small secretariat plans and manages the organization's activities. Each is based in a regional institution and draws on advice from a Steering Committee of local and international experts and policymakers. Each is experimenting with the use of web-based information and communication technologies to increase efficiency and facilitate communication among researchers (Figure 15.2).

The first network, the Economy and Environment Program for Southeast Asia (EEPSEA), was established in 1993 to support research and training in environmental and resource economics in the region, supporting and building the capacity of researchers in Vietnam, the Philippines, Indonesia, Lao PDR, Myanmar, Cambodia, and Thailand. The specific set of topics addressed included regional climate change studies, drinking water supply

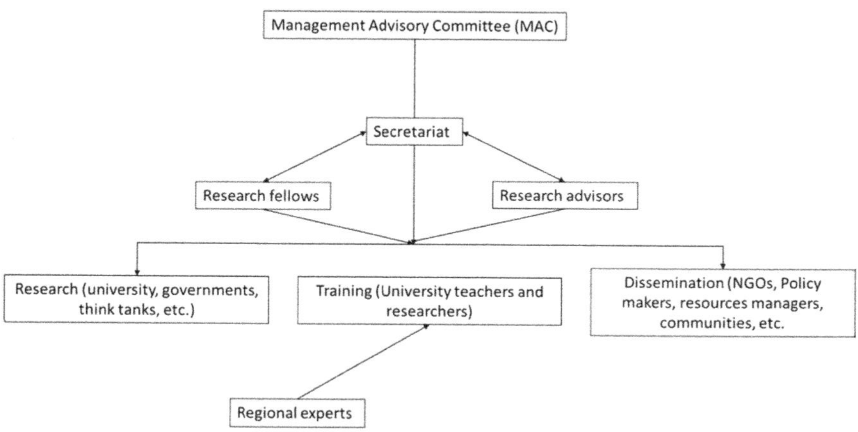


*Figure 15.2* Management structure of each network. *Source:* Author's illustration

improvement, protected area funding and management constraints, and willingness to pay for the conservation of endangered species.

Following the success of EEPSEA, the South Asian Network for Development and Environmental Economics (SANDEE) was launched in 1999. This network brought together key researchers and institutes from Bangladesh, Bhutan, India, Nepal, Pakistan, the Maldives, and Sri Lanka to address issues related to the linkages between development, poverty, and the environment but also included topics on trade-offs between ecosystem services and economic activities, locally relevant adaptation to climate change and related costs and benefits, and green development policies and programmes. As an important platform in the region, SANDEE facilitated policy-relevant research on the economics of the environment and enhanced the regional capacity for research.

The Centre for Environmental Economics and Policy in Africa (CEEPA) has worked with African researchers since 2001. It is housed at the Faculty of Agricultural and Natural Sciences of the University of Pretoria (South Africa), which provides core funding for its teaching and research activities. CEEPA's research strategy includes linkages between poverty and access to and dependence on natural resources: poverty and environmental health: globalization, trade, and the environment with special emphasis on macroeconomic and sectoral policies: improved measures and analyses of sustainability and well-being: institutional determinants of ecosystem change (depletion and degradation of natural capital) and consequences for human well-being: and impact of as well as adaptation to global environmental change.

The Latin American and Caribbean Environmental Economics Program (LACEEP) was launched in March 2005. Supported by International Development Research Center (IDRC) and Swedish International Development Cooperation Agency (SIDA), the LACEEP secretariat is administered by the Tropical Agricultural Research and Higher Education Center in Turrialba, Costa Rica.

The networks have been working on a variety of topics, each in response to local environmental issues and also linked to the goal of lowering a barrier or a set of barriers to the uptake of adaptation options. Their approach to capacity building includes:

- **knowledge custody, co-production, dissemination, and translation:** by increasing knowledge sharing across the scientific community, linking projects and people, thus creating a protected nursery of ideas and innovations.
- **outreach:** by increasing the outreach to users and processes unreachable or unknown by single participants or research teams.
- **capacity:** by acting as a pool of regional experts from which local organisations can draw to increase leadership and capacity in specific domains; and

- **coordination and legacy**: by coordinating sets of projects and actions, carrying learning in space and time, and looking for resources for subsequent phases.

The EEPSEA, LACEEP, CEEPA, and SANDEE networks share several similarities with other knowledge networks such as Intergovernmental Panel on Climate Change (IPCC), Third World Network, Global Development Network or the Climate and Development Knowledge Network, etc. In fact, they provide a platform for multidisciplinary and multistakeholder work, allow expertise to be pooled and enable communication and information sharing (Creech et al. 2012: Creech and Ramji 2004 and Mukhopadhyay et al. 2014). These networks are funded on the principle of social learning and aim to improve a certain practice, in this case, EE, and put a strong emphasis on participation and boundaries, peripheries, linkages, and interaction (Creech et al. 2012).

## 15.3 Outcomes

Most of the information and statistics used in this section were extracted from the various internal and external evaluations conducted over the years to assess the effectiveness of the networks. Each one of the networks was examined following three main factors: their achievements in terms of research and publications (working papers, journal articles, book chapters etc.), capacity building (regular training courses, specialized courses, etc.) and finally, policy influence (participation grantees to policy-related events, production, and dissemination of policy outputs) (for more details, see Glover 2010: Mukhopadhyay et al. 2014). Although it is a brave attempt from the authors to document all the achievements of these networks, the following section presents some high-level activities to provide the readers with some flavour of their contributions.

### *15.3.1 SANDEE*

SANDEE is one of the most successful networks in terms of capacity building and generating new knowledge on the economic and environmental problems in South Asia. The vast majority of SANDEE's funded studies in recent years focused on ecosystem services, climate change, and green growth-related issues. Several of these studies examined farmer responses to increasing risk and uncertainty posed by climate change and local adaptation measures. For example, two studies from Nepal and Pakistan have adopted similar methods, and a comparison of the results from them help enhance understanding of the difficulties and pitfalls that farmers in developing countries face in perceiving and adapting to climate change. Research also focused on interventions, particularly related to water, agriculture, and climate-related disasters, to understand how well these interventions may be working. SANDEE research on ecosystems has grown significantly in recent years, which examined the benefits of ecosystem services and trade-offs associated with managing these services. Another strand of ecosystem disservice research – research that analyses ecosystem functions whose effects are perceived to be harmful, unpleasant, or unwanted to human well-being (Lyytimäki 2015) – examined the costs of human-wildlife conflicts and benefits associated with mitigation measures in Bhutan, India, and Nepal. Some of this research received wide television coverage in mid-2014 in Bhutan. In Bangladesh, SANDEE supported a study on the impact of shrimp farming on paddy production. Shrimp farming changes the ecology of paddy due to saline ingress. In Nepal, a SANDEE study examined the appropriate design of a community-based insurance programme to cope with ecosystem disservices from elephant-human conflict.

Research emerging from the networks has been integrated into various national and regional initiatives. For instance, several SANDEE-trained researchers contributed to the REDD+ work[2] currently underway in Nepal. Under 'greener' policies and programmes, SANDEE research examined the implementation of environmental regulations in the region. For instance, SANDEE research highlighted as to why some municipalities are more successful than others in banning plastic bags. Many municipalities are now currently in discussion on a wider ban on plastics. Research in Pakistan examined clean production interventions in the tanning industry and whether firms continue to learn and innovate post such interventions. This research complements some previous studies on 'greening' the tourism sector in Sri Lanka. SANDEE also supported some new work that examined the new corporate social responsibility law in India and whether this is contributing to 'green' investments.

Several SANDEE-funded research has informed policy in many South Asian countries. For instance, research in Sri Lanka on shifting cultivation generated interest in the forest department because it provided some evidence on who participates in this form of agriculture and offered a solution to an ongoing debate between the courts and the forest department. Research in Nepal on banning plastic bags, crop residue burning, REDD+, and targeting of renewable energy subsidies have caught the attention of policymakers in several Ministries (Local Development, Agriculture, Forests, etc.). In India and other countries, SANDEE's policy influence continues to be mainly through the leadership provided by various researchers as they grow in seniority and participate in various research and policy activities. In India, SANDEE-related research has been cited in environmental legal cases, several SANDEE researchers were linked to the new Economics of Ecosystem and Biodiversity (TEEB) India programme and researchers served in advisory roles, particularly in their own states. These are a few examples of SANDEE's efforts in providing an evidence base for informed policymaking.

Capacity building is a core component of all the networks and has been particularly brought forward within this particular network. For instance, between 2011 and 2013, the networks organized more than 20 courses and 6 research and development workshops. The courses and workshops covered various topics: from introductory courses on Environmental and Resource Economics, Research & Proposal Writing, to basic training (microeconomics, policy dissemination, econometrics, and climate change research) and advanced topics on environmental economics (CGE Modeling, Advanced Econometrics, Household modelling, Survey Methods, Climate Change, Climate Science & Policy, Program Evaluation, Paying for Environmental Services, and Policy Tools for Climate Change). Overall, SANDEE contributed to two areas of the environment-economy interface in order to have an impact at scale: the use of environmental economics concepts such as environmental valuations in public decision-making processes and the use of environmental economics in education the media, and public discussion. It has continued to advocate for policy changes by using strategic grants or funding partnerships with other donors from the beginning (e.g., the World Bank, UNEP, ICIMOD, etc.). SANDEE facilitated the dissemination of outcomes in many forums (national and international conferences and workshops) to disseminate the knowledge generated by its research effort. Part of the over 800 participants and SANDEE's 'graduates' are now developing new courses and curricula on environmental economics at their respective universities. In addition, several SANDEE working papers and research papers have been used as teaching and reference materials in many universities across South Asia. Fostering intellectual dialogue and exchange across the region to generate impact at scale was one of SANDEE's main achievements. Another significant contribution of SANDEE was on the academic and professional development of younger environmental economists across the region. SANDEE-trained individuals are gradually occupying strategic posts within governments, NGOs, and academic institutions. SANDEE has also had an impact on the careers of some grantees in terms of connecting them to international organizations and networks that they would not have otherwise been able to reach. It is evident that, as individuals, quite a few SANDEE grantees are now in leadership positions to advise policymakers on important environmental and climate change issues in the region.

### *15.3.2 LACEEP*

Many research projects supported by this network have significantly contributed to policy debates in the regions. For example, LACEEP-funded study in Brazil assessed the impact of severe droughts on school attendance and performance in Northeast rural areas, a region where the frequency of droughts is expected to increase due to climate change. The findings from this study already informed a new initiative on the Schools with Cisterns

Program (*Programa Cisterna nas Escolas*) implemented by the Articulação Semiárido Brasileir (ASA), an association representing more than 1,000 NGOs whose activities are related to the Brazilian semi-arid region. The programme aims at providing cisterns to 5,000 rural schools in Northeast Brazil.

Another study explored whether protected areas can be used as a climate adaptation strategy in order to reduce the adverse effects of climate change. The study uses climatic information to describe how climate can affect health outcomes and explores whether protected areas are effective in reducing negative effects. The project conducted extensive consultations with experts and decision-makers, such as technicians and practitioners from the National Water Quality Lab and the Health Monitor Division of the Ministry of Health, as well as deep literature reviews on the mechanisms that link ecosystem changes and human health.

Another study from Chile explored the relationship between climate change adaptation and agricultural productivity and profitability. Using originally collected survey data from a representative sample of 400 farmers in Central Chile, this work concluded that climate change would have enormous impacts on agriculture in Central Chile. Due to the importance of the research, the author was invited to be part of a national expert panel to recommend the formulation process of a proposal presented by the Chilean Agriculture Ministry and Food and Agricultural Organization (FAO) to the Green Climate Fund. A LACEEP-funded study in Mexico City investigated how access to clean and safe water improves the well-being of urban dwellers as an important determinant of health. The study looks at ways to incentivize the consumption of municipally provided drinking water. This work contributes to our understanding of the role of policies and social norms in the construction of sustainable consumption patterns of urban dwellings. The authors worked closely with the National Laboratory of Sciences of the Sustainability of the National Autonomous University of Mexico (UNAM) and the Water System of the City of Mexico.

LACEEP's researchers analyzed how forest conservation relates to conflict in Colombia. They showed that civil conflict reduces the impact of Colombia's protected areas on deforestation. Findings from this study were presented to Colombian police and military forces, and the authors had conversations with the Environmental Agency of Antioquia in Colombia, given that this region has a large extension of protected areas but has faced significant armed conflict. This issue is highly relevant not only for Latin America but for other regions in the world where civil conflict and conservation interact. A team of LACEEP grantees studied the role of financial instruments, savings, and uncertainty in the decision to implement retrofits by households in central-south Chile. They concluded that the main obstacle for household investment is the cost, but that highlighting the saving side of the deal coupled with medium-term loans could trigger a decision to retrofit. These results were widely shared in policy discussions in Chile.

LACEEP had invested important resources in building the capacity of its grantees on policymaking to equip them with tools and methods to aim at influencing decisions and policymakers. Some LACEEP grantees are now in positions to advise policymakers on important environmental issues. For example, one of the researchers from Ecuador had to shorten the planned duration of his participation at a Workshop since he was involved in advising a cabinet minister in his country on an approach to secure international financing for a protected area where valuable hydrocarbon deposits are located. Similarly, investments in building human capital have placed many of the network's grantees in positions where they have the capacity, knowledge and power to influence key environmental policy issues in their respective countries.

The network invested a great effort to enhance the capacity to conduct high-quality research on the economic side of environmental problems. LACEEP identified the need for training in impact evaluation and economic valuation of environmental resources about ten years ago. At the time, those were incipient fields that were largely out of the reach of Latin American scholars in the region. By focusing on research and academic capacity building in the area of environmental economics, LACEEP undoubtedly generated new knowledge for large-scale positive impact.

Perhaps, the most important contribution of LACEEP was in field building. At the start of LACEEP (in 2005), capacity in environmental economics was virtually non-existent in most countries in the region, with a few exceptions, such as Chile. There was not one single master's programme in environmental economics in the region. This situation has now changed as EE is a well-established and thriving field, with a constant flow of master's and PhD students and strong teams in multiple countries. By focusing on research and academic capacity building in the area of environmental economics, LACEEP implicitly assumed an impact pathway that goes through the creation of high-level educators in universities first. These postdocs, PhDs and MScs are now seen as the new generation of environmental economists who are now part of the network committed to building capacity in the region. The region is now in a stage in which it can sustain both an increasing demand for environmental economics advice for policy design and a steady supply to match it.

### *15.3.3 EEPSEA*

EEPSEA was one of the largest environmental economics networks supported by Canada's International Development Research Center (IDRC) along with other like-minded donors. EEPSEA-funded research spans from climate change energy to the management of protected areas in Southeast

Asia with some major policy implications. For example, a study on establishing payment for environmental services for Sustainable Eco-Tourism in the Philippines largely informed the tourism master plan for the Partido area, the fourth congressional district of the Philippines' Camarines Sur province. The key insights and recommendations from this research were integrated into the strategies and action plans of the tourism master plan. An EEPSEA-funded study on the cost-benefit analysis of sustainability standards in smallholder oil palm farming in Sumatra attracted the attention of the Indonesia Estate Crop Fund for Palm Oil (IECFPO). This led to another research project on the valuation of the price determinants of fresh fruit bunches and crude palm oil, as well as the empowerment of cooperatives as smallholder institutions for replanting in the province of Jambi. The result from this study is currently being utilized by IECFPO to prepare Jambi's sustainable standards for palm oil replanting.

As a result of the EEPSEA cross-country research project on Fiscal Gap and Financing of Southeast Asia's Protected Areas, the Philippines Government amended the Republic Act No. 10629 (National Integrated Protected Areas System of 1992) to provide the retention by the Protected Area Management Board (PAMB) of 75% of the protected area revenue accruing to the Integrated Protected Area Fund. This was approved in September 2013. Previously, PAMB could only retain 25% of the revenue. EEPSEA research on the cost of illness of exposure to air pollution and the cost of an alternative mode of public transport in the city of Baguio, Philippines, received much attention from both the media and government agencies. The Principal Investigator of the project (Achilles Costales) was invited by the Environment Management Bureau (EMB) as the Academic Representative in the Technical Working Group on Air Quality Control Strategies – a five municipality agglomeration. The committee is currently finalizing the policy measures to be undertaken to improve the air quality within this jurisdiction.

Another study assessed the effectiveness of information provision and feedback on electricity consumption in influencing electricity conservation by households in Bangkok, Thailand. The Metropolitan Electricity Authority and the Provincial Electricity Authority (PEA) have already picked up several recommendations from this project as a measure to meet Thailand's commitment to reduce greenhouse gas emissions. A few years back, the Jakarta Disaster Mitigation Agency approached EEPSEA to help in conducting a training course on how to do flood damage assessment in reference to funded research on the Estimation of River Flood Damage in Jakarta. Another EEPSEA study, which determined the factors that affect the participation of the members of the waste bank in Indonesia's Depok municipality, led to two waste banks as a pilot project. More than 30 waste banks in the district are currently under operation after the successful outcome of this pilot project.

From research and dissemination activities discussed earlier, EEPSEA has created significant influence – not only towards improving environmental economics research capacity in the region but also in influencing environmental policy and decision-making. For example, from 2012 to 2017, EEPSEA organized 34 training courses in which many researchers from all over the region were trained, 53% of which were women. EEPSEA supported the participation of 132 researchers to attend international conferences during this period. The majority of the training participants (75%) are university-based researchers/lecturers who teach undergraduate and graduate courses: this increases the power of the Program's training courses through the multiplier effect. Twenty (20) of the 34 courses conducted by EEPSEA had its alumni as instructors, which highlights the programme's success in developing local leadership on the subject.

Another major achievement for EEPSEA was its capacity-building efforts for environment-economic policy research in Myanmar. With Myanmar's current efforts to advance their economic development parallel with environmental conservation, EEPSEA took advantage of this opportunity to build research capacity specifically designed for Myanmar researchers. EEPSEA conducted three in-country training courses on environmental economics during this period and funded 10 out of the 27 small research grants in this country. This was crucial for Myanmar researchers, who later were successful in receiving another big cross-country research project on land degradation that was funded by a German-based organization called 'GIZ' and the United Nations Convention to Combat Desertification (UNCCD).

EEPSEA also organized a high-level training which targeted Myanmar's policymakers in which 26 policymakers participated. Further, the Lower Mekong Sub-Region Environment Economics Institute (EEI-LMS) conducted several activities in the sub-region with funding support from EEPSEA, and many of its activities had focused on Myanmar. Another significant step of EEPSEA was cross-country research on coastal resources management, poverty, and value chain analysis in Cambodia, the Philippines, Thailand, and Indonesia.

Finally, the direct outcome of EEPSEA was the sustainability and devolution of this network at the local level. EEPSEA's transition phase managed to establish national environmental economics institutes in Vietnam, the Philippines, Indonesia, and Thailand. The sub-regional institute based in Thailand will cover the Lower Mekong Sub-region countries: Thailand, Lao PDR, Myanmar, and Cambodia. These institutes are independent but are connected under the umbrella of the Economy and Environment Partnership, a regional organization based in Vietnam administered by the University of Economics Ho Chi Minh City. They are made up of EEPSEA alumni who are committed to continue the capacity-building work of EEPSEA and to support their governments in environmental policymaking. A website for the newly developed Economy & Environment Partnership for Southeast

Asia (www.eepseapartners.org) was developed with funding support from the programme. It was launched in April 2016. The EEPSEA partnership is already assisting governments in the region in their efforts to foster greener, cleaner, and more inclusive development (Vincent 2008).

### *15.3.4 CEEPA*

Since its creation, CEEPA's activities have been focused on creating a continent-wide community of environmental economics researchers and build research capacity through competitive research grants from the outset. CEEPA-funded research has made some contribution to the field of environmental economics with policy-relevant research outputs in Africa. For example, one of the major CEEPA-funded flagship studies investigated the determinants of carbon dioxide emissions in six African countries. It found that the main driving force behind carbon emissions in the sample of countries was income per capita and that they were not determined by short-term fluctuations in real GDP per capita. Further, the growth of the service sector, other things being equal, does not reduce carbon emissions. The recommendation from this study has been taken forward by some countries in Africa to incorporate environmental concerns into their macroeconomic policies, reduce carbon emissions, and switch to a less polluting energy mix.

Several studies examined climate adaptation solutions being pursued by households and local authorities in Africa. A study from South Africa analyzes the risk attitudes of individuals living in flood-prone urban informal settlements (Bidwell et al. 2013). The results indicate that individuals adopting more effective (and costly) adaptation strategies are more risk-averse. It implies that attempts by local authorities to encourage uptake of adaptation strategies must consider risk attitudes. Another study from Nigeria found that high temperatures have significant negative impacts on yields of cassava, cotton, and maize. The findings were used to develop a weather index crop insurance scheme along with information from Nigeria's Meteorological Agency (NIMET) as a complement to the current nationwide multi-peril agricultural insurance scheme.

CEEPA made a great effort to boost the profile of researchers in Africa by providing them with opportunities to represent the continent in different international events (i.e., international environmental economics conferences). It is evident that African environmental economists are increasingly publishing articles in top international journals in the environment and development economics area. Africa's share of both submissions and published articles in the Cambridge University journal 'Environment and Development Economics' has increased substantially in the past decade, which can be directly attributed to this capacity-building programme. Statistics from the 2015 annual conference of the European Association of Environmental and Resource Economics (EAERE) confirmed a gradual increment of accepted papers for EAERE conferences were from countries served by CEEPA. This was an interesting finding and highlighted the solid contribution of this network in environmental economics rising importance.

## 15.4 Discussion

Networks are an important tool for empirical research and the development of innovative solutions. They are broadly understood to be a 'combination of persons [or organizations], usually dispersed over a number of geographically separate sites, with appropriate communications technology' (Clark 1998: Creech and Willard 2001). A subcategory, Development networks, has a 'well-defined theme and carefully chosen criteria for participation, existing to create knowledge and accelerate the application of that knowledge to economic and social development, and have a formal constitution and tight governance' (Clark 1998).

The use of networks for capacity building and sustainable development has had uncertain beginnings. They were created as a means to change public and private sector actions to be more supportive of sustainable development but have often failed to deliver on their objectives. The frameworks upon which the networks are modelled have proven to be well suited to address the various challenges that usually plague capacity-building networks. In fact, irregular interactions, little project collaboration and no demonstrable sign of the decision-makers having read or used the research and advice emerging from the networks (Creech and Willard 2001) were early signs that networks were not the most effective tool for capacity building.

Climate change and environmental degradation have profound, complex and uncertain social, political, cultural, and environmental consequences. The networks were made to internalize these challenges, having been based on a framework that provides various avenues and an all-encompassing pathway to build capacities. This inherent complexity and uncertainty have provoked the need for more effective and meaningful collaboration between researchers, policymakers, the private sector and other civil society stakeholders.

The Global South required strong EE research capacities to address these and complex environmental and social challenges. The capacity-building framework and the resulting networks have internalized this need and created key opportunities for innovation through the provision of information and a platform for the sharing of ideas. The framework has prompted the creation of networks with unique characteristics and governance structures. As a result, the four networks have supported several hundreds of researchers and projects in the field of Environmental Economics in Latin America and the Caribbean, Africa, South Asia, and South-East Asia for more than 25 years now. Below we review some of the lessons learned and challenges that have been faced as well as some of the issues that would need to be addressed in any future similar endeavours.

### *Lesson 1: Capacity Building and Collaboration Are at the Core of the Functioning of the Networks*

Partnerships and networks for capacity building are not new. Planning for sustainable development is a complex issue. Building the capacity of the people most equipped to address these issues does not simplify these challenges but provide them with the economic knowledge, tools, and skills to advise decision and policymakers. The core principle of all four networks is capacity building in the field of environmental economics. One of the foundations of the networks' strategies in the offering of courses, workshops, and other activities is building of each trainee's existing knowledge and skills in the conduct of EE. Capacities building through regional networks follow a user-centric approach: each network identifies local knowledge gaps and capacity-building needs and builds its programming accordingly. The strategy used by the networks goes beyond the simple learning and teaching strategies into creating an environment that can help leverage local best practices and foster cross-country collaboration. This fact has been particularly important in SANDEE, where researchers went beyond regional political tensions to implement cross-country projects, creating valuable opportunities to generate knowledge that transcend individual study sites. However, cross-country collaborative projects are not simple. They require strong coordination and are very demanding of researchers, resource persons, and the secretariat.

### *Lesson 2: Fostering Local Leadership Is Critical*

Efforts to build the local research capacity as local researchers are the best placed to address their local environmental problems. More often than not, capacity-building projects fail to deliver their intended impact to the beneficiaries and in general, projects that are replicated in several locations/phases which succeed in one location frequently fail, either partially or completely, in another location (Ika and Donnelly 2017), emphasizing the importance of grounding such initiatives within the local cultural context using local actors, in the creation and implementation of capacity building projects in an international development context.

All four regional networks have organized local scientific and technological expertise to facilitate learning and accelerate local policy and environmental problem-solving. To achieve this, each network has mobilized support throughout their respective regions to produce practical solutions and long-term pathways for economically sound sustainable development, promote high-quality training and research collaboration, and support transnational and local governments in understanding and addressing the social and technological challenges of climate change and environmental degradation to foster sustainable development.

The action-oriented research fostered by each one of these networks has provided support for each country to adopt and implement policies and practices that provide a cataclysm for change and foster local and regional leadership in sustainability. For instance, SANDEE's comparative advantages at present lie in its capacity-building efforts. They are especially important and noteworthy in South Asia, where transboundary academic collaboration has been difficult due to geopolitical tensions. SANDEE has provided a mechanism for environmental and resource economists across the South Asia region to meet and collaborate despite these tensions. Fostering intellectual dialogue and exchange across the South Asia region is one of SANDEE's main achievements.

Similarly, CEEPA has greatly contributed to the creation of a network of environmental economists in Africa. This has not just improved the quality of research funded, but the network has brought together experts from across the continent, providing a venue for people to develop personal networks and access senior researchers otherwise unavailable. The programme has spawned the Centre for Environmental Economic Research and Consultancy in Ghana, which provides similar network benefits at the national level.

The geographic variability of the effects of global environmental change emphasizes the need for 'place-based' approaches to research and planning (Adger and Kelly 1999: Cutter et al. 2000, Turner et al. 2003, Measham et al. 2011). Because each one of these networks operates regionally, they are well-positioned to provide solutions to locally specific problems. They nurture researchers with local lived experience that will, in turn, propose locally grounded solutions or recommendations for local problems, breaking down the western disciplinary monopole in their respective regions.

### *Lesson 3: Strengthening the Link between Research and Policy Is the Key to Sustainability*

Countries and policymakers are keen to understand how national budgets and plans can be applied to address climate-related challenges in the most cost-effective way. Bidwell et al. (2013) argue that forging network connections among communities of policymakers and researchers is an effective way to keep up with the growing supply of and demand for science for policy at the local level. This is especially important for networks or researchers that have direct links to policymakers and that have established long-term trust relationships with decision-makers and other stakeholders, thus raising the chances of producing and sharing information that is more salient, relevant, timely and legitimate (Cash et al. 2003: Dilling and Lemos

2011: Bidwell et al. 2013). As such, locally rooted networks of researchers can bolster the capacity of local governments to plan and implement sustainability initiatives, initiatives that are often able to shape local and regional policymaking. For instance, EEPSEA created an enabling environment that strengthened the dialogue between the regional network and local policymakers. In fact, since its creation, the network saw an increased focus on the preparation of policy recommendations and the organization of outreach conferences. One highlight of this dialogue was the Policy Impact Conference in Hanoi in 2010, which brought forward 40 projects where EEPSEA research contributed to policy change. CEEPA, on the other hand, in an effort to enable more interaction with the policy community, invited observers from the policy community and has organized short courses for local policymakers. While the reach has been relatively limited in the beginning, there have been important improvements in recent years. Similarly, LACEEP has been working on building and strengthening the capacities of junior researchers and, to a lesser extent, the capacities of those researchers' organizations, of other research users, and of institutions. Several of these trainees are now in positions to advise policymakers on important environmental issues.

An important effort was made in each network to better articulate and incorporate regional policy research needs and priorities into their work. In some cases, the reach has been quite limited, and in others, policymakers have been involved from the beginning of a specific project. Involving policymakers or natural resource managers at the start of each research project, especially on topics that are a high priority for governments, is particularly important, more so in countries where the government bureaucracy is a significant constraint. This realization has, in fact, increased the policy relevance and impact of funded research activities.

### *Lesson 4: Emphasize Peer Learning and Support*

Ensuring effective, dynamic, and timely exchange between peers and senior researchers is vital to strengthen capacity-building efforts beyond helping package research and providing training (EEPSEA impact report 1993–2000). As emphasized by the framework at the core of the creation of the networks (Figure 15.1), networking opportunities and mentorship are central to the success of these initiatives.

Peers learning to provide opportunities for members' joint reflection and knowledge co-creation, but also for solution sharing and policy recommendations that have been proven more or less successful to address comparable sustainability issues within similar local and cultural contexts. It helps create a repertoire of solutions and good practices that is dynamic and can be shared among members. Ultimately, the goal is to foster lasting systemic change within the policy areas that members will integrate in the future.

As mentioned before, a core aspect of the success and longevity of networks is their local relevance. Responding locally to global environmental challenges, it is important for these networks of learned communities to be inclusive, reflective, and build mutually supportive and collaborative groups of people. To be effective, they should go beyond just bounding social capital – with networks composed of people from similar demographics and socio-economic and educational backgrounds – towards bridging and linking social capital (as described by Grootaert et al. 2004) that foster both horizontal and vertical relationships and connections and operate across demographics, social characteristics, scientific disciplines, and power.

#### *Lesson 5: Creating a Representative and Inclusive Environment Is Primordial*

While peer exchange and learning are key to the functioning of these networks, creating an *enabling environment* to foster these activities is even more important. Economics has historically been a male-dominated profession around the world. Female presence in the field has historically been low – less than 15% of women in 2016 were full professors (Bhattacharjee 2007: Lundberg 2017). However, the participation of women in each one of the regional networks has been higher than the proportion of female researchers in economics. Grant recipients – 21–46% across all four networks were women. From their inception, there has been a real push from regional and international development agencies to encourage more programmes to address gender issues, including both awareness raising and policy research, but also in the management of the networks. While no intersectional data exist, it is important to note the effort of each network to be gender inclusive.

One of the main issues lies in the regional representativeness of some networks. In CEEPA, most of the countries are represented in the network: there is a notable absence of Francophone and Lusophone Africa. Similarly, in LACEEP, most of the Caribbean is absent from the proceedings, except for Jamaica. Developing a continent-wide community of environmental economics researchers require active investments in geographical participation, and future similar initiative should also aim to do so.

#### *Lesson 6: Increasing Policy Reach*

Influencing policymaking is one of the key goals of researchers and grantees involved in the networks. Most researchers face the challenge of translating research outputs in a way that is understood and usable to policymakers while remaining true to their original meaning (Perkin and Court 2005). While some networks provided courses on how to package research outputs to policymakers (notably SANDEE and EEPSEA), this practice was not common across all networks. In addition, some grantees were government employees: hence they were less likely able to critique and question government actions. Most notably, EEPSEA provided pathways to researchers to influence policymaking in the form of plenary lectures on the topic at biannual workshops and by offering specialized courses pertinent to it (e.g., on effective writing, policy analysis for environmental economists, and water and sanitation policy and planning).

Perkin and Court (2005) provided four ways through which networks can effectively influence policymaking within each stage of the policymaking process:

(i) At the agenda-setting stage, by the networks members can convince policymakers that a particular issue requires their attention and by providing the social, economic, and environmental reasons as to why this issue is important.
(ii) During the policy formulation process, by providing possible solutions, options and human resources (in the form of researchers or grassroots organizations) with the help of each network's expertise. It helps build a collaborative relationship with policymakers and build consensus.
(iii) During the policy implementation by complementing government activities and troubleshooting actions for better efficiency: and
(iv) During the policy implementation process, by providing good quality evidence and feedback, but also by facilitating and mediating dialogue between policymakers and end-users.

The goal is to create an atmosphere of interaction and knowledge exchange. However, collaboration and clear communication pathways are the keys to success.

## 15.5 Conclusions and Implications for Future Large-Scale Capacity-Building Projects

Knowledge-action networks in the field of environmental economics emphasize active collaboration and knowledge co-creation among all its members. In this chapter, we have presented four regional EE networks that work to build the capacity of local researchers and local sustainability issues. While all four networks share similar characteristics, they have proved that they operate within a specific niche to create quality research outputs. Much evidence indicates that the four regional EE networks have developed active communities of skilled environmental economics researchers and generated high-quality research output in Asia, Africa, Latin America, and the Caribbean. Here, we try answering one of the most important questions: what's next? Two main issues have been identified that can impact the sustainability of the networks and of the initiative as a whole, the first in terms of strategic direction and the second regarding the financial sustainability.

### 15.5.1 Devising a New Strategic Direction

Various evaluations have been conducted over the years, and numerous grantees have been interviewed in order to specifically bring forward some of the strategic issues that can arise with the networks' programming. Three main areas of change have been identified: exploring new capacity-building areas, focusing on in-country policy reach and finally facilitating cross-country research projects.

Most networks' members agree that policymaking should be an explicit new strategic direction, and as such, a specific capacity-building plan and communication strategy should be explored to inform this direction. For instance, a review by Creech and Willard (2001) has recommended that knowledge networks will gain in devising strategies, plans, and processes to engage decision and policymakers directly. It is important to note that the networks should not become a solution provider. Instead, they should continue advocating the use of EE in policymaking and create capacity-building courses that target policymakers. Working with policymakers from the research design will facilitate its intake and enable the translation of research outcomes into policy and practice.

In addition to policymaking, cross-country research projects and collaboration would be an important strategic direction to explore. Environmental degradation and climate change do not stop at borders. Similarly, water resources management is often a transboundary issue. However, political disagreements often prohibit comprehensive management, further aggravating the situation. SANDEE, for instance, facilitated cross-border collaboration on a research project between India and Pakistan. A specific cross-country research program will provide many opportunities for high-impact projects and improve policy reach, especially on topics that are a high priority for government bodies. Obviously, designing and implementing cross-country is not simple and would require more time and resources (financial and human). To do so, both the researchers and the networks' secretariat should have the required knowledge, capacity, and resources required to facilitate and help coordinate longer and cross-country projects. This would involve, for instance, providing more support for proposal development. However, cross-country initiatives will provide many opportunities for high-impact projects. This would be especially valuable in South Asia from a geopolitical perspective for demonstrating the importance of transboundary environmental research.

Finally, all these initiatives cannot come to fruition without the appropriate capacity building and communication strategy in place. The most vital advantage of the networks is their capacity-building work. Exploring new areas and formats for the creation of knowledge would keep the networks relevant and active. This goes not only for the choice of topics for workshops, webinars, and short courses but also for the way PhD scholarship recipients are mentored. Finally, recognizing the diversity of languages and cultures within each network, it would also be primordial to propose programmes and courses in Spanish, Portuguese, and French in order to support and sustain these growing networks.

### 15.5.2 Breaking Down Donor Dependency

With the support of external international organizations such as IDRC and SIDA, among others, the networks have thrived for several decades. However, the dependency on external donors limits the reach and sustainability of the networks. A number of ways have been explored to ensure that each network can keep its integrity, functions and programmes while breaking down its dependency on external funding. For instance, WorldFish, a member of the Consortium of International Agricultural Research Centre (CGIAR), was selected to host the EEPSEA Network in November 2012. Prior to its institutionalization, the network has been promoting more focused partnerships with key regional organizations/donors (e.g., ASEAN, Mekong River Commission) and exploring the possibilities of establishing a regional centre in one of the member countries with a local host institution. These avenues would facilitate the cost-effective management of activities and support. Similarly, since 2017, SANDEE has been an integral part of the International Center for Integrated Mountain Development (ICIMOD), institutionalizing the research brand that had been created over 15 years of investment (over four phases) by IDRC and SIDA. In both cases, the networks will continue to work in mentoring and training a new generation of researchers in the regions they operate.

### 15.5.3 Opportunities for Scaling Up and Addressing New Priorities

The final question is how we build on this success and scale up this initiative? The framework has provided an important foundation for future endeavours. It is important to reiterate that even if the framework has provided the guiding principles upon which the networks have been created, a specific approach, internalizing regional specificities, has been used for each one of the networks. It would be ideal if scaling up initiatives retained successful elements of the earlier networks while incorporating specific cultural elements for the creation of networks in francophone Africa or the Caribbean (see lesson 5), or even in the Pacific, for instance. Each one of these areas comes with its specific set of challenges. However, by partnering with policymakers and established organizations early on in each of these regions and building on the six lessons learned, it can overall improve the probability of success of these initiatives.

In addition to a possible new strategic direction, it is important for the networks to respond to new climate priorities to stay relevant. For a few years, EEPSEA has been supporting countries to explore new financial instruments for guiding countries towards building a Green Economy. The UN Environment defines a Green Economy as low carbon, resource-efficient and socially inclusive economy that allow for 'reduced carbon emissions and pollution enhanced energy and resource efficiency, and prevention of the loss of biodiversity and ecosystem services.'[3] Besides the development of new policies and economic instruments, capacity building is a central theme of the transitioning. This is a niche within which the EE networks can thrive.

All knowledge-action networks are born following the identification of a knowledge gap that inhibits proper policy responses for climate action and sustainable development. It is clear that all four of the presented networks have made a significant contribution in EE capacity building and also to the development of a local leadership trained in addressing local sustainability issues. It is also important to note that a strong emphasis has been made, since the creation of these networks, on the capacity building for early career researchers. These networks have funded research that provided the necessary evidence to create strong policies that address environmental issues in countries across each of their region of action. The networks' incorporation within strong, existing entities has solved some of the financial sustainability issues associated with networks. However, to continue to be relevant, efforts should be made to not only be inclusive and geographically representative but also pursue new strategic directions that will help in addressing the ever-evolving nature of climate change and environmental degradation.

## Acknowledgement

This chapter is informed by various technical reports from the four regional environmental economics networks to IDRC and mid-term evaluation reports of these networks. The first author also acknowledges the interactions with the network secretariats and researchers over the past ten years, whose comments and insights were helpful to prepare this manuscript.

## Notes

1 Agenda 21, the Rio Declaration on Environment and Development, and the Statement of principles for the Sustainable Management of Forests were adopted by more than 178 Governments at the United Nations Conference on Environment and Development (UNCED) held in Rio de Janeiro, Brazil, 3 to 14 June 1992. Agenda 21 is a comprehensive plan of action to be taken globally, nationally and locally by organizations of the United Nations System, Governments, and Major Groups in every area in which human impacts on the environment.

2 REDD+ is a framework created by the UNFCCC Conference of the Parties (COP) to guide activities in the forest sector that reduces emissions from deforestation

and forest degradation, as well as the sustainable management of forests and the conservation and enhancement of forest carbon stocks in developing countries.

3 See https://www.unenvironment.org/regions/asia-and-pacific/regional-initiatives/supporting-resource-efficiency/green-economy for more information (accessed on 12 June 2021)

## References

Adger, W.N. and P.M. Kelly. 1999. "Social Vulnerability to Climate Change and the Architecture of Entitlements." *Mitigation and Adaptation Strategies for Global Change* 4: 253–266. doi:10.1023/A:1009601904210.

Arrow, K., B. Bolin, R. Costanza, P. Dasgupta, C. Folke, C.S. Holling and Bengt-Owe Jansson et al. 1996. "Economic Growth, Carrying Capacity, and the Environment". *Environment and Development Economics* 1 (1): 104–110. doi:10.1017/s1355770x00000413.

Baland, J. and J. Platteau. 1996. *Halting Degradation of Natural Resources: Is there a Role of* Rural *Communities*? New York: FAO, Oxford University Press.

Barbier, E. 2005. *Natural Resources and Economic Development*. Cambridge: Cambridge University Press, doi: 10.1017/CBO9780511754036.

Bhattacharjee, S., J. A. Herriges and C. L. Kling. 2007. "The Status of Women in Environmental Economics". *Review of Environmental Economics and Policy* 1 (2): 212–227. doi:10.1093/reep/rem017.

Bidwell, D., T. Dietz and D. Scavia. 2013. "Fostering Knowledge Networks for Climate Adaptation". *Nature Climate Change* 3 (7): 610–611. doi:10.1038/nclimate1931.

Carpenter, S.R., H.A. Mooney, J. Agard, D. Capistrano, R.S. DeFries, S. Díaz, T. Dietz, A.K. Duraiappah, A. Oteng-Yeboah, H.M. Pereira and C. Perrings. 2009. "Science for Managing Ecosystem Services: Beyond the Millennium Ecosystem Assessment." *Proceedings of the National Academy of Sciences* 106(5): 1305–1312. https://asu.pure.elsevier.com/en/publications/science-for-managing-ecosystem-services-beyond-the-millennium-eco (accessed on 12 July 2020).

Cash, D.W., W.C. Clark, F. Alcock, N.M. Dickson, N. Eckley, D.H. Guston, J. Jäger and R.B. Mitchell. 2003. "Knowledge systems for sustainable development." *Proceedings of the National Academy of Sciences* 100(14): 8086–8091. https://www.pnas.org/content/100/14/8086 (accessed on 14 July 2020).

Cicin-Sain, B., R.W. Knecht, R. Knecht, D. Jang and G.W. Fisk. 1998. *Integrated Coastal and Ocean Management: Concepts and Practices*. Washington D.C., USA: Island Press. ISBN: 9781559636049. https://www.scirp.org/(S(351jmbntvnsjt1aadkposzje))/reference/ReferencesPapers.aspx?ReferenceID=1650941 (accessed on 7 August 2022)

Clark, H.C. 1998. *Formal Knowledge Networks: A Study of Canadian Experiences*. Ottawa, Canada: International Institute for Sustainable Development, 1998. https://www.iisd.org/system/files/publications/fkn.pdf (accessed on 12 June 2020).

Creech, H. and A. Ramji. 2004. *Knowledge Networks: "Guidelines for Assessment (Working Paper)."* International Institute for Sustainable Development. https://www.iisd.org/system/files/publications/networks_guidelines_for_assessment.pdf (accessed on 11 July 2020).

Creech, H. and T. Willard. 2001. *Strategic Intentions: Managing Knowledge Networks for Sustainable Development*. International Institute for Sustainable Development Report. ISBN 1-895536-48-0. https://idl-bnc-idrc.dspacedirect.org/bitstream/handle/10625/29290/117346.pdf?sequence=5 (accessed on 10 April 2020).

Creech, H., M. Laurie, L. Paas and J.E. Parry. 2012. *Performance Improvement and Assessment of Collaboration: Starting Points for Networks and Communities of Practice*. Manitoba: International Institute of Sustainable Development Report. https://www.iisd.org/system/files/publications/performance_improvement_networks.pdf (accessed on 2 February 2020).

Cutter, Susan L., J. T. Mitchell and M. S. Scott. 2000. "Revealing the Vulnerability of People and Places: A Case Study of Georgetown County, South Carolina". *Annals of the Association of American Geographers* 90 (4): 713–737. doi:10.1111/0004-5608.00219.

Dasgupta, P., S. Levin and J. Lubchenco. 2000. "Economic Pathways to Ecological Sustainability". *Bioscience* 50 (4): 339–345. doi:10.1641/00063568(2000)050[0339:eptes]2.3.co:2.

Davies, J. and M. Richards. 1999. *The Use of Economics to Assess Stakeholders Incentives in Participatory Forest Management: A Review*. European Union Tropical Forestry Paper 5, London: Overseas Development Institute. ISBN: 85003 476 0. https://odi.org/documents/2953/5706.pdf (accessed on 4 February 2020).

Delgado-Serrano, M. del Mar, J. Mistry, B. Matzdorf and G. Leclerc. 2016. "Community-Based Management of Environmental Challenges in Latin America and the Caribbean". *Ecology and Society* 21 (4): 1–12. doi:10.5751/es-08924-210449.

Department for International Development (DFID). 2010. Capacity Building in Research. https://assets.publishing.service.gov.uk/government/uploads/system/uploads/attachment_data/file/187568/HTN_Capacity_Building_Final_21_06_10.pdf (accessed on 8 June 2020).

Dilling, L. and M. C. Lemos. 2011. "Creating Usable Science: Opportunities and Constraints for Climate Knowledge Use and Their Implications for Science Policy". *Global Environmental Change* 21 (2): 680–689. doi:10.1016/j.gloenvcha.2010.11.006.

Glover, D. 2010. *Valuing the Environment: Economics for a Sustainable Future (1)*. IDRC. ISBN 978-1-55250-476-5. https://idl-bnc-idrc.dspacedirect.org/bitstream/handle/10625/44112/IDL-44112.pdf?sequence=1&isAllowed=y (accessed on 9 March 2020).

Grootaert, C., D. Narayan, V. Jones and M. Woolcock. 2004. *Measuring Social Capital*. Working paper no. 18. Washington, DC: The World Bank. https://openknowledge.worldbank.org/bitstream/handle/10986/15033/281100PAPER0Measuring0social0capital.pdf?sequence=1&isAllowed=y (accessed on 7 July 2020).

Hussen, A.M. 2004. *Principles of Environmental Economics*. Psychology Press. ISBN: 0-203-45581-9 Master e book. https://ashraffeps.yolasite.com/resources/Environmental_Eco./Principles%20of%20Environmental%20Economics.pdf (accessed on 9 June 2020).

Ika, L.A. and J. Donnelly. 2017. "Success Conditions for International Development Capacity Building Projects." *International Journal of Project Management* 35(1): 44–63. doi:10.1016/j.ijproman.2016.10.005

Jahn, T., M. Bergmann and F. Keil. 2012. "Transdisciplinarity: Between Mainstreaming and Marginalization." *Ecological Economics* 79: 1–10. doi:10.1016/j.ecolecon.2012.04.017.

Kaijser, A. and A. Kronsell. 2013. "Climate Change through the Lens of Intersectionality". *Environmental Politics* 23 (3): 417–433. doi:10.1080/09644016.2013.835203.

Mercer J., D. Dominey-Howes, I. Kelman and K. Lloyd. 2007. "The potential for combining indigenous and western knowledge in reducing vulnerability to environmental hazards in small island developing states." *Environmental Hazards* 7(4):245–256. doi:10.1016/j.envhaz.2006.11.001.

Lavell, A. and A. Maskrey. 2014. "The Future of Disaster Risk Management". *Environmental Hazards* 13 (4): 267–280. doi:10.1080/17477891.2014.935282.

Lundberg, S. 2017. Report: "Committee on the Status of Women in the Economics Profession (CSWEP)". *American Economic Review* 107 (5): 759–776. doi:10.1257/aer.107.5.759.

Lyytimäki, J. 2015. "Ecosystem Disservices: Embrace the Catchword". *Ecosystem Services* 12: 136. doi:10.1016/j.ecoser.2014.11.008.

Mäler, K.-G., S. Aniyar and Å. Jansson. 2008. "Accounting for Ecosystems". *Environmental And Resource Economics* 42 (1): 39–51. doi:10.1007/s10640-008-9234-8.

Marjanovic, S., R. Hanlin, S. Diepeveen and J. Chataway. 2012. "Research Capacity-Building in Africa: Networks, Institutions and Local Ownership". *Journal of International Development* 25 (7): 936–946. doi:10.1002/jid.2870.

Measham, Thomas G., Benjamin L. Preston, Timothy F. Smith, Cassandra Brooke, Russell Gorddard, Geoff Withycombe and Craig Morrison. 2011. "Adapting to Climate Change Through Local Municipal Planning: Barriers and Challenges". *Mitigation And Adaptation Strategies for Global Change* 16 (8): 889–909. doi:10.1007/s11027-011-9301-2.

Millennium Ecosystem Assessment (MA). 2005. *Ecosystems and Human Well-being: Synthesis*. Washington, DC: Island Press. ISBN 92 4 156309 5. http://www.bioquest.org/wp-content/blogs.dir/files/2009/06/ecosystems-and-health.pdf (accessed on 9 June 2020).

Milman, A. and Y. Arsano. 2014. "Climate Adaptation and Development: Contradictions for Human Security in Gambella, Ethiopia". *Global Environmental Change* 29: 349–359. doi:10.1016/j.gloenvcha.2013.11.017.

Mukhopadhyay, P., M. Nepal and P. Shyamsundar. 2014. "Building Skills for Sustainability: A Role for Regional Research Networks". *Ecology and Society* 19 (4): 1–10. doi:10.5751/es-07105-190445.

Muñoz-Erickson, Tischa A and Bethany B Cutts. 2016. "Structural Dimensions of Knowledge-Action Networks for Sustainability." *Current Opinion in Environmental Sustainability* 18: 56–64. doi:10.1016/j.cosust.2015.08.013.

National Research Council (NRC). 2007. *Research and Networks for Decision Support in the NOAA Sectoral Applications Research Program*. Washington, DC: National Academies Press. ISBN: 978-0-309-11202-4. https://www.nap.edu/catalog/12015/research-and-networks-for-decision-support-in-the-noaa-sectoral-applications-research-program (accessed on 23 May 2020).

Newell, P. 2005. "Citizenship, Accountability and Community: The Limits of the CSR Agenda". *International Affairs* 81 (3): 541–557. doi:10.1111/j.1468-2346.2005.00468.x.

PACJA. 2009. *The Economic Cost of Climate Change in Africa*. Pan African Climate Justice Alliance. https://www.preventionweb.net/files/12722_economiccostofclimatechangeinafrica.pdf (accessed on 9 March 2020).

Parks, J.E., G. Llewellyn, I.M. Dutton and R.S. Pomeroy. 2001. "Learning Networks Called for by Conservation Practitioners." *Intercoast Network* 32: 18–19. https://www.crc.uri.edu/download/2001_39_CRC_PowerofLearning.pdf (accessed on 12 June 2020).

Paul, S. 1995. "Capacity Building for Health Sector Reform." (No. WHO/SHS/NHP/95.8. Unpublished). World Health Organization. https://apps.who.int/iris/bitstream/handle/10665/62660/WHO_SHS_NHP_95.8.pdf?sequence=1&isAllowed=y (accessed on 27 January 2020).

Pearce, David W and R. Kerry Turner. 1990. *Economics of Natural Resources and the Environment*. New York: Harvester Wheatsheaf. ISBN: 0801839866.

Perkin, E. and J. Court. 2005. *Networks and Policy Processes in International Development: a Literature Review*. Overseas Development Institute. ISBN:0 85003 768 9. https://odi.org/documents/1943/160.pdf (accessed on 9 February 2020).

Richards, M. and J. Davies. 1999. *Internalising the Externalities of Tropical Forestry: A Review of Innovative Financing and Incentive Mechanisms*. European Union Tropical Forestry Paper. European Commission, Brussels. ISBN 0 85003 402. https://odi.org/documents/2946/5696.pdf (accessed on 10 February 2020).

The Economy and Environment program for Southeast Asia. *EEPSEA Impact Report. 1993–2000.* https://idl-bnc idrc.dspacedirect.org/bitstream/handle/10625/19217/116324.pdf?sequence=1&isAllowed=y (accessed on 10 February 2020).

Thomalla, F., M. Boyland, K. Johnson, J. Ensor, H. Tuhkanen, Å. Gerger Swartling, G. Han, J. Forrester and D. Wahl. 2018. "Transforming Development and Disaster Risk". *Sustainability* 10 (5): 1458. doi:10.3390/su10051458.

Turner, B.L., R.E. Kasperson, P.A. Matson, J.J. McCarthy, R.W. Corell, L. Christensen, N. Eckley, J.X. Kasperson, A. Luers, M.L. Martello and C. Polsky. 2003. "A framework for vulnerability analysis in sustainability science." *Proceedings of the National Academy of Sciences* 100 (14): 8074–8079. https://www.pnas.org/content/pnas/100/14/8074.full.pdf (accessed on 23 February 2020)

Turner, R.K. and D.W. Pearce. 1990. *The Ethical Foundations of Sustainable Economic Development*. International Institute for Environment and Development. ISBN: 978-94-017-6406-3. https://pubs.iied.org/sites/default/files/pdfs/migrate/8015IIED.pdf (accessed on 15 March 2020).

Vincent, J.R. 2008. "*Evaluation of Economy and Environment Program for Southeast Asia (EEPSEA), January 1, 2005, to June 30, 2008*." Unpublished report, Durham: Duke University. http://hdl.handle.net/10625/37574 (accessed on 2 July 2020).

# Index

For Product Safety Concerns and Information please contact our EU representative GPSR@taylorandfrancis.com
Taylor & Francis Verlag GmbH, Kaufingerstraße 24, 80331 München, Germany

www.ingramcontent.com/pod-product-compliance
Ingram Content Group UK Ltd.
Pitfield, Milton Keynes, MK11 3LW, UK
UKHW022318250926
475702UK00046B/942

*9781032182919*